HUNGRY?
B O S T O N

THE LOWDOWN ON

WHERE THE

REAL

PEOPLE

EAT!

Edited by
Esti Iturralde & Kaya Stone

D1369785

Printed in Canada

First Printing: November 2002

Library of Congress Cataloging-in-Publication Data
Hungry? Boston: The Lowdown on Where the Real People Eat!
Edited by Esti Iturralde & Kaya Stone
328 p. 8.89 x 22.86 cm
ISBN 1-893329-18-6
I. Title II. Food Guides III. Boston IV. Iturralde, Esti & Stone, Kaya

Production by Isaac Norton
Illustrations by Ingrid Olson, Tülbox Creative Group

Visit our Web site at www.HungryCity.com

To order Hungry? or our other Glove Box Guides, or for
information on using them as corporate gifts, e-mail us at
sales@HungryCity.com. or write to:

Glove Box Guides
P.O. Box 86121
Los Angeles, CA 90086

MANY THANKS

. . . To our contributors
Lauren Abbate, Jennifer Adams, Carol Alves, Michael Beckett, Leigh Belanger, Jenny Bengen, Jerry Berndt, Matt Bloomer, Reg Brittain, Melissa Carlson, Pete Carpenter, Mel Cartagena, Amélie Cherlin, Priti Chinai, Eric Cho, Amy Cooper, Nicole Cotroneo, Rhonda Cozier, Colleen Craig, Jesse Crary, Laura & Ben D'Amore, Tyler Doggett, Amanda Dorato, Mary Beth Doyle, Jamie Drummond, Sarah Duggan, Dorothy Dwyer, Alissa Farber, Mark Lynn Ferguson, Lara Fox, Paula Foye, Ankur Ghosh, Brendan Gibbon, Jon Gorey, Joe Goss, Nick Grandy, Melinda Green, Nick Grossman, James Haynes, Becky Hays, Ari Herzog, Hadley Hudson, Jodi Hullinger, Matthew Isles, Lisa Johnson, Sylvia Kindermann, Stephanie Kinnear, Amy Kirkcaldy, Kyle Konrad, Ted Kulik, Ana Laguarda, Christine Laurence, Tim Leonard, Kimberly Loomis, Joel Lowden, Donna M. Mancusi, Liz McEachern-Hall, Ray Misra, Kathy Morelli, Anna Morris, Meaghan Mulholland, John Newton, R.B. Michael Oliver, Dara Olmsted, Sarah Pascarella, Estelle Paskausky, Zachary Patten, Jesse Peck, Alison Pereto, Chris Railey, Dan Rosenberg, Sandy Ruben, Christopher Russell, Mark Sloan, Juan Smith, Heidi Solomon, Alex Speier, Caroline Stanculescu, Jason Stevenson, Katie Stone, Laura Stone, Glen Strandberg, Tina Tuminella, Megan Valentine, Charlene Wang, Nina West, Barry Willingham, Katie Wink, John Woodford

. . . To People Who Lent Suggestions and Support
Joe Cleemann and Marie Estrada for getting us started; Laura Stone and Sandy Ruben, for their contagious love of food; Nancy Kuo and Tinwah Wong, for putting up with the home office. We dedicate *Hungry? Boston* to the memory of Haley Surti, who always enjoyed a feast.

. . . To the Glove Box Guides Staff
Lindsey Blumenfeld, Anjali Kumuran, Jessica Weng, Molly Drexler, and Matt Shelbourn for their diligent fact-checking and research. Susan Jonaitis for her careful proofreading skills, and Janelle Herrick for her support and enthusiam. Isaac Norton for his interior book production expertise. Ingrid Olson, designer, for making everything look beautiful. Mari Florence, publisher, for making everything possible in the first place. And finally, to Kristin Petersen, managing editor, for giving us a chance and a wonderful example to use as a model.

—*Esti Iturralde & Kaya Stone,*
Editors

CONTENTS

Key to the Book VII

Map of Boston VIII

Please Read X

Boston Cheat Sheet XII

Introduction XIII

Downtown Boston

Faneuil Hall/Financial District/Waterfront 2

    Boston Baked Beans:
A Noble Legume Tradition 5

    Faneuil Hall:
The Original Place for Food, Folks, and Fun. . . 11

North End 15

    Little Italy:
Salumarias, Pastry Shops, and other
Delights of the North End 17

East Boston/Charlestown 26

    Know Your Chowdah 27

Beacon Hill 32

    R.I.P. Buzzy's Fabulous Roast Beef 32

Chinatown/Theater District 37

    Pearl Tea Mania 44

South End 53

    R.I.P. 1970s Downtown Boston at Night 58

Back Bay 62

    The Unhappy City 68

Fenway/Kenmore Square 80

    R.I.P. The Hedge School 85

Boston—Go West

Allston 88

    R.I.P. El Phoenix Room 93

Brighton 99

    Hungry? Boston College:
The Best Food Stops for the Starving Student . 101

Brookline: Coolidge Corner Circle 106

    The Honor Roll:
Where to Find the Best Baked Goods in Boston . 110

Brookline: Brookline Village 119

Brookline: Washington Square 124

Boston—Go South

Jamaica Plain 126
    The Boston Ice Cream Machine
    —Beach Weather Not Included 131

Roxbury/Mattapan/Dorchester 139
    New England Food Festivals 143

South Boston 148
    Beantown Eateries on the Big
    (and Little) Screen 150

Cambridge

Kendall Square 156
    Hungry? MIT:
    The Best Food Stops for the Starving Student . 158

Central Square 161

Inman Square 167
    Lowering the Bar on Fine Dining 168

Harvard Square 174
    R.I.P. The Blue Parrot 177
    R.I.P. The Tasty 183
    Hungry? Harvard:
    The Best Food Stops for the Starving Student . 191

Porter Square 194
    Of Pilgrims and Munchkins:
    The Story of Boston Donuts 195

West Cambridge/Alewife 203
    R.I.P. The Restaurants of Joyce Chen 204

Somerville

Davis Square/Ball Square 210
    Hungry? Tufts:
    The Best Stops for the Starving Student 212
    R.I.P. Steve's Ice Cream 219

Union Square 227

Western Suburbs

    The Farmer in the City 234

Arlington 235

Belmont 238

Watertown 239
    New England's Landmark Diners 241

Waltham. 244

Lexington. 248

Natick 249

Newton 249

Needham 254

Wellesley 255

Framingham. 256

North Shore 258

> *Of Gold, Glory, and Cod:*
> *A Fish 'n' Chips Tale* 261

South Shore 266

New England

> *Introduction to New England* 274

Western Massachusetts 274

Cape Cod. 276

> *The New England Cranberry:*
> *Where Sassamanash got its Start* 277

Rhode Island 280

Connecticut 282

> *New Haven Pizza* 283

Vermont. 285

> *Food Factory Fun* 286

New Hampshire 288

Maine. 290

Glossary. 292

Alphabetical Index 298

Category Index. 302

About the Contributors. 308

KEY TO THE BOOK

Most Popular Meals:

 Breakfast

 Lunch

 Dinner

Ambience

 It's late and you're hungry

 Sleep is for the weak

 Nice places to dine solo

 Get cozy with a date

 Fish or Seafood

 Vegetarian or Vegan-friendly

 Food on the run

 Desserts/Bakery

 Live music

 Patio or sidewalk dining

 Eat on the street

 In business since 1969 or before

 Editor's pick

Cost

Cost of the average meal:

$	**$5 and under**
$$	**$8 and under**
$$$	**$12 and under**
$$$$	**$13 and over**

Payment

Note that most places that take *all* the plastic we've listed also take Diner's Club, Carte Blanche, and the like. And if it says cash only, be prepared.

 Visa

 MasterCard

 American Express

 Discover

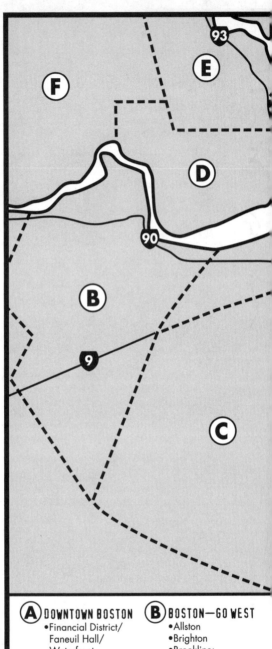

(A) DOWNTOWN BOSTON
- Financial District/ Faneuil Hall/ Waterfront
- North End
- East Boston/ Charlestown
- Beacon Hill
- Chinatown/ Theater District
- South End
- Back Bay
- Fenway/Kenmore

(B) BOSTON—GO WEST
- Allston
- Brighton
- Brookline: Coolidge Corner
- Brookline: Brookline Village
- Brookline: Washington Square

(E) SOMERVILLE
- Davis Square/ Ball Square
- Union Square

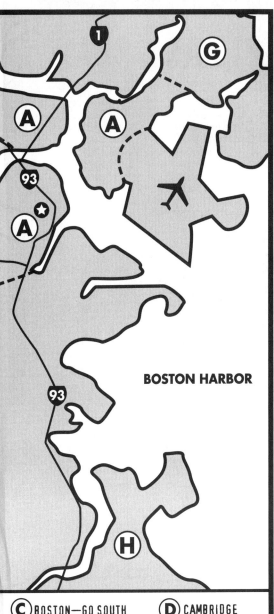

BOSTON HARBOR

C **BOSTON—GO SOUTH**
- Jamaica Plain
- Roxbury/Mattapan/Dorchester
- South Boston

D **CAMBRIDGE**
- Kendall Square
- Central Square
- Inman Square
- Harvard Square
- Porter Square
- West Cambridge/Alewife

F **WESTERN SUBURBS**
- Arlington
- Belmont
- Watertown
- Waltham
- Lexington
- Natick
- Newton
- Needham
- Wellesley
- Framingham

G **NORTH SHORE**

H **SOUTH SHORE**

PLEASE READ

Disclaimer #1

The only sure thing in life is change. We've tried to be as up-to-date as possible, but places change owners, hours, and menus as often as they open up a new location or go out of business. Call ahead so you don't end up wasting time crossing town and arrive after closing time.

Disclaimer #2

Every place in *Hungry? Boston* is recommended, for something. We have tried to be honest about our experiences of the each place, and sometimes a jab or two makes its way into the mix. If your favorite spot is slammed for something you think is unfair, it's just one person's opinion! And remember, under the Fair Use Doctrine, some statements about the establishments in this book are intended to be humorous as parodies. Whew! Got the legal stuff out of the way.

And wait, there's more!

While we list over 450 eateries in the book, that's just the beginning of the eating opportunities in Boston. Visit HungryCity.com for additional reviews, culinary itineraries, updates, and all the information you need for your next eating and drinking adventures.

Tip, Tip, Tip.

If you can't afford to tip you can't afford to eat and drink. In the United States, most servers make minimum wage or less, and depend on tips to pay the rent. Tip fairly, and not only will you get better service when you come back, but you'll start believing in karma (if you don't already).

Road Trip!

And, next time you hit the road, check the Glove Box Guides to destinations including: Chicago, Las Vegas, Los Angeles, Minneapolis/St. Paul, New Orleans, New York City, San Diego/Tijuana, San Francisco, Seattle, Toronto, Vancouver/Victoria, and many, many more!

Don't Drink and Drive.

We shouldn't have to tell you this, but we can't say it enough. Drink responsibly. Don't drive after you've been drinking alcohol, period. If a designated driver is hard to come by, take the T or call a cab to take you home. Split the costs with your friends to bring the cost down.

Share your secrets.

Know about a place we missed? Willing to divulge your secrets and contribute to the next edition? Send your ideas to *"Hungry? Boston* Update" c/o Glove Box Guides, P.O. Box 86121, Los Angeles, CA 90086 or e-mail Update@HungryCity.com. There's no guarantee we'll use your idea, but if it sounds right for us we'll let you know.

CHEAT SHEET

Nowhere But Here: The Boston Culinary Cheat Sheet

What if you only have a few days in town and you want to make sure you get the authentic Boston food experience? Don't miss the following items that you really can't get anywhere else—or you might, but it won't quite taste the same.

Lobster/Clam Bake: The ultimate New England meal experience: Strap on a bib and enjoy a boiled lobster, steamers, corn on the cob, boiled potatoes, and a cup of chowder.

Clam Chowder: The chili of Massachusetts. No two are alike, everyone has their own recipe, and few can agree on the best in town.

Fried Clams: Grab an overflowing pint of fresh, crispy fried clams, a six pack of Sam, and a sunset-view seat by the water and you'll have the classic New England picnic dinner.

Fish 'n' Chips: Maybe it's the British influence on Boston. Maybe it's the endless stream of cod arriving daily at the Bay State's docks. Either way, you can't go far in this state without finding a menu featuring a platter of thick, fresh, fried fish served over fries.

Boston Baked Beans: Boston is the Beantown after all. Back in the colonial days, a Boston favorite was slow-baked beans in molasses. Today, no local companies manufacture the treat and few Boston restaurants serve it.

Boston Cream Pie: In 1856, Boston's Parker House Restaurant popularized this vanilla custard-filled sponge cake. Since then, tourists have made it the Boston dessert of choice.

Maple Syrup: New Englanders scoff at mass-produced "pancake syrup." Once you try the rich sweetness of 100% pure Vermont maple syrup you'll know why.

Hot Apple Cider and Apple Pie: Come October, few things say New England Fall foliage season like hot spiced mulled cider and warm apple pie topped with vanilla ice cream.

Thick Frappes: What the rest of the country calls a milkshake, Bostonians call a frappe. The area's countless gourmet ice cream shops (see p. 131) boast thick frappes in every flavor from Kahlua to Dutch Orange Chocolate.

Sharp White Cheddar: Wisconsin may be the cheese state, but Vermont cheesemakers churn out over 70 million pounds of cheese a year. Try Cabot's Extra Sharp white cheddar and you'll never go orange again.

Guinness on Draught: It's not a food, but it might as well be. And thanks to the proximity to Ireland, in geography and spirit, with generations of Irish folks in Boston, Guinness in Boston is fresher and poured better than anywhere else in the U.S. A pint of Guinness from Doyle's (see p. 129), with a shamrock drawn in the thick foam, is the ideal companion to their bread bowl of creamy clam chowder.

INTRODUCTION

The Hungry? Challenge

You're in an unfamiliar neighborhood with just $5 for food? Not a problem. We'll show you how to get the best burrito you'll ever know, a chowder that will make you purr with delight, or a calzone revered by everybody within a ten-block radius. But these choices won't be obvious. While it's easy to get mediocre food for a lot of money, it's much harder to find an excellent meal somewhere cheap and unexpected—and what a feeling it is! You're in a tiny place and order the wonderful seafood, a perfect salad, and a beer—the bill arrives and it's only $10 a person. Wow, you say, and commit the restaurant's details to memory. Wouldn't it be great to know one place like this in every neighborhood? Wouldn't it be great to know 15 places like this in every neighborhood?

We thought so, too. That's why we wrote *Hungry? Boston*.

Our Criteria

We have chosen eateries where you can get a great meal for around $10, and often for less. We favor restaurants with real local character, mom-and-pop operations, and in the case of chains, small ones that are locally owned and usually family run. On rare occasions we stretch our budget a little—like for the best Afghan food in Boston, or a killer jazz brunch—but you won't see any $25 ravioli here. Every restaurant in this book represents an excellent value.

Real Character

You can't really know Boston until you've eaten your way through it. People from all over have descended upon this relatively compact area, bringing with them their own flavors and innovations. The restaurants in this book are thus organized by neighborhood (rather than alphabetically) so that you get a sense of each community through the restaurants they choose to patronize. We have chosen each restaurant in large part for its authentic neighborhood character. In many cases these restaurants have served their communities for over 30 years.

Real People

We elicited the help of over 80 contributors, among them many journalists, artists, and writers, but also programmers, lawyers, grantwriters, students, physicists, philosophers, textbook editors, consultants, and dot-commers. All of them are just ordinary locals who love their neighborhoods almost as much as they love to eat. They share with you a native's knowledge of not just where to eat but things like what the best dessert is, who their favorite servers are, and even where to sit for a nice view.

Exploration

We call this series the Glove Box Guides for a reason. Keep this book in your car (or if a car is still a distant dream, in your tote bag, backpack, briefcase, or handbag). That way, when you find yourself hungry in a new place, you won't have to settle for the last resort: a chain restaurant where ambience is something devised by the marketers at corporate headquarters. *Hungry? Boston* covers the entire Boston metro area, and we even provide some of the best roadside stops in all of the New England states. Now you can approach holes-in-the-wall throughout the area with confidence. Not to mention pizza parlors, 60-year-old diners, Indian buffets, crêpe makers, gourmet ice cream places, falafel takeouts, Brazilian cafés, Irish pubs, barbecue shacks, pancake houses. . .

So are you Hungry yet?

>   —*Esti Iturralde & Kaya Stone,*
>   *Boston*

DOWNTOWN BOSTON

FINANCIAL DISTRICT–
FANEUIL HALL–WATERFRONT

Bay State Chowda Co.

(see p. 27)
Seafood/Chowder
1 Faneuil Hall Marketplace, Boston 02109
Phone (617) 742-4441

Bertucci's

(see p. 175)
Gourmet Pizza
Faneuil Hall Marketplace:
22 Merchants Row, Boston 02109
Phone (617) 227-7889

Café 300

Cheap eats for the artsy crowd.
$$
300 Summer St., Boston 02210
(at D St.)
Phone (617) 426-0695

CATEGORY	Nouveau American
HOURS	Mon–Fri: 11 AM–3 PM
MASS TRANSIT	T: Red line to South Station
PAYMENT	VISA MasterCard AMERICAN EXPRESS
POPULAR FOOD	Runs the gamut from salads to exotic quesadillas, as well as a few wraps; the menu is small at this quick, sit-down lunch place
UNIQUE FOOD	Turkey meatloaf with mashed sweet potatoes
DRINKS	Soft drinks, espresso bar
SEATING	Small tables in very close proximity to each other
AMBIENCE	Frequented by business types on lunch break; the rest of the building is an art gallery and Café 300 takes up the open area of the lower level; it's bright, airy, and just a little artsy

—Melinda Green

Chacarero

A taste of Chile when you're on the run.
$
426 Washington St., Boston 02108
(beside Filene's)
Phone (617) 542-0392 • Fax (617) 895-3715

CATEGORY	Chilean
HOURS	Mon–Fri: 11 AM–6 PM
	Sat: 11 AM–4 PM
MASS TRANSIT	T: Red or Orange line to Downtown Crossing
PAYMENT	Cash only

POPULAR FOOD	The *only* food, *chacareros* and more *chacareros*: Chilean sandwiches served on traditional bread baked on the premises with ripe juicy tomatoes, mashed avocado, muenster cheese, homemade hot sauce, and marinated green beans; choose chicken, beef, or vegetarian; grilled with olive oil or barbecued; small (bagel-size) or large (about 6" across)
DRINKS	Nantucket Nectars, Orangina, bottled water, iced tea, soda
SEATING	In good weather, there are rod-iron tables and chairs for about 20 people outside
AMBIENCE	Clientele includes everyone from the CEO passing by between meetings to tourists shopping downtown to folks leaving the gym across the street; don't let the line at lunchtime scare you away; the wait is usually around 15 minutes
EXTRAS/NOTES	For large quantities, you can fax your order ahead of time.

—Heidi Solomon

Chart House

(see p. 27)
Seafood/Chowder
60 Long Wharf, Boston 02110
Phone (617) 227-1576

Country Life Vegetarian

Nirvana for vegans.
$$
200 High St., Boston 02110
(at Broad St. and Surface Artery)
Phone (617) 951-2534
www.countrylifeboston.home-page.org

CATEGORY	Vegetarian
HOURS	Mon: 11:30 AM–3 PM Tues–Thurs: 11:30 AM–3 PM, 5 PM–8 PM Fri: 11:30 AM–3 PM Sun: 10 AM–3 PM, 5 PM–8 PM
MASS TRANSIT	T: Red line to South Station
PAYMENT	VISA MasterCard AMERICAN EXPRESS
POPULAR FOOD	No animal products: no eggs, no dairy, no honey; meals are served buffet style with a different entrée, soup, and vegetable every day (lunch $7, dinner $8, brunch $9.45); huge salad bar by the pound; standouts include "chicken" salad; steamed veggies and rice; homemade minestrone soup; spaghetti and wheatballs; macaroni and "cheese"
UNIQUE FOOD	Soy Yummy Ice Cream; fake beef, sour cream, and eggs
DRINKS	Juices
SEATING	Multiple rooms surrounding the buffet table
AMBIENCE	Country setting wall murals and photos; fluorescent lighting

3

| EXTRAS/NOTES | This location is just one of 33 Country Life restaurants worldwide connected to the Seventh Day Adventist Church. |
| OTHER ONES | • New Hampshire: 15 Roxbury St., Keene, NH 03431, (603) 357-3975 |

—Kyle Konrad

Durgin Park

(see p. 5)
Boston Baked Beans
340 Faneuil Hall Market Place, Boston 02109
Phone (617) 227-2038

Fajitas & 'Ritas

(see p. 120)
Tex-Mex
25 West St., Boston 02111
Phone (617) 426-1222

The Hub Pub

*An unpretentious hideaway
for beer, sandwiches, and locals.*
$$$
18 Province St., Boston 02108
(off Bromfield St.)
Phone (617) 523-6168 • Fax (617) 227-9262

CATEGORY	Bar & Grill
HOURS	Daily: 11:30 AM–2 AM; food 'til 1 AM
MASS TRANSIT	T: Red line to Park St. or Downtown Crossing, Green line to Park St., Orange line to Downtown Crossing
PAYMENT	VISA AMERICAN EXPRESS
POPULAR FOOD	Turkey club with fries; big burgers; homemade ravioli or meatloaf
UNIQUE FOOD	The Park Square (roasted turkey, baked ham, and Swiss with "herb mayo")
DRINKS	Pitchers of Miller Lite; decent selection of beer, on tap and bottled; tea and coffee; sodas; don't even think about asking for a smoothie here
SEATING	Plenty of seating with small tables on the ground floor, stools around the bar, and an upstairs seating area for large parties or those seeking to escape the bar
AMBIENCE	A friendly, well-loved, efficient dive; end-of-week lunchtimes and evenings are busy, and the bar's usually full, but there's rarely a wait for a table; Irish waitresses, giant beer signs, video games, and jukebox tunes abound, not to mention the multitude of massive TV screens to keep you glued to the game. Clientele includes coworkers on lunch, guys yelling at the TVs over their beers, and smokers. This is not a good place for a heart-to-heart unless you're at the bottom of your pitcher; it is a place to have a convivial meal with friends.

EXTRAS/NOTES   No pretensions or high-profile clients here—warm yourself with "the Friendliest Pub in the Hub," get yourself a fine, earthy pint, and hole away with some worthy pub grub. Before you know it, chanting "Hub Pub!" when you're in the neighborhood may become irresistible. Tuesday is karaoke night.

—*Alison Pereto*

Boston Baked Beans, a Noble Legume Tradition

Baked beans have formed a part of Boston history for almost 400 years—in fact, they date back to the arrival of the Pilgrims. Boston may not be known as the Windy City, but given its bean-eating tradition, perhaps it should be.

For the Pilgrim, whose staunch religious beliefs advised against cooking on Sunday, baked beans were a convenient food that could be prepared on Saturday and eaten all weekend long—for breakfast, lunch, and dinner. These days, the most typical baked beans are dumped out of a can into a Teflon saucepan, served alongside ham or hot dogs, but those seeking authenticity can try the following classic recipe in a real ceramic bean pot—like those sold in souvenir shops around the city.

Soak two cups of navy or pea beans overnight (alternatively, cover beans with boiling water and soak for 4–5 hours) and then drain the beans and boil them slowly in a large amount of salt water for 1 hour. Drain the beans again. Combine 1–2 teaspoons of salt, 2 tablespoons of brown sugar, 1/4 cup of molasses, 1 bay leaf, 1/2 teaspoon of dry mustard, 1 tablespoon of chopped onion, and 1 cup of boiling water. Stir the beans into this mixture and pour into the bean pot. Press 1/2 pound of salt pork pieces into the beans, cover with more boiling water, and bake at 300 degrees F with the lid on for 2 1/2 hours. Take the lid off and bake for another 1 1/2 hours.

Given all this fuss, it's understandable why most people resort to the can approach instead.

Easier than both methods is going to **Durgin Park**, the classic Boston restaurant, whose baked beans are almost as famous as its wait staff's notoriously rude attitude. The only way to have a more classic Boston experience would be to drive through miserable traffic all the way home. *Downtown Boston: 340 Faneuil Hall Market Place, Boston 02109, (617) 227-2038.*

—*Amy Kircaldy*

J. Pace & Son

*An Italian, soup-to-nuts
lunch favorite.*

$$

2 Devonshire St., Boston 02109
(between State St. and Water St.)
Phone (617) 227-4949 • Fax (617) 227-5128

CATEGORY	Italian
HOURS	Mon–Fri: 6 AM–7 PM
MASS TRANSIT	T: Orange or Blue line to State St.
PAYMENT	VISA MasterCard DISCOVER
POPULAR FOOD	Calzones, chicken or eggplant parmesan; soups of the day; fresh salads; ziti, ravioli, or gnocchi with meatballs; manicotti and stuffed shells; deli stocked with fine meats and cheeses; aisles stocked with European cookies, pizelles, chips, and fresh fruit
UNIQUE FOOD	Roast lamb sub; spinach ravioli; gnocchi marinara
DRINKS	You name it, they've got it; hot coffees and teas
SEATING	Not an inch to spare for seating; Post Office Square is about a block away where cushions are provided to sit on the grass during warm days while a band serenades the crowds
AMBIENCE	Frequented mostly by the business crowd; at lunchtime, the Financial District descends on Pace's; it gets a little crazy, but they have everything down to a science
EXTRAS/NOTES	Over 18 different cakes, pies, and numerous pastries.
OTHER ONES	• Financial District: One Federal St., Boston 02110, (617) 556-8253
	• Beacon Hill: 75 Blossom Ct., Boston 02114, (617) 227-6141
	• North Shore: 325 Main St., Saugus 01906, (781) 231-9599

—*Heidi Solomon*

The Kinsale

*A Bostonified
Irish pub that dishes up
hearty Irish-American fare.*

$$$

2 Center Plaza, Boston 02108
(at Cambridge St.)
Phone (617) 742-5577 • Fax (617) 720-1330
www.classicirish.com

CATEGORY	Irish Pub
HOURS	Daily: 11 AM–2 AM
MASS TRANSIT	T: Blue or Green line to Government Center
PAYMENT	VISA MasterCard AMERICAN EXPRESS DISCOVER

POPULAR FOOD	Beer battered fish 'n' chips; eight-ounce burgers with cheddar and bacon; Gaelic four-onion soup (caramelized leeks, scallions, and red and white onions capped with a thick slice of bread with melted cheddar and smoked gouda); hot pastrami with melted Swiss
UNIQUE FOOD	Bangers and mash; beef and Guinness stew; full Irish breakfasts with black and white puddings (Sat/Sun only)
DRINKS	Frothy pints of Guinness and Harp; Poor Man's Martini—a tall 20-ouncer of Guinness; beers, wines, spirits, and soft drinks; strong Irish coffee or an O'Malley's coffee with whiskey and amaretto
SEATING	Cozy booths, tables made from beer barrels, and a massive carved wooden bar make for plenty of places to sit back and polish off a cold one (or five); warm weather patio and sidewalk seating
AMBIENCE	This pub was handcrafted in Ireland and shipped to Boston—then plopped down in the concrete monstrosity of Center Plaza; interior maintains a cozy feel of Celtic craftsmanship
EXTRAS/NOTES	Free live Irish music on weekdays. Free validated parking: Mon–Fri after 6 PM; all day Sat/Sun; three-hour maximum and a $20 check minimum.
OTHER ONES	Two identical sister bars:

- Central Square: The Asgard, 350 Massachusetts Ave., Cambridge 02139, (617) 577-9100
- Western Suburbs: Desmond O'Malley's, Rte. 9 East, Framingham 01702, (508) 875-9400

—Amanda Dorato

The Marshall House

*Fish so fresh, you'll hope
it stays on the plate.*

$$$$

15 Union St., Boston 02108

(at North St., east of City Hall Government Center)

Phone (617) 523-9396

CATEGORY	Seafood
HOURS	Daily: 11:30 AM–11 PM; bar open until 2 AM
MASS TRANSIT	T: Green line to Haymarket or Government Center
PAYMENT	VISA MasterCard AMERICAN EXPRESS DISCOVER
POPULAR FOOD	Featuring a full raw bar and a well-rounded pub menu, at the Marshall House you can get your fill of shrimp, lobster, schrod, mussels, and oysters; their clam chowder is chunky, savory, and loaded with clams, but not overbearingly buttery; the best bargain is the $6 plate of fried calamari; the burgers are enormous (served with equally giant steak fries); lobster is pricey, but still cheaper than some of the restaurants next door

UNIQUE FOOD	Seafood lovers can cozy up to the bar and order any number of raw shellfish to accompany a beer; the Haymarket vendors are just around the corner, so you can be sure you're getting it fresh
DRINKS	Full bar, beer, wine
SEATING	A skinny place: the bar seats 15 while tables line the left side of the front room; there's a dining room in back with some larger tables
AMBIENCE	A classy, beautiful restaurant exuding genuine warmth: lantern-lit, exposed brick walls, complete with rich, dark wooden beams and brass fixtures
EXTRAS/NOTES	They validate parking (up to three hours) at the Haymarket Garage ($3).

—Jon Gorey

Milk Street Café
*Kosher fare with
an international kick.*
$$

50 Milk St., Boston 02109
(between Devonshire St. and Arch St.)
Phone (617) 542-3663 • Fax (617) 451-5329
www.milkstreetcafe.com

CATEGORY	Kosher Café
HOURS	Mon–Fri: 7 AM–3 PM
MASS TRANSIT	T: Orange line to State St. or Downtown Crossing, Blue Line to State St., Red line to Downtown Crossing
PAYMENT	VISA MasterCard AMERICAN EXPRESS
POPULAR FOOD	No matzo or gefilte fish at this Kosher joint; standouts include teriyaki roast beef salad, roasted salmon salad, and their famous brownies
UNIQUE FOOD	The creamy vegetarian guacamole passion sandwich and the tangy Tuna '02 sandwich with tabouli; tomato-spinach feta soup
DRINKS	Soft drinks, tea, coffee, juices
SEATING	Grab a tray and get in line; granite-topped tables in large and somewhat sterile space; "get ya in, get ya out" dining experience
AMBIENCE	Suited banker/investor types mixed with Kosher tourists; bustling weekdays at noon; streamlined service keeps long lines moving quickly
EXTRAS/NOTES	This is *the* place to eat for Kosher diners. There's an extensive selection of healthy options, identified by the heart symbol on the menu. And although "healthy" and "Kosher" conjure up images of bland and lifeless food to many, Milk Street comes as close as possible to letting you have your cake and eat it too.
OTHER ONES	Deli-style cart with limited menu: • Financial District: Post Office Sq., Boston 02109, (617) 350-7275

—Amanda Dorato

New York Soup Exchange

Where stocks are traded—chicken stock, that is.

$$

133 Federal St., Boston 02118
(at Matthews St.)
Phone (617) 451-3500 • Fax (617) 695-2697
www.nysoupexchange.com

CATEGORY	Café
HOURS	Mon–Fri: 6:30 AM–6 PM
MASS TRANSIT	T: Green or Blue line to Government Center
PAYMENT	VISA MasterCard
POPULAR FOOD	At this version of the "NYSE," it's all about soup; popular ones like the chicken noodle and New England clam chowder appear most days; specials might include cream of broccoli or a meat-filled Italian sausage zucchini and tomato; the old-fashioned tomato and rice is rich, creamy, and nicely flavored with dill; all come with a piece of homemade bread and fruit; there are also plenty of sandwich options, such as CEO Roast Beef and the Dow Tuna Pocket
UNIQUE FOOD	Breakfast served until 11 AM, consisting primarily of cream of wheat, oatmeal, or southern-style grits, with coffee and fruit; bagels and muffins also available
DRINKS	Coffee, tea, bottled juices, and sodas; this location also offers chilled fruit soup smoothies, like Peachsickle and Strawberry Sunrise
SEATING	Fifteen small tables and another 12 stools at the bar by the window
AMBIENCE	From noon to 2 PM, the NYSE is hectic and harried, much like its marketplace namesake; enter through a giant plaster-cast copy of the New York Stock Exchange facade, complete with ionic columns; three television screens provide the menu and CNNfn; the clientele is almost exclusively Financial District workers grabbing a quick bite; no surprise, then, that NYSE closes at 6 PM, after which the neighborhood echoes like a giant concrete canyon
EXTRAS/NOTES	The web site is faithfully updated each morning with the soups of the day—plus you can have them emailed to you.
OTHER ONES	• Government Center: 3 Center Plaza, Boston 02108, (617) 973-6973
	• Post Office Square: 2 Oliver St. (behind Meridien Hotel), Boston 02109, (617) 695-3599

—Kimberly Loomis

No Name Restaurant

*Perhaps the speediest, cheapest,
and tastiest seafood dive in Boston.
Since 1917*

$$$

15 Fish Pier St. W, Boston 02210
(at Seaport Blvd., on the Harbor)
Phone (617) 338-7539

CATEGORY	Historic/Seafood
HOURS	Daily: 11 AM–10 PM
MASS TRANSIT	T: Red line to South Station
PAYMENT	Cash only
POPULAR FOOD	Big portions of fresh fish, either fried or baked; great clam and seafood chowder; a lobster special with fries and side of scallops or shrimp, cole slaw, and unlimited crusty garlic bread
DRINKS	Soda or water in Dixie cups; beer and wine in actual glasses
SEATING	Two floors of tables and more tables; when it's packed, be prepared to get hit with some of your neighbor's crumbs; some seats do offer a view of the harbor, but let's just say that it's not the restaurant's strongest suit
AMBIENCE	No Name's lack of ambience is precisely part of its charm; it's a roll-up-your-sleeves and get messy sort of joint; often visited by out-of-towners for the true Boston seafood experience
EXTRAS/NOTES	Free lot parking.

—Melinda Green

Pizzeria Regina

(see p. 24)
Pizza
Faneuil Hall Food Court, Boston 02109
Phone (617) 227-8180

Pizzeria Rico

*Some Little Italy
for those downtown.*

$

32 Bromfield St., Boston 02108
(at Tremont St.)
Phone (617) 423-7426 • Fax (617) 422-0059

CATEGORY	Pizza
HOURS	Mon–Fri: 10 AM–6 PM Sat: 10 AM–4 PM
MASS TRANSIT	T: Red or Orange line to Downtown Crossing
PAYMENT	
POPULAR FOOD	Huge pizza slices; Fridays bring the ever-popular cheese lasagna special, and for those so inclined, meatballs on the side; on Wednesdays enjoy stuffed chicken with cheese and spinach, or cheese and prosciutto

UNIQUE FOOD	The recently launched Box Lunch concept: small sub (eight choices from eggplant parmesan to salami and cheese), soup or salad, and chips for around $7; make-your-own pizza bag includes a homemade Rico's crust, cheese, and sauce for six bucks
DRINKS	IBC root beer and the standard soda selection; free refills on all fountain sodas
SEATING	Capacity for around 75; there are both booths and tables seating groups of various sizes
AMBIENCE	Home to one of the busiest weekday lunchtimes in downtown Boston; however, there is virtually no wait, and suits and shoppers alike stream through the cafeteria-style serving area without skipping a beat

—Liz McEachern-Hall

Faneuil Hall:
The Original Place for Food, Folks, and Fun

With over 40 indoor stands and 14 restaurants, Faneuil Hall offers a whole spectrum of different foods under one roof—Indian, Italian, Greek, Mexican, American, Chinese, coffee, candy, cakes, chocolate chip cookies, ice cream, fudge—the list goes on and on.

For centuries, Faneuil Hall has been the site of both food and spectacle. Constructed in 1746, it served as a meat, produce, and fish market, as well as the site of memorable speeches delivered by Revolutionary figures. By the mid-1900s Faneuil Hall had fallen into disrepair like much of the area (see p. 58) and was almost razed to the ground, but experienced a renaissance in 1976 when it was converted into the thriving marketplace of today.

These days, food stands tend to come and go in Faneuil Hall, bringing new favorite places with the changes. Yet there are a few classic stands, old standbys that have occupied a spot in the building for years. Perhaps the most famous is the **Brown Derby Deli,** (617) 742-3028, serving various types of hot dogs and sausages as well as deli-style sandwiches. Another favorite, **Mykonos Fair,** (617) 742-8349, puts together an excellent Greek salad with fresh feta cheese and delicious dressing. For dessert, you can smell your way to the **Boston Chipyard,** (617) 742-9537, whose freshly baked cookies can be found outside the main hall in the North Canopy.

—Amy Kircaldy

Rosie's Bakery

(see p. 111)
Bakery
2 South Station, Boston 02110
Phone (617) 439-4684

Silvertone Bar & Grill

Pub grub for all tastes.
$$$
69 Bromfield St., Boston 02108
(at Washington St.)
Phone (617) 338-7887 • Fax (617) 338-7890
www.cybermediary.com/silver/grill.html

CATEGORY	Bar & Grill
HOURS	Mon–Fri: 11:30 AM–11 PM
	Sat: 6 PM–11 PM
MASS TRANSIT	T: Red or Green line to Park St.
PAYMENT	VISA MasterCard AMERICAN EXPRESS
POPULAR FOOD	Homey comfort food like grilled cheese, mac 'n' cheese, and meatloaf; fried calamari; tomato and balsamic bruschetta; huge salads, including the excellent Summer Salad (with raisins, pine nuts, and goat cheese); shepard's pie
UNIQUE FOOD	Cold lo mein noodles in a spicy peanut and sesame dressing with crisp veggies served in a rustic wooden bowl
DRINKS	Bottomless sodas, root beer, beers on tap and bottled, wines by the glass; full bar (only premium spirits)
SEATING	Fifteen tables, mostly retro nostalgia border booths; bar seating
AMBIENCE	Loud lunch and after-work crowd; acid jazz music; quite smoky with slick, modern décor mixed with wood furnishings; hip, young, black-clad clientele that form something of a singles scene

—Jennifer Adams

South Street Diner

Providing greasy-spoon diner favorites through the night.
Since 1945
$$
178 Kneeland St., Boston 02111
(at South St.)
Phone (617) 350-0028

CATEGORY	Historic Diner
HOURS	24/7
MASS TRANSIT	T: Red line to South Station
PAYMENT	VISA MasterCard AMERICAN EXPRESS DISCOVER
POPULAR FOOD	Diner's Special, a hearty breakfast combination consisting of three eggs, two pancakes, homefries, toast, with a choice of bacon, sausage, or ham for around $6 and served around the clock

UNIQUE FOOD	Serving up good ol' standard diner favorites for years—the most unique aspect is the 24-hour service, exceedingly rare in Boston
DRINKS	1950s-style specialties like frappes, shakes, and raspberry lime rickeys; beer, wine, and soda
SEATING	The newspaper-littered counter overlooking sizzling hamburgers on the short-order grill offers the best seats in the house; in addition, four booths and a table offer limited seating of around 35
AMBIENCE	The peak hour here is 3 AM when everyone—from computer programmers pulling all-nighters to Lansdowne Street groupies released from the 2 AM club curfew to travelers from nearby South Station to long-haul truckers—line up out the door for something, anything, to satisfy the stomach. Once inside, diners are greeted by a life-sized James Dean cut-out on the restroom door, neon lights lining the wall, a jukebox pumping oldies, and patches of original tile floor and wooden paneling.
EXTRAS/NOTES	They also sell cigarettes—roll them up in your shirtsleeve to complete the flashback to the '50s.

—Charlene X. Wang

Sultan's Kitchen

To the claim that Turkish cuisine is one of the world's greatest, Sultan's food is the best supporting argument.

$$

72 Broad St., Boston 02110
(at Franklin St.)
Phone (617) 728-2828 • Fax (617) 695-9935

CATEGORY	Turkish
HOURS	Mon–Fri: 11 AM–5 PM
	Sat: 11 AM–3 PM
MASS TRANSIT	T: Orange or Blue line to State St.
PAYMENT	VISA MasterCard AMERICAN EXPRESS
POPULAR FOOD	Intensely flavorful *kofta* kebab made from ground lamb seasoned with herbs and spices; tender marinated chicken and lamb kebabs; crispy falafel; zingy hummus and tabouli
UNIQUE FOOD	Swooning Imam, a small eggplant stuffed and baked with sautéed onion, tomatoes, parsley, garlic and olive oil; curried lentil soup; *balik salatasi* sandwich made with poached tuna, sweet peppers, capers, black olives, red onion, lemon juice, olive oil, and spices; wonderfully creamy almond pudding
DRINKS	Turkish soft drinks, Turkish coffee; *ayran* (a yogurt drink); soft drinks, juices, beers, and a house wine

SEATING	Sixty seats upstairs, and another 20 downstairs, but mostly takeout
AMBIENCE	Far from a sultan's palace: austere white tiling, plastic forks, and paper plates; no Turkish adornments of any kind, except for the Turkish scene and Arabic-like font used on the menu and awning
EXTRAS/NOTES	Chef/owner Ozcan is becoming somewhat of a celebrity with his cookbook *The Sultan's Kitchen*.

—Amanda Dorato

Union Oyster House

(see p. 27)
Seafood
41 Union St., Boston 02108
Phone (617) 227-2750

Wildflower

The key word is "fresh" at this café serving imaginative takeout fare.
$$
99 High St., Boston 02110
(between Congress St. and Federal St.)
Phone (617) 423-5562 • Fax (617) 423-3618

CATEGORY	Café
HOURS	Mon–Fri: 6:30 AM–3 PM
MASS TRANSIT	T: Orange line to Downtown Crossing or State St., Red line to Downtown Crossing, Blue line to State St.
PAYMENT	VISA AMERICAN EXPRESS MasterCard
POPULAR FOOD	Salad and sandwich options such as the crisp and creamy Caesar salad and smoky grilled vegetable platter; fresh focaccia breads and pizzas with toppings such as sun-dried tomato, spinach, and feta; menu, written on a chalkboard, changes daily and uses only the freshest ingredients the season has to offer
UNIQUE FOOD	Curried chicken salad sandwich with ripe papaya and pineapple chunks; smoked turkey club wrap in a tomato tortilla
DRINKS	Soft drinks, tea, coffee, juices
SEATING	At lunch, tables are few and often hard to come by
AMBIENCE	At the base of a huge office building; cozy cafeteria-style café; bright, airy dining room; umbrella-covered tables on the outdoor patio

—Amanda Dorato

NORTH END

Bova's Bakery

The North End's round-the-clock source for Italian snacks. Since 1920

$$

134 Salem St., Boston 02113
(at Prince St.)
Phone (617) 523-5601

CATEGORY	Italian Bakery/Deli
HOURS	24/7
MASS TRANSIT	T: Green or Orange line to Haymarket
PAYMENT	VISA MasterCard AMERICAN EXPRESS
POPULAR FOOD	Excellent slices, all huge with thick, doughy crusts and great toppings; fresh bread baked daily on the premises; excellent subs and calzones; every pastry known to man, fresh baked *scala* bread, and a full deli with meats not found at the local grocery store; Sicilian Special Sub with mozzarella, salami, prosciutto, and provolone; eggplant parmesan
DRINKS	Coffee, soda, juices, milk, iced tea
SEATING	None in the bakery, but it's a short walk to the waterfront for a nice picnic
AMBIENCE	Family-owned eatery, and they know most of their clients by name, which creates a friendly and relaxed atmosphere
EXTRAS/NOTES	Bova's style is what makes the North End attractive to visitors from everywhere. Amid the throngs of tourists who crowd their bakery every weekend, they maintain their local ties and remain a sorely missed spot for those who have left the neighborhood.

—Colleen Craig & Jennifer Adams

Caffe Paradiso

(see p. 180)
Italian Café
253-255 Hanover St., Boston 02113
Phone (617) 742-1768

"And this is good old Boston

The home of the beans and the cod

Where the Lowells talk to the Cabots

And the Cabots talk only to God."

—John Collins Bossidy
(Holy Cross Alumni Dinner)

Caffe Vittoria

*Stylish café for
Italian coffee and dessert.
Since 1929*

$

290-296 Hanover St., Boston 02113

(at Wesley Pl.)

Phone (617) 227-7606 • Fax (617) 533-5340

CATEGORY	Italian Café
HOURS	Daily: 8 AM–1 AM
MASS TRANSIT	T: Green or Orange line to Haymarket
PAYMENT	Cash only
POPULAR FOOD	Tiramisu, cannoli, ricotta pie, and an impressive menu of gelati
UNIQUE FOOD	Not usually considered sustenance but a separate cigar menu is available upon request; the downstairs cigar parlor offers about eight dinner items (burgers, pizzas) made across the street at the Florentine Café, which is under the same ownership
DRINKS	Pistachio, blackberry, cinnamon, and mocha coffee; espresso and cappuccino; three full liquor bars—the upstairs one is more for coffees and wines, the downstairs for the cigar parlor, with an impressive menu of single-malt scotches, champagnes, grappa, martinis, and aperitifs
SEATING	Three different seating areas: a brightly lit front room with about 15 decent-sized marble tables; the older, and a bit shabbier Caffé Vittoria Originale next door with about 25 tables; and a dark, but cozy cigar parlor downstairs
AMBIENCE	A gathering spot for Italian-American locals by day, a trendy after-dinner spot by night, the ambience morphs from one room to the next. The front room is gleaming and a place to be seen, with towering, polished espresso machines, silver sconces, and coffee grinders on the walls, and a pounded tin ceiling; there's a jukebox in the back; the tunes of Sinatra or Italian opera accompany the hiss of espresso makers and clinking dessert forks. The slightly dingier original café next door is a bit more intimate and abuzz with socializing; downstairs an old-boy's club gathers to sip vermouth, smoke cigars, and take in Italian soccer games on a big-screen TV.
EXTRAS/NOTES	Claims to be the first Italian café in Boston. The service is aloof but decent— they pretty much let you be unless you need them.

—Kimberly Loomis

Little Italy:
Salumerias, Pastry Shops, and other Delights of the North End

To some, the North End is a slice of the Old Country; to others it's filled with kitsch and tourists than Disneyland. But whether or not it feels like old Roma, there is little in Boston that surpasses the energy, the great aromas, and the people-watching of this traditionally Italian neighborhood.

Maria's Pastry Shop creates a grand assortment of Italian sweets using traditional methods: cannoli are filled to order, and the *sfogliatelle* (clamshells) are made from layers of flaky pastry and filled with sweet orange- and cinnamon-flavored ricotta cheese. In the Fall, check out traditional seasonal specialties, such as *panettone* (an Italian version of fruitcake) and *osse di morti* (bones of the dead) for All Souls Day (Nov. 2)—a hard yet chewy cinnamon cookie topped with crisp meringue. *46 Cross St., Boston 02113, (617) 523-1196.*

Mike's Pastry owner Mike Mercogliano has been running this show for about 45 years, about as long as the debate over which shop serves the best cannoli in the North End. Some say Mike's, some say Modern Pastry, others say Maria's. With lines out the door and the ridiculous number of people in the North End toting blue-and-white Mike's Pastry boxes tied with white twine, few can dispute that Mike's is the most popular. The cannoli are generously sized and undeniably delicious. They also have rum cake, ricotta cheese pie, tiramisu, gelati, 50-plus varieties of cookies, lobster tails (pastry filled with thicker cheese and dried fruit), and tons of entertainingly shaped marzipan (sugary candy made with almond paste). Mike's has seating for about 50. *300 Hanover St., Boston 02113, (617) 742-3050.*

Modern Pastry—Three generations of Italian pastry chefs maintain the 70-year-old oven at this cheaper, less-crowded, and some might argue better-quality bakery than Mike's across the street. The signature product is the *torrone*, a very sweet and soft nougat log with chopped almonds—traditional white (just nougat and almonds) or caramel (nougat and almonds with a layer of soft caramel and covered in chocolate). There are only three small tables. *257 Hanover St., Boston 02113, (617) 523-3783.*

Monica's Salumeria is for the more demanding picnicker who wants to go beyond bread, cheese, and meat. From a Northern Italian veggie-stuffed eggplant, to chicken cutlets and pea salad, to stuffed portobello mushrooms, flank steak, homemade lasagna, and polenta pizzas, you have plenty of prepared food options to drool over. Don't forget a container of tiramisu for dessert. *130 Salem St., Boston 02113, (617) 742-4101.*

Parziale and Sons Bakery has been here for just about always and is a great place to get a loaf of crusty on the outside, angel-soft-fluffy on the inside hand-rolled bread for under $2. They supply bread to most of the restaurants in the neighborhood. *80 Prince St., Boston 02113, (617) 523-6368.*

Polcari's Coffee—Most places in the North End can brag about 40 years of ownership. However, Polcari's probably has earned more bragging rights than its neighbors, having been at this location for over 70 years. Current owner Ralph Polcari's dad opened up this shop in 1932 and since then has consistently won awards for the best coffee beans in town. Most folks come for the Colombian Supremo or Italian Roast, but the smell of fresh roasted coffee, spices, nuts, and candies is enough to warrant a visit. *105 Salem St., Boston 02113, (617) 227-0786.*

Purity Cheese Company—If you want to get the best ricotta possible for your ricotta dessert, schlep to this tiny little store on Endicott. You get a pound of this wonderful, creamy, flavorful stuff for $4, absolutely nothing like the chalky cheese from the grocery store. In addition, their regular mozzarella tastes just like fresh mozzarella, and is much cheaper. *81 Endicott St., Boston 02113, (617) 227-5060.*

Salumeria Italiana fills every nook and cranny with something edible. Since 1952, owner Erminio Martignetti has attracted North Enders with top-quality Italian cold cuts (including a melt-in-your-mouth prosciutto *cott*), sweets like biscotti, and fantastic zingy marinated artichokes. *151 Richmond St., Boston 02109, (617) 523-8743.*

Salumeria Toscana's counter is lined with all types of marinated marvels: white anchovies, mushrooms, roasted peppers, fresh mozzarella, olives of every hue and size. You can put together your own picnic with a mortadella sandwich from the counter (meat and a little mustard on fresh bread for $3 or some cherry peppers stuffed with a chunk of cheese and a sliver of prosciutto. The thick, raisiny syrup poured over fruit is worth every penny, as is the Calabria Gold cheese, a goat cheese with hot pepper flavors (exclusive to this shop). *272 Hanover St., Boston 02113, (617) 720-4243.*

Trio's Ravioli—Mr. and Mrs. Trio ran this shop for 45 years, making 25 kinds of pasta. Their daughter, the wonderfully friendly Catherine Cremaldi, oversees the operation now as well as Cremaldi's in Cambridge. You can't go wrong with any of the ravioli (meat, spinach, or cheese; $10.50 per dozen). Their famous meatless tomato sauce

($7 per pint) and homemade meatballs ($1.50 each) complete the meal. This stuff is so good, Catherine has prepared "suitcases" full of fresh pasta and sauce to send back overseas to Italy. *222 Hanover St., Boston 02113, (617) 523-9636.*

—Amy Cooper with Amanda Dorato, Kimberly Loomis, and Laura & Ben D'Amore

Corner Café

A cozy North End gem—with free food.
$$

87 Prince St., Boston 02113
(between Salem St. and Thatcher St.)
Phone (617) 523-8997

CATEGORY	Bar & Grill
HOURS	Mon–Sat: 8 AM–2 AM
	Sun: noon–2 AM
MASS TRANSIT	T: Green or Orange line to Haymarket
PAYMENT	Cash only
POPULAR FOOD	Most popular is the food that's free—drink Monday through Thursday 7 PM to 9 PM and chow down on all-you-can-eat tacos; there's also great grilled items (steak tips), franks and beans, and the homemade meatball sub
DRINKS	Wine, soft drinks, and cheap beer
SEATING	Four small tables, two booths, and room for about eight at the bar
AMBIENCE	North End locals who all know each other gather here for the relaxed atmosphere and cheap eats; small and cozily lit; gets busier, louder, and younger after 7 PM when the free food makes its appearance
EXTRAS/NOTES	Listen to classic tunes of the '70s, '80s, '90s, and today. A TV stays tuned to football for a crowd on Monday nights. There's also some arcade gambling games.

—Jenny Bengen

D'Amores

So much fresh pasta, so little time...
$$$
76 Salem St., Boston 02113
(at Stillman St.)
Phone (617) 523-8820
www.damores.com

CATEGORY	Italian
HOURS	Daily: 11:30 AM–10 PM
MASS TRANSIT	T: Green or Orange line to Haymarket
PAYMENT	

POPULAR FOOD	Huge portions of fresh, delicious pastas, sauces, and toppings; cheesy baked ziti; gnocchi sauté; lighter fare like penne al fresco combines olive oil, garlic, basil, black olives, fresh plum tomatoes, and grated Romano cheese; early-bird specials (Mon–Sat: 3 PM–5 PM, Sun: 11:30 AM–4 PM) include soup of the day, salad, beverage, and entree all for around $11
UNIQUE FOOD	Giant homemade sweet sausages drowned in fresh sauce and served over a bed of pasta; ravioli parmesan
DRINKS	Beer, wine, soft drinks, tea, coffee, cappuccino, espresso
SEATING	Sixty at small tables with plenty of windows to people-watch
AMBIENCE	Intimate tables, dim lighting, candles, and the opportunity to watch couples strolling the narrow streets of the North End; the wait staff won't rush you out the door, even on busy nights; a great place for a romantic outing or small gathering of friends

—Laura & Ben D'Amore
(no relation to restaurant, regretfully)

Dino's Café

Quick but delicious Italian in a casual atmosphere.
$$
141 Salem St., Boston 02113
(at Prince St.)
Phone (617) 227-1991

CATEGORY	Italian Café
HOURS	Daily: 11 AM–10 PM
MASS TRANSIT	T: Green or Orange line to Haymarket
PAYMENT	Cash only
POPULAR FOOD	Sixteen-inch mozzarella, basil, and tomato sandwiches; fresh prosciutto sandwiches on fresh baked bread; huge portions of pasta; pumpkin ravioli (by season); excellent gnocchi
UNIQUE FOOD	They'll tailor the menu to suit your own tastes—ask for a specific dish and there's a good chance they'll make it for you
DRINKS	Soft drinks and juices
SEATING	Several cozy tables, but also a substantial takeout business
AMBIENCE	Fast-paced and often packed, especially during lunch when businesspeople and Big Dig construction workers welcome the quick service; at dinner tourists without reservations and locals on their way home from work grab a quick bite

—Sarah Pascarella

Ernesto's Pizzeria

Large slices, low prices, great variety.

$

69 Salem St., Boston 02113

(just north of Cross St.)

Phone (617) 523-1373

CATEGORY	Pizza by the Slice
HOURS	Sun–Thurs: 9 AM–9 PM Fri/Sat: 9 AM–10 PM
MASS TRANSIT	T: Green or Orange line to Haymarket
PAYMENT	Cash only
POPULAR FOOD	The slices are enormous, each one a quarter of a whole pie, but it's quality, not quantity, that keeps Ernesto's customers loyal; an elegant crust, substantial enough to hold a raft of toppings without collapsing, yet light and crisp at the edges, is covered with a fine minimalist tomato sauce and good mozzarella, as well as a vast array of excellent toppings; well-stuffed calzones and subs
DRINKS	Beer, wine, soft drinks, and juices
SEATING	Three tables for four, three tables for two
AMBIENCE	A mixed crowd of locals, students, and workers share the small but cheery space, which is brightened by large windows opening onto the sidewalk

—*Michael Beckett*

La Famiglia Giorgio's

Will you finish YOUR plate?

$$$$

112 Salem St., Boston 02110

(between Cooper St. and Prince St.)

Phone (617) 367-6711 • Fax (617) 437-0339

CATEGORY	Italian
HOURS	Mon–Fri: 11 AM–9:30 PM Sat/Sun: 11 AM–10:30 PM
MASS TRANSIT	T: Green or Orange Line to Haymarket
PAYMENT	VISA MasterCard AMERICAN EXPRESS
POPULAR FOOD	Famously large portions; hearty chicken and veal parmesan; veal piccata; lunchtime special (11 AM–3 PM) of a five-item buffet offers assorted delicious pastas and ravioli for around $6
UNIQUE FOOD	The *misto di pesce*, three pounds of pasta smothered with clams, mussels, calamari, shrimp, and haddock sautéed in fresh marinara sauce, garlic, and oil; finish it yourself and get a T-shirt that says, "I finished the plate"; La Famiglia Special, chunks of chicken or veal sautéed with onions and mushrooms in an alfredo-pesto sauce over tri-colored cheese tortellini
DRINKS	Beer, wine, sodas, juices

SEATING	Two floors filled with tables
AMBIENCE	Large portions, cheap prices, and very casual atmosphere bring families and college students; summertime and weekends bring long waits; walls with murals of Italian countrysides and wood paneling on the bottom halves, with plenty of Sinatra wafting past; downstairs can get a bit noisy—the upstairs offers a more intimate setting
OTHER ONES	• Back Bay: 250 Newbury St., Boston 02116, (617) 247-1569

—Jenny Bengen

Galleria Umberto

Elemental pizza at old-fashioned prices.
$

289 Hanover St., Boston 02113
(at Richmond St.)
Phone (617) 227-5709

CATEGORY	Pizza by the Slice
HOURS	Mon–Fri: 11 AM–2:30 PM (or whenever they run out)
MASS TRANSIT	T: Green or Orange line to Haymarket
PAYMENT	Cash only
POPULAR FOOD	Pizza doesn't get any simpler: a not-too-thick pan pizza with sauce and cheese, cut into square slices, 85 cents each, no toppings offered or needed; variety is saved for the calzones, which come in several configurations of meat, spinach, and cheese, none for over three bucks
UNIQUE FOOD	Croquette lovers will rejoice at the *panzarotti*, substantial ovaloids of mashed potato, deep-fried to golden brown, with a core of molten mozzarella, and the exceptional *arancini*, baseball-sized rounds of risotto with a crunchy golden exterior and a savory filling of ground meat, peas, and cheese
DRINKS	Sodas, inexpensive beer (both domestics and imports), and even more inexpensive wine
SEATING	Plenty of cafeteria-style seating with capacity for at least 60 to 70
AMBIENCE	The long but fast-moving line to the counter is crowded with North End workers and residents—feel free to order in English or Italian; then carry your tray to a table in the cavernous L-shaped room. To say that the space lacks atmosphere would be unfair; there are several framed posters advertising Italian travel destinations, and a large aquatic-themed mural covers one wall. Still, most people come for the food.

—Michael Beckett

Giacomo's Ristorante

Quintessential North End and well worth the wait.

$$$$

355 Hanover St., Boston 02113
(at Fleet St.)
Phone (617) 523-9026

CATEGORY	Italian
HOURS	Mon–Thurs: 5 PM–10 PM
	Fri/Sat: 5 PM–10:30 PM
	Sun: 4 PM–10 PM
MASS TRANSIT	T: Green or Orange line to Haymarket
PAYMENT	Cash only
POPULAR FOOD	Some of the best fried calamari in the North End; they're especially known for the build-your-own linguine dishes—select from an assortment of seafood and sauces; the butternut squash ravioli with diced asparagus in a prosciutto mascarpone cheese cream sauce suits the sweet tooth; for those not craving carbs, the grilled swordfish steak is a tasty alternative
DRINKS	Beer, wine, soft drinks, sparkling water
SEATING	Thirteen tables and two bar seats make for a very close-knit atmosphere
AMBIENCE	No reservations, so it's best to arrive before 6 PM when a line of regulars and tourists forms on the sidewalk outside the restaurant. The tables are close together but somehow not crowded, and the open kitchen at the back fills the air with tantalizing scents.
OTHER ONES	• South End: 431 Columbus Ave., Boston 02116, (617) 536-5723

—Jennifer Adams

Il Panino Express

Impeccable, immediate, and inexpensive Italian.

$$

264-266 Hanover St., Boston 02113
Phone (617) 720-5720
www.ilpanino.com

CATEGORY	Italian
HOURS	Daily: 11 AM–11 PM
MASS TRANSIT	T: Green or Orange line to Haymarket
PAYMENT	Cash only
POPULAR FOOD	Masterful calzones; famed pizzas; perfect pasta (great meatballs); delectable panini sandwiches (homemade mozzarella, prosciutto, and other Italian meats); voluminous salads

UNIQUE FOOD	Potato and egg panini; *pizza 4 stagioni* (with ham, artichokes, mushrooms and sausage); *pasta amatriciana* with bacon, tomato, and onion
DRINKS	Beer, wine, sodas
SEATING	Tables for about 30; order at the counter
AMBIENCE	When local cops turn up regularly and in force for the hearty dining at a local establishment, you know you're on to something good; open and bustling kitchen; it may not be elegant dining, but it's high quality, great value food
OTHER ONES	• Harvard Square: 1001 Massachusetts Ave., Cambridge 02138, (617) 547-5818
	More expensive restaurants at:
	• Downtown: 295 Franklin St., Boston 02110, (617) 338-1000
	• North End: 11 Parmenter St., Boston 02113, (617) 720-1336

—Nick Grandy

Pizzeria Regina

The brick-oven queen.
Since 1926
$$

11 1/2 Thacher St., Boston 02113
Phone (617) 227-0765 • Fax (617) 227-2662

CATEGORY	Pizza
HOURS	Mon–Thurs: 11 AM–11 PM
	Fri/Sat: 11 AM–midnight
	Sun: noon–11 PM
MASS TRANSIT	T: Green or Orange line to Haymarket
PAYMENT	Cash only
POPULAR FOOD	Regina's Original North End Recipe is a thin-crust Neapolitan masterwork cooked in a fiery hot brick oven and made fresh to order, the kind with cheesy crust-bubbles, the kind for which you'll happily risk the roof of your mouth to take an immediate first bite; fresh ingredients and subtle seasonings go into every pie, which has been lovingly "stretched" and "painted," then cooked to your specification: light-cooked, regular, or well done; toppings run the gamut from olives and artichokes to jalapeño peppers and marinated steak
UNIQUE FOOD	Sausages like no other, made at Regina's according to the Polcari family way
DRINKS	Soft drinks, beer, and wine
SEATING	Booths and tables seat 70
AMBIENCE	Classic wooden booths with coat hooks; a 106-year-old brick oven; pizza boxes piled floor-to-ceiling and old-time Regina's photos and paraphernalia; a capacity crowd eats and talks noisily, while a line curls from the front stairs on down the street

EXTRAS/NOTES	No reservations, and with this reputation, expect at least a 30-minute wait. Regina's has often been copied but nothing beats the original.
OTHER ONES	• Faneuil Hall: Faneuil Hall Food Court, Boston 02109, (617) 227-8180
	Also in Braintree, Burlington, Kingston, Marlboro, Auburn, Holyoke; Paramus, NJ; Richmond, VA; Providence, RI; and Oviedo, FL.

—Esti Iturralde

Pomodoro Ristorante

You say tomato, I say pomodoro…
$$$$
319 Hanover St., Boston 02113
(near Richmond St.)
Phone (617) 367-4348

CATEGORY	Italian
HOURS	Daily: 11 AM–11 PM
MASS TRANSIT	T: Green or Orange line to Haymarket
PAYMENT	Cash only
POPULAR FOOD	If you love red sauce done well, this is your place; you'll pay more than at your local pizza joint, but less than at many of the other neighborhood places (and for better food); favorite dishes include the spicy calamari, the Seafood Diabolo entrée—cooked in a flavorful, fresh marinara, with a good kick of heat
UNIQUE FOOD	The pan-seared salmon with tomato *arancini* and arugula; *arancini* is Italian for "rice ball," which is exactly that—a ball of rice and various spices pressed into a yummy baseball-sized dumpling
DRINKS	A selection of sodas and beer; red and white house wine by the glass
SEATING	With only about 24 seats in a tiny room, be prepared to encounter your neighbor and your server up close; noisy, packed, hot, and lively; every seat has a great view—either of the bustling street outside or of the busy kitchen
AMBIENCE	Décor is simple, classic, and romantic; this place is packed to the gills after 6 PM; reservations are recommended, but do not necessarily eliminate a wait; the crowd is a mix of locals, families, and hip, dressy people out on dates; no restroom—you have to go to the coffeeshop across the street
EXTRAS/NOTES	Sometimes you get an earful of some really funky '80s mix tapes. Depeche Mode and Kate Bush seem a little funny in an Italian place, but hey, we've all heard enough of *That's Amore.*

—Amy Cooper

EAST BOSTON/CHARLESTOWN

Jeveli's

An old-school Italian legend. Since 1927

$$$

387 Chelsea St., East Boston 02128
(in Day Sq.)
Phone (617) 567-9539

CATEGORY	Italian
HOURS	Mon–Sat: 11 AM–1 AM
	Sun: noon–1 AM
MASS TRANSIT	T: Blue line to Maverick
PAYMENT	VISA MasterCard AMERICAN EXPRESS
POPULAR FOOD	Huge portions of chicken or veal parmesan, sausage cacciatore; at lunch the prices get knocked way down
UNIQUE FOOD	Good tripe is becoming a rarer find in the city's restaurants these days
DRINKS	Full bar; there is also a bar with a table where you can eat; the wine list is limited to house wines and the beer selection is small—but it's all really cheap
SEATING	Room for over 200 in three dining rooms; the upstairs dining room doubles as a function hall for large catered gatherings
AMBIENCE	A lively family atmosphere, great for a large outing of friends; everything here is a throwback to a different time; even the waitresses have some old-fashioned feisty Boston attitude
EXTRAS/NOTES	Bill Clinton ate here when he was President.

—*Matt Stauff*

Lori-Ann Donut Shop

(see p. 196)
Donut Shop
198 Bunker Hill St., Charlestown 02129
Phone (617) 241-7808

> "It seems to me that our three basic needs,
> for food and security and love, are so mixed and mingled
> and entwined that we cannot straightly think
> of one without the others. So it happens that when
> I write of hunger, I am really writing about love and the
> hunger for it, and warmth and the love of it and the
> hunger for it; and then the warmth and richness
> and fine reality of hunger satisfied; and it is all one."
> —*M. F. K. Fisher,* The Art of Eating

Know Your Chowdah

Any self-respecting Bostonian will tell you that only their clam chowder is worthy of the name. According to them, the brothy Manhattan variety, with tomatoes and no dairy, is more of a soup than a proper chowder. However, ask Rhode Islanders and they will tell you that tomato soup is a recommended addition. In stark contrast, the creamiest chowders are found in Maine and Massachusetts, where potatoes and salt pork also figure largely. Little exemplifies these recipe rivalries more than a piece of legislation that was nearly passed by the state of Maine in 1939, which would have made it *illegal* to put tomatoes in any chowder made of clams.

Why such strictness? One might expect, at least in Massachusetts, some kind of loyalty to early chowder recipes—perhaps dating back to the Pilgrims—the same way the French trace their methods of cheese-making back to centuries-old traditions. But this is hardly the case with chowder. New England clam chowder, despite its old-fashioned appearances, is a pretty newfangled idea. It would have been inconceivable to put clams, cream, broth—not to mention tomatoes—in the first New England chowders. Indeed, today's chowder is so decadent and unorthodox it would have made a Pilgrim blush.

The word *chowder* probably came from the French *chaudière*, a Breton cauldron used by fishermen to make big stews, or *chaudée*, a fish soup, particularly one made over an open outdoor fire. This idea for a fish stew probably got to New England from the French colonies up north. Because the first chowders were made on ships, the availability of ingredients was fairly limited: the day's catch, some cured pork, maybe some biscuits. Fresh water was too scarce for much broth. Forget fresh ingredients like milk or tomatoes.

The earliest known record of New England "chowder" in print came in 1732, when the most common ingredient was cod, not clams. Unlike in the case of cod (see p. 261), New Englanders did not discover a passion for clams right away, and did not put them in chowders until much later. Both the tomato and the clam were suspected by early white North Americans to be poisonous. Thomas Jefferson helped champion the cause of the former, while clams did not become popular until the 19th century, when improvements in ice-making and refrigeration made shellfish more widely available.

By the 1830s, Boston's **Ye Olde Union Oyster House** was well known for its clam chowder and still serves gallons of it today. But even then, there was no definitive New England chowder recipe. Some cooks stayed true to the use of cod, pork, onions, and crackers; later came sliced potatoes, clams, and water for broth. In the latter half of the 1800s, the last new ingredients were introduced: tomato and cream, though rarely in the same recipe. Tomatoes appeared in New York, Rhode Island, and Connecticut, probably adopted from the recipes of Southern European immigrants. Around the same time, milk and cream became mainstays of upper New England chowders. And thus was born the tomato-versus-cream chowder controversy that has persisted ever since.

With this history of diversity, it's no wonder that New Englanders like to battle it out over their many chowder recipes. A good way to quickly discern between Boston's many versions is at **Chowderfest**, held annually in July at Boston City Hall Plaza. We also recommend the following for a bowl of New England's best.

Atlantic Fish Co., *Back Bay: 761 Boylston St., Boston 02116, (617) 267-4000.*

Bay State Chowda Co., *Faneuil Hall: 1 Faneuil Hall Marketplace, Boston 02109, (617) 742-4441.*

Chart House, *Waterfront: 60 Long Wharf, Boston 02110, (617) 227-1576.*

Legal Sea Foods, *Kendall Square: 5 Cambridge Ctr., Cambridge 02141, (617) 864-3400. (and 11 other Boston locations.)*

The Marshall House, *see p. 7, Faneuil Hall: 15 Union St., Boston 02108, (617) 523-9396.*

No Name, *see p. 10., Waterfront: 15 1/2 Fish Pier St. W., Boston 02210, (617) 338-7539.*

Union Oyster House, *Faneuil Hall: 41 Union St., Boston 02108, (617) 227-2750.*

—Esti Iturralde

Santarpio's Pizza

Pizzerias come and pizzerias go, but Santarpios... Since 1930

$$

111 Chelsea St., East Boston 02128
(corner of Porter St., first exit in East Boston after Callahan Tunnel)
Phone (617) 567-9871

CATEGORY	Pizza
HOURS	Mon–Sat: 11:30 AM–midnight Sun: noon–midnight
MASS TRANSIT	T: Blue line to Airport
PAYMENT	Cash only
POPULAR FOOD	Toppings are limited to the basics—garlic, peppers, sausage, onions, pepperoni, and anchovies—but plain cheese is best; the pie here is like no other: a very crispy crust that's charred on the outside with a soupy middle of cheese and sauce
UNIQUE FOOD	Behind the bar, Italian sausage cooks over a grill and is served with marinated peppers and a hunk of white bread

DRINKS	Bottled beers, none more exotic than Heineken, served in juice-sized glasses
SEATING	A long bar with stools seats a dozen, while dilapidated booths accommodate 40 more
AMBIENCE	Santarpio's is a dive in the noblest sense; ask somebody for directions to it and they'll invariably begin, "It don't look like much on the outside…"; years' worth of awards share the walls with pictures of boxing legends and Old Blue Eyes himself (Frank ate here once); wood paneling, oldies music—even the patrons at the bar look like they've been here since 1973
EXTRAS NOTES	Where else would the waiters smoke? Santarpio's, we salute you.

—Esti Iturralde

Sorelle

Sweet and savory, locals-meet-yuppies, lunch spot near the Monument.
$$

1 Monument Ave., Charlestown 02129
(corner of Main St.)
Phone (617) 242-2125 • Fax (617) 241-9675

CATEGORY	Bakery/Café
HOURS	Mon–Fri: 6:30 AM–5 PM Sat/Sun: 8 AM–3 PM
MASS TRANSIT	T: Orange line to Bunker Hill Community College; bus: #93
PAYMENT	Cash only
POPULAR FOOD	Don't blink because the muffins and buttery cinnamon-packed pecan rolls go quickly in the morning; Tuesday's meatball sandwich is excellent; other popular sandwiches are the Southwestern chicken and the roast beef with Swiss and onion; various chicken, veggie, and pasta salads; pizza, calzones, and soups; the sinfully fantastic cakes need to be ordered 48 hours ahead of time
UNIQUE FOOD	Perfectly chosen condiments: horseradish mayo with roast beef, orange mayo with turkey, olive-and-herb vinaigrette with tuna
DRINKS	Soft drinks, espresso, cappuccino, tea
SEATING	Three tables inside and a few out back when it's warm; largely a takeout place
AMBIENCE	Cute lunch spot and bakery; can get competitive during the grab-coffee-and-muffin-before-work period when everybody is lunging for the baked goods
EXTRAS/NOTES	The two owners, Mark and Marc, are very easy-going, friendly people who are good to their regulars—and anyone who tries Sorelle once becomes one.

—Hadley Hudson

La Terraza

When you're in need of an empanada fix.

$$

19 Bennington St., East Boston 02128

(at Porter St.)

Phone (617) 561-5200

CATEGORY	Colombian
HOURS	Daily: 10 AM–11 PM
MASS TRANSIT	T: Blue line to Maverick
PAYMENT	VISA MasterCard
POPULAR FOOD	Huge cornmeal *empanadas* stuffed with beef, pork, potatoes, and onions; *arroz con pollo*; fish cakes; *maduros* (plantains); flan
UNIQUE FOOD	*Bevas con queso* (figs and cheese); *tomate de arbol* (tamarillo and cheese)
DRINKS	*Aguapanela*, a sugarcane drink with lime
SEATING	Plenty of seating at small tables
AMBIENCE	Plain atmosphere: white walls, murals, and the murmurs of television.

—*Kyle Konrad*

Uncle Pete's Hickory Ribs

The American dream—life, liberty, and the pursuit of slow-smoked ribs.

$$$

309 Bennington St., East Boston 02128

(at Chelsea St., in Day Sq.)

Phone (617) 569-RIBS

www.unclepetes.com

CATEGORY	Barbecue
HOURS	Sun–Tues: 3 PM–9:30 PM Wed/Thurs: 11:30 AM–9:30 PM Fri/Sat: 11:30 AM–10 PM
MASS TRANSIT	T: Blue line to Maverick
PAYMENT	Cash only
POPULAR FOOD	Tender, juicy pork ribs, hand rubbed and wood smoked; it takes three days to make these ribs; pulled pork; brisket; chili; sweet potato biscuits
UNIQUE FOOD	Thai chicken in peanut sauce and Asian cole slaw (after all, Pete's wife is Thai); ziti (after all, owner Pete is Italian)
DRINKS	Soft drinks served in mason jar mugs
SEATING	Booths with red and white checked tablecloths and thick rolls of paper towels
AMBIENCE	Christmas lights twinkle year-round at this wood shingled former Dairy Queen
EXTRAS/NOTES	Owners Pete and Pha Cucchiara are not your typical barbecue connoisseurs. The two met when Pha came to work at The King & I, a Thai restaurant Pete co-owned for a while (see p. 34). Pete sold it and decided to try the barbecue business. After traveling from rib joint to rib joint in the Southeast, the couple bought a smoker, put it in their basement, honed their skills, and Uncle Pete's was born.

—*Kaya Stone*

Warren Tavern

History, hamburgers, and heavenly chowder at one of Paul Revere's old haunts.
Since 1780

$$$

2 Pleasant St., Charlestown 02129

(between Main St. and Warren St.)

Phone (617) 241-8142

CATEGORY	Historic American Pub
HOURS	Mon–Fri: 11:30 AM–10:30 PM
	Sat/Sun: 10:30 AM–10:30 PM
MASS TRANSIT	T: Orange line to Bunker Hill Community College
PAYMENT	VISA MasterCard AMERICAN EXPRESS
POPULAR FOOD	The Tavern Burger—a half-pound of Angus beef with boursin cheese and honey dijon mustard, with fried-to-perfection Tavern potato chips; though numerous Boston-area restaurants boast "award-winning chowdah," the Warren clam chowder is just as the menu describes: fresh, thick, and creamy—a must-try for those seeking the authentic Boston experience; lobster ravioli
DRINKS	Full bar; well-poured Guinness
SEATING	A quaint, dark wooden room with six intimate tables and low ceilings; another larger room with an open bar area and a few additional wooden tables
AMBIENCE	Cozy pub with broad wooden floors, exposed beams, antique murals on the walls and lace curtains on the windows, dark wood paneling, fireplaces, and wooden tables; casual locals hangout, bar stays open later than restaurant
EXTRAS/NOTES	Great quality food in good portions—not your typical tourist grub. Believed to be the first building erected in Charlestown after the British razed the area during the Battle of Bunker Hill, the tavern reportedly hosted George Washington sometime after independence was won. It was founded by Captain Eliphelet Newell, believed to have been a Boston Tea Party conspirator, who named his tavern after General Joseph Warren, the fallen hero of Bunker Hill. It came to be an important gathering place—one of Paul Revere's favorite watering holes—and a center of debate and discussion in the early days of the Revolutionary War.

—*Meaghan Mulholland*

"If you are ever at a loss to support a
flagging conversation, introduce the subject of eating."
—*Leigh Hunt*

BEACON HILL

Antonio's Cucina Italiana
Homestyle Italian in casual elegance.

$$$

288 Cambridge St., Boston 02114

(at Anderson St.)

Phone (617) 367-3310 • Fax (617) 367-2070

CATEGORY	Italian
HOURS	Mon–Thurs: 11 AM–10 PM
	Fri/Sat: 11 AM–10:30 PM
MASS TRANSIT	T: Red line to Charles/MGH
PAYMENT	VISA MasterCard AMERICAN EXPRESS
POPULAR FOOD	An array of simple veal, chicken, and seafood dishes in sauce and served with a side of pasta; Old World comfort foods like gnocchi, homemade fusili, and other pastas served with pesto or garlic and oil; wonderful cannoli
DRINKS	Beer, wine, cappuccino
SEATING	A single room that seats about 50 at intimate tables
AMBIENCE	A neighborhood favorite for a delicious traditional meal; elegant, framed figure drawings decorate the cream-colored walls; waiters blend the right amount of American efficiency, Boston attitude, and European aloofness

—*Esti Iturralde*

R.I.P.
Buzzy's Fabulous Roast Beef

Sitting in the shadow of old-time Charles Street Jail and in a prime spot between Beacon Hill and the West End, Buzzy's was *the* all-night joint for just about anyone. MGH doctors, late-night cops, drunk students, and retired townies all stopped in for heaps of 3 AM grease. Legend has it that even the jail's inmates had the dive's notorious roast beef sandwich tossed in between cell bars. And when it closed down in early 2002, the city's night owls were left with nary a food option.

Opened in the mid-1960s, Buzzy's was finally forced to shut its doors when developers acquired the 24/7 eatery and tore it down in order to reconstruct the area as a four-star hotel set to open in mid-2004.

Like most late-night spots, Buzzy's sold cheap grease in a grimy but kitschy atmosphere. And while at times it seemed like they were operating by their own health code, their thick roast beef and shake could cure any case of the midnight munchies.

—*Kaya Stone*

Istanbul Café

Authentic Turkish in a bohemian, basement setting.

$$$

37 Bowdoin St., Boston 02114

(at Derne St.)

Phone (617) 227-3434 • Fax (617) 227-4616

CATEGORY	Turkish
HOURS	Mon–Wed: 11 AM–10 PM
	Thurs–Sat: 11 AM–11 PM
	Sun: noon–10 PM
MASS TRANSIT	T: Red or Green line to Park St.
PAYMENT	VISA MasterCard AMERICAN EXPRESS
POPULAR FOOD	Lamb kebabs; *yaprak doner* and *izgara kofte*, both lamb dishes served with strong but not overbearing Turkish spices; *yaprak dolma*, a stuffed grape leaf appetizer is a meal unto itself with olive oil, rice, and nuts mixed together inside the leaves; for those on a budget, the free bread plus one appetizer is enough for a lunch; swordfish skewers (*kilic sis*) with tender and tasty fish and vegetables, the red lentil soup, and baked rice pudding are perfect for a cold Boston day
UNIQUE FOOD	*Beyaz peynir*, a white cheese; thin crusted *krymali* pizza with ground beef and sautéed onions; *mucver* appetizer, a zucchini fritter with cold yogurt
DRINKS	Turkish beer, Turkish red or white wine, sweet and rich Turkish coffee; *aroma visne*, a fresh sour cherry drink
SEATING	Fourteen intimate wooden tables for two, and two tables for four in a small room; expect a wait at lunchtime
AMBIENCE	A combination of political staff and law students; Old World feel with Turkish rugs, plates, and paintings everywhere

—*Ted Kulik*

J. Pace & Son

(see p. 6)

Italian

75 Blossom Ct., Boston 02114

Phone (617) 227-6141

Joe and Nemo's

The hot dog kings are back.
Since 1909

$

138 Cambridge St., Boston 02114

(at Hancock St.)

Phone (617) 720-4342

www.joeandnemo.com

CATEGORY	Hot Dogs
HOURS	Daily: 9 AM–9 PM
MASS TRANSIT	T: Red line to Charles/MGH

PAYMENT	Cash only
POPULAR FOOD	Not all wieners were created equal—Joe and Nemo's serves original pork and beef, deep fried, garlic spiced, and even a blasphemous veggie dog
UNIQUE FOOD	Dirty fries—strips of deep-fried hot dog wieners with chili, cheese sauce, and onions
DRINKS	House-brand root beer
SEATING	Mostly takeout; fewer than a dozen seats
AMBIENCE	Modern fast food look mixed with old-time pictures of Boston and Fenway Park
EXTRAS/NOTES	A fixture of Scollay Square throughout the first half of the twentieth century, Joe and Nemo's remained when all else in the area disappeared. In the '40s, the restaurant owed much of its popularity to its location across from the Old Howard burlesque theater. The "Hot Dog Kings" grew to 27 restaurants in the early 1960s, serving over a million franks per year, but in 1963 the city took over the Scollay Square location as part of an ever-widening circle of urban renewal. In 2001, the current Cambridge St. location opened, a mere two blocks from where the original once stood.

—Kyle Konrad

The King and I

Thai delicacies fit for Anna and her king.

$$$

145 Charles St., Boston 02114

(at Revere St.)

Phone (617) 227-3320

CATEGORY	Thai
HOURS	Mon–Thurs: 11:30 AM–9:30 PM
	Fri: 11:30 AM–10:30 PM
	Sat: noon–10:30 PM
	Sun: 5 PM–9:30 PM
MASS TRANSIT	T: Red line to Charles/MGH
PAYMENT	VISA MasterCard AMERICAN EXPRESS DISCOVER
POPULAR FOOD	Drunken Chicken (in chili sauce with string beans) and the Rama Garden (chicken in peanut sauce); plenty of vegetarian options; papaya salad
DRINKS	Beer, wine, coffee, tea, Thai iced tea
SEATING	Two rooms with tables
AMBIENCE	A cozy and elegant place with candelabras on the ceilings, beautiful drawings and paintings on the walls, and tiny candles on the tables; a varied crowd ranging from college kids to couples to large families, all of whom come here to enjoy great food in a relatively quiet atmosphere

—Jenny Bengen

Panificio

*Friendly brunch and lunch
secret downtown.*

$$

144 Charles St., Boston 02114
(near Cambridge St.)
Phone (617) 227-4340

CATEGORY	Italian Café
HOURS	Mon–Fri: 7 AM–9:30 PM
	Sat/Sun: 10 AM–4 PM
MASS TRANSIT	T: Red line to Charles/MGH
PAYMENT	VISA MasterCard AMERICAN EXPRESS
POPULAR FOOD	French toast, pancakes, Sicilian pizza slices, upscale Italian sandwiches, salads
UNIQUE FOOD	A brunch item called *formaggio*: perfectly toasted country bread spread generously with mascarpone cheese, topped with fresh berries (blueberries, strawberries, raspberries, and/or blackberries), and drizzled with honey
DRINKS	Most of the day, they are an authentic coffee-and-espresso kind of establishment, also with a good selection of imported Italian sodas; in the evening, there's a limited wine and beer selection
SEATING	Order at the counter and the staff brings big, beautiful plates to you; there are tables for about 30 people, mostly at small, intimate two-person tables
AMBIENCE	This comfy-casual place is very busy on weekends, especially Sunday from 10:30 AM to 12:30 PM; the crowd is as diverse as a Beacon Hill place can be: yuppie-types in their ponytails and fleece vests, professorial types reading the *New York Times*, young families with their babies in strollers, and the random (lucky) tourist who wanders in while on a break from the Trolley Tour
EXTRAS/NOTES	It's an appetizing symphony of clanking silverware, accompanied by the coffee grinder and espresso machine, and the sounds and smells of cooking in the kitchen—all at close quarters. Sit on a stool at the bar overlooking Charles St. for a solo meal and people-watching. Eating is tight at certain times, but the turnover is pretty quick. The décor transports you to what an Italian grandmother's place in Sicily might look like. The walls are covered with gaudily framed family photos of the owners, signed pictures of celebrities, and scenes from Italy. The shelves hanging on the side wall are packed full of small trinkets, including porcelain plates perched for looking, not touching.

—Jodi Hullinger

The Paramount

Charming café/bistro at cobblestone's edge.

$$$

44 Charles St., Boston 02114

(at Chestnut St.)

Phone (617) 720-1152

CATEGORY	Café
HOURS	Mon–Thurs: 7 AM–10 PM
	Fri/Sat: 7 AM–11 PM
MASS TRANSIT	T: Red line to Charles/MGH
PAYMENT	VISA MasterCard AMERICAN EXPRESS
POPULAR FOOD	Potentially boring burgers and sandwiches are transformed here into mouthwatering wonders with creative changes; try the pumpkin and smoked mozzarella ravioli; entrees such as the grilled sirloin are well worth their extra nibbling of your wallet; the sweet potato fries are a must
UNIQUE FOOD	Turkey burger with cranberry sauce
DRINKS	Beer, wine, soft drinks, tea, coffee
SEATING	Tables for four and two, including more intimate and romantically lit two-seaters
AMBIENCE	Plenty of locals come in the morning for the café, but tourists and regulars alike crowd tables in the evenings when Paramount goes bistro

—Jenny Bengen

The Upper Crust

Even Brahmins need their pizza.

$$

20 Charles St., Boston 02114

(at Beacon St.)

Phone (617) 723-9600 • Fax (617) 723-6685

www.theuppercrustpizzeria.com

CATEGORY	Gourmet Pizza
HOURS	Mon–Wed: 11:30 AM–10 PM
	Thurs–Sun: 11:30 AM–10:30 PM
MASS TRANSIT	T: Red line to Charles/MGH
PAYMENT	VISA MasterCard AMERICAN EXPRESS
POPULAR FOOD	The definitive thin-crust pizza: high-quality mozzarella, fresh-tasting chunky tomato sauce, and a crust perfectly balanced between crunch and chew, all combined to make beautifully simple pizza; whole pies are available with a wide range of excellent toppings
UNIQUE FOOD	White (canned) clam pizza; uncommon combos such as the Uncommon, with bacon, pineapple, bits of jalapeños; spinach leaf, chopped garlic, and ricotta
DRINKS	Soft drinks and juices
SEATING	Ten seats at the long table; counter stools
AMBIENCE	As you enter, your eyes are drawn upward to the brushed metal ceiling which seems to undulate, then down again to the pizza

maker stretching dough at a counter overlooking the dining area; a mix of local college students and well-heeled Beacon Hill residents sit at one long table and two narrow counters along each side of the small but well-designed space

EXTRAS/NOTES   Check out the pizza-box cartoon art hanging behind the register.

—*Michael Beckett*

CHINATOWN-THEATER DISTRICT

Buddha's Delight

For the vegan, the vegetarian, and others who love "meat."

$$$

3 Beach St., 2nd Fl., Boston 02111

(at Washington St.)

Phone (617) 451-2395

CATEGORY	Pan-Asian/Vegetarian
HOURS	Sun–Thurs: 11 AM–9:30 PM Fri/Sat: 11 AM–10:30 PM
MASS TRANSIT	T: Orange line to Chinatown
PAYMENT	VISA MasterCard
POPULAR FOOD	Typical Asian dishes but instead of chicken or beef, they use chicken-like and beef-like substitutes made out of wheat gluten and similar products; the "beef" is really tasty and the closest to actual meat; other attempts, such as the "shrimp," are downright weird (and weird-looking); recommended are #22 "beef" and yellow noodles stir-fried with vegetables, #84 sweet-and-sour "pork" tofu, #42A fried wontons, and #37 steamed wheat gluten spring rolls
UNIQUE FOOD	Especially notable are the barbecued dishes and combination specials, which usually feature a mixture of "beef," "shrimp," and "pork"; the "roast skin" is mighty tasty, whatever it is
DRINKS	Vietnamese-style coffee; tea; an exotic array of milkshakes (green bean, jackfruit, carrot-tomato); juices; bottled beer; wine
SEATING	Plenty of seating at small tables in a large room; a few bigger tables as well
AMBIENCE	Cavernous and blue, with devotional art on the walls; lunch (an especially notable deal) is sometimes busy, and service varies widely, but there is rarely a wait for a table; first dates will find plenty to talk about as they debate the merits of the "shrimp" versus the "duck" or hypothesize about what "roast skin" could possibly be; vegetarians, thrill seekers, and bargain hunters alike make repeat customers

EXTRAS/NOTES	Buddha's Delight has the unique distinction of being one of the few places in Boston where a vegetarian can order anything—and that's *anything*—on the menu. Newcomers eventually get over the sheer number of quotation marks.
OTHER ONES	Smaller and a bit cozier than the one in Chinatown: • Coolidge Corner: Buddha's Delight Too, 404 Harvard St., Brookline 02446, (617) 739-8830

—Alison Pereto

China Pearl

The classic for no-frills dim sum.
$$

9 Tyler St., Boston 02111
(between Beach St. and Kneeland St.)
Phone (617) 426-4338

CATEGORY	Chinese Dim Sum
HOURS	Daily: 8:30 AM–10:30 PM
MASS TRANSIT	T: Orange line to Chinatown
PAYMENT	VISA MasterCard AMERICAN EXPRESS DISCOVER
POPULAR FOOD	Probably the best dim sum in Boston (served until 3:30 PM), with traditional dishes like *shumai*, *cha sui bao* (steamed pork buns), and mango pudding; whatever you choose, it's sure to be hot, fresh, and tasty
UNIQUE FOOD	Servers bring around carts with a number of delicacies; you look and point, and because there's sometimes no telling what you'll get—chicken whosits, crab whatsits—it's bound to be an adventure
DRINKS	Tea, soda
SEATING	A huge restaurant with over 900 seats in large, sometimes shared, tables
AMBIENCE	Travel up the large golden staircase lined with mirrors and push through the crowds of waiting hungry people; it's loud and bustling; avoid Saturday and Sundays between noon and 1 PM, unless you don't mind an hour wait
OTHER ONES	• Western Suburbs: 288 Mishawum Rd., Woburn 01801, (781) 932-0031

—Christopher Russell

"Our lives are not in the lap of the gods,
but in the lap of our cooks."
—Lin Yuntang (The Importance of Living)

Chinatown Café

Five dollars, once a day, guarantees you will never have to cook again.

$

262 Harrison Ave., Boston 02111
(corner of Marginal St.)
Phone (617) 695-9888

CATEGORY	Cantonese
HOURS	Daily: 10:30 AM–8:30 PM
MASS TRANSIT	T: Orange Line to New England Medical Center
PAYMENT	Cash only
POPULAR FOOD	Their Chinese take on *pad* Thai could be cause for an addiction recovery group; black pepper T-bone beef and General Gao's Chicken also have cult-like followings that border on compulsion; Cantonese favorites *won ton mein* (wonton noodles) and *cha siu fan* (the barbecued pork hanging in the window served over rice) are platinum hits
UNIQUE FOOD	Three Treasures Rice (cuts of chicken, barbecue pork, and barbecue duck with sauce on rice) provides a nice sampling of their specialty, barbecued meats
DRINKS	Soybean milk and soft drinks; in the tradition of any proper Chinese restaurant they provide free hot tea
SEATING	Two rows of booths and two large round tables in the back seat about 45 people
AMBIENCE	Historic and community-related pictures of Chinatown decorate the otherwise plain, fluorescent-lit walls; consistently noisy and pretty clean (for Chinatown standards); Chinatown locals, police officers, New England Medical Center workers, poor students, and cute senior citizens provide a steady stream of customers; Sundays at lunchtime are the busiest and noisiest with crowds from Chinatown churches chatting it up over their favorite rice and noodle dishes
EXTRAS/NOTES	Just when you approach your eating limit you look into the Styrofoam container and find that the food looks more or less untouched; you can't even see the bottom—either the food has self-multiplying amoeba qualities, the Styrofoam containers are manufactured by the people who make Mary Poppins's bag, or they give you a lot a lot of food. You are squandering your time in Boston if you fail to eat here.

—Charlene X. Wang

Ding Ho

China in a shoebox.

$

88 Harrison Ave., Boston 02111
(at Kneeland St.)
Phone (617) 357-4150

CATEGORY	Chinese
HOURS	Daily: 8:30 AM–7 PM
MASS TRANSIT	T: Orange line to Chinatown
PAYMENT	Cash only
POPULAR FOOD	The specials are the most noteworthy feature of this tiniest of eateries; every day there's something new—from curried beef to kung pao chicken—all for a mere $2
DRINKS	None
SEATING	Ding Ho is literally the size of a walk-in closet; there's really only one perfect place to feast on your $3 meal, and that's on a bench in Chinatown Gateway Park, which you can reach by taking a left down Kneeland and another left onto Hudson
AMBIENCE	Chinatown denizens, Financial District yuppies, and impecunious vegetarians

—*Ray Misra*

East Ocean City

Those giant fish tanks aren't just for show.

$$$

27 Beach St., Boston 02111
(west of Harrison Ave.)
Phone (617) 542-2504

CATEGORY	Chinese
HOURS	Mon–Thurs: 11 AM–3:30 AM
	Fri/Sat: 11 AM–4 AM
	Sun: 11 AM–3 AM
MASS TRANSIT	T: Orange line to Chinatown
PAYMENT	VISA MasterCard AMERICAN EXPRESS
POPULAR FOOD	Still swimming seafood straight from the tanks; steamed whole fish, geoduck clams, conch, eels, crabs; clams in black bean sauce, *chow foon*, Peking duck
UNIQUE FOOD	You'll see the enormous Alaskan king crabs when you first walk in—you sure you're up to the challenge?
DRINKS	Beer, wine, full bar
SEATING	A number of large tables in two rooms
AMBIENCE	One of the nicer rooms in Chinatown; very attentive service, and a number of large families sharing huge platters of fresh seafood; there can be a wait on weekends, but luckily, they are open until 4 AM for those late-night cravings
EXTRAS/NOTES	It's impossible to resist the fresh seafood that's still swimming when you order it.

The servers will even bring your selection to the table for your approval before sending it back to the kitchen. A great place to take Chinatown first timers, with a lot of action, and a huge menu to please everyone.

—Pete Carpenter

Grand Chau Chow

Because lazy fish taste great.

$$$

45 Beach St., Boston 02111

(at Harrison St.)

Phone (617) 292-4646

CATEGORY	Chinese
HOURS	Sun–Thurs: 10 AM–2:30 AM Fri/Sat: 10 AM–3:30 AM
MASS TRANSIT	T: Orange line to Chinatown
PAYMENT	VISA MasterCard AMERICAN EXPRESS DISCOVER
POPULAR FOOD	The haggard fish on display may look like asthmatics having just completed an underwater relay, but they are fresh and delicious; the crab rangoon actually tastes like crab; other popular dishes are the soft lo mein noodles, crispy sesame chicken, and beef with scallions
UNIQUE FOOD	Southern Cantonese fish head with ginger and scallions; braised duck feet with oyster sauce
DRINKS	Tea, wine, Tsingtao, and soft drinks
SEATING	Seats 100, mostly at tables, but also a few booths
AMBIENCE	Entering through a narrow channel of beveled mirrors, Grand Chau Chow at first seems like a glittering, gaudy noodle palace; once inside, the dining room is actually large, casual, and usually bustling; ultra-late hours and heaping servings make this grand dame of Chinatown popular with hungry students of every race and creed
OTHER ONES	The sister restaurant around the corner, which also offers dim sum: • Chinatown: Chau Chow City, 81 Essex St., Boston 02111, (617) 338-8158

—Mark Ferguson

Ho Yuen Bakery

(see p. 110)

Bakery

54 Beach St., Boston 02111

Phone (617) 426-8320

Jacob Wirth

Updated German classics that are definitely wirth the trip.
Since 1868
$$$

31-37 Stuart St., Boston 02116
(between Tremont St. and Washington St.)
Phone (617) 338-8586 • Fax (617) 426-5049
www.jacobwirth.com

CATEGORY	German
HOURS	Sun/Mon: 11:30 AM–8 PM Tues–Thurs: 11:30 AM–11 PM Fri/Sat: 11:30 AM–midnight
MASS TRANSIT	T: Orange line to New England Medical Center
PAYMENT	VISA MasterCard AMERICAN EXPRESS DISCOVER
POPULAR FOOD	Anything involving German sausages—the mixed grill features smoked bratwurst and *weisswurst*, while Jake's Special prepares the same meats, only boiled; the meats are fresh and flavorful, and meant to mix with the side dishes in the same forkful; only the mixed grill includes sauerkraut, but both dishes are served with German potato salad and *rotkohl*, a.k.a. pickled red cabbage (see below); German potato salad (made with bacon and onions); for an updated version of traditional German comfort food, try the potato pancake appetizer—the flavor of the green onions within the pancake is complemented by a chestnut *crème fraîche* sauce and applesauce
UNIQUE FOOD	The *rotkohl* stands out for its sweetness and finely chopped texture, which proves a great combination; the *sauerbrauten*: thin slices of beef served with sweet and sour sauce, and dill *spaetzle*, the German answer to pasta; the smoked salmon and brie strudel appetizer—served on top of fresh baby arugula and capers
DRINKS	The perfect place for a drink, the establishment's most exquisite feature is its long mahogany bar. Above, a Latin motto proclaims SUUM CUIQCE—translation: "to each his own"—and they probably have enough different drafts to go around, especially imported German, Dutch, Belgian, and English brews. There's everything a serious beer drinker would need, from Pilsners to Hefeweizens to dark beers. Two are brewed locally and exclusively for the restaurant: Jake's Special Lite and Special Dark. Also a nice array of Reislings.
SEATING	Catering to packed theater crowds, JW's can seat up to 265 people: spaces for eating directly at the bar; tables around

the bar; small and large wooden tables are the options in the dining area; busiest during pre- (4 to 7 PM) and post- (10 PM to midnight) theater hours

AMBIENCE Lively and gregarious, with a knowledge-able and friendly staff. Mahogany tables are decorated with thin tall vases filled with fresh flowers. The place hasn't changed all that much in 134 years—sepia-toned photos (largely of Wirth's family and the restaurant) and former wine lists and menus adorn the walls, reminding modern patrons that Jacob Wirth's is truly a 100 percent authentic Bostonian landmark.

EXTRAS/NOTES Live free music Wednesday through Saturday nights: Every Friday, Mel Stiller leads a piano sing-a-long (8 PM–midnight); on Saturdays, the Steve Fells Jazz Quartet, comprised for years of ever-changing Berklee students and graduates, performs.

—*Christina Tuminella*

Jumbo Seafood

Normal-sized fish, jumbo-sized flavors.
$$$
5-7-9 Hudson St., Boston 02111
(south of Beach St.)
Phone (617) 542-2823

CATEGORY Chinese

HOURS Daily: 11:30 AM–12:15 AM

MASS TRANSIT T: Orange line to Chinatown

PAYMENT VISA MasterCard AMERICAN EXPRESS

POPULAR FOOD Whole steamed sea bass, striped bass, or black fish; live shrimp that jump out of the tank; fresh Chinese vegetables like pea tendrils and Chinese broccoli; picking your own fish out of the tank is always a fun experience

DRINKS Beer, wine, and soft drinks

SEATING A long room with large tables to accommodate a number of large families

AMBIENCE A large Asian clientele; well lit and clean with an attractive dining room; hardly ever a wait

EXTRAS/NOTES There are many seafood restaurants with live fish tanks in Chinatown. What sets Jumbo apart is the freshness and lightness of the cuisine—and watching the servers chase down shrimp that have escaped from the tank.

—*Pete Carpenter*

"I will not eat oysters. I want my food dead. Not sick, not wounded, dead."

—*Woody Allen*

Pearl Tea Mania

The sight of teen girls, middle-aged men, and mothers with strollers all sipping a milky liquid with ball-shaped globs floating in it—and those telltale enormous straws—has mystified many. What is this phenomenon that has swept the Chinese-American community and beyond? It's *zhen zhu nai cha* (a.k.a. *bo ba nai cha* on the West Coast), a craze that has spilled over from Asia and spread worldwide. This Taiwanese drink, consisting of tea, milk, and chewy black tapioca beads is also known as Pearl Milk Tea, Bubble Milk Tea, and Bo Ba Milk Tea, and comes in an endless array of flavors, served both hot and cold.

The most common and standard drink, *zhen zhu nai cha*, is sweetened red tea with milk. Also popular is *ying yang zhen zhu*, which is half-iced coffee and half-iced tea. While all purveyors of *zhen zhu nai cha* carry these basic drinks, their selection beyond these varies greatly, and in light of the growing competition in the market, businesses have become more and more creative. Some fancy flavors include taro milk tea, green tea, almond tea, red bean milk, mint tea, mango, strawberry, passion fruit, and lychee—all with tapioca pearls.

The following Boston-area stores have caught on to the fact that people are, well, suckers for the pearls. So what is it about these drinks that have entranced masses of people enough to dish out $2 to $4 a cup on a regular basis? Simultaneously drinking and sucking up the pearls makes for a fun, tasty, and addictive drinking challenge.

Cindy's Planet

A small cute eatery that, in addition to a tremendous offering of different pearl drinks, also sells Chinese homemade snacks, desserts, and packaged Japanese candy and snacks. The pearls are especially buoyant. *Chinatown: 70 Tyler St., Boston 02111, (617) 338-8837.*

Eldo Cake House and Bakery

This bakery is known for its pastries, but it also sells a small assortment of pearl drinks. *Chinatown: 36 Harrison Ave., Boston 02111, (617) 350-7977.*

Harrison Café

Their pearls are a bit too soft, but tasty, and the green tea drink is delicious. *Chinatown: 177 Harrison Ave., Boston 02111, (617) 426-2828.*

Hu Tieu Nam Vang

This Vietnamese restaurant surprises with the freshest and best fruit concoctions—especially their mango shake—accompanied with impeccable pearls. *Chinatown: 7 Beach St., Boston 02111, (617) 422-0501.*

Juice Bar

The selection is extensive, and the fruity flavors are their specialty—you must try their strawberry drink with pearls. *Chinatown: 44-46 Beach St. (on the 2nd floor food court at the corner of Harrison St. and Beach St.), Boston 02111.*

Wisteria House

Overpriced (well it is Newbury St.) and just so-so quality drinks. *Back Bay: 264 Newbury St., Boston 02116, (617) 536-8866.*

—*Charlene X. Wang*

King Fung Garden

Step inside one of Chinatown's best-kept secrets.

$$$

74 Kneeland St., Boston 02111

(at Hudson St.)

Phone (617) 357-5262

CATEGORY	Chinese
HOURS	Daily: 11 AM–10 PM
MASS TRANSIT	T: Orange line to New England Medical Center or Chinatown
PAYMENT	Cash only
POPULAR FOOD	Hot and sour soup, beef *chow foon*, Shanghai chow mein, rice cakes, scallion pancakes, pork dumplings, and pork buns
UNIQUE FOOD	The famous three-course Peking duck feast (must be ordered 24 hours in advance); Mongolian fire pots: you get lamb, chicken, pork, beef, squid, and tripe along with bean curd, noodles, veggies, and sauce, then cook it all up in a soup-filled fire pot right on your table
DRINKS	Soft drinks and tea; BYO everything else
SEATING	A cramped room consisting of a few rickety tables and three red pleather booths
AMBIENCE	This place is truly a diamond in the rough; it looks like a rundown, abandoned trailer (it used to be a pizza parlor) and the lighting inside is too bright, but do not let that scare you off
EXTRAS/NOTES	Many of Boston's top chefs can be found here on their nights off.

—*Pete Carpenter*

New Lei Jing

*An indecisive appetite
is no obstacle.*

$$

20 Hudson St., Boston 02111
(at Kneeland St.)
Phone (617) 338-9777 • Fax (617) 338-9799

CATEGORY	Pan-Asian
HOURS	Mon–Thurs: 10 AM–10 PM
	Fri–Sun: 10 AM–2 AM
MASS TRANSIT	T: Orange line to Chinatown
PAYMENT	
POPULAR FOOD	Outstanding Chinese buffet lunch; the familiar offerings are all here, and quite lovingly prepared—lo mein, General Gau's chicken, Peking ravioli, perfect crab rangoon—but it's the little extras that make New Lei Jing special; the appetizing sushi assortment, the Chinese cookies and pastries, the urns of egg drop and hot and sour soup laid out right on the table; the sliced watermelon (by season); all this for around $7 a plate; for three dollars more, you can attack the buffet table and choose anything from the dim sum cart—pork buns and chicken feet galore
UNIQUE FOOD	A full Chinese menu *and* a full Korean/Japanese menu; $25 all-you-can-eat sushi
DRINKS	Full bar
SEATING	Eighteen large round tables, each seating up to ten, with different parties sharing tables
AMBIENCE	Chinatown locals and professionals are the primary clientele, with the occasional karaoke enthusiast singing and gazing lovingly at the video monitor during less busy hours (3 PM–6 PM)

—*Ray Misra*

New Shanghai

*Where some of Boston's best chefs
have learned a thing or two.*

$$$

21 Hudson St., Boston 02111
(at Kneeland St.)
Phone (617) 338-6688 • Fax (617) 338-0732

CATEGORY	Chinese
HOURS	Sun–Thurs: 11:30 AM–10 PM
	Fri/Sat: 11:30 AM–11 PM
MASS TRANSIT	T: Orange line to Chinatown
PAYMENT	
POPULAR FOOD	Sizzling platters of fresh meats and seafood in spicy sauces, cold appetizers, pan-fried lobster with ginger and scallions
DRINKS	Beer, wine, full bar
SEATING	Two large rooms with a number of smaller tables; much quieter than most Chinatown establishments

AMBIENCE	The table linens, carpeted floors, and attentive service set New Shanghai apart from its neighbors; a good place for a date or business dinner
EXTRAS/NOTES	Chef C.K. Sau is considered one of the best in the city, let alone Chinatown. Ask the managers what to order, and they won't steer you wrong. It's been said that Boston chefs Jasper White and Lydia Shire learned their pan-fried lobster technique from Chef Sau.

—Pete Carpenter

Peach Farm

The dishes come fast and furious at this Chinatown eatery.

$$$

4 Tyler St., Boston 02111

(sout of Beach St.)

Phone (617) 482-1116

CATEGORY	Chinese
HOURS	Daily: 11 AM–2 AM
MASS TRANSIT	T: Orange line to Chinatown
PAYMENT	VISA MasterCard AMERICAN EXPRESS
POPULAR FOOD	Fresh seafood dishes: steamed or fried whole fish; spicy fried squid; spicy salted shrimp with heads on: lobster with ginger and scallions; steamed pea pod tendrils with garlic; steamed oysters or clams in black bean sauce
UNIQUE FOOD	Braised chicken hot pot (perhaps the best chicken dish in town); whole fried flounder; salt and pepper fried squid
DRINKS	Beer, wine, soft drinks
SEATING	A somewhat claustrophobic basement restaurant split into two rooms, with large, family-style tables
AMBIENCE	Perfect for celebrating a birthday or for a group outing; with the staff sprinting to and from the kitchen the energy level is high
EXTRAS/NOTES	There are a number of similar Hong Kong-style seafood restaurants in Chinatown, but the freshness and speed of Peach Farm is unmatched. Many of their best dishes benefit from getting to the table as soon as they come off the fire.

—Pete Carpenter

> "The devil has put a penalty
> on all things we enjoy in life.
> Either we suffer in health
> or we suffer in soul or we get fat."
>
> *—Albert Einstein*

Penang

The jungle comes to Boston.

$$$

685-691 Washington St., Boston 02111
(at Kneeland St.)
Phone (617) 451-6373 • Fax (617) 451-6300
www.penangboston.com

CATEGORY	Malaysian
HOURS	Daily: 11:30 AM–11:30 PM
MASS TRANSIT	T: Orange line to Chinatown
PAYMENT	VISA MasterCard AMERICAN EXPRESS
POPULAR FOOD	*Roti canai*, a crispy pancake with curry chicken and potato sauce; mango chicken served in a mango shell; *masak lemak*, stir-fried meat with sweet peppers, onions, and carrots in a chili sauce; crispy fried squid; *rendang*, tender pieces of beef simmered with cinnamon, cloves, and lemongrass in coconut milk
UNIQUE FOOD	Shaved ice with red bean, corn, palm seed, jelly, red rose syrup, and milk; sizzling beef, chicken, or seafood platters; Malaysian steamed fish with ginger and garlic; Buddhist yam pot—veggies cooked in a garlicky soy sauce in a ring of fried mashed taro root
DRINKS	Nice wine list
SEATING	Big tables for large groups
AMBIENCE	A bit of a faux tropical jungle feel with bamboo, rope, all wooden tables and exposed brick; noisy open kitchen
EXTRAS/NOTES	Penang Boston is part of well-known New York City chain.

—Kyle Konrad

Pho Pasteur

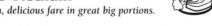

(see p. 187)
Vietnamese
123 Stuart St., Boston 02116
Phone (617) 742-2436
and
682 Washington St., Boston 02111
Phone (617) 482-7467

Pho Vietnam

Fresh, delicious fare in great big portions.

$$

1 Stuart St., Boston 02116
(at Washington St.)
Phone (617) 292-0220

CATEGORY	Vietnamese
HOURS	Daily: 9:30 AM–9:30 PM
MASS TRANSIT	T: Orange line to New England Medical Center
PAYMENT	VISA MasterCard AMERICAN EXPRESS

POPULAR FOOD	Spicy lemongrass soup filled with meat and noodles; chicken and noodle soup with basil and sprouts; vermicelli and various meats; a variety of lemongrass dishes; fabulous spring rolls; vegetarian offerings
DRINKS	Fresh lemonade, beer, wine, soft drinks, tea, coffee
SEATING	Capacity for 40 to 50, with a range of intimate and larger tables; never a wait
AMBIENCE	A simple dining room decorated with flowers and Asian art; it's the stellar food over the ambience that matters here

—Sarah Pascarella

Remington's

A comfortable pub and restaurant in the theater district.

$$

124 Boylston St., Boston 02116
(between Tremont St. and Washington St.)
Phone (617) 574-9676

CATEGORY	American Pub
HOURS	Daily: 11:30 AM–2 AM
MASS TRANSIT	T: Red or Green line to Park St.
PAYMENT	VISA MasterCard AMERICAN EXPRESS
POPULAR FOOD	Treats such as Remy's Rathskeller, a reuben stacked with extras like potato salad, lettuce, and tomato; though Remy's is open late for the after-theater crowd, the lunch specials are the best deal, ranging from linguine with meatballs to sirloin tips for around $7; the roast beef melt lunch special is a rare achievement, stacked with cheese, doused with 999 dressing, served on dark rye, and accompanied by your choice of fries, baked beans, or potato salad
UNIQUE FOOD	The Remy Whaler, fresh haddock served on a tuna melt
DRINKS	Bottle or draft beers, as well as a fine spirits menu
SEATING	Remington's is rectangular, with a bar on one side and booths lining the other; seats around 35
AMBIENCE	Cozy-looking and inviting on the outside, private and comforting inside, a place where you'll rest your feet after shopping downtown or meet with a friend for a slow, lazy round of drinks; high wooden ceilings are contrasted by low-hanging light fixtures, creating a dimly lit though not menacing atmosphere; promo posters for *Les Miserables* and *Miss Saigon* remind you of nearby attractions
EXTRAS/NOTES	Live music and stand-up comedy on certain nights.

—Melvin Cartagena

Rod Thai

*Tiny Thai wonder
in the heart of Chinatown.*
$$

44 Beach St., 2nd Fl., Boston 02111
(east of Harrison Ave.)
Phone (617) 357-9188

CATEGORY	Thai
HOURS	Daily: 11 AM–10 PM
MASS TRANSIT	T: Orange line to Chinatown
PAYMENT	Cash only
POPULAR FOOD	For just over a fiver, you get a huge, steaming plate of some of the best *pad* Thai around
UNIQUE FOOD	The Pad Paradise features chicken, shrimp, big flavorful cashews, and loads of veggies in a spicy soy-flavored sauce over rice
DRINKS	Free tea, sodas, juices, bottled water, Thai iced tea, and Thai iced coffee
SEATING	Rod Thai is inside the Chinatown Eatery, along with three other take-out-or-eat-in restaurants all sharing the same seating area; most people are there to pick up their order and leave, so you can usually find a table without any trouble, though it may be close quarters
AMBIENCE	Pretty cramped and altogether bustling; a lot of Chinatown locals eat here, a sure indication of the quality, as well as business lunchers, late-night drunkards, and hungry masses; great for groups, as you can all choose from Chinese, Vietnamese, or Thai, but still sit together

—Jon Gorey

Sam Hop Eatery

*For the best helping
of squid, head to the Hop*
$$

44 Beach St. 2nd Fl., Boston 02111
(east of Harrison Ave.)
Phone (617) 482-1188

CATEGORY	Chinese
HOURS	Daily: 11 AM–1 AM
MASS TRANSIT	T: Orange line to Chinatown
PAYMENT	Cash only
POPULAR FOOD	Request a bowl of hot and sour soup (at no charge) and order a #166, an artfully arranged helping of delicate, tender squid, strikingly green Chinese broccoli, and white rice smattered with fresh red pepper and scallions; once you've tried #166, it could easily become a weekly fix; in fact, some have said to need it as much as three times per week
DRINKS	Free hot tea; soda
SEATING	Seating shared with other eateries

AMBIENCE	Located in the Chinatown Eatery, Samhop is one of the smallest vendors of the lot; you can sit by the window overlooking a segment of the bustling street below, or share one of the other tables that comprise the communal seating of the second-floor cafeteria; although the place is low on frills and pretense, it's one of the liveliest on the block, more so past midnight

—Darla Bruno

Taiwan Café

A Taiwanese original.
$$$
34 Oxford St., Boston 02111
(at Beach St.)
Phone (617) 426-8181

CATEGORY	Taiwanese
HOURS	Daily: 11 AM–1 AM
MASS TRANSIT	T: Orange line to Chinatown
PAYMENT	Cash only
POPULAR FOOD	Steamed flounder; sauteed eggplant with basil; steamed vegetable dumplings; tofu with mustard greens; cheap lunch specials
UNIQUE FOOD	Spicy anchovies with green chilis
DRINKS	Tsingtao, wine, tea
SEATING	One small room
AMBIENCE	This is as un-Americanized as it gets: untranslated specials on the wall, chopsticks only, mostly Chinese clientele

—Kyle Konrad

Tu Do

*The Vietnamese, Cambodian,
and Chinese connection.*
$$
5 Beach St., Boston 02111
(between Washington St. and Harrison St.)
Phone (617) 451-9550

CATEGORY	Pan-Asian
HOURS	Sun–Thurs: 9 AM–10 PM Fri/Sat: 9 AM–11 PM
MASS TRANSIT	T: Orange line to Chinatown
PAYMENT	VISA MasterCard
POPULAR FOOD	Vietnamese staple *pho* noodle soup, Cambodian noodle dishes
UNIQUE FOOD	Vietnamese "pizza" (*banh xeo*); noodle dishes from the Phnom Penh region of Cambodia (*hu tieu nam vang*); pungent caramel specialties like catfish, pork chops, and sliced pork simmered in pungent caramel (*thit kho hoac ca kho*)
DRINKS	Vietnamese specialties: sugarcane and mung red bean drinks; excellent iced coffee (don't underestimate the French colonial influences); also, fresh fruit shakes
SEATING	Wooden tables and chairs seat about 50

AMBIENCE	Vietnamese and Vietnamese-American Bostonians, Chinatown locals, and cheap-eat groupies fill this spacious (for Chinatown) establishment; light blue walls, fake plants, and half-wooden interior evoke a quasi-country charm accented by random attempts at glamour: a mini chandelier hangs from the ceiling
EXTRAS/NOTES	Classic American success story: a refugee from Saigon who cleaned houses and now owns three restaurants, one of them being Tu Do, which means "liberty" in Vietnamese.

—Charlene X. Wang

Yan's Best Place Restaurant

Who can argue with Yan when it comes to heapings of Cantonese food?

52 Beach St., Boston 02111

(between Tyler St. and Harrison Ave.)

Phone (617) 338-6223

CATEGORY	Cantonese
HOURS	Daily: 11 AM–9 PM
MASS TRANSIT	T: Orange line to Chinatown
PAYMENT	VISA MasterCard
POPULAR FOOD	General Gao's Chicken; sweet and sour chicken with crab rangoon; hot and sour soup; lunch specials—under $5—supply more than a meal with a mountain of chicken, pork, or beef piled over a healthy serving of rice and steamed vegetables
UNIQUE FOOD	Extensive vegetarian menu with bean curd dishes and broccoli; seasonal seafood offerings include flounder, lobster, and squid
DRINKS	Hot tea, soft drinks
SEATING	Small tables jammed into a truly cozy dining environment
AMBIENCE	An eat-and-talk dining experience with no other frills considered; red checkered tablecloths and faded wall posters; a mix of elderly Chinatown regulars and the much louder salary-men and -women from the nearby Financial District; lunch is the busiest time of the day
EXTRAS/NOTES	Not as big or as well known as some of its Chinatown rivals, Yan's took over the space of the original Chau Chow in late 2000.

—Jason Stevenson

"My tongue is smiling."

—Abigail Trillin

SOUTH END

Addis Red Sea Ethiopian Restaurant

Who knew eating with your hands could be so civilized?

$$$

544 Tremont St., Boston 02118

(at Clarendon St.)

Phone (617) 426-8727 • Fax (617) 695-3677

www.addisredsea.com

CATEGORY	Ethiopian
HOURS	Mon–Fri: 5 PM–11 PM Sat/Sun: noon–midnight
MASS TRANSIT	T: Orange line to Back Bay
PAYMENT	VISA MasterCard AMERICAN EXPRESS
POPULAR FOOD	Chopped, largely stewed beef and lamb served on a spongy flatbread called *injera*; vegetarian options include purees of lentils and split peas and chick peas with oil, lemon, and green and black pepper
UNIQUE FOOD	Using the spongy flatbread, you eat with your hands; dishes are all served directly on an unconventional bread-covered, woven, straw table making for a communal eating experience
DRINKS	Beer and wine, including Ethiopian wine
SEATING	Seats 40 to 50 at small, low wicker tables
AMBIENCE	Intimate, relaxed atmosphere created by colorful rugs, Ethiopian crafts, dim lighting, and the serene seating and serving style.

—Nick Grossman

Anchovies

Cheap Italian eats and good greets in the South End.

$$

433 Columbus Ave., Boston 02116

(between Braddock Park and Holyoke St.)

Phone (617) 266-5088

CATEGORY	Italian
HOURS	Daily: 4 PM–1 AM
MASS TRANSIT	T: Orange line to Back Bay, Green line to Prudential Center
PAYMENT	VISA MasterCard AMERICAN EXPRESS
POPULAR FOOD	Best pizza in the South End; huge slices topped with your choice of seven garlic-driven sauces; clams or mussels marinara; eggplant and chicken parmesan
UNIQUE FOOD	Pizza you can eat without draining the grease off first
DRINKS	Full bar, with six beers on tap and a nice list of wines

SEATING	Many claim that "everyone knows your name" at Anchovies; they probably learned your name because of how close you were sitting to them; with a mix of booths and tables, and plenty of room at the bar
AMBIENCE	An eclectic band of followers, from South Enders (including its gay denizens), having their nightly cocktail, to outlanders seeking late-night eats many hundred cuts above your standard diner; some find the intimate front section a bit too claustrophobic; booths in the back give a great opportunity to spread out and savor the huge meals while pondering the cow skulls hanging on the wall; don't miss the trophy deer adorned with Mardi Gras beads or the large portrait of Andy "Old Hickory" Jackson at his creepiest— nothing says you're in the South End like a décor that doesn't care if you "get it"
EXTRAS/NOTES	The service is congenial and generally on-the-spot. Anchovies is the South End version of the band that few know about that you want to keep for yourself.

—Chris Railey

Appleton Bakery

A one-stop gourmet picnic pit-stop.
$$

123 Appleton St., Boston 02116
(at Dartmouth St.)
Phone (617) 859-8ABC • Fax (617) 859-9898
www.appletonbakerycafe.com

CATEGORY	Café
HOURS	Mon–Fri: 6:30 AM–8 PM Sat: 7 AM–5 PM Sun: 7 AM–2 PM
MASS TRANSIT	T: Orange line to Back Bay
PAYMENT	VISA　MasterCard　AMERICAN EXPRESS
POPULAR FOOD	Famous for its muffins; everything from pineapple and coconut to raspberry white chocolate chip to classic blueberry; old-fashioned sour cream coffee cake; granola; gourmet sandwiches filled with portabellos, prosciutto, pesto, and other tasty toppings; soups, and more elaborate ready-to-take-home-and-devour deli and grill foods such as potato salad, crab cakes, and roast pork loin
UNIQUE FOOD	Daily luncheon specials include a great meat-loaf (Thursday) and pan-fried crab cakes (Tuesday); they also sell their own gelato
DRINKS	Coffee, soda, fruit juices
SEATING	Seats 15 at small tables with stools
AMBIENCE	Nothing special; a takeout place

—Nick Grossman

Bob the Chef's

*Soul food with
a sophisticated twist.
Since the late 1950s*

$$$$

604 Columbus Ave., Boston 02118
(at Northampton St.)
Phone (617) 536-6204 • Fax (617) 536-0907
www.bobthechefs.com

CATEGORY	Soul and Southern Food
HOURS	Tues/Wed: 11:30 AM–10 PM
	Thurs–Sat: 11:30 AM–midnight
	Sun: 10 AM–9 PM
MASS TRANSIT	T: Orange line to Massachusetts Ave.
PAYMENT	VISA MasterCard AMERICAN EXPRESS
POPULAR FOOD	Sweet potato fries; collared greens; mac 'n' cheese; fall-off-the-bone ribs coated in a surprisingly sweet sauce; jambalaya packed with shrimp and chicken; crab cakes; candied yams; sweet potato pie with whipped cream; peach cobbler à la mode; Bob's Famous Chicken can be ordered baked, barbecued, or "glorifried"
DRINKS	Bottled beer and pricey mixed drinks; small, but diverse selection of wine
SEATING	Seats about 60 tightly; small bar with a few seats; reservations only for parties of six or more and essential on weekends after 6 PM
AMBIENCE	Lively atmosphere after 7 PM and during the famous albeit pricey Sunday jazz buffet brunch; casual is OK, but the dinner crowd tends to be a little dressier; fun-loving, diverse crowd of young and old, black and white, local and tourist
EXTRAS/NOTES	Live jazz and R&B Thursday through Saturday and of course with brunch. The $3 to $7 cover charge is added to your check.

—Ted Kulik

Charlie's Sandwich Shoppe

*The South End's landmark
greasy spoon.
Since 1927*

$$

429 Columbus Ave., Boston 02116
(at Dartmouth St.)
Phone (617) 536-7669

CATEGORY	Diner
HOURS	Mon–Fri: 6 AM–2:30 PM
	Sat: 7:30 AM–1 PM
MASS TRANSIT	T: Orange line to Back Bay
PAYMENT	Cash only

POPULAR FOOD	Breakfast served all day: French toast; hash and eggs; cranberry, blueberry, banana, and strawberry pancakes; spinach and feta omelettes; cornbread; cheeseburgers; the hash here is legendary
UNIQUE FOOD	Fried oysters for breakfast
DRINKS	Coffee, soda, juice
SEATING	Seats 25 at a long counter with stools
AMBIENCE	A timeless, local hangout perfect for a cheap and casual breakfast alone at the counter; photographs adorn walls; no restrooms
EXTRAS/NOTES	Charlie's is a South End and Boston institution. It used to be open around the clock until 1960 when limited hours were introduced. A locksmith had to be called in—since they had never locked the door before, the owners had long ago lost the key. In the old days, Sammy Davis Jr. tap-danced out front for spare change, and Charlie's was among the first in Boston to serve non-white customers, notably jazz greats like Duke Ellington who played in downtown hotels but were barred from eating and sleeping there.

—Nick Grossman

Delux

It's Christmas Eve every night at this cozy bar and grill.

$$$

100 Chandler St., Boston 02116

(at Clarendon St.)

Phone (617) 338-5258

CATEGORY	Bar & Grill
HOURS	Mon–Sat: 5 PM–1 AM (food served until 11:30 PM)
MASS TRANSIT	T: Orange line to Back Bay
PAYMENT	Cash only
POPULAR FOOD	A small but eclectic menu of tasty dishes changes every six weeks, from burritos to beef bolognese, nothing for more than $10, and never with ketchup—there is none; dishes are far above average for a bar
DRINKS	Locally brewed Tremont Ale and Guinness on tap; fully-stocked bar
SEATING	A tiny place; intimate tables seat just 30; no more than five people per table
AMBIENCE	Almost always busy and buzzing, often with a short wait for a table; frequented by locals, Delux is a popular after-work meeting spot; the walls are adorned with album covers and Christmas lights, the Cartoon Network plays at all times, and a glowing Santa guards the bathroom doors; funky décor, dim lighting, and original music create a fun and lively atmosphere

—Nick Grossman

Formaggio Kitchen

A culinary expedition to Europe without leaving Massachusetts.

$$

268 Shawmut Ave., Boston 02118
(between Hanson St. and Milford St.)
Phone (617) 350-6996
www.formaggiokitchen.com

CATEGORY	Gourmet Grocery
HOURS	Mon–Fri: 9 AM–7 PM
	Sat: 9 AM–6 PM
	Sun: 9 AM–3 PM
MASS TRANSIT	T: Orange line to Back Bay
PAYMENT	VISA MasterCard AMERICAN EXPRESS
POPULAR FOOD	An amazing selection of artisinal cheeses and meats from Europe; olive oils, spices, sea salt, and other stock for an extraordinary pantry; they also have exquisite pressed sandwiches; but the pride here is the cheese; the savvy staff can educate you on the different varieties and give you small tastes; every cheese here is painstakingly chosen and cared for, and each has its own story, such as the hearty Garrotxa, made from the goat's milk of a family farm in a remote Pyrenean village
DRINKS	Juices, soda, coffee, tea, and that perfect pairing to cheese, wine, mostly from France and Italy
SEATING	None
AMBIENCE	One cannot help but be overwhelmed—in a good way—by the quantity of fine food items on display; the meats and artisanal cheeses transport you to the Old World
EXTRAS/NOTES	Occasional events are organized to teach the rest of us about cooking and cheeses. This fairly recent addition to the South End spun off the world-famous original in Cambridge, where they actually keep the cheeses for both stores aging in their cellar cheese cave. Nothing says passion for cheese more than having your own cheese cave.
OTHER ONES	• Harvard Square: 244 Huron Ave., Cambridge 02138, (617) 354-4750

—Meg & Devin Grant

Franklin Café

(see p. 168)
Gourmet Café
278 Shawmut Ave., Boston 02118
Phone (617) 350-0010

R.I.P.
1970s Downtown Boston at Night

In the early '70s, at night, downtown Boston pretty much turned into a ghost town. Faneuil Hall had not been renovated into the successful tourist destination that it is now; it was run-down and half vacant, with a few butchers and cheese shops selling to the residents of the North End. Lewis Wharf, Commonwealth Pier—almost all of the waterfront—was generally abandoned, with the exception of the Combat Zone, Boston's red light district. It got its name because it was where all the service men on leave would duke it out after the bars had closed. As a respite, places like the **Hayes Bickford**—a cafeteria-style chain—and **Mondo's** were some of the only bright lights downtown at those quiet hours.

I had moved back to Boston in 1973 after a three-year stint as a newspaper photographer in Detroit, and was determined to become an artist. I moved into a small room at 36 Bromfield Street, a beautiful turn-of-the-century building, still standing, which mirrors old Boston City Hall on the other end of Province Street. At the time, 36 Bromfield was filled with old Italian artisans—tailors, letterpress printers, silversmiths—and then a much younger group of painters, musicians, and photographers. At night, all the old Italians would walk home to the North End, but the youngsters all lived in the building illegally. It was the beginning of the downtown loft movement. All of us were poor, struggling, and generally cold in the winter because 36 had no heat at night or on the weekends, no hot water, and D/C electricity, which meant no A/C radios, hi-fi's, or anything with A/C motors for us.

The Hayes Bickford was located kitty-corner across from the Old State House on Washington Street (it's now a McDonald's). When it got too cold at 36, or when we had been up most of the night talking and critiquing each others' work, or playing music in jam sessions, we would head over to the Bick. During the day the Bick served the blue- and white-collar workers of downtown, but at 3 AM or so, the usuals were old guys who had spent the night at the dog track. Neon lights, formica tables and chairs, steam table food, and a grill. Hand-painted placards over the serving counter advertised the daily specials of meat loaf, hamburgers, and corned beef and cabbage. "Oatmeal 25 cents" was what I usually ordered, not because I liked oatmeal all that much, but because I didn't usually have much more than 25 cents, and you could ask for honey and cream at no extra cost. The guy behind the counter was Vinny, a man in his 60s, ex-merchant marine, cigar clamped and smoking in his jaw. He could spend hours talking about his passion, Noah's Ark—he spent days in Boston's old public library reading anything he could find on the subject. He always made me feel better during the worst of times by saying, "So how's the Picasso business?"

Mondo's was an even better deal, on the north side of the Faneuil Hall building, sort of in the center, as I remember it. You either knew where it was or you didn't—there was no sign outside. Mondo's was open all night, and for 99 cents you could have three eggs any way you wanted them, plus sausage, ham, or bacon, plus white, rye, or whole-wheat toast, plus home-fried potatoes, plus orange, grapefruit, or tomato juice, plus coffee or tea. There was sawdust on the floor, a ratty collection of tables and mismatched chairs, a counter, and a fantastic jukebox. At 3 and 4 AM the place was jammed with truck drivers, cab drivers, hookers, musicians getting off work, and night owls of all kinds. There may have been other items on the menu, but I don't remember them—the 99-cent "Special" was what made the place. Mondo himself was a large man, and I don't remember him saying much. He was usually at the grill, cracking three eggs at a time with one hand, or sleeping in the back of his Cadillac. When Faneuil Hall was renovated, Mondo's moved for a short while to a place on Kneeland Street, Chinatown, and then to a place on A street, in Southie. But by then the energy of the Faneuil Hall Mondo's was lost. Ten years later I heard that after a night of cracking eggs, Mondo had died in his sleep, in the back seat of his Cadillac.

—Jerry Berndt

Garden of Eden

Fun neighborhood conversation and eavesdropping spot.

$$$

571 Tremont St., Boston 02118

(at Clarendon St.)

Phone (617) 247-8377 • Fax (617) 247-8493

CATEGORY	Café
HOURS	Mon–Fri: 7 AM–11 PM Sat/Sun: 7:30 AM–11 PM
MASS TRANSIT	T: Orange line to Back Bay
PAYMENT	VISA MasterCard AMERICAN EXPRESS
POPULAR FOOD	Great sandwiches and French-influenced comfort food; weekend brunch; a market with breads, cheeses, cookies, pastries; a good value for the portions
UNIQUE FOOD	Paté and cheese plates
DRINKS	Coffee, beer, and wine
SEATING	Seats 50; sit at long, wooden tables with others, or at more intimate small tables; also an outdoor patio

AMBIENCE	Laid-back but upbeat atmosphere; great for people-watching; young male hipsters wait tables; perfect for a casual meal
EXTRAS/NOTES	Garden of Eden used to be just a café and lunch place, but was expanded to a full restaurant last year.

—*Nick Grossman*

Giacomo's Ristorante

(see p. 23)
Italian
431 Columbus Ave., Boston 02116
Phone (617) 536-5723

Le Gamin

A street café right out of the Left Bank.
$$$
550 Tremont St., Boston 02116
(at Clarendon St.)
Phone (617) 654-8969 • Fax (617) 654-8969
www.legamin.com

CATEGORY	Crêpes
HOURS	Daily: 9 AM–midnight
MASS TRANSIT	T: Orange line to Back Bay
PAYMENT	Cash only
POPULAR FOOD	An extensive menu with a full range of sweet and savory crêpes in addition to sandwiches, bistro entrees, quiches, and salads; they specialize in authentic Parisian café food with crêpes as the highlight
DRINKS	A great Parisian-style hot chocolate; beer, wine, coffee
SEATING	Seats 50 at café-style tables
AMBIENCE	Le Gamin strives for a minimalist, rustic, wood-accented French style; it's comfortable, but lacks atmosphere
OTHER ONES	• Five other locations in New York (which might explain the above-average prices for café food)

—*Nick Grossman*

Mike's City Diner

Harmony through homecookin'.
$$
1714 Washington St., Boston 02118
(at E. Springfield St.)
Phone (617) 267-9393

CATEGORY	Diner
HOURS	Daily: 6 AM–3 PM
MASS TRANSIT	T: Orange line to Massachusetts Ave.
PAYMENT	VISA MasterCard
POPULAR FOOD	Breakfast classics including their famous corned beef hash and the Emergency Room special (two eggs, two pancakes,

bacon or sausage, home fries or grits, and toast), fittingly named for the diner's proximity to the city's hospitals and, well, the sheer cholesterol content; no canned veggies here—Mike's prepares its dishes from fresh ingredients daily

UNIQUE FOOD	Visiting or expatriate Southerners rejoice—there's grits here!
DRINKS	Coffee, tea, juice, soft drinks, and beer
SEATING	Seats 49 at tables for two or four; or counter seating with a view of the bustling kitchen
AMBIENCE	Clean and bright; a fairly new restaurant but looks like a classic diner with black-and-white checkered tablecloths and vintage light fixtures
EXTRAS/NOTES	How many restaurants bring together the gay brunch crowd, construction workers, and local politicos? Just one by our count. At Mike's, social barriers melt away like butter on a stack of pancakes. And it's no wonder: who has room for hate with a belly full of fresh baked turkey, real mashed potatoes, and homemade squash? These freshly prepared dishes have attracted everyone from President Bill Clinton to Mathew Broderick to players from the Boston Celtics. Don't be surprised if the guy loaning you salt from the next table is Mayor Menino or your plumber. One is just as likely as the other.

—*Mark Ferguson*

Nashoba Brook Bakery

Perhaps the best sandwiches in the South End.

$$

288 Columbus Ave., Boston 02116
(at Clarendon St.)
Phone (617) 236-0777
www.slowrise.com

CATEGORY	Café
HOURS	Mon–Fri: 7 AM–6 PM
	Sat: 8 AM–5 PM
	Sun: 9 AM–5 PM
MASS TRANSIT	T: Orange line to Back Bay
PAYMENT	VISA MasterCard
POPULAR FOOD	Gourmet sandwiches on their freshly baked bread, the best are the turkey-avocado and the chicken curry; cinnamon swirl pastries filled with pecans and butter
DRINKS	Coffee and juices
SEATING	Seats 20 at small tables
AMBIENCE	Great place to quietly read the paper in the morning or take a long lunch; locals go in and out in the morning for fresh loaves and coffee; a long line forms at lunch

—*Nick Grossman*

Tim's Bar & Grill
The place for big, juicy burgers.
$$$

329 Columbus Ave., Boston 02116
(at Dartmouth St.)
Phone (617) 247-7894

CATEGORY	Bar & Grill
HOURS	Mon–Sat: 11 AM–midnight
MASS TRANSIT	T: Orange line to Back Bay
PAYMENT	Cash only
POPULAR FOOD	Renowned for its bulky, juicy, flame-grilled hamburgers; this is the only reason to come here but a decent enough reason if you really like burgers; also serving steak tips, ribs, and seafood
DRINKS	Full bar; cheap Bud and Boston Ale on tap; Red Stripe
SEATING	Seats over 60 at a bar and tables in back rooms
AMBIENCE	A dark place where older locals tan themselves via the TVs, watching sports and casually drinking beer; more of a small-town, backwoods bar with no frills except for a jukebox

—Nick Grossman

BACK BAY

Atlantic Fish Co.
(see p. 27)
Seafood/Chowder
761 Boylston St., Boston 02116
Phone (617) 267-4000

Baja Cantina
That was delicious, but I cantina 'nother bite.
$$$

111 Dartmouth St., Boston 02116
(between Huntington Ave. and Columbus Ave.)
Phone (617) 262-7575

CATEGORY	Mexican
HOURS	Mon–Thurs: 11:30 AM–11 PM
	Fri: 11:30 AM–midnight
	Sat: 5 PM–11 PM
	Sun: 11:30 AM–4 PM, 5 PM–11 PM
MASS TRANSIT	T: Orange line to Back Bay
PAYMENT	VISA MasterCard AMERICAN EXPRESS
POPULAR FOOD	All-you-can-eat nights: Monday means endless fajitas for $10; Tuesday, unlimited tacos for around $8; Wednesday, $5 buys all the fine Mexican desserts you can swallow; during Happy Hour (Sun–Thurs 4 PM–7 PM) all appetizers are half price with the purchase of a drink

UNIQUE FOOD	The *memela*, a Mexican pizza, but with toppings like roasted peppers, cilantro pesto, goat cheese, and pumpkin seeds; grilled salmon or ground turkey burritos; fajitas with duck breast or Cajun catfish
DRINKS	Full bar with 95 varieties of tequila (or over 3,000 margarita possibilities)
SEATING	Seating at tables and at the bar for 60 to 70
AMBIENCE	A moderately priced, boisterous place that attracts a lot of yuppies, guppies, fabulous South Enders, college students, and culture vultures on their way to a show at the Boston Center for the Arts; piñatas and pink day-glo paintings of cacti adorn the restaurant, while the corrugated metal above adds to the feel of a cantina in the Southwest

—*Ray Misra*

Bangkok City

Elegant Thai dining, convenient location.
$$$
167 Massachusetts Ave., Boston 02115
(between St. Germain St. and Belvidere St.)
Phone (617) 266-8884 • Fax (617) 266-8629
www.bkkcity.com

CATEGORY	Thai
HOURS	Mon–Fri: 11:30 AM–3 PM, 5 PM–10 PM Sat: 11:30 AM–3 PM, 3 PM–10:30 PM Sun: 3 PM–10 PM
MASS TRANSIT	T: Green line to Hynes/ICA
PAYMENT	VISA MasterCard AMERICAN EXPRESS DISCOVER
POPULAR FOOD	Three-Chili Shrimp and Shrimp Mermaid; vegetarian rolls; lemon chicken; garlic fish; crispy duck; *pad* Thai; the Create Your Own section of the menu offers a dozen possible ways to prepare chicken, tofu, duck, scallops, and the like
UNIQUE FOOD	The daring may order very spicy traditional Thai dishes from a special menu; glass noodle salad with cilantro, chili, and lime
DRINKS	Beers, wine, soft drinks, Thai iced tea, and coffee
SEATING	Twenty intimate tables that seat either two or four; three traditional low tables; a private dining room for 10 to 15
AMBIENCE	An elegant, relaxed atmosphere; Thai wall hangings and paintings decorate the low-lit indigo blue walls; candles and flowers adorn the tables for evening diners; clientele includes students and faculty of Berklee College of Music, local businesspeople, and Thai food enthusiasts from all over; kind and attentive service—your water glass is always full

—*Matthew Isles*

Bertucci's

(see p. 175)
Gourmet Pizza
43 Stanhope St., Boston 02116
Phone (617) 247-6161

Betty's Wok and Noodle Diner

Funky Asian-Cuban fusion.

$$$

250 Huntington Ave., Boston 02115
(across from Symphony Hall)
Phone (617) 424-1950 • Fax (617) 638-3242
www.bettyswokandnoodle.com

CATEGORY	Asian and Latin
HOURS	Tues–Thurs: noon–10 PM
	Fri/Sat: noon–11 PM
	Sun: noon–10 PM
MASS TRANSIT	T: Green line-E to Symphony
PAYMENT	VISA MasterCard AMERICAN EXPRESS
POPULAR FOOD	Meat, veggies, and rice or noodles in big bowls; choose jasmine or brown rice; egg, chow fun, soba, wheat flour, or broth noodles; beef, chicken, shrimp, or veggies (pick your own from the 15-item veggie bar or let the chefs pick for you), and then select a sauce (Fiery Kung Pao, Cantonese Hoisin, Asian Pesto, Red Thai Coconut, Madras Curry, Cuban Chipotle-Citrus, or Thai-Tiki)
UNIQUE FOOD	Crispy Cabana Juan-Tons (chili beef won-tons with a Cuban-Citrus dip), Cool Cucs and Weed (cucumbers and seaweed in a wasabi ginger dressing); chili orange noodles; golden shrimp balls
DRINKS	Wine, sangria, Sparklers (sparkling wine with fruit juice), sake, and bottled beers; Shirley Temples, root beer floats; Cafe Cubano; Moon Glow specialty-brewed iced tea
SEATING	Plenty of seating at funky tables
AMBIENCE	Stylish, retro feel with black tables, dark red leather banquettes, lots of mirrors, and exposed sandstone; mix of Symphony goers, students, and South End hipsters; Cuban music

—Kyle Konrad

"Almost every person has something
secret he likes to eat."

—M.F.K. Fisher

Bodhi Café

*An original sandwich and
smoothie shop.*

$$

335 Newbury St., Boston 02110
(at Massachusetts Ave.)
Phone (617) 536-6977

CATEGORY	Café
HOURS	Daily: 7 AM–6 PM
MASS TRANSIT	T: Green line to Hynes/ICA
PAYMENT	VISA MasterCard
POPULAR FOOD	The panini (sandwiches); fantastic ones include the blackened ranch chicken served on a crunchy baguette and the turkey served with lettuce, tomatoes, cucumbers, and a tasty mayonnaise dressing; the soups are thick and filling— the mushroom is recommended
UNIQUE FOOD	The sandwiches here are creative and scrumptious, all with a unique twist on the traditional; the specials change weekly
DRINKS	Smoothies, soft drinks, coffee
SEATING	Mainly counter seating with a few tables
AMBIENCE	Cheery and well lit, Bodhi is a great place to sit and enjoy lunch after a long day of window shopping on Newbury; enjoy the photographs on the walls or chat with the always friendly counter staff

—Jenny Bengen

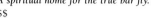

Bukowski Tavern

A spiritual home for the true bar fly.

$$

50 Dalton St, Boston 02115
(at Belvedere St.)
Phone (617) 437-9999

CATEGORY	Bar & Grill
HOURS	Mon–Sat: 11 AM–2 AM
	Sun: noon–2 AM
MASS TRANSIT	T: Green line to Hynes/ICA
PAYMENT	Cash only
POPULAR FOOD	The burgers are widely known as the main attraction
UNIQUE FOOD	Why put vegetarian chili on a hot dog? Any doubts will evaporate at first bite.
DRINKS	More beer than one can safely shake a stick at, suiting tastes from the pragmatic Pabst enthusiast to the ultra-refined Lambic tippling beer snob; a commemorative en-graved mug awaits you if you sample the entire selection before dying of liver disease
SEATING	Almost as scarce as the parking outside, and every bit as cutthroat; if you have ethical qualms about glaring at a patron to hurry him through his meal, you will have a hard time getting a table

AMBIENCE	A very egalitarian dive; the clientele tends to be late 20s and early 30s, but there is little to no socioeconomic polarization; ultra-hip art school kids compare their indie rock record collections while rubbing elbows at the bar with young MOTUs (Masters of the Universe) discussing the latest bond issues; about the only people who will feel uncomfortable here are those sensitive to secondhand smoke, present in such quantities as to qualify practically as part of the décor
EXTRAS/NOTES	Having successfully beaten 16 other people to one of the few tables in the place, now you must begin lobbying your waitress or waiter in earnest; the competition for the overworked and understaffed waitstaff's attention is an integral part of dining here; earn it, and free drinks have a way of making their way to your table; alienate them, or fail to appear on their radar screen, and you may find yourself waiting upwards of half an hour for your salad.

—*James Haynes*

Café Jaffa

A little den of tahini treats.

$$

48 Gloucester St., Boston 02110
(between Boylston St. and Newbury St.)
Phone (617) 536-0230

CATEGORY	Middle Eastern
HOURS	Mon–Thurs: 11 AM–10:30 PM Fri/Sat: 11 AM–11 PM Sun: 1 PM–10 PM
MASS TRANSIT	T: Green line to Hynes/ICA
PAYMENT	VISA MasterCard
POPULAR FOOD	Huge sandwiches filled with chicken or lamb schwarma; excellent tabouli; grape leaves stuffed with lemon and rice; falafel and hummus
UNIQUE FOOD	*Shishlik*, a spicy ground beef patty
DRINKS	Beer, wines from Israel, Turkish coffee
SEATING	Ten small tables
AMBIENCE	Plain, brick-lined coffeeshop feel; soft rock music

—*Kyle Konrad*

"I hate people who are not serious about their meals."
—*Oscar Wilde*

Crazy Dough's

*The mad genius of
pizza-making.*

$

1124 Boylston St., Boston 02215
(between Massachusetts Ave. and Hemenway St.)
Phone (617) 266-5656

CATEGORY	Pizza by the Slice
HOURS	Mon–Fri: 11 AM–11 PM
	Sat/Sun: noon–11 PM
PARKING	T: Green line to Hynes/ICA
PAYMENT	VISA MasterCard
POPULAR FOOD	Although Crazy Dough does serve various pastas and salads, their staple is their unique slices (regular and Sicilian) with toppings such as pesto shrimp, potato/bacon/cheddar, and beef taco
UNIQUE FOOD	The pizza toppings get even more obscure with creations like pesto tortellini, chicken ziti broccoli, pastrami and sauerkraut with Russian dressing, buffalo chicken with bleu cheese dressing, and spinach and artichoke dip pies
DRINKS	The owners pride themselves as much on their esoteric approach to beer as on their esoteric approach to pizza; you'll find Heineken and Sam Adams side by side with Duvel's and Seadog Blueberry Ale; also red and white wine by the glass
SEATING	Between counterspace and tables, it seats about 35
AMBIENCE	Berklee students and any number of sincere devotees of the pizza as an artistic medium
EXTRAS/NOTES	Antonio, the late and fondly remembered owner of the eponymous pizza-by-the-slice-eria in Amherst, trained the chef/owners of Crazy Dough. Also, a BYOCD atmosphere rules here. Anyone hoping to promote their local band (or just turn the customers on to something new) can submit a CD to the management for potential play. You're bound to hear anyone from Angelique Kidjo to Belle & Sebastian.

—Ray Misra

Herrell's

(see p. 131)
Ice Cream Shop
224 Newbury St., Boston 02116
Phone (617) 236-0857

The Unhappy City

In most places, Happy Hour is an after-work tradition. What better way to blow off steam after a crappy day at the office than $1 drafts and two-for-one shots? In Boston, however, there's little to be happy about daily from 4 to 7 PM.

Hundreds of years after the Mayflower landed at Plymouth, Bostonians still suffer from the party-pooping personality of their Puritan forefathers. In 1984, Massachusetts became the first state in the nation to ban the early-evening liquor fest that is Happy Hour. Only five other killjoy states have followed its lead.

According to state law, establishments cannot "sell a drink at a price less than the price regularly charged for such drinks during the same calendar week," "increase the volume of alcoholic beverages contained in a drink without increasing proportionately the price regularly charged for such a drink during the calendar week," or hold "any contest which involves drinking or the awarding of drinks as prizes."

There is a bright side to all of this. Bostonians also share their Puritan forefathers' sense of entrepreneurship, meaning that if liquor can't be used to entice customers, food certainly will be. Stress can be drowned in grease just as easily as in beer, as proven by the following great Happy Hours in the Boston area.

Baja Cantina
Free nachos and half-price appetizers Sun–Thurs: 4 PM–7 PM. See p. 62. *Back Bay: 111 Dartmouth St., Boston 02116, (617) 262-7575.*

Cactus Club
Half-price appetizers Mon–Thurs: 4 PM–6 PM. *Back Bay: 939 Boylston St., Boston 02115, (617) 236-0200.*

Corner Café
Free all-you-can-eat tacos with drink purchase Mon–Thurs: 7 PM–9 PM. See p. 19. *North End: 87 Prince St., Boston 02113, (617) 523-8997.*

Grendel's Den
Everything on the menu but the cheese fondue costs $2.50 with a $3 beverage purchase, including spinach lasagna, mussels, sirloin-steak sandwich, and pasta bolognese daily: 9 PM–11:30 PM; Sun–Thurs: 5 PM–7 PM. See p. 184. *Harvard Square: 89 Winthrop St., Cambridge 02138, (617) 491-1160.*

John Harvard's Brewhouse
Half-priced appetizers Mon: 10 PM–midnight. *Harvard Square: 33 Dunster St., Cambridge 02138, (617) 868-3585.*

McCormick and Schmick's
$1.95 menu often includes mussels, burgers, and wings Mon–Fri: 3:30 PM–6:30 PM; Mon–Thurs: 10 PM–midnight. *Faneuil Hall: Faneuil Hall Marketplace, Boston 02109, (617) 720-5522. Back Bay: 34 Columbus Ave., Boston 02116, (617) 482-3999.*

Our House

Two-for-one burgers and nachos Mon–Fri: 4 PM–7 PM. See p. 94. *Allston: 1277 Commonwealth Ave., Allston 02134, (617) 782-3228.*

Pour House

All grilled chicken sandwiches are $2.50 Wed: 6 PM–10 PM. All Mexican food half price Thurs: 6 PM–10 PM. All burgers half price Sat: 6 PM–10 PM. See p. 73. *Back Bay: 909 Boylston St., Boston 02115, (617) 236-1767.*

Sunset Grill and Tap

All-you-can-eat buffet with purchase of two drinks Mon–Wed: midnight–1 AM. See p. 97. *Allston: 130 Brighton Ave., Allston 02134, (617) 254-1331.*

White Horse Tavern

Pizza, burgers, or a pound of wings for $3 with purchase of a drink Mon/Tues: 6 PM–midnight. Steak tips for $5 with drink purchase Wed/Thurs: 6 PM–midnight. See p. 98. *Allston: 116 Brighton Ave., Allston 02134, (617) 254-6633.*

—*Kaya Stone*

Island Hopper

Asian cuisine with zen chic atmosphere.

$$$

91 Massachusetts Ave., Boston 02115

(at Newbury St.)

Phone (617) 266-1618 • Fax (617) 266-1617

www.islandhopperrestaurant.com

CATEGORY	Pan-Asian
HOURS	Mon–Thurs: 11:30 AM–11 PM Fri/Sat: 11:30 AM–midnight Sun: noon–11 PM
MASS TRANSIT	T: Green line to Hynes/ICA
PAYMENT	VISA MasterCard AMERICAN EXPRESS
POPULAR FOOD	Lemongrass wings and crab rangoon; roti; tofu cake with black mushroom sauce; Chinese eggplant with black bean sauce
UNIQUE FOOD	The crispy calamari (*satong goring*) is wonderful, coated with a dried chili seasoning and tossed in a fresh and spicy red pepper chutney
DRINKS	A wide variety of smoothies served in tall glasses and garnished with fresh fruit; excellent Thai iced tea
SEATING	Room for 110; individual chairs face one long shared booth against the wall; large tables in the center and near the windows
AMBIENCE	Art deco look with bold purple accents, exposed brick, and contemporary lighting; full of young couples and small groups of friends

—*Rhonda Cozier*

J.P. Licks

(see p. 131)
Ice Cream Shop
352 Newbury St., Boston 02115
Phone (617) 236-1666

La Famiglia Giorgio's

(see p. 21)
Italian
250 Newbury St., Boston 02116
Phone (617) 247-1569

Little Stevie's Pizza

And the word is P-I-Z-Z-A,
plain and simple.
$

1114 Boylston St., Boston 02215
(between Fenway St. and Hemenway St.)
Phone (617) 266-5576

CATEGORY	Pizza by the Slice
HOURS	Daily: 9 AM–3 AM
MASS TRANSIT	T: Green line to Hynes/ICA
PAYMENT	VISA MasterCard AMERICAN EXPRESS
POPULAR FOOD	From backpackers to club kids, people pack into this no-frills joint for their massive slices, pies, and subs; with perfectly crisp and chewy crust, tasty sauce and gooey mozzarella, it's hard to go wrong whether you order a pepper or pepperoni slice; nice veal parmesan and meatball subs as well
UNIQUE FOOD	New York Extra Special Pie, with everything but the kitchen sink loaded on top
DRINKS	Basic soft drinks, beers, juices, and milk
SEATING	Although there is ample seating and counter space for standing, this place can be crowded, especially at night
AMBIENCE	The ambience comes from a decided lack thereof; booths, tables, and countertops are covered in well-worn formica in various shades from red to pink to orange due to years of repair and random replacements

—*Amanda Dorato*

"Happy is said to be the family which
can eat onions together.
They are, for the time being, separate from the world,
and have a harmony of aspiration."
—*Charles Dudley Warner* (My Summer in a Garden)

Marché

*A unique marketplace-
style gathering of international foods.*
$$

The Prudential Center, Boston 02115
(on Boylston St. and Huntington St.)
Phone (617) 578-9700 • Fax (617) 578-9886
www.marcheusa.com

CATEGORY	Cafeteria
HOURS	Daily: 11:30 AM–midnight
MASS TRANSIT	T: Green line to Hynes/ICA
PAYMENT	VISA MasterCard
POPULAR FOOD	Sixteen food stations, each representing a different cuisine: soups, salads, pasta, pizza, and breakfast; grill and rotisserie items; seafood; Asian dishes; excellent desserts like freshly baked pastries and made-to-order crêpes, with a large choice of fillings
DRINKS	Coffees; a full bar downstairs called the Caveau; wine is also available from their Old World-style grocery store
SEATING	The 36,000-square-foot space seats about 900 in five unique seating areas, each with its own distinct atmosphere, including a restaurant, grocery, bistro, and takeout
AMBIENCE	Modeled on a charming European marketplace, every dish is picked, prepared, and finished right before your eyes; an eclectic atmosphere with its five different seating areas and an abundance of fake trees; a clientele consisting of locals and tourists, with international diversity; Marché is busy at lunch, evenings (6–8 PM), and during the occasional late-night rush from 11 PM to midnight
EXTRAS/NOTES	This is the only U.S. location of the Mövenpick Marché chain, which originated in Switzerland in the '50s; it employs almost 400 workers, and cost nearly $14 million to build.

—Eric Cho

The Other Side Cosmic Café

Where the (wheat) grass is always greener.
$

407 Newbury St., Boston 02115
(at Massachusetts Ave.)
Phone (617) 536-9477

CATEGORY	Café
HOURS	Mon–Fri: 11 AM–midnight
	Sat: 11 AM–1 AM
	Sun: noon–midnight
MASS TRANSIT	T: Green line to Hynes/ICA
PAYMENT	Cash only
POPULAR FOOD	Huge cheese-smeared Cosmic Burrito with homemade guacamole, salsa, and sour cream; chicken salad specials, such as

tarragon chicken salad with pears and almonds; lovely, fresh salads; soups made from scratch

UNIQUE FOOD The fruit, cheese, and bread platter feeds two and comes with a yogurt-honey dipping sauce; a brie cheese sandwich with apples, pears, onions, lettuce, tomato, and choice of mustard

DRINKS French and Italian sodas; beers by draught or bottle ranging from Bud to organic microbrews; wine by the glass or bottle; every permutation of fruit or coffee drink imaginable; organic teas; sodas and seltzers of all varieties; the "Pharmacy" section on the menu with at least 20 fresh juices, plus smoothies and wheatgrass shots; homemade strawberry lemonade

SEATING Small, tucked-away tables downstairs, booths and plush chairs upstairs

AMBIENCE Dark, grotto-esque with pink lighting under a cloud-painted ceiling; Boston's recent ban on restaurant smoking now means you can more or less see who's sitting across from you; music tends to be of the loud James Brown/punk rock variety, and customers are generally young, hip, and slightly scruffy, with lots of bike couriers and Berklee musicians brooding over their coffee

—Alison Pereto

Parish Café

A sampling of Boston's best—between two slices of bread.

$$$

361 Boylston St., Boston 02116

(at Arlington St.)

Phone (617) 247-4777 • Fax (617) 247-3210

CATEGORY Sandwich Shop

HOURS Mon–Sat: 11:30 AM–1 AM
Sun: noon–1 AM

MASS TRANSIT T: Green line to Arlington

PAYMENT VISA MasterCard AMERICAN EXPRESS

POPULAR FOOD Original sandwiches with names to match: the English (almond-coated chicken breast with red onions and cheese), Norma's Zuni Roll (smoked turkey, bacon, and cheese wrapped in a flour tortilla), the Regal Regis (sliced steak and portobello mushrooms)

UNIQUE FOOD Most of the menu consists of sandwich "creations" from renowned local chefs: the Schlesinger, of East Coast Grill fame (jack cheese, smoked ham, and mango chutney on warmed banana bread), Elephant Walking on Eggs, from the Cambodian/French Porter Square favorite (julienne vegetables with goat cheese and baked eggs on a baguette); Lydia (Biba) Shire's lobster salad on pepper brioche

DRINKS	Coffee, soft drinks, wide selection of bottled and draft beers (e.g. blueberry beer), great mixed drink list
SEATING	Between its tables and bar stools, the Parish seats approximately 50 people inside; patio seating on Boylston St. is the most popular choice among patrons, and adds another 20 to the café's capacity during the warmer months
AMBIENCE	Dark red walls, polished hardwood floors, and the dim lights of the bar that spans the right side of the café; the patio seating consists of steel chairs and tables with sun umbrellas on a slightly raised platform; the Parish is a favorite among area professionals—for lunch, dinner, or an after-work drink

—*Matt Bloomer*

Pho Pasteur

(see p. 187)
Vietnamese
119 Newbury St., Boston 02116
Phone (617) 262-8200

Pour House

*A cheap sit-down meal
in the Back Bay.*
$$
909 Boylston St., Boston 02115
(at Hereford St.)
Phone (617) 236-1767

CATEGORY	Bar & Grill
HOURS	Daily: 8 AM–2 AM (food until 1:45 AM)
MASS TRANSIT	T: Green line to Hynes/ICA
PAYMENT	VISA MasterCard
POPULAR FOOD	Dirt-cheap specials (6 PM–10 PM): on Wednesday, all grilled chicken sandwiches are $2.50; on Thursday, all Mexican food is half price; and on Saturday night burgers are half price; great Sunday brunch and the cheapest lunch specials in the area; grab a hamburger, fries, nachos, and a beer and still have a few quarters left over to play one of the many arcade games
UNIQUE FOOD	Just wandering home from partying the night before? This bar serves breakfast
DRINKS	Two full bars (one at street level and one in the basement) in addition to the standard drink offerings
SEATING	Two floors of booths and tables; bar seats
AMBIENCE	During the day, it's not too loud and pretty slow; at night, frat brothers, sports enthusiasts, and other all-American twentysomethings come to grab a cheap drink with 20 of their closest friends

—*Christopher Russell*

Scoozi

*Where the beautiful people
enjoy bargain panini.*

$$

237 Newbury St., Boston 02116
(at Fairfield St.)
Phone (617) 247-8847 • Fax (617) 266-7868

CATEGORY	Gourmet Pizza
HOURS	Mon–Thurs: 11 AM–9 PM
	Fri/Sat: 11 AM–10 PM
	Extended summer hours
MASS TRANSIT	T: Green line to Copley
PAYMENT	VISA MasterCard AMERICAN EXPRESS
POPULAR FOOD	Creative homemade thin-crust pizza and panini made with high-quality fresh produce; Scoozi offers a different Mediterranean-inspired pizza, pasta, and soup of the day every day; consider yourself very lucky if you happen upon the garlic shrimp and caramelized onions slice of the day; the margherita pizza with fresh tomatoes is also a good bet
UNIQUE FOOD	White pizza with mozzarella, caramelized onions, arugula, and olive oil
DRINKS	Beer and moderately priced wine; variety of soft drinks, including microbrewed ones like Black Cherry; coffees of American and European origin; tea, iced tea, and mineral water
SEATING	Thirty inside, 50 outside—the sidewalk terrace is open in warmer months
AMBIENCE	Casual elegance, from the wrought-iron tables and chairs outside to the wicker chairs, comfy padded benches, small wood tables, and black-and-white prints hanging inside
EXTRAS/NOTES	Scoozi feeds a wide range of ages and backgrounds, including employees of Newbury's fashionable shops, Back Bay locals, and tourists. The most noticeable of Scoozi's clientele, however, are the designer-clad foreign students who are a fixture of the open-air terrace in warmer months, and who belie the gourmet pizzeria's reasonable prices. Thanks to the international house music often playing on weekends, Scoozi is a great place to come on a Friday or Saturday afternoon to gear up for a night out.

—Anna Morris

Shino Express

*Cheap sushi in the
unlikeliest of places.*

$$

144 Newbury St., Boston 02116
(at Dartmouth St.)
Phone (617) 262-4530

CATEGORY	Sushi
HOURS	Daily: noon–9 PM
MASS TRANSIT	T: Green line to Arlington
PAYMENT	VISA MasterCard
POPULAR FOOD	Especially good tuna and a nice eel roll; most rolled sushi is about $2 for six pieces; miso soup around $1; 12 kinds of nigiri sushi for a buck each
UNIQUE FOOD	Bring a group of your hungriest friends to get the buy-in-bulk special worthy of Costco: 140 sushi rolls for $100
DRINKS	Soda
SEATING	Around 20 stools at the counter
AMBIENCE	A cute, but sparsely decorated little basement luncheonette and a great place to stop in for a quick bite in between shopping excursions

—Amélie Cherlin

Steve's Restaurant

*Even before the hipster migration
to Newbury, this taverna was dishing out
great Greek standards.*

$$

316 Newbury St., Boston 02115
(between Gloucester St. and Hereford St.)
Phone (617) 267-1817 • Fax (617) 424-6965

CATEGORY	Greek
HOURS	Mon–Sat: 7:30 AM–11 PM Sun: 10 AM–10 PM
MASS TRANSIT	T: Green line to Kenmore
PAYMENT	VISA MasterCard AMERICAN EXPRESS
POPULAR FOOD	Terrifically tasty gyros and chicken kebabs—a wonderful blend of savory meats, fresh vegetables, and tangy sauce; extremely sweet Greek cookies and pastries, like the baklava
UNIQUE FOOD	The *Pikilia* appetizer, which offers an assortment of dips and little nibbles such as tangy *taramosalata* (a caviar spread), spiced *skordalia* (a potato dip), zingy hummus, and stuffed grape leaves; they also have burgers, steak sandwiches, and other non-Greek options
DRINKS	Soft drinks, juices, alcohol, beers, and coffee drinks including the eye-poppingly strong hot or iced Greek coffee
SEATING	This place is very popular, especially for weekday lunch; in an apparent effort to

get as many people in as possible, tables are jammed together so closely that it's often hard to tell where one ends and another begins; service, though, is friendly and fast, making any waiting time minimal

AMBIENCE   Located in a parlor floor bowfront, the décor is simple and clean with small Greek touches displayed on the cream-colored walls, such as classical columns and a star of Macedonia, the restaurant's symbol; the perfect place (and a temporary wallet reprieve) for casual business lunchers and the shopping-weary

—*Amanda Dorato*

Tealuxe

Unpretentious toast and tea for the masses.

$

108 Newbury St., Boston 02116

(at Clarendon St.)

Phone (617) 927-0400

www.tealuxe.com

CATEGORY	Café
HOURS	Sun–Thurs: 8 AM–11 PM Fri/Sat: 8 AM–midnight
MASS TRANSIT	T: Green line to Copley
PAYMENT	VISA MasterCard AMERICAN EXPRESS DISCOVER
POPULAR FOOD	Sandwiches to please vegetarians and omnivores alike: the Veggie Toastite sandwich has garlic portobello mushrooms, basil, and tomato, while the Providence Club is stocked with ham, turkey, bacon, greens, tomato, and mayo; the tuna salad is reliably fresh and tasty; nibble on a maple scone or a chocolate-tangerine cookie with your tea
UNIQUE FOOD	The Toastites—grilled sandwiches—are enormously comforting, and include the strawberry and cream cheese, and peanut butter and honey sweetite; there are crumpets, too, and the Devon cream shortcake is a decadently special treat—all without the cost of High Tea at the Ritz
DRINKS	Over 100 loose teas: bewitching Creme de la Earl Grey, ruby herbal Rote Grutze, cardamom-spiked decaf Highland Chai, and, of course, Golden Tippy Assam, for starters; daily variety of iced teas, hot chocolate, Zen Blenders (iced fruit/tea drinks); intrepid souls will enjoy the peppery Kashmiri Chai—it ain't your Starbucks chai, that's for sure
SEATING	Takeout and ephemeral clients sit at the couple of small tables upstairs; those more engrossed, or perhaps dining, head to the small tables in the basement; tables can be pushed together, but more than four people in a party gets crowded

AMBIENCE	Decked out in hammered bronze and navy blue, Tealuxe is a kind of postmodern café with throwbacks to the 1920s, with the advantage of Bose speakers on which to play funky old jazz; typically patrons are in their 20s and up, with the occasional elderly lady lost in a book over her teapot; the downstairs space fills up fast during dinner and especially on weekends
EXTRAS/NOTES	Tealuxe began as an almost unbelievably tiny café in Harvard Square, serving ceramic personal or party pots to visitors and offering tall paper cups of tea as takeout. Immediately it was mobbed at all hours—even without serving anything more substantial than a blueberry scone. When Tealuxe expanded into its other locations, by trial and error it introduced meals and has since become the ideal respite from the homogenization of coffee-oriented chain cafés.
OTHER ONES	• Harvard Square: 0 Brattle St., Cambridge 02138, (617) 927-0400 (baked goods only) • Rhode Island: 231 Thayer St., Providence 02906, (401) 734-9920

—Alison Pereto

Thai Dish

Affordable pad *Thai on Newbury St.*

$$$

259 Newbury St., Boston 02116

(between Gloucester St. and Fairfield St.)

Phone (617) 437-9691 • Fax (617) 437-8862

CATEGORY	Thai
HOURS	Mon–Thurs: 11:30 AM–3 PM, 5 PM–10 PM Fri: 11:30 AM–3 PM, 5 PM–11 PM Sat: noon–11 PM Sun: noon–10 PM
MASS TRANSIT	T: Green line to Copley or Hynes/ICA
PAYMENT	VISA MasterCard AMERICAN EXPRESS DISCOVER
POPULAR FOOD	Delicious masaman curry and *pad* Thai
UNIQUE FOOD	Interestingly named menu items include Seafood Orgy (scallops, shrimp, squid, crab, and mussels with a touch of curry) and Cave Man Chicken (half-chicken grilled with a tangy chili sauce)
DRINKS	Sodas and limeade; Thai iced tea and iced coffee; beer
SEATING	Room for 50 at 16 tables of varying size
AMBIENCE	The atmosphere is pleasant and the staff extremely friendly; when the weather is nice there are three tables outside, perfect for people-watching on Newbury

—Amélie Cherlin

Torrefazione Italia

A liquid trip to Italy.
$

85 Newbury St., Boston 02116
(between Clarendon St. and Berkeley St.)
Phone (617) 424-0951 • Fax (617) 424-0953
www.titalia.com

CATEGORY	Italian Café
HOURS	Mon–Fri: 7 AM–9 PM
	Sat: 8 AM–9 PM
	Sun: 9 AM–9 PM
MASS TRANSIT	T: Green line to Copley
PAYMENT	VISA MasterCard AMERICAN EXPRESS
POPULAR FOOD	Served in gorgeous Italian ceramic ware: fresh panini, salads, and desserts; opt for the super tasty "pizza"—toppings like prosciutto and spinach on a sauceless bread-like crust; they'll grill all sandwiches
DRINKS	Several varieties of Italian coffee, served hot and iced; San Pellegrino flavored carbonated drinks; *granita di caffe latte*, an ice blended coffee drink, and a refreshing *granita di frutta*
SEATING	Seats 25 inside at small wooden and tile tables that line the wall of the somewhat narrow café; additional seats outside on the terrace in warmer months
AMBIENCE	Elegant and inviting, the walls are warm oranges and yellows, and the pretty tiled tables and the colorful ceramic cups give the café the feeling of being much fancier than the prices would have you believe; a mixed crowd of Beacon Hill grandes dames, professionals from Boston and Paris alike, and med students; even though the terrace, shaded by great big canvas umbrellas in the summer, is a great spot for people-watching, don't expect to find the poseurs of other Newbury St. environs joining you there.

—Anna Morris

Trident Booksellers and Café

*Excellent taste—in books
and in food.*
$$

338 Newbury St., Boston 02115
(a block from Massachusetts Ave.)
Phone (617) 267-8688

CATEGORY	Café
HOURS	Daily: 9 AM–midnight
MASS TRANSIT	T: Green line to Hynes/ICA
PAYMENT	VISA MasterCard AMERICAN EXPRESS

POPULAR FOOD	Perpetual breakfast ranging from eggs to lemon ricotta-stuffed French toast; mild bean chili with cashews; Trident fries (potatoes, beets); lovely desserts and a reliable chunk of sour cream coffee cake big enough to get into and drive home
UNIQUE FOOD	Momos (traditional Tibetan dumplings served with salad and "racy dipping sauce")
DRINKS	The juice bar should meet most emotional, psychological, or physical needs, with offerings like Immune Builder, Slimmer, and Wheatgrass Hopper (although this reviewer has tiptoed warily around the ominously named Depression); also many loose teas, chai, smoothies, frappes, floats, wine, and beer
SEATING	Two seating areas, one at the front for the window-watchers (see and be seen by the glitterati of Newbury St.) and another at the back for those requiring more seclusion; tables are perfect for two, and can be pushed together for larger groups; singles can cozy up to the juice bar with a $1 Dover Classic from the shelf
AMBIENCE	Clean, serene, welcoming, artsy, accepting of solitude or romance; friendly staff will allow patrons to nestle into their tables for hours at a stretch, though on the busy weekend nights they'll have to order more than coffee—the place fills up fast when everything else in Boston closes; clientele includes dates (first, last, and in-between), artists, writers, philosophical college types, bike couriers; warm, yellow walls with ever-changing art
EXTRAS/NOTES	When Gail and Bernie Flynn opened the bookstore/café in the dog-eat-dog early 1980s, they wanted it to be a place where one could "sit down with a fine cup of coffee and linger over a conversation or a book." As such, it's enormously successful, an embodiment of the Flynns' desire to live the Buddhist concept of right livelihood. On a street known for its glamour and material snobbishness, the Trident offers the perfect antidote to the urban whirl. Be sure to check out the huge magazine selection, wander amid the tall stacks of thoughtfully chosen books, and try and figure out if that shaggy poet-type in the corner is scribbling a love letter or a manifesto.

—*Alison Pereto*

"Shallots are for babies. Onions are for men.
Garlic is for heroes."

—*Anon*

FENWAY-KENMORE SQUARE

Audubon Circle

Casual chic.

$$$

838 Beacon St., Boston 02215

Phone (617) 421-1910

CATEGORY	Bar & Grill
HOURS	Mon–Fri: 11:30 AM–1 AM
	Sat/Sun: 4 PM–1 AM
MASS TRANSIT	T: Green line to Kenmore
PAYMENT	
POPULAR FOOD	Great burgers, both traditional and new; inventive sandwiches (hot-pressed apples, brie, watercress); and great appetizers
UNIQUE FOOD	Grilled jerky turkey sandwich, served with roasted potatoes, with Thai-chili ketchup for dipping; New Zealand lamb chops with tart cherry glaze at an amazing price
DRINKS	Full bar with a great selection of beers and wines, soft drinks, coffee, tea
SEATING	Intimate tables along the walls and overlooking the street seat around 50; a long bar accommodates 20 or more
AMBIENCE	Simple, chic, inviting—just like the clientele; lunch hour is a bustling time, as is any weekend night, where you'll see and be seen by a stylish but approachable crowd

—John Newton

Brown Sugar Café

A sweet Thai experience.

$$$

1033 Commonwealth Ave., Boston 02215

(at Babcock St.)

Phone (617) 787-4242

www.brownsugarcafe.com

CATEGORY	Thai
HOURS	Mon–Thurs: 11 AM–10 PM
	Fri: 11 AM–11 PM
	Sat: noon–11 PM
	Sun: noon–10 PM
MASS TRANSIT	T: Green line-B to Babcock St.
PAYMENT	
POPULAR FOOD	An extensive menu that highlights seafood and every kind of curry; try the popular Brown Sugar Mango Fried Rice or Old Lady Spicy, an array of vegetables and sweet basil in the chef's intense special sauce; or choose your favorite ingredient like pineapple, snow peas, or bok choy, and then add meat, fish, or tofu to see the chef work his magic
UNIQUE FOOD	Seafood Volcano, a foil bubble filled with seafood and vegetables set on fire at your table; papaya salad; mango curry chicken
DRINKS	Coconut milk-frothed Thai iced tea quells the flames best; sodas and beers, including Singha, are also available

SEATING	Candlelit, mock marble-topped tables for two or four are set so close together that intimacy is obliterated on busy nights; however, as the café is next door to Boston University, surrounding conversations are bound to be either educational or amusing
AMBIENCE	Despite the cramped seating, the café tries hard to maintain a romantic atmosphere; the overhead lights are kept dim and iridescent swarms of butterflies suspended in Plexiglas swoop across the walls, while little Christmas lights twinkle around the cove that deftly hides the kitchen
EXTRAS/NOTES	Although located on busy Comm. Ave, Brown Sugar is a cozy haven of sweet and spicy experience that successfully shelters you from the roar of the cars and passing T. The service is extremely swift—your entrée may come before you've finished your appetizer.
OTHER ONES	• Fenway: 129 Jersey St., Boston 02215, (617) 266-2928

—Nicole Cotroneo

Burrito Max

A fresh-Mex place with a sinful taste.

$

642 Beacon St., Boston 02215
(at Raleigh St.)
Phone (617) 266-8088

CATEGORY	Burrito Joint
HOURS	Daily: 11:30 AM–11 PM
MASS TRANSIT	T: Green line to Kenmore
PAYMENT	Cash only
POPULAR FOOD	Big burritos with your choice of tortilla (white, spinach, chili, tomato, whole wheat) and filling (grilled veggies, black beans and rice, chicken, barbecued pork, ground beef, grilled steak); crispy and soft tacos, vegetarian chili, and quesadillas; some of the best fries around (regular, cheese, chili, and sweet)
UNIQUE FOOD	Barbecued tofu or Texas chili burrito or taco; California-style fried snapper with salsa and guacamole
DRINKS	Soft drinks, bottled juices, bottled teas
SEATING	Sixty seats at rustic, crowded tables; a small window-lining wooden counter
AMBIENCE	This place is a true dive with brightly painted walls, an eclectic late-night crowd, and punk-rock line cooks; one of the best places in the Kenmore area to people-watch, this tiny restaurant has two mostly glass walls, leaving just about any seat in the house with an open view of passersby.
OTHER ONES	• Allston: Big Burrito, 160 Brighton Ave., Allston 02134, (617) 562-0440

—Laura & Ben D'Amore

Buteco Restaurant

*Join the loyal following at
Boston's oldest Brazilian joint.*

$$$

130 Jersey St., Boston 02215
(between Queensberry St. and Park Dr.)
Phone (617) 247-9508

CATEGORY	Brazilian
HOURS	Mon–Thurs: noon–10 PM
	Fri: noon–11 PM
	Sat: 3 PM–11 PM
	Sun: 3 PM–10 PM
MASS TRANSIT	T: Green line to Kenmore
PAYMENT	VISA MasterCard AMERICAN EXPRESS DISCOVER
POPULAR DISHES	The Brazilian national dish *feijoada*, a stew of black beans, pork, sausage, and dried beef; chicken and cheese enchiladas with a spicy green sauce; *vegetariano*, steamed vegetables with garlic and a little olive oil
UNIQUE FOOD	*Mandioca*, a lot like steak fries but made from yucca, served with homemade carrot sauce
DRINKS	Assorted beers, Xingu (a Brazilian beer), soft drinks, and wine
SEATING	Just one small dining room that seats just over 30; gets busy on Saturday nights
AMBIENCE	Friendly, very homey, even romantic; full of in-the-know diners who look like they could afford a more expensive place but have gotten hooked on Buteco

—*Glen Strandberg*

Café Belo

(see p. 88)
Brazilian
636 Beacon St., Boston 02215
Phone (617) 236-8666

Cornwall's

*Hearty grub and authentic
suds at this laid-back British pub.*

$$

654 Beacon St., Boston 02215
(at Raleigh St.)
Phone (617) 262-3749
www.cornwalls.com

CATEGORY	English Pub
HOURS	Mon–Fri: noon–2 AM
	Sat/Sun: 5 PM–2 AM
MASS TRANSIT	T: Green line to Kenmore
PAYMENT	VISA MasterCard
POPULAR FOOD	Though the many varieties of burgers are popular (blue cheese to guacamole), try the authentic English fish 'n' chips (the vinegar is already on the table), or a sandwich named for a famous Brit, like the Thomas Beckett (a grilled ham and

cheese with tomato and onion); killer grilled portobello mushroom salad

UNIQUE FOOD Should you need some game-sustaining grub, the grilled bangers (British sausage made of beef) with mashed potatoes and gravy will, according to one waiter, "really stick with you all night!"; shepherd's pie or Welsh cottager's chicken pie topped with mashed potatoes and gravy provide hearty pub experience

DRINKS Amazing beer list, wine, full bar, soft drinks

SEATING Seats about 100

AMBIENCE A game-playing sort of place: guess the infamous Brits painted on the wall, tackle one of the many board games available for use, or get drunk and play darts; situated in the vicinity of several Boston area schools and in the heart of BU, this is a mostly academic crowd; suits and ties share the space with jeans and tees at any hour, the after-dinner crowd is mostly students, and the place stays humming until 2 AM; on weekends, Cornwall's opens earlier in the afternoon on game days

—Laura & Ben D'Amore

Herrell's

(see p. 131)
Ice Cream Shop
350 Longwood Ave., Boston 02115
No phone

India Quality

A rare gem and a Boston legend.
$$$
484 Commonwealth Ave., Boston 02215
Phone (617) 267-4499 • Fax (617) 267-4477
www.indiaqualityrest.com

CATEGORY Indian

HOURS Mon–Fri: 11:30 AM–3 PM, 5 PM–11 PM
Sat/Sun: 11:30 AM–11 PM

MASS TRANSIT T: Green line to Kenmore

PAYMENT VISA MasterCard AMERICAN EXPRESS DISCOVER

POPULAR FOOD Any of the *vindaloos*; fresh, buttery *naan*; famous lunch specials that start at $6 and include chutneys, *papadum*, and basmati rice

UNIQUE FOOD The menu invites that the *shahi paneer*, homemade cheese cooked in a tomato cream sauce, "may very well become your favorite"

DRINKS Mango *lassi*; over 35 bottled beers both from India (Taj Mahal, Flying Horse) and just about every other country; a good wine selection, by glass and bottle; tea, coffee, and a few juices

SEATING Comfortable tables with plenty of room

AMBIENCE	Clean without being sterile, friendly without being fake, India Quality has a long-standing clientele of Boston residents and BU students; the room is very blue, with tasteful Indian scenes on the wall of people engaged in wholesome tasks; lunch is extremely popular but not especially crowded, while dinner around the weekend attracts many
EXTRAS/NOTES	The India Quality is a Boston legend, having risen like a phoenix from the fire that gutted its previous location at 536 Comm. Ave. in 1998. The restaurant boasts a sandwich board positively stuffed with accolades won over years of service to hungry locals and travelers.

—Alison Pereto

El Pelón Taquería

Fenway's favorite tacos.

$

92 Peterborough St., Boston 02111
(between Kilmarnock St. and Jersey St.)
Phone (617) 262-9090
www.elpelon.com

CATEGORY	Mexican
HOURS	Daily: 11:30 AM–10:30 PM
MASS TRANSIT	T: Green line to Fenway
PAYMENT	VISA MasterCard AMERICAN EXPRESS
POPULAR FOOD	Pulled pork tacos with beans, pickled red cabbage, and limed onions; homemade chips and salsa; fried plantains; the Burrito Bravo with three cheeses, pinto beans, and poblano peppers; *carne asada*
UNIQUE FOOD	Tamales and *tortas* (toasted bread topped with beans, guacamole, lime onions, and meat); fish tacos; red mole or green mole
DRINKS	*Horchata*, self-service soda machine
SEATING	Seats 15; plus outdoor tables in summer
AMBIENCE	Just a few tables and counter service; Mexican decorations and bullfight posters; food served on cardboard and foil with plastic silverware
EXTRAS/NOTES	On Tuesdays, $10 gets you all you can eat tacos (5 PM–10 PM). Owner Loretta Huguez used to cook at upscale eateries East Coast Grill, Tremont 647, and Blue Room.

—Kyle Konrad

"Since Eve ate the apple, much depends on dinner."

—Lord Byron

Rod Dee Thai Cuisine

(see p. 115)
Thai
94 Peterborough St., Boston 02215
Phone (617) 859-0969

Sausage Guy

*Greasy Italian sausages,
a Fenway tradition as old
as The Curse.*
$
Lansdowne St., Boston 02215
(next to the garage)
www.sausageguy.com

CATEGORY	Sausage Cart
HOURS	Before and after all Red Sox home games Thurs–Sat: 10 PM–2 AM
MASS TRANSIT	T: Green line to Fenway
PAYMENT	Cash only
POPULAR FOOD	Italian sausages with grilled onions and peppers
DRINKS	Sodas
SEATING	None
AMBIENCE	A man, his grill, his cart, his cooler—a recipe for success among the drunk clubgoers and boisterous Sox fans who make up the regular clientele
EXTRAS/NOTES	The Sausage Guy himself, David Littlefield, began hawking boneless wings at Patriots games. He quickly turned to sausages, became known as "The Sausage Guy" and moved his cart to Fenway. He also owns Salsa's, a South Boston Mexican restaurant (see p. 152).

—*Kyle Konrad*

R.I.P.
The Hedge School

Where does a nice young anarchist go to meet another young anarchist? It used to be at the Hedge School. Serving up the finest vegetarian food in Boston, for years this underground restaurant (in both a literal and figurative sense), resided in the basement of a Boston University building and served lunch to a variety of counterculture types. Run by a collective of six hardworking cooks who made a memorable quiche, the Hedge School was named for the secret 18th century Catholic schools of Ireland. Despite the support of numerous BU faculty members, the Hedge School eventually closed down under the leadership of university president John Silber.

—*Sandy Ruben*

Thornton's Fenway Grill

A cheap little neighborhood treasure.

$$$

100 Peterborough St., Boston 02215

(at Kilmarnock St.)

Phone (617) 421-0104

CATEGORY	Bar & Grill
HOURS	Mon–Fri: 10 AM–midnight Sat/Sun: 9 AM–midnight
MASS TRANSIT	T: Green line to Kenmore
PAYMENT	VISA MasterCard AMERICAN EXPRESS DISCOVER
POPULAR FOOD	Huge portions; buffalo wings with homemade ranch dressing; vegetarian options like the Big Dig, a large hummus plate; early bird dinner specials (Daily: 3 PM–6 PM) for $8; all-you-can-eat ribs (Wed: 5 PM–midnight) for $12
UNIQUE FOOD	All of the chicken sandwiches are named after Jack Nicholson films, and many of the other menu items feature Boston landmarks in their names
DRINKS	An impressive list of alcoholic and non-alcoholic blender drinks; full bar
SEATING	Tables in two rooms, plus an outside patio that gets packed on warm nights
AMBIENCE	Busy before Red Sox games; on weekends, the extensive brunch menu (also Mon–Fri 10 AM–3 PM) attracts crowds and substantial waits
EXTRAS/NOTES	Matt Damon has dined here, as has the kid in *American Pie* who got busy with Stifler's mom. If you're bored, watch one of the two televisions or wander around and look at the random wall hangings and knick knacks adorning the dining areas and bar.

—*Melinda Green*

BOSTON—GO
WEST ON
THE GREEN
LINE

ALLSTON

Big Burrito

(see Burrito Max, p. 81)
Burrito Joint
160 Brighton Ave., Allston 02134
Phone (617) 562-0440

Café Belo
Meat-eaters rejoice!
$$
181 Brighton Ave., Allston 02134
(at Quint Ave. in Brooks Plaza)
Phone (617) 783-4858

CATEGORY	Brazilian
HOURS	Daily: 8 AM–10 PM
MASS TRANSIT	T: Green line-B to Harvard Ave.; bus: #57 or #66
PAYMENT	VISA MasterCard AMERICAN EXPRESS
POPULAR FOOD	Spit-roasted *churrasco* (Brazilian rotisserie barbecue meats); everything from chicken hearts to charred pork and *linguica* (Portuguese sausage), all sliced to order and less than $6 a pound; black beans and rice, spicy collard greens, and fried plantains
UNIQUE FOOD	In addition to the barbecue carving station, the buffet also includes salads and entree specials that vary by day; specials include dried codfish with potatoes; *feijoada* (the Brazilian national dish of meat and beans), and roast pork loin
DRINKS	Guarana, passionfruit nectar, Brazilian coffee
SEATING	Seats about 40
AMBIENCE	Much like a Brazilian community center with lively music, mostly Brazilian locals, and postings of upcoming cultural events; no wait service—just grab a plate, pile on the meat, and pay as you go out
OTHER ONES	• Fenway: 636 Beacon St., Boston 02215, (617) 236-8666
	• Union Square: 120 Washington St., Somerville 02108, (617) 623-3696
	• Western Suburbs: 94 Union Ave., Framingham 01702, (508) 620-9354

—Kaya Stone

Café Brazil

*A gluttonous display
of Brazilian homecooking.*

$$$

421 Cambridge St., Allston 02134

(at Harvard Ave.)

Phone (617) 789-5980

CATEGORY	Brazilian
HOURS	Sun–Thurs: 11 AM–10 PM Fri/Sat: noon–11 PM
MASS TRANSIT	Bus: #66 along Cambridge St. and Harvard Ave.
PAYMENT	VISA MasterCard AMERICAN EXPRESS
POPULAR FOOD	The *mondioca frita com linguica* appetizer (fried cassava root and grilled sausage); some of the best beans even for Beantown (the stewed black turtle variety); popular entrees include *minas especial* (grilled boneless chicken in a lemon-garlic marinade), and for the hearty appetite, Brazil 2001 (chicken, pork, sausage, and beef with sautéed cabbage and fried bananas); *bife rolet*, slices of beef rolled up with cheese and ham, is also excellent
UNIQUE FOOD	*Rabada*, a painstakingly simmered stew of oxtail and vegetables
DRINKS	Brazilian and domestic beers, wine, soft drinks, coffee, tea, Guarana, and *suco tropicais* (tropical fruit juices)
SEATING	Capacity for about 70; the space can accommodate small and large parties
AMBIENCE	Blue walls, background Brazilian music, and colorful holiday lights welcome a large South American crowd, especially during dinner hours
EXTRAS/NOTES	A live guitarist plays Thursday, Friday, and Saturday night.

—Sarah Duggan

El Cafetal

A delicious and cheap Andean gem.

$$$

479 Cambridge St., Allston 02134

(at Brighton Ave.)

Phone (617) 789-4009 • Fax (617) 789-4253

CATEGORY	Colombian
HOURS	Daily: 10 AM–10 PM
MASS TRANSIT	Bus: #66 along Cambridge St.
PAYMENT	VISA MasterCard AMERICAN EXPRESS
POPULAR FOOD	Great big Colombian specialty platters with rice, beans, yucca, and plantains on the side, featuring mouthwatering filets of usually pork or beef; the sides are a meal unto themselves—indeed, the rice and beans are plated separately—with crispy renditions of *chicharrón* (ultra-fried pork strips) and delicious *maduros fritos* (sweet

plantains); the steaks here tend to be thin cuts and cooked well-done in one of several ways: breaded, covered in a cream sauce, or grilled

UNIQUE FOOD The enormous *bandeja paisa* or "mountain dish," with steak, rice, beans, sweet plantains, pork strips, *arepa* (corn cake), and topped for good measure, in case you were still hungry, with a fried egg; *picadillo de higado* (liver hash); *mondongo* soup (made with beef tripe); grilled tongue; a long list of seafood dishes including trout, striped bass, cod, and red snapper; and, for those seeking a real experience, *mazamorra*, which could be described as a not-so-sweet milk-and-corn-flour concoction

DRINKS No alcohol; the drinks of choice are the tropical fruit juices, which you can have beaten into a milky shake (*con leche*); also, Colombian sodas

SEATING Two substantial rooms with tables for four

AMBIENCE A cheerful and busy dinnertime ambience, with the musical sound of chatter in a Bogotá accent. The staff switches readily between languages to accommodate its loyal non-Latin and Latin clientele, some of whom become glued to the Spanish-language soaps playing on the overhead TV. This is one ethnic restaurant that delivers both in food and in looks, but not in an uptight or particularly sophisticated way. There are the red tablecloths so typical of restaurants in the Andes, and a pastoral mural depicting coffee-growers complete with little donkeys carrying bags of beans. It's a place where one can spend a long time with friends and a long time eating—in part because it would take forever to finish a whole plate.

—*Esti Iturralde*

Camino Real

Get ready for a no-frills heaping of South American chow.

$$$

48 Harvard Ave., Allston 02134

(near Cambridge St.)

Phone (617) 254-5088 • Fax (617) 254-9475

CATEGORY Colombian

HOURS Daily: 10 AM–10 PM

MASS TRANSIT Bus: #66 along Cambridge St. and Harvard Ave.

PAYMENT VISA MasterCard AMERICAN EXPRESS DISCOVER

POPULAR FOOD Big hunks of pork, beef, or chicken prepared *a la plancha* (grilled) or *a la criolla* (in a sauce) with sides that threaten to steal the show: sweet plantains, rice and beans, yucca, potatoes, and salad

UNIQUE FOOD	The sampler plate, or Picada Camino Real, may require belt loosening with three meats plus sausage, *chicharrón* (pork strips), cheese, plantains, fries, and tomatoes; breakfast is served until 1 PM: start the day South American style with dishes of steak, pork, eggs, rice, and beans for a few dollars
DRINKS	Colombian sodas, tropical fruit juices mixed with milk, Latin milkshakes like *horchata* (wheat flavored) and *avena* (oatmeal)
SEATING	Spacious dining room for 50
AMBIENCE	Seen through the slats of vertical blinds, Camino Real doesn't look like much. Go inside, and it still doesn't look like much—sort of a Midwestern Chinese restaurant crossed with the lobby of an EconoLodge. Green carpeting basks in the glow of a ridiculously large chandelier.
EXTRAS/NOTES	People come here to eat, and judging by the largely immigrant clientele, the authentic food and cheap prices explain why. Catch up with the latest hit singles in the Spanish-speaking world by watching MTV *en español*.

—*Esti Iturralde*

Carlo's Cucina Italiana

Why can't all kitchens be like Carlo's?
$$$
131 Brighton Ave., Allston 02134
(at Harvard Ave.)
Phone (617) 254-9759

CATEGORY	Italian
HOURS	Sun–Thurs: 11 AM–10 PM Fri/Sat: 11 AM–11 PM
MASS TRANSIT	T: Green line-B to Harvard Ave.; bus: #66
PAYMENT	VISA MasterCard
POPULAR FOOD	Large portions of excellent gnocchi dishes, including gnocchi *spezzatino* (chicken, sun-dried tomatoes, mushrooms, and capers over gnocchi with plum tomato sauce); wonderful bruschetta; veal saltimbocca; huge salads; lobster ravioli
DRINKS	Beer, good wine list, cordials, espresso, soft drinks, tea, coffee
SEATING	About 35 people crammed into a very tight space
AMBIENCE	Extremely casual; expect at least a 30-minute wait on weekends; murals covering the walls and wooden wine racks

—*Christine Laurence*

Grasshopper

Taking a leap back to nature.

$$$

1 N. Beacon St., Allston 02134

(at Brighton Ave.)

Phone (617) 254-8883

CATEGORY	Asian/Vegetarian
HOURS	Mon–Thurs: 11 AM–10 PM Fri/Sat: 11 AM–11 PM Sun: noon–10 PM
MASS TRANSIT	T: Green line-B to Harvard Ave.; bus: #66
PAYMENT	VISA MasterCard
POPULAR FOOD	Vermicelli noodles and spring rolls; chow foon noodles with snow peas, carrots, and choice of fake meat; spicy Chinese eggplant; spicy stir-fried chicken seitan and vegetables in a yellow coconut curry
UNIQUE FOOD	Wheat gluten takes the place of chicken; faux-barbecued pork; the House Nest is a taro basket full of veggies and five fake meats
DRINKS	Jack fruit and soy shake; jasmine tea
SEATING	Black tables lit with candles or small beaded lamps; seats for about 30
AMBIENCE	Botanical all the way: botanical illustrations on the green walls, a number of real plants and pictures of plants, a tank with very small fish, and loads of ivy

—Kyle Konrad

Harvard Business School Dining Hall

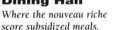

Where the nouveau riche score subsidized meals.

$$

117 Western Ave., Boston 02163

(at corner of Travis St.)

No phone

www.hbs.edu/about/campus/spangler.html

CATEGORY	Cafeteria
HOURS	Mon–Thurs: 7 AM–2 PM, 5:30 PM–8 PM Fri/Sat: 7 AM–2 PM Sun: 9 AM–2 PM
MASS TRANSIT	Bus: #70
PAYMENT	Cash only
POPULAR FOOD	This atypical dining hall offers a varying ensemble of excellent international dishes at obscenely low prices; flavorfully spiced Mediterranean, Caribbean, and Asian dishes take center stage, complemented by salad and sandwich bars
DRINKS	Bottled juices, beer, wine, tea, coffee
SEATING	Seats for 340 at large tables, limited outdoor seating
AMBIENCE	The between-classes home of those who are training to hire and fire; smartly dressed (dare we say "business casual"?)

students flood the Spangler Center between noon and 1:30 PM; despite the somewhat sterile decor, the atmosphere is lively with dining hall-style banter

EXTRAS/NOTES   Though it is part of the HBS Spangler Student Center, non-students can enjoy the cheap food and plush environs without having taken the GMAT.

—Alex Speier

R.I.P.
El Phoenix Room

While the El Phoenix Room wasn't exactly trendy or cozy or, well, clean, it *was* a landmark in the college-kid-infested neighborhood of Allston-Brighton for 35 years. The "upstairs" (which was, in fact, only three stairs higher than the downstairs) was a shabby Mexican restaurant where a few bucks could buy you a lot of burrito.

A sign of days gone by, each booth had its own miniature jukebox, though I never actually saw anyone using them, which led me to believe that they had stopped working long ago. Descend the three steps to the "downstairs" and you entered, in all senses of the term, a dive bar. The most prominent feature of the El Phoenix bar through the smoky haze was a multitude of neon beer signs. It was generally packed with college kids and older men from the neighborhood, all buying bottles of Bud, and maybe a few young couples waiting uncomfortably by the steps for a table to open upstairs.

I happened upon this place in the early '90s when I had just moved to Boston and was entertaining company from out of town. I didn't know the city yet. Driving down Comm. Ave. from Newton, it was the first place we came upon. We parked illegally out front and wandered in, sliding into a lumpy, dimly lit booth. Every time the kitchen door would swing open at the far end of the room, the whole restaurant would be swathed in fluorescent light, and then return to semi-darkness. Portions were huge, and we were poor; I ate leftover quesadilla for about three days. There was little that was truly Mexican on the menu, much of which seemed poured out of a can.

About five years later, I moved two blocks away from the El Phoenix; but alas, this was shortly before it closed its doors for the last time.

The El Phoenix Room finally bid Brighton *adiós* around the end of 2000, when it was elbowed out of its Comm. Ave. location to make way for the more sophisticated **Elbow Room** (see p. 104), which opened in late 2001.

—Kimberly Loomis

Herrell's

(see p. 131)
Ice Cream Shop
155 Brighton Ave., Allston 02134
Phone (617) 782-9599

Our House

*Comfort, couches,
and Connect Four.*
$$

1277 Commonwealth Ave., Allston 02134
(near Harvard Ave.)
Phone (617) 782-3228 • Fax (617) 782-6769

CATEGORY	Bar & Grill
HOURS	Mon–Fri: 4 PM–2 AM
	Sat/Sun: noon–2 AM
MASS TRANSIT	T: Green line-B to Harvard Ave.
PAYMENT	VISA MasterCard
POPULAR FOOD	Burgers and nachos, with a two-for-one deal weekdays from 4 PM to 7 PM; other typical pub fare like jalapeño poppers, potato skins, subs, and club sandwiches
DRINKS	Shot of the week; full bar, plenty of beer choices, soft drinks
SEATING	Numerous tables, funky, curving couches, and raised bars with stools spread out over three rooms
AMBIENCE	A laid-back, smoke-filled bar atmosphere, strictly 21+ after 8 PM. Below street level and decorated with dim lights, low ceilings, and dark colors, Our House makes the mostly student crowd feel at home with board games (Scattegories to Operation), a pool table, foosball, and funky-chill music.
EXTRAS/NOTES	While a great place to chill, the food is of average quality and service is so-so at best. Extremely popular *Simpsons* television marathon on Tuesday nights.

—*Meaghan Mulholland*

Pho Pasteur

(see p. 187)
Vietnamese
137 Brighton Ave., Allston 02134
Phone (617) 783-2340

"Sex is good, but not as good as fresh sweet corn."
—*Garrison Keillor*

Rangoli

*Distinctive Southern
Indian cuisine.*

129 Brighton Ave., Allston 02134
(between Harvard Ave. and Linden St.)
Phone (617) 562-0200 • Fax (617) 562-0447
www.rangoliboston.com

CATEGORY	Indian
HOURS	Sun–Thurs: 11:30 AM–3 PM, 5 PM–10:30 PM Fri/Sat: 11:30 AM–3 PM, 5 PM–11 PM
MASS TRANSIT	T: Green line-B to Harvard Ave.; bus: #66
PAYMENT	VISA MasterCard AMERICAN EXPRESS DISCOVER
POPULAR FOOD	While Rangoli's menu is extensive and all over the Indian map, its focus on Southern Indian cuisine is unique in the Boston area. The excellent *naan* comes stuffed with garlic, onion, lamb, or cashew and raisin. Vegetarians enjoy the *aloo ghobi* (cauliflower and potatoes cooked in herbs and spices), *malai kofta* (vegetable croquettes stuffed with nuts and herbs, simmered in gravy), or one of several *paneer* dishes made with a homemade cottage cheese. Tandoori dishes are decent, though by nature somewhat drier because of the clay oven cooking. Excellent desserts include rice pudding with cardamom, milk dumplings in rose syrup, and homemade mango ice cream.
UNIQUE FOOD	Rangoli's unique specialty (even its sister restaurants don't offer it) is the *dosa*, a thin, 18-inch rice flour crêpe, which can be ordered plain or stuffed with potatoes and your choice of onion, chicken, or lamb.
DRINKS	Smooth yogurt-based rose *lassi*; beer and wine; sodas (including a lemon Kashmiri soda); Indian coffee and pots of Eastern tea
SEATING	About 20 tables that are easily pushed together for larger parties; on weekend nights when the restaurant is full, you might feel a little too close to your neighbors, but it's comfortable and never seems to get too loud
AMBIENCE	A decent date spot for couples and an inexpensive enough option for local college students; the dominating color in the dining area is pink, the music is generally quiet sitar, and décor is minimal but appropriate with a few wooden masks and decorative Indian triptych panels on the walls
OTHER ONES	The owners, the Majmudar family, also operate two sister restaurants: • Coolidge Corner: Bombay Bistro, 1353 Beacon St., Brookline 02446, (617) 734-2879 • Harvard Square: Tanjore, 18 Eliot St., Cambridge 02138, (617) 868-1900

—Kimberly Loomis

Sài Gòn

*Bargain Vietnamese that's a hidden gem
in Boston's Asian food scene.*

$$

431 Cambridge St., Allston 02134

(at Harvard Ave.)

Phone (617) 254-3373

CATEGORY	Vietnamese
HOURS	Mon–Thurs: 11:30 AM–10 PM
	Fri/Sat: 11:30 AM–11 PM
	Sun: 5 PM–10 PM
MASS TRANSIT	Bus: #66
PAYMENT	Cash only
POPULAR FOOD	Noodle soups; spring rolls and fresh rolls; grilled meats with vermicelli; curries
UNIQUE FOOD	*Banh xeo*, a crisp pancake rolled up with chicken, shrimp, bean sprouts, and scallions; fisherman's soup; caramel entrees; every weekend there is a special entrée—if you're lucky enough to find curried sea bass with eggplant, don't miss out on this fabulous red curry blended with peanuts
DRINKS	Juices, soda, coffee, complimentary tea
SEATING	Two small rooms with tables that start out as twos but are put together to accommodate more as necessary
AMBIENCE	Bamboo blinds line the windows in this serene, wood-paneled restaurant; generally quiet at lunchtime, the restaurant picks up in the evenings with an eclectic mix of students, families, and couples

—*Katie Stone*

Seoul Bakery

(see p. 110)

Korean Bakery

58 Harvard Ave., Allston 02134

Phone (617) 787-6500

Steve's Kitchen

Friendly all-day Greek breakfast.

$

120 Harvard Ave., Allston 02134

(near the corner of Brighton Ave.)

Phone (617) 254-9457

CATEGORY	Greek Diner
HOURS	Mon–Sat: 6:30 AM–8 PM
	Sun: 6:30 AM–7 PM
MASS TRANSIT	T: Green line-B to Harvard Ave.
PAYMENT	Cash only
POPULAR FOOD	Steve's all-day breakfast keeps hungover students and hungry stragglers pouring in until late in the afternoon most weekends. Great coffee comes super hot and refills are easy to come by. All breakfast specials

come with home fries (the big, clumpy variety) and buttered toast; later on in the day, burgers, sandwiches, and gyros attract the hungry.

UNIQUE FOOD   Spinach and feta pie with soup for around three bucks; a dollar and some change buys really nice baklava—not excessively sweet, though not as flaky as you'd find at a bakery

DRINKS   Tea, coffee, fruit juices, soft drinks, hot cocoa with whipped cream and milk

SEATING   The smallish, diner-style setup can seat about 50 people; mostly four-person tables with a couple of two-seaters by the window and a large counter

AMBIENCE   In the heart of Allston, Steve's gets its fair share of college kids and grubby musician types to complement the usual diner crowd. The atmosphere is simple and nice: wooden tables, friendly low-key conversations, and a wide assortment of chalkboards and hand-scrawled menus combine to create the homemade sort of feeling you'd want from any diner.

EXTRAS/NOTES   Steve's is family-owned and it shows; the service is quick, clean, and absolutely friendly. And you won't leave hungry.

—*Jon Gorey*

The Sunset Grill and Tap

Beer bar, but better.

$$$

130 Brighton Ave., Allston 02134

(at Harvard Ave.)

Phone (617) 254-1331 • Fax (617) 254-3766

www.allstonsfinest.com

CATEGORY   Bar & Grill

HOURS   Daily: 11:30 AM–1 AM

MASS TRANSIT   T: Green line-B to Harvard Ave.; bus: #57 or #66

PAYMENT   VISA MasterCard AMERICAN EXPRESS DISCOVER

POPULAR FOOD   Burgers (ground sirloin, vegetarian, ground turkey, chicken, or fried cod) that can be done literally thousands of ways thanks to The Sunset's Toppers—seven cheeses, Canadian bacon, sprouts, and 16 other items in between; nachos; "world renowned" buffalo wings; Meltdowns (creativity with sandwich melts)

UNIQUE FOOD   Raspberry Mako shark sticks; chicken fajita potato skins; shrimp po' boy; lunch taco and fajita buffet (Mon–Fri: 11:30 AM–3 PM)

DRINKS   A patron or two have gotten drunk at the Sunset: 112 beers on tap, 400+ bottled; also wine, champagne, sangria, hard cider, sake, shooters, cocktails, "beertails," frozen drinks, and concoctions featuring that energetic bovine, Red Bull

SEATING Seats for 288 spread over three rooms and two floors

AMBIENCE On weekend nights, the Sunset is packed and vivacious—or noisy, depending upon your state of mind at the time; some of the mostly college age and young professional crowd come for the beer, some for the food, but most come for both

EXTRAS/NOTES A discount coupon was available on their web site at the time of this writing. Monday through Wednesday nights, your two-drink minimum gets you all you can eat, from midnight to 1 AM. The Sunset's beer selection is unmatched in Boston. If you know what dunkel weizen is (and you like it), go to the Sunset for a bottled selection. Sometimes you can even find one on tap.

—Reg Brittain

White Horse Tavern

Abercrombie at nite.
$$
116 Brighton Ave., Allston 02134
(near Harvard Ave.)
Phone (617) 254-6633
www.whitehorseallston.com

CATEGORY English Pub

HOURS Daily: 11:30 AM–2 AM

MASS TRANSIT T: Green line-B to Harvard Ave.; bus: #57 or #66

PAYMENT VISA MasterCard AMERICAN EXPRESS

POPULAR FOOD Award winning chili; sandwiches, burgers, and pizza; on Wednesdays and Thursdays get steak tips for $5 with the purchase of a drink; Monday and Tuesday get pizza, burgers, or a pound of wings for $3 (6 PM–midnight)

UNIQUE FOOD All-you-can-eat Sunday brunch buffet (until 3:30 PM; $10)

DRINKS White Horse is primarily a bar, so you can order whatever your little alcoholic heart desires: margaritas, mudslides, beer or wine.

SEATING Open and airy with many tables and a large bar

AMBIENCE Bright red front with large windows that open in warm weather; a vibrant and bustling place packed with college students and recent grads; a good pick-up joint judging from the canoodling that seems to escalate during the night

—Melinda Green

Wing-It

For when that craving strikes—21 flavors and free delivery.

$$

1153 Commonwealth Ave., Allston 02134
(at Fordham Rd.)
Phone (617) 783-2473 • Fax (617) 783-8677

CATEGORY	Wings
HOURS	Mon–Thurs: 4 PM–midnight
	Fri/Sat: noon–2 AM
	Sun: noon–11 PM
MASS TRANSIT	T: Green line-B to Fordham Rd.
PAYMENT	VISA MasterCard AMERICAN EXPRESS
POPULAR FOOD	Wings! Regular or boneless, mild, medium, hot, or Suicide Wings; also burgers and ribs
UNIQUE FOOD	Honey-glazed garlic wings, Teridactil wings (a blend of barbecue and teriyaki), garlic and parmesan wings, sweet and sour wings, sweet dijon wings—the list goes on and on
DRINKS	Canned soda
SEATING	There are only five tables, three small aluminum tables with two chairs each and two larger tables with two stools each
AMBIENCE	A favorite dive among the surrounding colleges; although they specialize in takeout and delivery, the tables get extremely crowded on weekends between midnight and 2 AM as the bar crowd trickles in; no place for casual conversation, the music is always loud and the genre changes with the staff from Sinatra to punk

—Donna M. Mancusi

BRIGHTON

Angora Café 2
(see p. 102)
Café
153 Sutherland Rd., Brighton 02135
Phone (617) 277-5400

Bamboo

Crispy, fresh Thai that's a pleasure to devour.

$$$

1616 Commonwealth Ave., Brighton 02135
(at Washington St.)
Phone (617) 734-8192

CATEGORY	Thai
HOURS	Mon–Thurs: 10:30 AM–10 PM
	Fri/Sat: 11:30 AM–11 PM
	Sun: 5 PM–10 PM
MASS TRANSIT	T: Green line-B to Washington St.
PAYMENT	VISA MasterCard AMERICAN EXPRESS

POPULAR FOOD	Mango curry with chunks of chicken and veggies; *tom yum goong* (Thai hot and sour shrimp soup); crispy *pad* Thai; most dishes come with heaps of cooked but crunchy vegetables
UNIQUE FOOD	Crispy tamarind duck; soft shell crab with yellow curry; crispy whole bass with chili sauce
DRINKS	Full bar, Singha, soft drinks
SEATING	Room for about 35
AMBIENCE	Dimly lit with orange and green walls, brightly colored lamps, fresh flowers, and candles; as might be expected, a bamboo motif right down to the bamboo-shaped glasses
EXTRAS/NOTES	Owner Sam Chindapanich is the former general manager of Jae's Café in Cambridge. Like Jae's, Bamboo will make any dish with your choice of meat or seafood, rice, or noodle.

—*Kyle Konrad*

Bangkok Bistro

Keeping the flavor of Cleveland Circle alive.
$$$
1952 Beacon St., Brighton 02135
(at Chestnut Hill Ave.)
Phone (617) 739-7270

CATEGORY	Thai
HOURS	Mon–Fri: 8 AM–7:30 PM
	Sat: 11:30 AM–6 PM
	Sun: 9 AM–3 PM
MASS TRANSIT	T: Green line-B, C, D to Cleveland Circle
PAYMENT	VISA MasterCard AMERICAN EXPRESS
POPULAR FOOD	Flavorful, classic Thai food: chicken basil, *pad* Thai, beef rendang; green, yellow, red, or masaman curry
UNIQUE FOOD	One Night in Bangkok is the hottest and spiciest dish on the menu with chicken, beef, or pork sautéed with basil leaf and hot pepper—it's a socially acceptable way to have a sweaty one-night stand
DRINKS	Thai iced tea and coffee, juice, soda, bottled water, beer, wine
SEATING	Banquettes line two walls of the somewhat triangular room; small, Formica tables fill the awkward space in adjustable combinations
AMBIENCE	Wall-mounted lamps illuminate teal walls, giving the place—and diners wearing white—a funky green-blue glow; Boston College students and casual Cleveland Circle locals keep the place rocking every evening, while the open kitchen noticeably elevates the noise level
EXTRAS/NOTES	Though a bit startling, the pink facade is actually appropriate, as Bangkok is a major muscle keeping the pulse of Cleveland Circle strong.

—*Nicole Cotroneo*

Hungry? Boston College: The Best Food Stops for the Starving Student

BC kids enjoy some of the best restaurant options in Boston, with eateries in Brookline and Brighton earning top accolades. And, befitting a large student population, there are a number of cheap greasy spoons and grungy hangouts. Here is a selection of BC students' favorite haunts.

Best Burger: Eagles Deli

Though named after the BC mascot, it's not university pride that attracts BCers to Eagles Deli but the famous Godzilla Burger. If you can clean up a pound of beef capped with four slices of cheddar and an equal amount of fries they add your picture to the back wall already plastered with the Polaroids of the Godzilla slayers that have come before. *Cleveland Circle: 1918 Beacon St., Brighton 02135, (617) 731-3232.*

Best Place to Eat While Drinking: Roggie's Brew & Grille

At this laidback joint, friends catch up or watch a game over beers and typical grille fare. Roggie's is a BC institution like Mary Ann's (see below), but much more qualified to be so; they actually put in effort here. *Cleveland Circle: 356 Chestnut Hill Ave., Brighton 02135, (617) 566-1880.*

Best Ice Cream: White Mountain Creamery

Right across the street from campus, White Mountain is a BC addiction that even the frigid winters can't cure. The smell of warm waffle cones fills the shop where tables are always packed with students enjoying homemade ice cream. Even the nonfat peanut butter frozen yogurt tastes sinfully delicious. *Chestnut Hill: 19 Commonwealth Ave., Chestnut Hill 02467, (617) 527-8790.*

Best Happy Hour Special: Mary Ann's

What attracts generation after generation of BCers to this unattractive hole-in-the-wall, most lovingly called "Scary Ann's" is truly a mystery. The only conceivable explanation is the free wings and $1 bottles at Happy Hour. *Cleveland Circle: 1937 Beacon St., Brighton 02135, no phone.*

Best Place to Impress: Tasca

When BC students want to feel cultured, they turn to the "exotic" experience of eating Spanish tapas at Tasca. Sipping wine beneath dim light, serenaded by Spanish guitar on Thursdays, Tasca is a world away from Lower Dining Hall. *Brighton: 1612 Commonwealth Ave., Brighton 02135, (617) 730-8002.*

Best Late Night: Angora Café and Angora Café 2

To BC's delight, Angora has crept even closer to campus with the opening of its second café on Sutherland. What other place will satisfy a hankering for frozen yogurt at midnight—and deliver! Here toppings are folded into the yogurt instead of glopped on top. *Angora Café—Fenway: 1020 Commonwealth Ave. # A, Boston 02215, (617) 232-1757. Angora Café 2—Brighton: 153 Sutherland Rd., Brighton 02135, (617) 277-5400.*

Best Pizza: Presto Pizzeria Restaurant

The cheese and oil oozes as any good neighborhood pizza should, but not enough to create a sloppy mess. Warm from the Presto's oven, the crust has a delightfully crispy bite. Try the popular thin-crust Neopolitan. Delivery hours are limited. *Cleveland Circle: 1936 Beacon St., Brighton 02135, (617) 232-4545.*

Best Pizza Delivery: Pizza Etc.

Located right in Oak Square, Pizza Etc. is a 10-minute scoot from Boston College. With free delivery and a deal of two large pies for $10, Pizza Etc. is irresistible for BC students too famished to leave their dorms. *Oak Square: 2 Tremont St., Brighton 02135, (617) 254-2022.*

Best Sandwich: Shawarma King

When BCers feel like breaking out of their white bread mold, they head over to this Middle Eastern sandwich shop for shawarma or falafel stuffed in pita. See p. 115. *Coolidge Corner: 1383 Beacon St., Brookline 02446, (617) 731-6035.*

Most Underrated: Bluestone Bistro

Stuck on a corner amid apartment houses, next to a grocery store with a tacky blue sign, this bistro hides its magic inside. Bluestone offers creative dishes, gourmet pizza, live music, and outdoor seating in the spring. Unfortunately only those BC juniors kicked off campus and living on Chiswick Rd. tend to know what a gem Bluestone is. See p. 103. *Brighton: 1799 Commonwealth Ave., Brighton 02135, (617) 254-8309.*

—Nicole Cotroneo

"Hunger: One of the few cravings that cannot be appeased with another solution."
—Irwin Van Grove

Bluestone Bistro

*West Coast eclectic served in
New England portions.*

$$$

1799 Commonwealth Ave., Brighton 02135
(at Chiswick Rd.)

Phone (617) 254-8309 • Fax (617) 782-2875

www.bluestonebistro.com

CATEGORY	Gourmet Pizza
HOURS	Mon–Wed: 11 AM–10:30 PM
	Thurs: 11 AM–11 PM
	Fri: 11 AM–midnight
	Sat: 10 AM–midnight
	Sun: 10 AM–10:30 PM
MASS TRANSIT	T: Green line-B to Chiswick Rd.
PAYMENT	VISA MasterCard AMERICAN EXPRESS DISCOVER
POPULAR FOOD	Contemporary pasta dishes like the Checkerboard Ravioli—spinach and black pepper pasta stuffed with ricotta and spinach—are great, but the pizza is what it's all about here. Get deep dish or thin crust, share a pie, or get a personal eight-inch pizza with its puffy crust as delectable as pastry. Or go for the excellent five-cheese calzone.
UNIQUE FOOD	Build your own pasta dish or pizza pie with nearly any ingredient/topping imaginable (pine nuts or shrimp to smoked turkey); also predetermined creations like Southern Comfort (sweet potato, onion, corn) or Calypso (blackened chicken and banana)
DRINKS	Surprisingly extensive wine and beer list; soft drinks served in huge glasses
SEATING	Intimate tables; outdoor seating in the warmer seasons
AMBIENCE	Bluestone Bistro defines itself as "the coziest eatery this side of the Milky Way": blue, pink, and yellow walls covered with mythological constellations, lit by flickering candles and dim lights, transform the pizzeria into a celestial hideaway for loyal neighborhood residents and BC students
EXTRAS/NOTES	Thursday through Saturday night there is live acoustic entertainment. Tuesdays indulge yourself on all-you-can-eat pizza for $6; on Wednesdays it's all-you-can-eat pasta; on Mondays they have half-price appetizers.

—*Nicole Cotroneo*

Corrib Pub

(see p. 108)
American
396 Market St., Brighton 02135
Phone (617) 787-0882

Eagles Deli

(see p. 101)
Burger Joint
1918 Beacon St., Brighton 02135
Phone (617) 731-3232

Elbow Room

Sophisticated neighborhood eatery in a neighborhood that needs it.
$$$$

1430 Commonwealth Ave., Brighton 02135
(at Kelton St.)
Phone (617) 738-9990

CATEGORY	Nouveau American
HOURS	Daily: noon–2 AM
MASS TRANSIT	T: Green line-B to Warren St.
PAYMENT	VISA MasterCard AMERICAN EXPRESS
POPULAR FOOD	Grilled portobello mushroom sandwich with fresh ricotta on focaccia, served with great fries; cobb salad; thin-crust gourmet pizzas like shrimp scampi; meatloaf with wild mushroom gravy; seafood *fra diavolo*; pan-roasted chicken breast with maple-pecan glaze and butternut squash gratin; apple cobbler; crème brulée
UNIQUE FOOD	Crispy tuna spring rolls, a roll of tuna sushi wrapped, fried, and sliced into four thick pieces, with a soy-ginger sauce
DRINKS	Harpoon and Magic Hat on draft, martinis, red wine
SEATING	Two levels: a lower-level bar with about ten tall bar tables with stools and a long oak bar with about a dozen bar stools and a fair amount of standing room; the upper level has ten cozy booths and more intimate tables; during summer, the large windows fold out for a taste of open air
AMBIENCE	Hip young professionals and students crowd in on weekends; subtle techno music and dim lighting; white votive candles burn on all the tables and along the bar, and strings of white lights wrap the railings; the brick wall behind the bar and the industrial ceiling give it character, and a giant mirror over the bar works well here to open up the space; a heavy velvet curtain encircles the area just inside the front door to keep the draft from chilling those seated near the bar
EXTRAS/NOTES	The chef, Stephen Sherman, used to be at New York City's Union Square Café, and the owner, Doug Bacon, also owns the White Horse Tavern in Allston, and the Last Drop in Back Bay and Brighton's Oak Square.

—*Kimberly Loomis*

Guido's

A panini paradise.

$

256 Washington St., Brighton 02135
(at Shepard St.)
Phone (617) 254-8436

CATEGORY	Sandwich Shop
HOURS	Daily: 11:30 AM–11 PM
MASS TRANSIT	T: Green line-B to Washington St.
PAYMENT	VISA MasterCard AMERICAN EXPRESS
POPULAR FOOD	Panini sandwiches are the choice here; buffalo chicken and chicken parmesan stand out from the crowd; all cold cuts are Boar's Head meats
DRINKS	Soft drinks
SEATING	Mainly takeout, but one lone table by the soda machine
AMBIENCE	Get takeout and light some candles back at your place if you're looking for ambience

—Melinda Green

Mary Ann's

(see p. 101)
Dive Bar/Happy Hour
1937 Beacon St., Brighton 02135
No Phone

Pizza Etc.

(see p. 102)
Pizza
2 Tremont St., Brighton 02135
Phone (617) 254-2022

Presto Pizzeria Restaurant

(see p. 102)
Pizza
1936 Beacon St., Brighton 02135
Phone (617) 232-4545

Roggie's Brew & Grille

(see p. 101)
Bar & Grill
356 Chestnut Hill Ave., Brighton 02135
Phone (617) 566-1880

Tasca

A most divine form of finger food.

$$$$

1612 Commonwealth Ave., Brighton 02135
(at Washington St.)

Phone (617) 730-8002

www.tascarestaurant.com

CATEGORY	Spanish Tapas
HOURS	Sun–Thurs: 5 PM–11 PM
	Fri/Sat: 5 PM–midnight
MASS TRANSIT	T: Green line-B to Washington St.
PAYMENT	VISA MasterCard AMERICAN EXPRESS DISCOVER
POPULAR FOOD	As in Spain, one really shouldn't leave Tasca without trying *tortilla*, an onion and potato omelette much like an Italian frittata and a staple of the Spanish diet; other winning tapas include sizzling shrimp in garlic, calamari, and *chorizo* sausage
UNIQUE FOOD	Baby octopus in red wine; black bean crabcakes
DRINKS	A nice selection of mostly Spanish wines
SEATING	Romantic dim lighting and intimate wooden tables—classy *taverna*-style
AMBIENCE	Tasca lures preppy folk with adventurous tongues; the weekends are always full but reservations are often unnecessary
EXTRAS/NOTES	Thursdays bring live Spanish guitar. Ironically, Tasca was not only started by a native Irishman but features an executive chef who is also Irish.

—*Nicole Cotroneo*

BROOKLINE: COOLIDGE CORNER

Anna's Taqueria

(see p. 196)

Mexican

1412 Beacon St., Brookline 02446

Phone (617) 739-7300

and

446 Harvard St., Brookline 02446

Phone (617) 277-7111

Boca Grande

(see p. 198)

Mexican

1294 Beacon St., Brookline 02446

Phone (617) 739-3900

Bombay Bistro

(see Rangoli, p. 95)
Southern Indian
1353 Beacon St., Brookline 02446
Phone (617) 734-2879

Boston Daily Bread Company

(see p. 110)
Bakery
1331 Beacon St., Brookline 02446
Phone (617) 277-8810

Bottega Fiorentina

Fresh, addictive Tuscan takeout.
$$
41 Harvard St., Brookline 02145
(at Linden St.)
Phone (617) 738-5333 • Fax (617) 738-5414

CATEGORY	Italian
HOURS	Mon–Wed: 11 AM–8 PM
	Thurs–Sat: 11 AM–8:30 PM
	Sun: noon–6 PM
MASS TRANSIT	T: Green line-C to Coolidge Corner
PAYMENT	VISA MasterCard AMERICAN EXPRESS
POPULAR FOOD	A variety of fresh sauces and pastas you can mix and match including pumpkin ravioli and gnocchi that melt in your mouth; each day of the week brings a different pasta, soup, and meat special; fresh-baked focaccia, sandwiches made with imported cheeses and meats; tiramisu
UNIQUE FOOD	Pasta specials like salmon ravioletti and fettucine al gorgonzola; pasta pesce, a sampling of fresh seafood in a buttery cream sauce
DRINKS	Pellegrino, espresso, cappuccino
SEATING	Mostly takeout, but one long picnic-style, wooden table in front
AMBIENCE	You will often hear Italian spoken, both by the staff and clientele; also an impressive grocery collection including Italian coffees, olive oils, and biscotti
EXTRAS/NOTES	Free fresh Italian bread and olive oil with any dinner. Bottega rivals any North End Italian restaurant, and many say it is the most authentic Italian eatery in the area.
OTHER ONES	• Coolidge Corner: 313B Harvard St., Brookline 02446, (617) 232-2661

—Estelle Paskausky

Buddha's Delight, Too

(see Buddha's Delight, p. 37)
Pan-Asian/Vegetarian
404 Harvard St., Brookline 02446
Phone (617) 739-8830

Chef Chang's

Few know General Gau like Mr. Chang.

$$$

1004-1006 Beacon St., Brookline 02446

(near St. Marys St.)

Phone (617) 277-4226 • Fax (617) 277-2834

CATEGORY	Sichuan Chinese
HOURS	Mon–Fri: 11:30 AM–9:30 PM
	Sat: 11:30 AM–10:30 PM
MASS TRANSIT	T: Green line-C to St. Mary's St.
PAYMENT	
POPULAR FOOD	Some of the best General Gau's chicken in the area; tangy and spicy green beans; flavorful, but not greasy chicken fried rice
UNIQUE FOOD	Peking duck carved at your table; sizzling platters with white or brown sauce; translucent fish fillets
DRINKS	Full bar with a small selection of tropical drinks
SEATING	Seats for about 60
AMBIENCE	Impeccable service; poorly lit and bland, but spacious atmosphere; the large BU crowd definitely comes for the food

—Laura Stone & Carol Alves

Clear Flour Bread

(see p. 110)

Bakery

178 Thorndike St., Brookline 02446

Phone (617) 739-0060

Corrib Pub

Typical bar menu, with reasonably priced entrees.

$$$

201 Harvard St., Brookline 02446

(near Marion St.)

Phone (617) 232-8787

CATEGORY	American Pub
HOURS	Mon–Fri: 8 AM–2 AM
	Sat: 8 AM-1 AM
	Sun: noon–2 AM
MASS TRANSIT	T: Green line-C to Coolidge Corner
PAYMENT	
POPULAR FOOD	Half-pound burgers; fish 'n' chips; reubens
UNIQUE FOOD	Complete turkey dinner every Sunday
DRINKS	Full bar
SEATING	Booths and tables seat 40; small bar on the other side has three tables
AMBIENCE	Clean and friendly bar atmosphere with a large following of locals
OTHER ONES	• West Roxbury: 2030 Centre St., West Roxbury 02132, (617) 469-4177
	• Brighton: 396 Market St., Brighton 02135, (617) 787-0882

—Juan Smith

Gourmet India

Delicious Indian food
for the harried city-goer.

$$

1335 Beacon St., Brookline 02446
(at Harvard St.)
Phone (617) 734-3971

CATEGORY	Indian
HOURS	Mon–Sat: 11:30 AM–10 PM Sun: 11:30 AM–8:30 PM
MASS TRANSIT	T: Green line-C to Coolidge Corner
PAYMENT	VISA MasterCard AMERICAN EXPRESS
POPULAR FOOD	The food is displayed in a buffet allowing you to look at your food before ordering it; chicken *tikka masala* with creamy tomato-based sauce and tender chicken; spicy lamb *vindaloo*; vegetarian options include *saag paneer*, cubed mild cheese with creamed spinach, and *gobhi mutter*, a flavorful medley of curried cauliflower, peas, and potatoes
UNIQUE FOOD	Mint *naan*; *onion bhaji*, a fried vegetable and potato appetizer; *rasgulla*, cheese dumplings with honey dessert
DRINKS	Sodas and juices, plus mango *lassis* and delicious chai
SEATING	A large dining area with a variety of seating options; even when it's busy you can find a place to sit comfortably
AMBIENCE	Open, modern, and fun atmosphere with Indian music playing and local newspapers and entertainment magazines available to read
EXTRAS/NOTES	The $5 lunch special includes one meat entrée, one vegetarian entrée, and either rice or *naan*.
OTHER ONES	• Western Suburbs: Burlington Mall Food Court, 75 Middlesex Turnpike, Burlington 01803, (781) 270-0200

—*Estelle Paskausky*

J.P. Licks

(see p. 131)
Ice Cream Shop
311 Harvard Ave., Brookline 02446
Phone (617) 737-8252

"Part of the secret of a success in life is to eat
what you like and let the food fight it out inside."
—*Mark Twain*

The Honor Roll:
Where to Find the Best Baked
Goods in Boston

Bread, sustenance of the ages, comes in all shapes and sizes, and almost every culture has some form of it—unleaven or yeasty, dark or light, dry or moist, sour or sweet. Boston's ethnically diverse neighborhoods offer a cornucopia of regional specialties. If you're hankering for challah, pining for pizzelles, longing for *lahmejune*, or aching for almond cookies, you've come to a place that can provide.

Brookline has traditional Jewish bakeries, with bagels and rugelach galore. Try Chinatown for Asian specialties like lotus seed sponge cake and the North End, of course, for biscotti, tiramisu, and cannoli (for North End bakeries, see p. 17). Watertown, with its influx of Armenians, has wonderful places for Middle Eastern fare like *lahmejune*—flat bread soaked with oil, herbs, chicken or beef, and a bit of tomato—and long displays of olives, nuts, and a profusion of baklava. Bakeries in East Cambridge and Union Square carry Portuguese sweet bread. Dorchester and South Boston are *the* places to find Irish Soda Bread. For donut shops, see p. 195.

Ho Yuen Bakery provides traditional almond paste cookies, nutcake, and two-egg-yolk lotus seed mooncake along with sticky rice and peanuts stuffed in a leaf with some twine. Sweets sit alongside steamed dumplings, roast pork buns, and beef curry pie. *Chinatown: 54 Beach St., Boston 02111, (617) 426-8320.*

Seoul Bakery has the Korean sweet tooth covered with peanut cream pastries, sweet bean paste, and custard rolls. A shaved ice, mixed with milk, sweet bean sauce, rice gummies, and slices of strawberries, is a great alternative to ice cream on a hot day. *Allston: 58 Harvard Ave., Allston 02134, (617) 787-6500.*

Athan's is a true European Bakery that dates back to 1938, from the Italian gelato (try the amazing fig flavor) and sorbet to the Middle Eastern pastries and baklava. *Washington Square: 1621 Beacon St., Brookline 02446, (617) 734-7028.*

Boston Daily Bread Company bakes every kind of bread you can imagine—including challah, Irish soda bread, fresh peach raspberry muffins, and French baguettes. Don't leave without a pumpkin raisin walnut muffin. *Washington Square: 1331 Beacon St., Brookline 02446, (617) 277-8810.*

Kupel's glass counter boasts a full array of dense, gooey pastries and sweet bread loafs, huge raspberry and chocolate bear claws, strudel, and cinnamon raisin, chocolate cheese, and chocolate cinnamon pastries. A half-dozen bagels with a small cream cheese goes for $4. *Coolidge Corner: 421 Harvard Ave., Brookline 02446, (617) 566-9528.*

Clear Flour Bread bakes different types of bread every day. Loaves to look out for include: the Sunflower Sourdough, the cake-like Golden Fruit

Tea, Paris Night (a mix of organic rye and whole wheat with walnuts, raisins, milk, and honey), the challah (after 10 AM on Friday in time for Sabbath), and wonderful shortbread cookies with little surprises like bits of dried cranberries and nuts. *Coolidge Corner: 178 Thorndike St., Brookline 02446, (617) 739-0060.*

Fornax Bread Company is a lovely place to spread out the Sunday paper across a wide wood table while nibbling on a buttermilk biscuit, or a sandwich on their wonderful bread. The tin roof is painted cream and yellow. Tiffany-style lamps and art deco advertising posters adorn the burnished red walls. *27 Corinth St., Roslindale 02131, (617) 325-8852.*

Rosie's Bakery wins so many awards that their brownies, chocolate chip cookies, apple pie, and cakes all carry little certificates of recognition. You can't go wrong with the intense, serious, wonderfully fudgy brownies, whether the Harvard Squares or the excruciating-to-order-but-worth-it Chocolate Orgasms. *Inman Square: 243 Hampshire St., Cambridge 02138, (617) 491-9488. Waterfront: 2 South Station, Boston 02110, (617) 439-4684. Western Suburbs: Chestnut Hill Shopping Center, 9 Boylston St., Newton 02467, (617) 277-5629.*

Central Bakery may be a bit hard to spot—some of the letters in its old neon sign have broken off. The oldest bakery in Cambridge, opened in 1919, it supplies its baked goods to sub shops, restaurants, schools, and hotels, as well as the pedestrian willing to look beyond a faded sign for their specialty Portuguese corn bread. *Inman Square: 732 Cambridge St., Cambridge 02141, (617) 547-2237.*

Royal Pastry Shop next door provides Italian fare, biscotti, almond macaroons, pizzeles, anise with chocolate, napoleons, and lots of Italian cookies, with sugar-free options, too. There's pan pizza slices for those in need of something savory. Sample wedding cakes line the top shelves. *Inman Square: 738 Cambridge St., Cambridge 02141, (617) 547-2053.*

L.A. Burdick upholds the European tradition of making chocolates by hand rather than by mold. Among the painstakingly made selections include a two-inch tall milk chocolate mouse with mocha in its belly and a penguin whose dark-and-white chocolate body and almond-filled arms conceal a heart of sugary-sweet lemon. There are baked goods as well, and many patrons come just for the *chocolat chaud*, which, true to European tastes, seems to contain much more melted chocolate than milk. *Harvard Square: 52 Brattle St., Cambridge 02138, (617) 491-4340. Other locations in Walpole, NH and Martha's Vineyard.*

Panini Bakery has large and small rounds, baguettes, rolls, scones, and a few sweeter goodies. They also have light lunch fare. Mesclun salad with soft goat's cheese, pecans, and cranberries, goes well with a cheddar cheese scone and a great cup of rich dark coffee. With seating for about 15, it's another great place to hang out for a couple of hours. *Union Square: 406 Washington St., Somerville 02143, (617) 666-2770.*

Massis Bakery offers Armenian and Middle Eastern specialties: anise-flavored cookies and bread-sticks, all kinds of pretty packaged baklava, *lahmejune*, *maniesh*, and a long bar full of olives of all kinds, even pickled turnip—great with falafel. *Western Suburbs: 569 Mt. Auburn St., Watertown 02472, (617) 924-0537.*

Sevan Bakery is another option for *lahmejune*. Homemade baklava dripping in honey at the front counter comes in all shapes and sizes. Like Massis, a long display of olives, dried fruits, and nuts takes center stage. *Western Suburbs: 599 Mt. Auburn St., Watertown 02472, (617) 924-3243.*

Iggy's two retail outlets are wonderful places to get their traditional hearth-baked breads, composed from organic ingredients and available at local, high-quality groceries. Pick up an unusual sandwich or a torpedo on your way to the beach or day hike. *Western Suburbs: 2054 Arlington St., Watertown 02472, (617) 924-0949. North Shore: 5 Pleasant St., Marblehead, 01945, (781) 639-4717.*

—*Paula Foye with Stephanie Kinnear, Amy Cooper, & Lara Fox*

Khao Sarn

Upscale, unusual, unforgettable Thai.
$$$$
250 Harvard St., Brookline 02446
(at Webster St.)
Phone (617) 566-7200 • Fax (617) 566-7207

CATEGORY	Thai
HOURS	Sun–Thurs: 11 AM–10 PM Fri/Sat: 11 AM–11 PM
MASS TRANSIT	T: Green line-C to Coolidge Corner
PAYMENT	VISA MasterCard AMERICAN EXPRESS DISCOVER
POPULAR FOOD	Atypical northern Thai specialties like *haw moak* chicken or salmon wrapped in a banana leaf with coconut milk and a hot red curry; *miang kum*, a Thai spinach leaf with dried shrimp, coconut, peanuts, ginger, lime, and onions; mango with coconut sticky rice; an excellent rendition of the typical *tom yum goong*, Thai hot and sour soup with shrimp
UNIQUE FOOD	Stuffed omelette with ground chicken, onions, carrots, peas, onions, shrimp, and garlic; steamed whole sea bass in a spicy lime sauce
DRINKS	Full bar; wine list; Singha; gorgeous cocktails like mango martinis; papaya smoothies
SEATING	Seats for about 40
AMBIENCE	Modern and fancy feel with silk hangings on the walls, swank bar, and dramatic evening lighting

—*Kyle Konrad*

Kupel's

(see p. 110)
Bagels/Bakery
421 Harvard Ave., Brookline 02446
Phone (617) 566-9528

Mr. Sushi

*The place to go for fresh sushi,
minus Boston prices.*
$$$
329 Harvard St., Brookline 02446
(at Babcock St.)
Phone (617) 731-1122 • Fax (617) 739-7377

CATEGORY	Japanese
HOURS	Mon–Thurs: noon–2:30 PM, 5 PM–10:30 PM Fri/Sat: noon–2:30 PM, 5 PM–11 PM Sun: noon–2:30 PM, 5 PM–10 PM
MASS TRANSIT	T: Green line-C to Coolidge Corner
PAYMENT	VISA MasterCard AMERICAN EXPRESS DISCOVER
POPULAR FOOD	The 60 or so items on the sushi list (all of which can be modified to your own specification, e.g. sashimi, maki with tobiko, inside out, etc.) span the sushi spectrum. The combos are very popular for their variation and reasonable price. The generous Sushi Deluxe with nine pieces of *nigiri* and six pieces of *tekka maki* goes for under $14. Mr. Sushi, despite the name, also does popular appetizers such as *shumai*, tempura, and *yu-dofu*.
UNIQUE FOOD	A short list of Korean specialties, including *bi bim bab* and *bulgogi*
DRINKS	Beer and wine, soft drinks, and tea
SEATING	Their space accommodates small and large groups or single seating at the sushi bar, with a total capacity of 70
AMBIENCE	Befitting Coolidge Corner, Mr. Sushi is family-friendly and draws a regular crowd of all ages. Comfortable seating allows for good eating and conversation. The decor is the usual for many small sushi restaurants: fish tanks, bamboo, and wooden boat sculptures.
EXTRAS/NOTES	Expect a wait between 7:30 and 8:30 PM. You'll be remembered after a few visits to Mr. Sushi where the service is admirably attentive.
OTHER ONES	• Western Suburbs: 693 Massachusetts Ave., Arlington 02476, (781) 643-4175

—Sarah Duggan

Pho Lemongrass

*The magic combination of lemongrass
and Asian sauces.*

$$$

239 Harvard St., Brookline 02446
(between Marion Rd. and Stearns Rd.)
Phone (617) 731-8600 • Fax (617) 731-9639

CATEGORY	Vietnamese
HOURS	Sun–Thurs: 11 AM–10 PM Fri/Sat: 11 AM–midnight
MASS TRANSIT	T: Green line-C to Coolidge Corner
PAYMENT	VISA MasterCard AMERICAN EXPRESS
POPULAR FOOD	Lemongrass shrimp; fresh summer rolls served with peanut sauce; *pho* (Vietnamese noodle soup), served with rare steak, brisket, or beef meatballs; vermicelli dishes with stir-fried meat, sprouts, scallions, and roasted peanuts
UNIQUE FOOD	Soft shell crab flavored with ginger, scallion, and garlic sauce; *pho* shrimp ball; crispy bass in a sweet and sour sauce; *banh xeo* crêpe stuffed with shrimp, pork, and bean sprouts
DRINKS	Full bar, decent wine list; smoothies; salty limeade
SEATING	Seats for 120 at booths and tables
AMBIENCE	A lively place that is busy every night with semi-diverse Brookline diners and takeout customers

—Tim Leonard

Rami's

*Coolidge Corner's Middle
Eastern delight.*

$$

324 Harvard St., Brookline 02446
(at Babcock St.)
Phone (617) 738-3577

CATEGORY	Israeli/Kosher
HOURS	Sun–Thurs: 10 AM–10 PM Fri: 10 AM–3 PM
MASS TRANSIT	T: Green line-C to Coolidge Corner
PAYMENT	Cash only
POPULAR FOOD	Legendary falafel—crispy on the outside, soft on the inside; hummus, baba ganoush, shawarma, and kebabs
UNIQUE FOOD	*Bourekas*, a puffed sesame pastry filled with potatoes, spinach, or apples
DRINKS	Israeli fruit juices, mango nectar, sodas
SEATING	Eight comfortable tables and a short counter top seat a total of about 20
AMBIENCE	Simple décor; office workers, young adults, families, and a large Jewish contingent
OTHER ONES	• Western Suburbs: 341 Cochichuate Rd. (Rte. 30), Framingham 01701, (508) 370-3577

—Ari Herzog

Rod Dee
Thai Cuisine

So-so looks, yum-yum food.
$$
1430 Beacon St., Brookline 02446
(at Summit Ave.)
Phone (617) 738-4977 • Fax (617) 738-9002

CATEGORY	Thai
HOURS	Daily: 11:30 AM–11:30 PM
MASS TRANSIT	T: Green line-C to Summit Ave.
PAYMENT	Cash only
POPULAR FOOD	Killer *pad* Thai; not greasy spring rolls; large vegetarian-friendly menu; every one of their nearly 100 dishes is freshly made to order
UNIQUE FOOD	The Drunken Squid earns three hot chilis for its spice; the Pad Paradise is a little less frisky, combining tasty shrimp, chicken, veggies, and cashews with a delicious sauce
DRINKS	Soft drinks, Thai iced tea
SEATING	Mostly takeout, but with six small tables in the storefront window
AMBIENCE	Not much atmosphere, with bright menu panels above the takeout counter; med students, Thai families, and other smart people make the trip for the colorful, happy food
OTHER ONES	• Fenway: 94 Peterborough St., Boston 02215, (617) 859-0969

—*Caroline Stanculescu*

Shawarma King

Shawarma, yes, but much, much more.
$$
1383 Beacon St., Brookline 02446
(at Park St.)
Phone (617) 731-6035

CATEGORY	Middle Eastern
HOURS	Tues–Sun: noon–9:45 PM
MASS TRANSIT	T: Green line-C to Coolidge Corner
PAYMENT	VISA MasterCard
POPULAR FOOD	Falafel, shish-kabob, *baba ghanoush*, grape leaves, tabbouli, *zaatar*: the food is incredibly fresh, thoughtfully prepared, and served with good humor
UNIQUE FOOD	Vegetarian *kibby* (ground pumpkin and cracked wheat stuffed with raisins, chick peas, and onions)
DRINKS	Soft drinks, fresh fruit smoothies, coconut juice, tamarind juice, *jallab* (raisin drink with rose water)
SEATING	Small tables; mostly takeout
AMBIENCE	Locals and lots of Middle Eastern customers; busiest in the evenings for dinner

—*Becky Hays*

Sushi Express

*Where happiness is a
plate of raw fish.*

$$$

1038 Beacon St., Brookline 02446

(between St. Mary's St. and Carleton St.)

Phone (617) 738-5658

CATEGORY	Japanese Sushi
HOURS	Daily: 11:45 AM–10 PM
MASS TRANSIT	T: Green line-C to St. Mary's St.
PAYMENT	VISA MasterCard
POPULAR FOOD	Simple, affordable sushi at an incredible price ($2 to $4 for *maki*, $1 to $2 for *nigiri*); very few gourmet rolls, but everyone's favorite is bound to be on the menu: from vegetarian *kappa* (cucumber) or *ume-shiso* (plum) to *unagi* (broiled eel), *tekka* (tuna) and the ever-popular California roll; their $6 lunch special, includes miso soup, *maki* and *nigiri*, and sweet egg
UNIQUE FOOD	California roll with flying fish roe; Eliot Roll (named after the swank hotel up the road) with eel, lettuce, cucumber, and mayo; the *futo-maki* (thick roll) with sweet egg, crab, squash, pickles, and cucumber
DRINKS	Soda, juices, free green tea
SEATING	Fifteen seats at small tables and a counter
AMBIENCE	The tiny restaurant is jam-packed at lunch and dinner hours. The décor is minimal: sushi calendars and mini posters cover old stains on the semi-white walls.

—Laura & Ben D'Amore

Via Via Café

*Bound to satisfy even your
finicky friends.*

$$

1032 Beacon St., Brookline 02446

(between St. Mary's St. and Carleton St.)

Phone (617) 264-2266 • Fax (617) 264-4926

CATEGORY	Mediterranean
HOURS	Sun–Wed: 11 AM–1 AM Thurs and Sat: 11 AM–1:45 AM Fri: 3 PM–1:45 AM
MASS TRANSIT	T: Green line-C to St. Mary's St.
PAYMENT	Cash only
POPULAR FOOD	Self-proclaimed "best gourmet pizza in Rhode Island"; it may not be the best in Boston, but one can't go wrong with any of the 21 unique wood-fired pies; fabulous pocket sandwiches (falafel, chicken kabob, and baba ganoush); grape leaves; smoky rotisserie chicken
UNIQUE FOOD	Via Via Salad with spinach, goat cheese, dates, pine nuts, and a creamy mustard dressing; clam cakes; *kafta* kabob, Middle Eastern ground beef with seasoning

DRINKS	Juices, teas, sodas, coffee
SEATING	Eighty seats at large, well-spaced tables
AMBIENCE	Ultra informal; order at the counter and they'll bring the food to your table
EXTRAS/NOTES	Locals will tell you that this Beacon St. location is cursed—it seems a new restaurant moves in every year or two. Viva Via Via!
OTHER ONES	• Providence, RI: Three locations • Newport, RI: Two locations • New Hampshire: 219 Ocean Blvd., Hampton, NH 03842, (603) 926-6860

—Laura & Ben D'Amore

Zaftigs Delicatessen

Delicatessen extraordinaire and self-proclaimed neighborhood Jewish mother.
$$$

335 Harvard St., Brookline 02446
(at Shailer St.)
Phone (617) 975-0075 • Fax (617) 975-0775
www.zaftigs.com

CATEGORY	Jewish Deli
HOURS	Daily: 8 AM–10 PM
MASS TRANSIT	T: Green line-C to Coolidge Corner
PAYMENT	VISA MasterCard AMERICAN EXPRESS DISCOVER
POPULAR FOOD	Breakfast served all day: from banana-stuffed French toast to lox, onion, and eggs. Known for quirky reinterpretations of classic Jewish and American fare, you can get a Raphel (turkey dinner sandwich on challah bread) or borscht soup with a meat and potato knish combo. Also, brisket and roast beef sandwiches, salmon and roasted corn salad, and cheese blintzes.
UNIQUE FOOD	Hot beef tongue or chopped liver sandwiches; meatloaf melt; carrot soup; veggie burger with cajun ketchup; tomato, scallion, and cream cheese omelette with caviar; apple and cheddar omelette
DRINKS	A menu in itself: wines, beers, sodas, coffee/tea, juices, chocolate egg cream, Dr. Brown's root beer float
SEATING	Fairly big, but usually a long line for weekend brunch; booths and comfortable chairs line the walls, and you will inevitably be fairly close to your neighbors
AMBIENCE	Artwork lines the walls, much of it depicting the signature well-fed zaftig momma in a red dress
EXTRAS/NOTES	The word *zaftig* is a slang term for full-bosomed or having a shapely figure—from the Yiddish word meaning juicy—and amply describes the effect the owners of Zaftigs wish to impart on their clientele.

—Estelle Paskausky

Zathmary's Specialty Foods Marketplace

Unique gourmet dining and shopping for every appetite.

$$

299 Harvard St., Brookline 02446

(at Beacon St.)

Phone (617) 731-8900 • Fax (617) 731-1736

www.zathmary.com

CATEGORY	Gourmet Cafeteria/Market
HOURS	Mon–Fri: 10 AM–10 PM
	Sat: 8 AM–10 PM
	Sun: 8 AM–8 PM
MASS TRANSIT	T: Green line-C to Coolidge Corner
PAYMENT	VISA MasterCard AMERICAN EXPRESS DISCOVER
POPULAR FOOD	Zathmary's is known for variety: you can get gourmet pizza by the slice, a fresh salad from their well-equipped salad bar with items from tofu to fresh tabouli, or sample one of their hot entrees like a rotisserie chicken or vegetable lasagna. Get a turkey and gravy sandwich on fresh whole grain bread with a bowl of their creamy clam chowder.
UNIQUE FOOD	Watch your sushi made to order, sample cheeses fresh from France, or watch oranges squeezed into fresh OJ. Zathmary's is a tactile eating experience: you see, smell, and watch your entrée being prepared for you, and then, with your meal in hand, you can browse the market for imported sodas or fresh fruits or *tapenades* and *crostini*, and decadent desserts, from fantastic linzer tortes to rich chocolate mousse cakes.
DRINKS	French pink lemonade to Swedish Kristal soda with loganberry flavor; also, a ZBAR with a variety of alcoholic beverages
SEATING	Kind of like a cafeteria, but clean; plenty of seats, some overlooking Harvard St.
AMBIENCE	A wonderful place even to just browse. Breeze by the pastries and cakes that smell and look mouth-watering. Next, enter the displays of the night's entrees, and the market opens up to your left. At every turn, there is something interesting to look at or sample.
OTHER ONES	• Western Suburbs: 1000 Highland Ave., Needham Heights 02494, (781) 449-9090

—Estelle Paskausky

BROOKLINE: BROOKLINE VILLAGE

Allandale Farm

(see p. 234)
Farm Stand
259 Allandale Rd., Brookline 02467
Phone (617) 524-1531

Baja Betty's

*We wish they all could be
California burritos.*
$$
3 Harvard Sq., Brookline 02445
(at Davis Ave.)
Phone (617) 277-8900

CATEGORY	Burrito Joint
HOURS	Mon–Sat: 11:30 AM–9 PM Sun: noon–8 PM
MASS TRANSIT	T: Green line-D to Brookline Village
PAYMENT	Cash only
POPULAR FOOD	California burrito with your choice of two fillings (vegetables, chicken in a red *mole* sauce, *carne asada*, lean pork in a spice *guajillo* sauce, or slow cooked shredded beef), pico de gallo, guacamole, cheese, sour cream or non-fat yogurt, and lettuce
UNIQUE FOOD	San Joaquin burrito filled with home-fried potatoes and *chile relleno*; tostadas and *chalupas*, crisp flat tortillas with beans (refried or black), pico de gallo, cheese, and sour cream or non-fat yogurt for less than $3; tamales
DRINKS	Jarritos Mexican sodas in flavors like guava, pineapple, sangria, and lime; fresh lemonade; *mango bebida*
SEATING	Seats about 16
AMBIENCE	Baja Betty's takes you back to a place when Jefferson Airplane, the Doors, and Buffalo Springfield ruled the pop charts; life is easygoing inside and worries drift away

—*Heidi Solomon*

Bertucci's

(see p. 176)
Gourmet Pizza
4 Brookline Pl., Brookline 02215
Phone (617) 731-2300

"One cannot think well, love well, sleep well,
if one has not dined well."

—*Virginia Woolf*

Fajitas & 'Ritas

Laid-back, tasty Tex-Mex.

$$$

49 Boylston St., Brookline 02445

(at White St.)

Phone (617) 566-1222 • Fax (617) 566-5074

www.fajitasandritas.com

CATEGORY	Tex-Mex
HOURS	Mon: 5 PM–9 PM
	Tues–Thurs: 5 PM–10 PM
	Fri: 11:30 AM–11 PM
	Sat: noon–11 PM
	Sun: 4:30 PM–9 PM
MASS TRANSIT	T: Green line-D to Brookline Village
PAYMENT	VISA MasterCard AMERICAN EXPRESS
POPULAR FOOD	The fajitas: steak and chicken combos (under $10) come sizzling with a basket of warm tortillas; create your own nachos by checking off your desired toppings
UNIQUE FOOD	Tequila wings; smoked brisket and pulled pork
DRINKS	The 'ritas: strawberry is lip-smackingly good; full bar, draft and bottled beer, wine, soft drinks, juices
SEATING	Plenty of tables in casual seating arrangements
AMBIENCE	A boisterous young T-shirt-and-jeans crowd comes after work or in large groups; crayons are provided for drawing on the tablecloths
EXTRAS/NOTES	Do-it-yourself ordering: your order form is plopped down on the table and you get to fill it out yourself.
OTHER ONES	• Financial District: 25 West St., Boston 02111, (617) 426-1222

—*Jenny Bengen*

Matt Murphy's Pub

Traditional Irish fare and brew in an intimate neighborhood setting.

$$$

14 Harvard St., Brookline 02445

(at Kent St.)

Phone (617) 232-0188

CATEGORY	Irish Pub
HOURS	Mon–Wed: 11 AM–10 PM
	Thurs–Sat: 11 AM–11 PM
	Sun: 11:30 AM–10 PM
MASS TRANSIT	T: Green line-D to Brookline Village
PAYMENT	Cash only
POPULAR FOOD	Huge portions of shepherd's pie (made with potatoes and lamb chunks in a wine sauce) and hearty beef stew; the fish 'n' chips come wrapped in the *Irish Times*, and the thick pork chop belongs on display at the MFA; excellent homemade bread

DRINKS	Full bar with popular beers from the Emerald Isle on draught (Guinness, Murphy's Stout); Irish teas
SEATING	Twelve rustic tables (about 30 people); bring what you have to pass for Gaelic charm to make nice with the folks at the next table, eight inches away
AMBIENCE	You'll need a four-leaf clover to get a table right away; Matt's isn't traditional Irish the way the pretenders do it downtown— followers come for the food, the friendliness, and the perfect pints
EXTRAS/NOTES	Traditional Irish Seissun music every Thursday. Wednesday Quiz Night.
OTHER ONES	• Across the pond in West Cork, Ireland
	—Chris Railey

New England Soup Factory

Good old-fashioned (and not-so-old-fashioned) soup for all seasons.

$$

2-4 Brookline Pl., Brookline 02445
(at Washington St.)
Phone (617) 739-1695 • SoupLine (617) 739-1899

CATEGORY	Soup
HOURS	Mon–Fri: 10:30 AM–8 PM
	Sat: 10:30 AM–5 PM
MASS TRANSIT	T: Green line-D to Brookline Village
PAYMENT	VISA MasterCard
POPULAR FOOD	The Comfort Soups are a daily staple (chicken soup, chili, stew, etc.); about four or five additional soups vary daily; the chowders are excellent, especially the lobster newburg chowder; they also let you sample all the soups before you buy
UNIQUE FOOD	Unusual, but popular (and very good) soups include the Thai butternut, the tomato, bacon, and cheddar, and the chicken potpie
DRINKS	Soda, juice
SEATING	Just a few tables, but there are public benches outside near the T stop
AMBIENCE	Mostly takeout; very busy at lunch with local workers coming for a quick bite
EXTRAS/NOTES	The SoupLine, updated daily, is a convenient way of finding out what the day's selection is. Soups are also sold frozen, and store for a long time in your freezer.
OTHER ONES	• Western Suburbs: 244 Needham St., Newton 02464, (617) 558-9988
	—Hadley Hudson

Sichuan Garden

Unassuming suburban setting for truly unique Sichuan spice.

$$$

295 Washington St., Brookline 02445
(at Holden St.)
Phone (617) 734-1870 • Fax (617) 734-1898

CATEGORY	Sichuan Chinese
HOURS	Mon–Thurs: 11 AM–10 PM Fri/Sat: 11 AM–11 PM Sun: noon–10 PM
MASS TRANSIT	T: Green line-D to Brookline Village
PAYMENT	VISA MasterCard AMERICAN EXPRESS DISCOVER
POPULAR FOOD	Respectable versions of all the usual standards, but look on the menu under Sichuan Delicacies and Chef's Signature and you'll find gutsy, authentically spicy Sichuan cuisine that delivers both serious heat and deep flavor. Any dish marked "with roasted chili" is a treat, offering the essential Sichuan combination of a powerful, complex chili burn and the citrusy zing of Sichuan peppercorns. Among the non-spicy dishes, the Steamed Mini Juicy Pork Buns are a standout—delicate dumpling skins encasing a moist, savory pork filling.
UNIQUE FOOD	More adventurous diners can ask for a copy of the special Sichuan menu (with teenie-tiny English translations—a hint?) and order house specialties, from Dong-Puo Pig Feet to sea cucumber, home style.
DRINKS	Beer, wine, full bar
SEATING	Tables for two and four, and round tables for larger groups
AMBIENCE	A mixed clientele of Chinese and Westerners relax in the rather plush surroundings; comfortable chairs, classical music in the background

—Michael Beckett

Village Pizza House

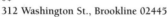

The neighborhood pizza place.
$$

312 Washington St., Brookline 02445
(at Holden St., across from Town Hall)
Phone (617) 731-4210 • Fax (617) 731-9713

CATEGORY	Pizza by the Slice
HOURS	Daily: 10 AM–11 PM
MASS TRANSIT	T: Green line-D to Brookline Village
PAYMENT	VISA MasterCard
POPULAR FOOD	Crispy, doughy-crust pizza with rich tomato sauce and loads of five gooey cheeses; chicken parmesan; grinders ranging from traditional roast beef to veggie and egg salad; gyros and chicken souvlaki

UNIQUE FOOD	Greek salads and entrees, including Greek-inspired pizza toppings like feta cheese and olives; also, baklava
DRINKS	Bottled beer, wine, and a selection of sodas
SEATING	Ample booths
AMBIENCE	Pictures of Greece and ocean scenes line the walls; photos of family children sit on the front counter
EXTRAS/NOTES	For over 30 years, the folks at this family-run business have been joking with regulars and dishing out good pizza.

—*Estelle Paskausky*

Village Smokehouse

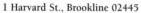

Texas open-pit barbecue in Brookline.
$$$$
1 Harvard St., Brookline 02445
(at Kent St.)
Phone (617) 566-3782
www.villagesmokehouse.com

CATEGORY	Barbecue
HOURS	Sat–Wed: 4 PM–10:30 PM
	Thurs/Fri: 11:30 AM–10:30 PM
MASS TRANSIT	T: Green line-D to Brookline Village
PAYMENT	VISA MasterCard AMERICAN EXPRESS
POPULAR FOOD	Pork or beef ribs, brisket, and Texas sausage all cooked on an open-pit barbecue with a sweet sauce and served with tasty cornbread and family-style baked beans (serving for the whole table); burgers, Texas chili; stuffed jalapeños; homemade pies
DRINKS	Longhorn Lemonade, beer and wine, margaritas, coffee concoctions
SEATING	Seats for138; gets busy after 7 PM most nights
AMBIENCE	Definitely Texan: a sign above the barbecue pit states "No Fighting Here"; waitstaff wear shirts that say "Don't Mess with Texas," and pictures of Waylon Jennings and other beloved cowboys line the wooden walls
EXTRAS/NOTES	Some of the most exciting moments during dinner are when the barbecue pit fills up with red flames—it makes for great entertainment.

—*Estelle Paskausky*

BROOKLINE: WASHINGTON SQUARE

Athan's

(see p. 110)
Bakery
1621 Beacon St., Brookline 02446
Phone (617) 734-7028

B&D Deli

Comfort food epitomized.
Since 1923
$$$
1653 Beacon St., Brookline 02445
(between University Rd. and Winthrop Rd.)
Phone (617) 232-3727 • Fax (617) 738-0460

CATEGORY	Jewish Deli
HOURS	Sun–Thurs: 7 AM–9 PM
	Fri/Sat: 7 AM–10 PM
MASS TRANSIT	T: Green line-C to Washington Sq.
PAYMENT	VISA MasterCard AMERICAN EXPRESS DISCOVER
POPULAR FOOD	Huge three-egg omelettes with homefries and challah French toast for breakfast; matzo ball soup; amazing sandwiches, including a well-known Reuben and a great hot pastrami on rye; all of the meat is cooked and carved on the premises
UNIQUE FOOD	Knishes, blintzes, whitefish, lox, stuffed latkes (corned beef, brisket, or pastrami between two potato pancakes)
DRINKS	Coffee and espresso, Dr. Brown's, egg cream, fresh squeezed OJ, beer, and wine; bloody marys and mimosas for Sunday brunch
SEATING	Ninety-two seats in very cramped seating; when the weather gets warm there's seating outside on Beacon St.
AMBIENCE	A young sweatpants-and-baseball-cap crowd congregates here on weekend mornings; be prepared for a bit of a wait

—*Stephanie Kinnear*

BOSTON—GO
SOUTH

JAMAICA PLAIN

Bella Luna

Pizza with its own sublime gravitational pull.

$$$

403-405 Centre St., Jamaica Plain 02130
(at Perkins St.)
Phone (617) 983-6060

CATEGORY	Gourmet Pizza
HOURS	Mon–Wed: 11 AM–3 PM, 5 PM–10 PM Thurs/Fri: 11 AM–3 PM, 5 PM–11 PM Sat: 11 AM–11 PM Sun: noon–10 PM
MASS TRANSIT	T: Orange line to Jackson Sq.; bus: #39 to Perkins St. and walk east
PAYMENT	VISA MasterCard AMERICAN EXPRESS DISCOVER
POPULAR FOOD	Complimentary roasted garlic olive oil with bread; spinach salad with mushrooms, roasted red peppers, glazed walnuts, and gorgonzola; Gypsy King Pizza with caramelized onions, spinach, and ricotta; homemade tiramisu
UNIQUE FOOD	Manny's Grand Slam (a white pizza with garlic mashed potatoes, bacon, and cheddar); Breakfast Pizza during Sunday's famous jazz brunch; over 30 pizza toppings from the basics to green olives, steak tips, and soy cheese
DRINKS	Beer by tap or bottle; wine by the glass or bottle; soft drinks; coffee, tea, cappuccino
SEATING	Small, intimate tables on the ground floor, extending out back in warmer weather; long, open, more casual tables downstairs by the bar and bowling alley—yes, there's a bowling alley!
AMBIENCE	Cozy, cheery, warm with vibrantly colored walls, exuberant white plastic plates decorated with markers, and similarly funky painted chairs. It leans towards the romantic, but also a fine place to catch up with a friend or have a birthday celebration (reservations accepted). Also welcoming to the solitary diner with a glass of wine and a book on a quiet evening. Even weeknights can get markedly busy by 7:30 PM, and on weekends expect a line—fortunately it moves fast. The clientele ranges from college students to musicians and longtime JP residents, and the neighborhood vibe is intensified by the local art on the walls.
EXTRAS/NOTES	Word has it that some people have actually moved to Jamaica Plain to be closer to Bella Luna, so entrancing is the pizza. Thin-crust lovers may become peevish, but those favoring a thicker, chewy crust will be more than satisfied. Recently Bella Luna expanded into the area beneath it, reviving the old bowling

alley, adding two bars as well as a concert space, and calling it the Milky Way Lounge and Lanes. Since then, Bella Luna has become *the* place in Jamaica Plain to see great shows.

—*Alison Pereto*

Centre Street Café

Rioting vegetables and shrimp nirvana: a JP institution

$$$

669A Centre St., Jamaica Plain 02130

(at Seaverns Ave.)

Phone (617) 524-9217

CATEGORY	Nouveau American
HOURS	Mon–Fri: 11:30 AM–3 PM, 5 PM–10 PM
	Sat: 9 AM–3 PM, 5 PM–10 PM
	Sun: 9 AM–3 PM, 5 PM–9:30 PM
MASS TRANSIT	T: Orange line to Green St.; bus #39
PAYMENT	VISA MasterCard
POPULAR FOOD	Burrito with smoky black beans; tender, naturally-raised chicken; bluefish cakes with homemade tartar sauce; orgasmic brunch; gorgeous, tasty salads
UNIQUE FOOD	Danno's Szechwan Shaboom (veggies, greens, egg noodles in spicy garlic-ginger soy sauce); Potatoes Santa Cruz (potatoes with a "mountain" of fresh veggies, onions, cheddar, and homemade *salsa cruda*); transcendent key lime pie and chocolate mousse
DRINKS	Bottled beer, wine by the glass or bottle, soda, juice, tea, coffee (self-serve)
SEATING	One center aisle with a row of small tables on either wall for a total of 28 seats
AMBIENCE	Convivial, friendly, and bustling atmosphere, with rockabilly on the stereo and neighboring tables at each elbow. This is a place to go whether you're pierced and dreadlocked or showing your parents what a nice neighborhood you live in (or, even better, both). Crunchy, warm, and laid-back vibe with fast, efficient service. Expect a line on the sidewalk during dinner or brunch, but don't be scared, it moves quickly, and in the winter, the wait staff has been known to pass out paper cups of steaming beverages to those holding vigil for a table.
EXTRAS/NOTES	The Centre Street Café has long been JP's culinary beacon. For several years it squeezed into the tiny space further north on Centre St. now occupied by the upscale restaurant Perdix. Business boomed until the café could hold no more and moved to its present location (the space formerly occupied by Five Seasons restaurant). Its reputation has been built on healthy, colorful dishes friendly to both

vegetarians and omnivores (although you're not likely to find beef here). The menu favors terms like "a riot of fresh veggies," and when it uses the word "mountain," you'd better be prepared to either run or share.

—*Alison Pereto*

Coffee Cantata Bistro and Beans

The best sunlight with your coffee in JP.

$$

605 Centre St., Jamaica Plain 02130
(at Pond St.)
Phone (617) 522-2223

CATEGORY	Café
HOURS	Mon: 7 AM–6 PM
	Tues–Fri: 7 AM–10 PM (food until 9:30 PM)
	Sat: 8:30 AM–10 PM (food until 9:30 PM)
	Sun: 9 AM–6 PM
MASS TRANSIT	T: Orange line to Stony Brook; bus: #39
PAYMENT	Cash only
POPULAR FOOD	French Suite (with homemade compôte); Cantata Prelude (fruit, cheese, and homemade bread); porcini and wild mushroom ravioli in rose cream sauce; Queen of Sheba chocolate torte
UNIQUE FOOD	Sweet potato gnocchi; lavender shortbread cookies
DRINKS	Coffee drinks from straight-up to foamy; loose tea; bottled sodas; BYOB
SEATING	Mostly tables for two, plus a tiny counter and one large table for a group
AMBIENCE	Comforting, hip, and romantic, with its warm walls reflecting the sunlight coming over Pond St. Real plants, climbing vines painted on the wall, and ever-changing artwork from local artists. Early afternoon is busiest as patrons linger at their tables. The staff is funky and friendly, there's always music on the speakers (but not intrusively), and you can nestle in with the hipsters, the couples, and the parents.
EXTRAS/NOTES	Brunch is served daily until 4 PM. Everything is handmade, and even the cheapest brunch is so aesthetically pleasing it will make a hardened diner weep. Small touches matter here, and they'll keep all your senses occupied when your book (or date) begins to flag. Open since October 1993, the Cantata is a reliable JP neighborhood landmark. Get a cup of the Cantata Blend to-go and walk around the Pond after you eat.

—*Alison Pereto*

Doyle's Café

A scotch-lover's mecca,
a home away from home,
a Boston institution.
Since 1882

$$

3484 Washington St., Jamaica Plain 02130
(at Williams St.)
Phone (617) 524-2345
www.doylescafe.com

CATEGORY	Historic Irish Pub
HOURS	Daily: 9 AM–1 AM (food until 11 PM)
MASS TRANSIT	T: Orange line to Green St.
PAYMENT	Cash only
POPULAR FOOD	Fish 'n' chips; stellar clam chowder in a bread bowl; sublime fruit pancakes bigger than your head; great omelettes; Braddock Hot 'n' Spicy Buffalo Wings; pizza
UNIQUE FOOD	Knockwurst plate with sauerkraut and fries; meatless reuben (a sauerkraut and Russian dressing sandwich on grilled dark rye); corned beef and cabbage; Irish lamb stew; thin and crispy sweet potato fries
DRINKS	Dozens of beers on tap, ranging from lite beers to the occasional lambic; perfectly built pints of Guinness; multi-paged scotch list; soda, tea, and the only bottomless 75¢ cup of coffee you can find these days; champagne splits, mimosas, and bloody marys available at brunch
SEATING	Flat-out huge; a bar with booths and tables in the front smoking section, plus two nonsmoking rooms, one large enough for functions; the wooden booths are private, with hard seats and tall backs reminiscent of old Puritan church pews
AMBIENCE	Clean and bustling, yet divey in the most venerable and comforting way. Brunch and weekend nights draw a wait even with the place's seemingly endless capacity. Clientele ages range from infancy to second childhood. Some of the waitresses have been here most of their adult lives. The posters and clippings papering the wall display JFK, infamous Boston mayor Michael Curley, beer signs, and wartime warnings of the "Loose Lips Sink Ships" variety. Depending on the time, you can see families, hangovers in progress, hangover brunches, and deep, involved State of the Union relationship discussions.
EXTRAS/NOTES	Doyle's is the only area bar to stay open throughout Prohibition and survive to this day. It's well worth getting there and digging in for an hour or three. Look for glimpses of Michael Dukakis or that former teacher; it's well known that simply everyone goes to Doyle's at some point, from famous Boston politicos to local

college students. As an added bonus, the nearby Sam Adams Brewery runs shuttle buses on Saturday afternoons from Doyle's for tours. Really, it doesn't get much better than that.

—Alison Pereto

Fornax Bread Company

(see p. 111)
Bakery/Café
27 Corinth St., Roslindale 02131
Phone (617) 325-8852

J.P. Licks

(see p. 131)
Ice Cream Shop
659 Centre St., Jamaica Plain 02130
Phone (617) 524-6740

Jake's Boss BBQ

Down-home barbecue in JP.
$$$
3492 Washington St., Jamaica Plain 02130
(at Williams St.)
Phone (617) 983-3701 • Fax (617) 983-4900

CATEGORY	Barbecue
HOURS	Sun, Tues/Wed: 11 AM–10 PM Thurs–Sat: 11 AM–11 PM
PARKING	T: Orange line to Green St.; bus: #39
PAYMENT	VISA MasterCard DISCOVER
POPULAR FOOD	A full menu of ribs, beef brisket, chopped pork, and chicken (smoked and jerk); the chicken is notably good—falling-off-the-bone tender, with a deep smoky flavor
UNIQUE FOOD	Burnt Ends Sandwich (smoked brisket simmered in barbecue sauce until it falls apart and melds with the sauce, served on a bun with a choice of slaw, potato salad, or beans); also, chocolate bread pudding
DRINKS	Soft drinks and bottled juices
SEATING	Several tables
AMBIENCE	The decor is minimal, mainly a wall of Kenton "Jake" Jacobs' trophies from various barbecue competitions. The crowd is friendly and mostly local.

—Michael Beckett

The Boston Ice Cream Machine—Beach Weather Not Included

Bostonians are true ice cream aficionados. It was here that the gourmet ice cream craze unofficially began (see p. 219), and Boston consumes more ice cream per capita than any other city in the world. Ice cream shops on every other block battle for business with creative flavors like Burnt Sugar, Grapenut, Guinness, and Kahlua. While no two people will agree on the absolute best in Boston, our contributors have presented below their cases for the top contenders.

J.P. Licks has become a Boston favorite for its soft frozen yogurt, thick frappes, and ice cream flavors like Tiramisu and Kahlua. The cow-inspired décor and notoriously eccentric staff give it additional character. *Back Bay: 352 Newbury St., Boston 02115, (617) 236-1666. Jamaica Plain: 659 Centre St., 02130, (617) 524-6740. Coolidge Corner: 311 Harvard Ave., Brookline 02446, (617) 737-8252. Western Suburbs: 46 Langley Rd., Newton 02459, (617) 244-0666.*
—Kyle Konrad

Ice Creamsmith has been a Dorchester landmark since 1976. The ice cream is rich and creamy and there are 14 flavors including Pumpkin and Banana. Fourteen mix-ins and eight sauces, including homemade hot fudge and whipped cream are available to accompany your ice cream selection. *Dorchester: 2295 Dorchester Ave., 02124, (617) 296-8567. Closed in winter.*
—Ari Herzog

Herrell's is the second child of Steve Herrell, the former high school English teacher who started then later sold Steve's Ice Cream (see p. 219). Like Steve's, Herrell's offers smoosh-ins, the art of mushing nuts and candies into their gourmet flavors. *People Magazine* once chose the Crème de Cocoa as one of the top ten ice cream flavors in the country. *Allston: 155 Brighton Ave., 02134, (617) 782-9599. Back Bay: 224 Newbury St., Boston 02116, (617) 236-0857. Fenway: 350 Longwood Ave., Boston 02115, No phone. Harvard Square: 15 Dunster St., Cambridge 02138, (617) 497-2179. Western Massachusetts: 8 Old South St., Northampton 01060, (413) 586-9700.*
—Kaya Stone

Toscanini's is said to be Ben Cohen's (of Ben & Jerry's fame) favorite ice cream—not counting his own. Maybe it is the buttery bite of burnt caramel, or the subtle spiciness of cardamom or the pistachio-laden khulfee. Chocolate aficionados will delight in the Belgian chocolate, and the grapenut ice cream is a selection that might be familiar to a few Canadians. But the ultimate flavor for those who might want a break from the bar but need a hoppy flavor fix? Guinness. *Harvard Square: 1310 Massachusetts Ave., Cambridge 02139, (617) 354-9350. Central Square: 899 Main St., Cambridge 02139, (617) 491-5877. Kendall Square: 84 Massachusetts Ave., Cambridge 02139, (617) 491-1558.*
—Paula Foye

Christina's is an ice cream-lover's paradise. The constantly rotating menu of 30-odd flavors (including ice cream, frozen yogurt, and sorbet) are all homemade, all rich and creamy, and all divine. The incredibly inventive flavors at Christina's at times may seem inappropriate (caramel prune?), but even the most out-there combinations are almost always delicious. Pumpkin is a popular seasonal treat (like pie à la mode, only better). Mexican chocolate is a sweet and zingy (from cinnamon) favorite, as is azuki bean (a malty sweet red-bean flavor). *Inman Square: 1255 Cambridge St., Cambridge 02139, (617) 492-7021.*
—*Ankur Ghosh*

Denise's shines when it comes to risqué flavors like Sex on the Beach Sorbet, Bailey's Irish Cream, and Guinness. Cherry Denise, mint-chip, and burnt sugar are slightly more traditional but still exquisite. All flavors are handmade, very rich, and served in good-sized portions. *Davis Square: 4 College Ave., Somerville 02144, (617) 628-2764.*
—*Kyle Konrad*

Lizzy's owner, Nick Pappas, dropped out of the corporate world in order to start an ice cream parlor in 1995. His dream was to combine his perfectionist tendencies with the finest ingredients in order to make the best ice cream possible, and to back it up he was willing to put his own name on the label. "Unfortunately," Pappas tells us, "Nick's sounded too much like a seedy night club." Instead, he named the business after his daughter, Lizzy. Some of the most popular flavors include black raspberry, coconut, Mocha Chocolate Lace, ginger, and Chocolate Orgy. Lizzy's makes one mean frappe—a traditional recipe of ice cream, milk, and flavored syrup. On a dairy-free diet? Have no fear. Lizzy's tofuti has literally sprouted a cult following in the vegan and lactose intolerant communities. *Western Suburbs: 367 Moody St., Waltham 02453, (781) 893-6677.*
—*Jesse Crary*

Rancatore's doles out some of the finest homemade ice cream this side of Cambridge (owner Joe Rancatore's brother owns and operates Toscanini's). Top flavors include bittersweet or callebaut chocolate ice cream and lemon walnut or mango sorbet. *Western Suburbs: 283 Belmont St., Belmont 02478, (617) 489-5090.*
—*Paula Foye*

Crescent Ridge Dairy Bar rests among storybook Holstein cows grazing on open pasture; from the udders of these and similarly hormone-free bovines springs the milk that yields 70-year-old Crescent Ridge's 31 delicious ice cream flavors including pumpkin, ginger, butter crunch, and cherry vanilla. At its busiest, lines at each of the eight ordering windows run ten-people deep; that's not even counting its counter inside, where ice cream, frozen yogurt, and milk can be bought by the gallon. *New England: 355 Bay Rd., Sharon, MA 02067, (781) 784-2740.*
—*Nina West*

James's Gate

Home is where the hearth is.

$$

5-11 McBride St., Jamaica Plain 02130
(at South St.)
Phone (617) 983-2000 • Fax (617) 983-2288
www.jamessgate.com

CATEGORY	Irish Pub
HOURS	Sun, Tues–Thurs: 5:30 PM–10 PM Fri/Sat: 5:30 PM–11 PM
MASS TRANSIT	T: Orange line to Forest Hills; bus: #39
PAYMENT	VISA MasterCard
POPULAR FOOD	Pub menu includes the Prince Edward Island mussels (with garlic, chili pepper, basil, and white wine butter broth) are perfection; traditional pub offerings like homemade shepherd's pie, pot roast, and fish 'n' chips are revamped without losing the Old World appeal; great clam chowder
UNIQUE FOOD	Chips and curry; grilled vegetable quesadilla; tuna nicoise salad, with rare tuna; bangers and mash
DRINKS	Over 15 beers on tap including Old Speckled hen, Tremont Ale, Ipswich Ale, and the usual pub suspects; good selection of wines
SEATING	The space is divided into two halves: the pub with a long bar, a huge communal table in the center, and many small tables around the periphery; and a restaurant with seating for about 40
AMBIENCE	The outside is meant to replicate the appearance of St. James's Gate Brewery in Dublin, the home of Guinness Stout since 1759. Inside, the dim glow from the stone fireplace, flickering candles, and lively music set the mood. Whether you're with a large group or on your first date, the atmosphere seduces you into lingering a little longer over your entrée or your final pint.
EXTRAS/NOTES	The restaurant portion of James's Gate offers fancier entrees in the $14-18 range. Pub open Tues–Sun: 11:30 AM–1 AM and Mon: 4 PM–1 AM.

—*John Newton*

"Making coffee has become the great compromise
of the decade. It's the only thing "real" men do
that doesn't seem to threaten their masculinity.
To women, it's on the same domestic entry level as
putting the spring back into the toilet-tissue holder
or taking a chicken out of the freezer to thaw."

—*Erma Bombeck*

JP Seafood

The freshest seafood short of wading into the harbor and getting it yourself.

$$$

730 Centre St., Jamaica Plain 02130

(at Harris Ave.)

Phone (617) 983-5177

www.jpseafoodcafe.com

CATEGORY	Korean
HOURS	Tues–Sat: 11:30 AM–2:30 PM, 5 PM–10 PM Sun: 5 PM–10 PM
MASS TRANSIT	T: Orange line to Green St.; bus: #39 drops you off in front
PAYMENT	VISA MasterCard AMERICAN EXPRESS DISCOVER
POPULAR FOOD	Sushi of all sorts, *bibimbop* (exotic veggies, egg, meat if you want it, on rice with Korean chili paste), scallion pancakes, seafood or vegetable tempura, seafood stir fry, miso soup; superb lunch specials
UNIQUE FOOD	*Ok-dol bibimbop* worth the extra $2 for the sizzling hot pot; Phil's JP Blues Maki (tobiko, sesame, mayo, crabmeat covered with salmon, tuna, and fluke)
DRINKS	Sam Adams to Sapporo, soft drinks, green tea, full wine list
SEATING	Intimate wooden tables that can be pushed together for large groups; plenty of room but still cozy; busy takeout business in lobby
AMBIENCE	Romantic, but singles-friendly; a diverse crowd discussing art, music, childrearing, travel, deep emotions, and *SNL*; a soothing, sparse setting, with fish mural, green lanterns, tribal masks, glowing candles; soft, empowering chick-folk music on the sound system; expect a wait during the peak dinner hours
EXTRAS/NOTES	JP Seafood started up the street, where Hi-Fi Records now stands, as a simple fish counter that also ran a takeout business. When word got out about the quality fish, business boomed and eventually they had to relocate to the present, spacious locale. Sadly, you can no longer get a pound of salmon for tonight's dinner, but you can take yourself out for a classy, cheap lunch. —*Alison Pereto*

"After a good dinner one can forgive anybody, even one's own relatives."

—*Oscar Wilde*

Miami Restaurant

If you like Cuban food and know what you want.

$$

381 Centre St., Jamaica Plain 02130
(near Day St. in Hyde Square)
Phone (617) 522-4644

CATEGORY	Cuban
HOURS	Daily: noon–11 PM
MASS TRANSIT	T: Orange line to Jackson Sq. bus: #39
PAYMENT	VISA MasterCard DISCOVER
POPULAR FOOD	Outstanding Cubano sandwiches; breaded steak with rice, beans, and plantains; flan
UNIQUE FOOD	Steamed yucca; *majarete*, a dessert with sweet red beans, milk, and shredded coconut
DRINKS	*Café con leche*, cooler of drinks
SEATING	Seats 25 at a counter, a couple tables, and five booths
AMBIENCE	Mainly a lunchtime place with a cafeteria-like atmosphere.

—Nick Grossman

El Oriental de Cuba

Locals go loco for JP's best Cuban food.

$$

416 Centre St., Jamaica Plain 02130
(at Paul Gore St. in Hyde Sq.)
Phone (617) 524-6464

CATEGORY	Cuban
HOURS	Daily: 10 AM–10 PM
MASS TRANSIT	T: Orange line to Jackson Sq.; bus: #39
PAYMENT	VISA MasterCard DISCOVER
POPULAR FOOD	*Mondongo* (beef tripe) on Sundays; Cuban sandwiches with roast pork (requiring two days to prepare), ham, melted Swiss, pickles, and mustard; hearty chicken soup; excellent breakfasts; *tostones* (fried green plantains); you never knew black beans and rice could be this good
UNIQUE FOOD	*Ropa vieja* (pulled beef) with rice and beans; oxtails; *mofongo* (mashed plantains mixed with crispy pork rinds and garlic)
DRINKS	The shakes (*batidos*) are the best in town; try *parcha* (passionfruit) or *guarapo* (sugarcane); Caribbean juices, *malta*, and sodas; *café con leche*; Cuban espresso for 75¢
SEATING	Seating for 40 at tables
AMBIENCE	JP has a significant Cuban population and for Cuban food, this is the place to go; a local atmosphere and authentic, delicious food at great prices

—Nick Grossman

La Pupusa Guanaca

Hot little pockets of Central American goodness.

$

378 Centre St., Jamaica Plain 02130
(at Sheridan St. in Hyde Sq.)
Phone (617) 524-4900

CATEGORY	Salvadoran
HOURS	Daily: 9 AM–9 PM
MASS TRANSIT	T: Orange line to Jackson Sq.; bus: #39
PAYMENT	Cash only
POPULAR FOOD	One-buck *pupusas*, two corn tortillas filled with meat, beans, and cheese, and a tomato sauce and pickled cabbage relish to top it off; Salvadoran-style tacos; great rice and beans; tamales filled with chicken, potato, peas, egg, garlic, and onion
UNIQUE FOOD	Fried yucca; fried cassava with fried pork; Salvadoran quesadilla (an egg, cheese, and sesame dessert)
DRINKS	Juices, sodas
SEATING	Twelve seats, two counters, three tables
AMBIENCE	Small, mostly takeout joint with lively Latin music
EXTRAS/NOTES	Everything is made to order so even when there is no line, food can take a bit.

—*Kyle Konrad*

Purple Cactus

Mexican meets Gen-X.

$

674 Centre St., Jamaica Plain 02130
(at Seaverns Ave.)
Phone (617) 522-7422 • Fax (617) 522-7552

CATEGORY	Wraps
HOURS	Daily: 11 AM–10 PM
MASS TRANSIT	T: Orange line to Green St.; bus: #39
PAYMENT	VISA MasterCard Discover
POPULAR FOOD	Yuppies love the quick, fresh, healthy wraps filled with shrimp, steak, chicken, or vegetables
UNIQUE FOOD	Asian ginger peanut, tofu, and hummus wraps
DRINKS	Non-dairy smoothies, limeade, fresh juices
SEATING	Seats 15 at counters
AMBIENCE	None really; watch the foot traffic on Centre St. or do takeout

—*Nick Grossman*

Sorella's

*Vegetarian hash
with your bacon?*

$$

388A-386 Centre St., Jamaica Plain 02130
(at Perkins St. in Hyde Square)
Phone (617) 524-2016

CATEGORY	Café
HOURS	Daily: 6:30 AM–2:30 PM
MASS TRANSIT	T: Orange line to Jackson Sq.; bus: #39
PAYMENT	Cash only
POPULAR FOOD	Forty kinds of omelettes, some with as many as 15 ingredients; French toast with sesame, apricot, and strawberries; raspberry-banana-walnut or carrot-walnut pancakes; oatmeal; a dozen homemade breads for French toast such as challah or banana bread
UNIQUE FOOD	Potential omelette ingredients include asparagus, shitake mushrooms, avocado, gouda, and pesto (as well as the basics); vegetarian "hash"; polenta specials; one of the only places in Boston with a choice of several vegetarian club sandwiches
DRINKS	Coffee, tea, Sanka; fresh-squeezed orange, grapefruit, or carrot juices; sodas and bottled juices; milk; bottled beer and inexpensive glasses of wine at lunch
SEATING	Two seating areas next door to each other: the main one, with two rows of small tables that can morph to seat larger parties; the newer, upstairs one, with slightly bigger tables and a little more elbow room (but less organically grown ambience).
AMBIENCE	The walls are packed with handwritten signs advertising a dizzying array of specials. A shrine to the Three Stooges hovers by the cash register, while random, 3-D maps of various countries hang on the walls. Customers are mainly locals and the place has a good, cluttered, efficient vibe. Almost always crowded—get there by 9:15 AM on weekends or face a line.
EXTRAS/NOTES	On a bitter winter day, this writer dragged a friend to Sorella's extolling its magnificent variety of omelettes and breads, its pure-ray-of-sunshine fresh OJ, and its friendliness to both vegetarians and omnivores alike. The wait was at least 15 minutes. As we debated waiting, a server came outside carrying a tray laden with small paper cups of steaming hot apple cider to warm the huddled masses. We stayed. Plenty to eat, plenty to look at, and good neighbors besides, Sorella's makes the wait worthwhile.

—Alison Pereto

Tacos El Charro

*Mariachi madness and some of
the best sangria in town.*

$$

349 Centre St., Jamaica Plain 02130

(at Jackson Sq.)

Phone (617) 522-2578

CATEGORY	Mexican
HOURS	Daily: noon–11 PM
MASS TRANSIT	T: Orange line to Jackson Sq.
PAYMENT	VISA MasterCard DISCOVER
POPULAR FOOD	Burritos, fajitas, *tacos al pastor* with tender pork marinated in pineapple juice; delicious 36-ingredient *mole poblano* made with dry peppers, almonds, peanuts, tomatoes, and chocolate; homemade chips and salsa
UNIQUE FOOD	Great goat meat stew; beef tongue; tamales; cactus salad; marinated seafood ceviche
DRINKS	Some of the best sangria in Boston; beer; no margaritas
SEATING	Seats 40 at tables and booths
AMBIENCE	Piñatas hanging from the ceiling; upbeat and busy but with a friendly and relaxed family atmosphere
EXTRAS/NOTES	Known for authenticity, many locals claim El Charro is the best Mexican food in Boston. Live mariachi band on weekends.

—*Nick Grossman*

Wonder Spice Café

*A Cambodian-Thai mix
that tastes better with every visit.*

$$$

697 Centre St., Jamaica Plain 02130

(at Burroughs St.)

Phone (617) 522-0200

CATEGORY	Thai and Cambodian
HOURS	Mon–Thurs: 11:30 AM–3 PM, 5 PM–10 PM Fri: 11:30 AM–3 PM, 5 PM–10:30 PM Sat: noon–3:30 PM, 5 PM–10:30 PM Sun: noon–3:30 PM, 5 PM–10 PM
MASS TRANSIT	T: Orange line to Green Street; bus: #39
PAYMENT	VISA MasterCard
POPULAR FOOD	Classic Thai in large portions, with an emphasis on fish, particularly salmon; crispy *pad* Thai
UNIQUE FOOD	From pear and prawn to sizzling fruits, the sweetness of this Cambodian savory food is an exciting foray into an underrepresented cuisine
DRINKS	Beer and wine
SEATING	Tables indoor and an outdoor patio
AMBIENCE	A true East meets West vibe here; Buddhist images abound, yet stylish lamps hang overhead; typical JP crowd—people of all colors and personalities

—*Zachary Patten*

ROXBURY-MATTAPAN-DORCHESTER

Ali's Roti Restaurant

Looking for genuine West Indian food?
$$

118 Blue Hill Ave., Mattapan 02126
(at Morton St.)
Phone (617) 298-9850

CATEGORY	West Indian
HOURS	Mon–Thurs: 11 AM–9 PM Fri/Sat: 11 AM–10 PM
MASS TRANSIT	Bus: #21, 26, 28, 29, or 31 to the corner of Morton St. and Blue Hill Ave.
PAYMENT	
POPULAR FOOD	Ali's is *the* place to come for authentic, delicious Trinidadian *roti* with a variety of fillings; the curry boneless chicken *roti* is always a crowd pleaser
UNIQUE FOOD	*Roti*, a Trinidadian dish originating in the island's East Indian communities, is a sort of wrap filled with meat or vegetable curry, anything from chickpeas (*channa*) to stewed oxtail
DRINKS	Juice, soft drinks, and a variety of West Indian soft drinks
SEATING	Seats 24
AMBIENCE	Red cafeteria-like tables; bland atmosphere; locals and West Indians alike come to get seriously good food fast
OTHER ONES	• Roxbury: 1035 Tremont St., Roxbury 02120, (617) 427-1079 • Roslindale Village: 25 Poplar St., Roslindale 02131, (617) 325-8079

—Anna Morris

Boston Speed's Famous Hot Dogs

Not your ordinary hot dog.
$

Western corner of Newmarket Square, Boston 02118
(between Massachusetts Ave. and Southampton St.)
No phone

CATEGORY	Hot Dog Stand
HOURS	Tues–Fri: 11:30 AM–2 PM (weather permitting)
MASS TRANSIT	Bus: #8 or #10
PAYMENT	Cash only
POPULAR FOOD	Half-pound, eight-inch hot dogs for $5
DRINKS	Sodas in the cooler
SEATING	None
AMBIENCE	A cross-section of truck drivers, local workers, and in-the-know eaters who make the pilgrimage for some of the best hot dogs in Boston
EXTRAS/NOTES	From his wagon parked on a corner of Newmarket Square, home to Boston's wholesale food distributors, "Speed"

Anderson serves up seriously oversized kosher dogs, slow-grilled over charcoal until infused with maximum smoky flavor, then garnished with your choice of mustard, onions, and Speed's secret sauce and relish.

—Michael Beckett

Chef Lee's

Bring on the soul food.

$$

1160 Blue Hill Ave., Dorchester 02124

(at Morton St.)

Phone (617) 436-6634

CATEGORY	Soul Food
HOURS	Mon–Sat: 10 AM–8 PM
PARKING	T: Orange line to Ruggles, then take bus #22; Orange line to Forest Hills, then take bus #31
PAYMENT	VISA MasterCard AMERICAN EXPRESS DISCOVER
POPULAR FOOD	Famous for their renowned Steakburger with fries for the bargain price of $5; large portions of fried, barbecued, or baked chicken; sweet potato pie
UNIQUE FOOD	Fried catfish with warm corn bread and a choice of two sides (collard greens, string beans, black-eyed peas, candied yams, cheesy mac 'n' cheese, corn, potato salad, beans, and rice); oxtail
DRINKS	Iced tea, coffee, soda
SEATING	1950s-style diner
AMBIENCE	Friday and Saturday nights are the busiest, but there's a pretty steady crowd all day long; the walls offer a walk through time with pictures of Martin Luther King, Jr., Etta James, Langston Hughes, and old Celtics greats

—Heidi Solomon

Chris' Texas B.B.Q.

Real Texas ribs, Dorchester-style.

$$$

1370 Dorchester Ave., Dorchester 02122

(at Orchardfield St.)

Phone (617) 436-4700

CATEGORY	Texas Barbecue
HOURS	Mon–Thurs: 11 AM–11 PM Fri/Sat: 11 AM–midnight Sun: noon–10 PM
MASS TRANSIT	T: Red line-Ashmont to Fields Corner
PAYMENT	Cash only
POPULAR FOOD	Texas-style beef ribs in a sweet and spicy sauce; baby back ribs; steak tips; samplers like the Sheriff's Platter (pork chops, wings, barbecued chicken breast, and pork ribs); traditional sides such as collard greens, sweet potatoes, and pork and beans

UNIQUE FOOD	Some of their dishes are more "Dorchester ethnic" than "Texas barbecue": beef, chicken, and shrimp kebabs; pasta with meatballs; pizza with a variety of toppings
DRINKS	Soda
SEATING	Order at the counter and receive your grub in a Styrofoam container; mostly a takeout place
AMBIENCE	A stand-alone building in a parking lot; the eatery mostly consists of a kitchen with vats of sauce-laden meats ready to be scooped and served
EXTRAS/NOTES	The original owner Chris, the Texas ribs enthusiast, originally hailed from Greece. The eatery recently switched management to a Kurdistani family from Northern Turkey.

—Esti Iturralde

Common Ground Café

Incense, flowing robes, and wholesome food.

$$

2243 Dorchester Ave., Dorchester 02124
(two blocks from Adams St.)
Phone (617) 298-1020
www.twelvetribes.com

CATEGORY	Café
HOURS	Mon–Thurs: 10 AM–9 PM Fri: 10 AM–3 PM
PARKING	T: Red Line-Ashmont to Milton; bus: #217
PAYMENT	Cash only
POPULAR FOOD	Peanut butter, banana, and honey sandwich on whole wheat bread; salads served in three sizes; burritos; cheese and tomato and tuna melt; homemade muffins
UNIQUE FOOD	No red meat here—honey is used instead of sugar, whole grains rather than refined flour; several times a week there are specials of the day, usually soup and either a salmon or chicken sandwich
DRINKS	Fruit juices, yogurt smoothies, hot and iced teas, lemonade, mocha, smoothies, and fruit concoctions
SEATING	Approximately 20 can sit at one of several wooden tables or along the small three-stool bar
AMBIENCE	Very dark and resembling a cottage straight out of a Grimm's fairytale: polished tree trunks as table tops, hanging bushel basket lamps, a fire in the stone hearth, and worldly chants and melodies coming over the sound system. The bathrooms are hand-painted with country scenes. Promotional pamphlets on the tables remind you that this café is run by a religious group; very serious, almost somber, staff.

EXTRAS/NOTES	Owned and operated by the Twelve Tribes spiritual brotherhood, they also manage the Common Sense Wholesome Food Market next door. While not officially open on weekends, they will often leave their doors open to greet visitors. Live Irish and folk music on Wednesday nights.
OTHER ONES	The Messianic community also runs cafes in: • Cape Cod: 420 Main St., Hyannis 02601, (508) 778-8390 • New Hampshire: 55 Main St., Lancaster, NH 03584, (603) 788-4729

—Ari Herzog

Ice Creamsmith

(see p. 131)
Ice Cream Shop
2295 Dorchester Ave., Dorchester 02124
Phone (617) 296-8567

Irie Jamaica

Hole-in-the-wall source for island specialties.
$$
310 Bowdoin St., Dorchester 02122
(near Geneva Ave. and Columbia Rd.)
Phone (617) 929-3866 • Fax (617) 282-5145

CATEGORY	Caribbean
HOURS	Mon–Thurs: 7 AM–10 PM Fri/Sat: 7 AM–11 PM Sun: 9 AM–5 PM
MASS TRANSIT	T: Red line to Field's Corner, then take bus #17; Orange line to Ruggles, then take bus #19
PAYMENT	Cash only
POPULAR FOOD	Grilled jerk chicken, stewed chicken, spicy oxtail sautéed and then simmered with beans and tomato
UNIQUE FOOD	Ackee (a fruit) and saltfish—a traditional Jamaican breakfast; lots of freshly prepared fish dishes: steamed, fried, served in a brown stew gravy, or escovish—a spicy marinade of onions, herbs, and spices
DRINKS	West Indian drinks such as Sorrell, ginger beer, and carrot juice
SEATING	There are seven tables, but the business is mostly takeout
AMBIENCE	A dive that does a ton of business

—Rhonda Cozier

"Hunger is the best sauce in the world."
—Miguel De Cervantes

A Taste of New England Food Festivals

Most festivals, whatever the occasion, are not complete without a greasy Italian sausage or some sugar-caked hunks of fried dough. Once in a while comes a food junkie's dream: a festival that skips the frivolous games and rides to pay homage to a single delicacy. Endless rows of vendors come together to battle for best in show, while hungry Bostonians gorge themselves on all-you-can-eat samples. For a true taste of New England, check out these fantastic food fests.

Chowderfest

Whether it's your heaven or hell, there's not much else quite like a never-ending bowl of hot, creamy chowder on a sweltering July day. For over 20 years thousands of Bostonians have descended on Boston City Hall Plaza to sample the city's best chowder recipes. Over 2,000 gallons of the Boston staple get scooped out, with Turner Fisheries Bar, Chart House, and Captain Parker's Pub the perennial favorites. *July 4th Weekend, Boston City Hall Plaza, (617) 227-1528.*

North End Summer Street Festivals

In theory these festivals pay homage to various saints, but it's really all about the food. Countless food stands, thousands of eaters, and Italian crooners take over one or two of the North End's narrow streets for a weekend of non-stop eating and celebration. The Fisherman's Feast, held in mid-August on North, Fleet, and Lewis streets takes top honors with four days of food, entertainment, and carnival games. *Almost every weekend, late July to August, North End, Boston, (617) 720-2283. www.northendboston.com*

Scooper Bowl

Twelve creameries from Ben and Jerry's to Häagen Dazs, plus 12 tons of ice cream, plus 36 flavors, equals the nation's largest all-you-can-eat ice cream festival—and one big bellyache—all to support the Jimmy Fund for cancer care and research at Dana-Farber Cancer Institute. *Second week of June, Boston City Hall Plaza, (800) 52-JIMMY. www.jimmyfund.org/eve/*

Vegetarian Food Festival

Pick up free samples of soy milk, vegan soups, and flavored tofu. Tofurkey-Jerky, anyone? Educational presentations with titles such as "Going Vegetarian? A How-to Guide for Making the Change" and "Protein Myth: The Plain Truth about High Protein Diets" cater to herbivores of every stripe. *Mid-October, Reggie Lewis Athletic Center, Roxbury Community College, 1350 Tremont St., Boston, (617) 424-8846. www.bostonveg.org/foodfest*

Some other New England festivals to check out include:

Chinatown Festival *Early August, Chinatown, Boston, MA*

Hot Dog Safari *Mid-May, East Boston, MA www.hotdogsafari.com*

Taste of Northampton *Mid-August, Northampton, MA www.northamptonuncommon.com/taste/*

Gloucester Seafood Festival *Late September, Gloucester, MA www.capeannchamber.com/gsf/*

Cranberry Harvest Festival *Columbus Day Weekend, Edaville Cranberry Bogs, South Carver, MA www.cranberries.org/hfestival/festival.html*

Taste of Rhode Island *Late September, Newport, RI www.newportfestivals.com*

Taste of Hartford *Early June, Hartford, CT www.tasteofhartford.com*

New England Barbecue Championships *Late July, at Harpoon Brewery, Windsor, VT www.harpoonbrewery.com/events/index.htm*

Hampton Beach Seafood Festival *Early September, Hampton Beach, NH www.hamptonbeach.org/calendar/*

Maine Lobster Festival *Early August, Rockland, ME www.mainelobsterfestival.com*

—*Kaya Stone*

Keith's Place

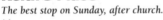

The best stop on Sunday, after church.
$$

469 Blue Hill Ave., Dorchester 02121
(at Georgia St. in Grove Hall)
Phone (617) 427-7899

CATEGORY	Southern
HOURS	Tues–Fri: 6:30 AM–6 PM
	Sat: 7 AM–5 PM
	Sun: 7 AM–3 PM
MASS TRANSIT	Bus: #21, 26, 28, 29, or 31
PAYMENT	Cash only
POPULAR FOOD	Country-fried steak; sweet potatoes; collard greens; black-eyed peas; fried catfish; mac 'n' cheese; homemade buttermilk biscuits; sweet potato pie; banana pudding; very popular Sunday Brunch, featuring banana pecan pancakes, homemade fish hash, fried porgies, and great omelettes
UNIQUE FOOD	Sweet potato pancakes; Southern fish fry every Friday at lunch with fixings like fried okra and hushpuppies
DRINKS	Iced tea, soft drinks
SEATING	Tables for two and four
AMBIENCE	Down-home atmosphere with large windows

—*Kyle Konrad*

M&M Ribs

*Southern-style ribs
served from a food truck,
courtesy of Big Moe.*

$$

Columbia Rd., Dorchester 02121

(corner of Quincy St.)

Phone (617) 825-6852 • Fax (617) 288-0577

CATEGORY	Southern Barbecue
HOURS	Wed: 11 AM–6 PM
	Thurs: 11 AM–8 PM
	Fri/Sat: 11 AM–midnight
	Sun: noon–6 PM
PARKING	Free lot
PAYMENT	Cash only
POPULAR FOOD	In a dirt lot on a street corner of Dorchester, M&M's has served Carolina pork ribs for years—chosen for their meatiness and shipped, despite the name, specially from Virginia. Other favorites include chopped barbecue (a.k.a. pulled pork) sandwiches, with a spicy vinegar sauce. There's been a recent addition of beef ribs to the menu, now that Moe has found a supplier up to his standards. Classic sides like collard greens, corn bread, and macaroni are winners, as are the desserts: sweet potato pie and peach cobbler.
UNIQUE FOOD	Pig feet; oxtail; banana pudding; Big Moe's own sauce by the quart
DRINKS	Soda, root beer
SEATING	A couple of picnic tables near the van in the lot
AMBIENCE	On the five days when M&M's is open, expect an assortment of locals stopping by during lunch or after work; Moe's is an easy stop by car too—just park in the lot and place your order
EXTRAS/NOTES	In 1982, Maurice "Big Moe" Hill had a dream. He was leased his first barbecue truck on the promise of a dollar (that he never actually paid). The truck led to a trailer in 1985, and then the silver van of today in 1990. The mobile kitchen makes catering a snap, and M&M ribs have attended rib festivals up and down the Eastern seaboard. According to Moe, "We go anywhere."

—Esti Iturralde

Pat's of Lower Mills

The identity of Dorchester's best calzones is out.

$

2254 Dorchester Ave., Dorchester 02124

(at Washington St.)

Phone (617) 298-9625

CATEGORY	Pizza by the Slice
HOURS	Mon–Sat: 10 AM–10 PM
	Sun: 11 AM–8 PM
MASS TRANSIT	T: Red Line-Ashmont to Milton; Bus: #217
PAYMENT	VISA MasterCard AMERICAN EXPRESS DISCOVER
POPULAR FOOD	Solid cheese pizzas and enormous calzones filled with a host of ingredients: chicken parm, steak, the cheese bomb (onions, mushrooms, and peppers), ham, cold cuts, even turkey with all the fixings; they take awhile and are worth it; everything made fresh to order
UNIQUE FOOD	Marinated Dinners are a slight departure from the usual Italian, consisting of steak tips, grilled chicken, turkey tips, pork loin, or swordfish tips brushed with sauces like teriyaki or Jamaican Jerk made on site
DRINKS	Soda, juice, iced tea, lemonade
SEATING	Booths seat 16 with small tables for six more
AMBIENCE	A no-frills pizza parlor with the requisite booths and long counter for ordering, Pat's is beloved by this Irish-American section of Dorchester and certain staff members of the nearby *Boston Globe*
EXTRAS/NOTES	Owner Pat McDonagh whose Irish name is "spelled the correct way" hadn't found his calling until he learned the art of pizza-making from a Sicilian in West Roxbury 20 years ago. Pat's popularity has soared of late after some *Globe* regulars made mention of the pizzeria in the paper's calendar section, spreading news of the Lower Mills pizza parlor to stoops across New England.

—Esti Iturralde

Pho Hòa

The health-conscious choice.

$

1356 Dorchester Ave., Dorchester 02122

(at Kimball St.)

Phone (617) 287-9746

CATEGORY	Vietnamese
HOURS	Mon–Wed: 9 AM–10 PM
	Thurs/Fri: 9 AM–11 PM
	Sat: 8 AM–11 PM
	Sun: 8 AM–10 PM
TRANSPORT	Take Morrisey Blvd. Exit off I-93 (#13 on 93N, #12 on 93S)
PAYMENT	VISA MasterCard AMERICAN EXPRESS DISCOVER

POPULAR FOOD	Thirty-one varieties of *pho* (meaning soup, pronounced *phwah*) *hoa* (meaning noodles, pronounced *hwa*); almost all are beef-based, and come in a huge bowl packed with rice noodles and brisket or steak, as well as fresh basil, bean sprouts, lime, hot chilis, and various chili sauces (all optional); *pho ga*, a natural chicken broth with shredded chicken, meat, and noodles; homemade Vietnamese puddings
UNIQUE FOOD	*Pho tai gan sach*, a noodle soup with eye round steak, soft tendon, and tripe; *pho nam, gan ve don*, a noodle soup with well-done flank, soft tendon, and skirt steak
DRINKS	Free tea; avocado juice made with condensed milk, sugar, and ice; soda; fruit drinks (durian, plum, coconut)
SEATING	Seats about 100
AMBIENCE	A neighborhood hot spot for the local Vietnamese community; it gets packed on Sunday mornings; very little English spoken
EXTRAS/NOTES	There's a numerical system that allows you to design your ideal *pho*: choose nonfat broth (*05), more noodles (*16), no onion and parsley (*19), white meat only (*26), etc. This location is part of a chain of 80 franchised Vietnamese noodle shops worldwide.

—*Heidi Solomon*

Pit Stop Barbecue

Mattapan's pork rib legend.

$$

888A Morton St., Mattapan 02126
(at Evans St.)
Phone (617) 436-0485

CATEGORY	Southern Barbecue
HOURS	Thurs–Sat: 11 AM–midnight
MASS TRANSIT	T: Red line to Ashmont
PAYMENT	Cash only
POPULAR FOOD	Meaty hickory smoked ribs, chopped pork, barbecued chicken; standout sides include candied yams, mac 'n' cheese, and collard greens
UNIQUE FOOD	Tender brisket
DRINKS	Soda machines
SEATING	Just one table; mostly takeout
AMBIENCE	With its limited hours, it becomes packed around dinnertime—show up early to avoid the wait.

—*Kyle Konrad*

SOUTH BOSTON

Amrheins

*It changes by
not changing at all.*
Since 1890
$$$
80N W. Broadway, South Boston 02127
(at A St.)
Phone (617) 464-4009

CATEGORY	Historic Bar & Grill
HOURS	Mon–Thurs: 11 AM–8 PM
	Fri/Sat: 11 AM–11 PM
	Sun: 9 AM–2 PM
MASS TRANSIT	T: Red line to Broadway
PAYMENT	VISA MasterCard AMERICAN EXPRESS
POPULAR FOOD	Clam chowder, lobster filled mushrooms, chicken portobello
UNIQUE FOOD	Wiener schnitzel, lobster pie, famous homemade grapenut pudding
DRINKS	Full bar
SEATING	Home to the oldest hand-carved bar in Boston; also plenty of booths
AMBIENCE	Frequented by longtime Southie residents, including local Irish politicos past and present whose photos decorate the walls; a true neighborhood spot where folks go for a beer and meal to watch the game with their friends

—Colleen Craig

The Fish Pier Restaurant and Market

It ain't pretty but the seafood rocks.
$$$
667 E. Broadway, South Boston 02127
(at K St.)
Phone (617) 269-2111 • Fax (617) 269-5590

CATEGORY	Seafood
HOURS	Sun–Tues: 10:30 AM–9:30 PM
	Wed–Sat: 10 AM–9:30 PM
MASS TRANSIT	T: Red line to Broadway, then take #9 bus
PAYMENT	VISA MasterCard
POPULAR FOOD	Known as one of the best places for fast, cheap, and tasty seafood; the fish 'n' chips are some of the best in the city; the fried seafood plate combines scallops, whitefish, whole clams, and shrimp; plenty of non-seafood selections for whole families of finicky eaters
UNIQUE FOOD	Squid and chips, Cajun catfish, smelts, and baked stuffed sole
DRINKS	Soft drinks
SEATING	About ten booths
AMBIENCE	The smell of grease and fish definitely fills the air.

—Joel Lowden

L Street Diner

*Mingle with locals and politicians
for a cheap, low-key dining experience.*

$$

108 L St., South Boston 02127
(at Fifth St.)
Phone (617) 268-1155 • Fax (617) 268-5524

CATEGORY	Diner
HOURS	Mon–Thurs: 8 AM–10 PM Fri–Sun: 7 AM–10 PM
MASS TRANSIT	Bus: #11 bus to Sixth St. and L St., or #9 or #7 to L St. and Broadway
PAYMENT	VISA MasterCard
POPULAR FOOD	Breakfast every day until 3 PM; deli sandwiches, burgers, pastas, salads, calzones, and pizza are always available; standouts include roast turkey dinner and a grilled ham steak served with mashed potatoes and veggies
UNIQUE FOOD	Boasts "real Southern BBQ in Southie"
DRINKS	Beer and wine, gourmet coffee and hot chocolate, tea, milk, soft drinks, and juices
SEATING	Seats up to 40 at any one of its intimate two-person tables, which can be consolidated to seat more
AMBIENCE	The L St. Diner may not have hired a master interior decorator, but the fairy lights, plentiful plastic plants, and obvious care taken to the upkeep of the dining room will endear you to it immediately; expect to dine with lots of locals and young professionals
EXTRAS/NOTES	A separate take-out entrance keeps the coming and going in the dining room to a minimum.

—*Anna Morris*

Loaf and Ladle

*A better Irish breakfast can only
be found on the Emerald Isle.*

$$

483 E. Broadway, South Boston 02127
(where E. and W. Broadway meet)
Phone (617) 268-7006

CATEGORY	Irish
MASS TRANSIT	T: Red line to Broadway, then take #9 bus
PAYMENT	Cash only
HOURS	Mon–Sat: 7 AM–4 PM Sun: 8 AM–3 PM
POPULAR FOOD	Irish breakfast served all day: bacon, sausage, homefries, eggs, and grilled tomato; burgers and sandwiches; black-and-white pudding sausages; everything very inexpensive
DRINKS	Soft drinks and really good Irish tea
SEATING	Twenty-five seats
AMBIENCE	Small but cozy lunch counter, rarely crowded; frequented by local Irish

—*Joel Lowden*

Beantown Eateries on the Big (and Little) Screen

When Boston is portrayed in movies or on TV, more often than not, the crew is on location in a Hollywood backlot. Nevertheless there have been a few Boston-area eateries to take their place in the spotlight.

Good Will Hunting (1997)

L Street Tavern

Blue-collar genius Will (Matt Damon) and goofball friend Chuckie (Ben Affleck) hang out here in the beginning of the film. According to *Hunting* director Gus Van Sant, the neon shamrocks and bumper sticker over the bar proclaiming "No Liberals" best exemplified the Southie experience. *South Boston: 58 E. 8th St. #A, South Boston 02127, (617) 268-4335.*

Bow & Arrow Pub

Formerly located on the corner of Mass. Ave. and Bow St. in Cambridge. Over drinks at the Bow, Will impresses Harvard coed Skylar (Minnie Driver) by embarrassing her arrogant male classmate with an impromptu analysis of pre-Revolutionary economic theory. In 2000 the Bow closed when its landlord, Harvard University, raised the rent. It has since been replaced, in part, by a swanky Irish pub.

The Tasty

Formerly located on JFK St. in Cambridge. After leaving the Bow, Will and Skylar exchange a sloppy kiss while eating greasy cheeseburgers at this legendary greasy spoon. See p. 183.

Cheers

Bull & Finch

In the 1970s this turn-of-the-century Beacon Hill mansion-turned-basement pub truly was where everyone knew your name. A few Hollywood producers stumbled upon it in their search for an American neighborhood bar and soon the outside of the Bull & Finch could be seen on NBC's top-rated *Cheers*. The inside of the Bull slightly resembles the bar where Norm, Cliff, Sam, and the gang wasted their days. However, the entire show was filmed at a replicated setting on a Hollywood lot. These days, the bar is an overpriced tourist-trap shrine to the show—you might not be glad you came. *Back Bay: 84 Beacon St., Boston 02108, (617) 227-9605.*

Boston Public

Doyle's Café

While the inside has been reproduced on a Hollyood lot, the outside of this century-old watering hole serves as the inspiration for the teachers' after-school hangout on Fox's *Boston Public*. See p. 129. *Jamaica Plain: 3484 Washington St., Jamaica Plain 02130, (617) 524-2345.*

—Kaya Stone

Mul's Diner

The real people's diner.

$$

73-75 W. Broadway, South Boston 02127
(at A St.)
Phone (617) 268-5748

CATEGORY	Diner
HOURS	Daily: 5 AM–3 PM
MASS TRANSIT	T: Red line to Broadway
PAYMENT	Cash only
POPULAR FOOD	Belgian waffles with strawberries; gorgeous muffins; reliable burgers
UNIQUE FOOD	It will strike some as odd to be able to get a chai tea or a Broadway latte in the heart of old Irish Boston, but here you can, right along with your two eggs "your way."
DRINKS	Coffee and espresso, tea, hot chocolate, juices, soda, frozen lemonades, Berry Blend smoothies
SEATING	Small tables with some booths; a bit tight on space, but it turns over quickly
AMBIENCE	Clean, vaguely retro diner with red vinyl seats on the chairs and posters of Elvis and Marilyn on the walls; watch for a pre-lunch lull on Saturday and a churchgoing lull on Sunday—otherwise crowded and popular, with a fast-moving line
EXTRAS/NOTES	Mul's is a classic, non-divey diner where you have a fighting chance at being called "hon." In the morning you can get your coffee fix and Special #3 with a minimum of fuss or attitude.

—*Alison Pereto*

Quiet Man Pub

Sshhh! A home-cooked meal away from home.

$$

11 W. Broadway, South Boston 02127
(at Dorchester Ave., near T stop)
Phone (617) 269-9878

CATEGORY	Irish Pub
HOURS	Mon–Wed: 11 AM–9 PM Thurs–Sat: 11 AM–10 PM Sun: noon–8 PM
MASS TRANSIT	T: Red line to Broadway
PAYMENT	Cash only
POPULAR FOOD	Steak tips, sausage, turkey tips, teriyaki chicken—all served in hearty portions with your choice of potato or rice, and salad
UNIQUE FOOD	John Wayne Platter, a dinner for two that features steak tips, chicken, sausage, a half rack of ribs, rice pilaf, and salad
DRINKS	Beer, wine, and a full bar
SEATING	Go ahead and seat yourself in the back
AMBIENCE	Not the fanciest joint in town; cooks tend to shout orders (or greetings to friends); always friendly servers

—*Colleen Craig*

R&L Deli

Superior Southie sandwich shop
with a sense of humor.

$$

313 Old Colony Ave., South Boston 02127

(at Columbia Rd.)

Phone (617) 269-3354 • Fax (617) 269-3358

CATEGORY	Deli
HOURS	Mon–Fri: 6 AM–9 PM
	Sat: 8 AM–9 PM
MASS TRANSIT	T: Red line to JFK/UMass or Andrew
PAYMENT	VISA MasterCard AMERICAN EXPRESS DISCOVER
POPULAR FOOD	The menu is huge but the sandwiches rule: the Abie O'Brien (corned beef with cheese and mustard on marble bread), the Rachel (extra lean roasted pastrami topped with Swiss cheese, cole slaw, and Russian dressing), and the Big Bird (turkey stuffing and cranberry sauce on your choice of bread)
UNIQUE FOOD	One of the only places in Southie that has healthy choices on the menu; great names for sandwiches, too (e.g. Baked Honey Moon, Dallas Cowboy, and the Porky Pig)
DRINKS	Soft drinks, shakes, frappes
SEATING	About 15 tables
AMBIENCE	Bright and busy; no wait service; very popular with local police and firefighters

—Joel Lowden

Salsa's

Taco Hell for dinner? Never again.

$$$

118 Dorchester St., South Boston 02127

(at E. Broadway and W. Broadway)

Phone (617) 269-7878

www.sausageguy.com

CATEGORY	Mexican
HOURS	Mon–Sat: 11 AM–11 PM
	Sun: 2 PM–10 PM
MASS TRANSIT	T: Red line to Andrew
PAYMENT	VISA MasterCard AMERICAN EXPRESS
POPULAR FOOD	The basics: burritos, tacos, enchiladas, and fajitas; *pollo en almendras* (grilled chicken in an almond salsa)
UNIQUE FOOD	*Chile en Nogada* (peppers stuffed with beef, almonds, raisins, apples and honey); Papa Taco, a baked potato stuffed with chicken, steak, or beans
DRINKS	Sangria, beer, wine, and soda
SEATING	Ample seating, but on weekends you may have to wait a few minutes for a table
AMBIENCE	Festive, casual, and bright red, with hanging piñatas, sombreros, and cacti
EXTRAS/NOTES	One of three restaurants owned by David Littefield, of Fenway Park Sausage Guy fame (see Sausage Guy in Fenway, p. 85).

—Colleen Craig

Sullivan's

One of the cheapest deals in town.
Since 1951
$$

2080 Day Blvd., South Boston 02127
(at the very end of Day Blvd.)
Phone (617) 268-5685

CATEGORY	Food Stand
HOURS	Daily: 9 AM–sunset (Mar.–Nov. only)
MASS TRANSIT	T: Red line to Andrew
PAYMENT	Cash only
POPULAR FOOD	Hot dog, fries, soda, and ice cream all for $5; fried clam strips, onion rings, chicken nuggets, some sandwiches and salads, clam chowder, Hood hard ice cream, and soft serve ice cream
DRINKS	Soda, milk, bottled water, milkshakes
SEATING	No indoor seating; several wooden benches and tables in front of the enclosed stand
AMBIENCE	Everyone comes here: parents with strollers and small children, high schoolers, construction workers, business people, cabbies, senior citizens, young adults
EXTRAS/NOTES	Sullivan's is located next to Fort Independence and offers a skyline view of Boston across the harbor—although the serenity of this view is often broken by the airplanes flying directly overhead.

—*Ari Herzog*

Taste of Home Bakery

A taste of real Irish cooking.
$

32 W. Broadway, South Boston 02127
(at Dorchester St.)
Phone (617) 269-3800

CATEGORY	Irish Bakery
HOURS	Mon–Sat: 5:30 AM–3 PM Sun: 6 AM–3 PM
MASS TRANSIT	T: Red line to Broadway
PAYMENT	Cash only
POPULAR FOOD	Crumbly scones and other pastries, including specially made cakes and soda bread; limited lunch menu featuring sand-wiches with delicious fresh baked bread
UNIQUE FOOD	Irish bacon, bangers, and white or black pudding
DRINKS	Tea, coffee, soda
SEATING	Tables are sparse, but there is always one avail-able as most people take their orders to go
AMBIENCE	A quiet, friendly place best visited in late morning or early afternoon when the morning rush has passed

—*Colleen Craig*

Terri's Place

The cheapest breakfast in Southie.

$

676 E. Broadway, South Boston 02127

(at K St.)

Phone (617) 268-3119

CATEGORY	Diner
HOURS	Mon–Sat: 5:30 AM–2 PM
	Sun: 6 AM–2 PM
MASS TRANSIT	T: Red line to Broadway; bus: #11
PAYMENT	Cash only
POPULAR FOOD	The breakfast special: two eggs, bacon, homefries, and coffee for only $2; on weekends, top your homefries with a special cheese sauce; eggs benedict
UNIQUE FOOD	Stuffed French toast, breakfast burrito, morning glory muffins
DRINKS	Coffee, juice
SEATING	Booths and counters seat 35
AMBIENCE	Mostly locals; friendly waitresses know everyone by name

—Joel Lowden

CAMBRIDGE

KENDALL SQUARE

Amelia's Trattoria

(see Amelia's Kitchen, p. 210)
Italian
111 Harvard St., Cambridge 02139
Phone (617) 868-7600

Boca Grande

(see p. 198)
Mexican
149 First St., Cambridge 02142
Phone (617) 354-5550

Cambridge Brewing Company

Grub and ale oasis in the land of the brainy.
$$$
One Kendall Sq., Cambridge 02118
(at Kendall St. and Shawnut Ave.)
Phone (617) 494-1994 • Fax (617) 494-8958
www.cambrew.com

CATEGORY	Bar & Grill
HOURS	Mon–Fri: 11:30 AM–closing
	Sat: noon–closing
	Sun: 3 PM–closing
	Closing varies depending upon the crowd; call ahead
MASS TRANSIT	T: Red line to Kendall/MIT
PAYMENT	VISA MasterCard AMERICAN EXPRESS
POPULAR FOOD	Blackened chicken or roasted portobello sandwiches; Mediterranean brick-oven pizza; southwestern turkey burger with chipotle barbecue sauce
UNIQUE FOOD	Red curry seared tofu dinner appetizer; $8 lunch entrees, including Moroccan spiced chicken and jambalaya
DRINKS	Informative drink menu caters to the beer snob; CBC brews a variety of ales and features Regatta Golden, Tall Tale Pale, Cambridge Amber, and Charles River Porter; by-the-glass wine palette for any palate ranges from chianti to pinot grigio
SEATING	The bar and front room hold 100; the back room can handle 79 and the covered patio seats 75
AMBIENCE	The nerdy set discusses nanotechnology or mapping the human genome while enjoying ample servings and consistent, flavorful brewed-on-premises beers. Wood, brick, and forest-green give a natural feel to the airy front room and bar, and distract the eye from the exposed ductwork and pipe above. In the slightly more elegant back room, one finds earth tone-painted walls and subtle sconces; mellow throughout.

EXTRAS/NOTES	You'll see a lot of geeks, not freaks, here—from MIT students to tech geniuses to pharmaceutical lab technicians to college-educated lovers stopping in for a bite before their film starts. For a great date that doesn't feel cheap, split a pizza, choose a pint for each of you from the excellent ale selection, add conversation, and enjoy.

—Reg Brittain

Emma's

Pizza and a movie have never had it so good.
$$$
40 Hampshire St., Cambridge 02139
(at Cardinal Medeiros Ave.)
Phone (617) 864-8534 • Fax (617) 864-EMMA

CATEGORY	Gourmet Pizza
HOURS	Tues–Fri: 11:30 AM–10 PM
	Sat: 4 PM–10 PM
MASS TRANSIT	T: Red line to Kendall/MIT
PAYMENT	VISA MasterCard AMERICAN EXPRESS
POPULAR FOOD	Pizza, pizza, and more pizza; also a small assortment of salads and Italian *pagnotelle*, warm pressed sandwiches made daily with a variety of fresh, local ingredients
UNIQUE FOOD	The pizza here has an almost paper thin crust and is topped with everything from Italian sausage to dried cranberries and roasted sweet potatoes; lemon fluff dessert
DRINKS	Italian fruit juices, soda, beer, and wine
SEATING	A small counter in the window serves slices; table service for about 40 in the back; come early, especially on weekend nights when the place fills up with pre- and post-movie crowds
AMBIENCE	Funky is the word in this happy mish-mash of a dining room with yard sale tables and chairs, and assorted antique silverware and place settings. The clientele is appropriately diverse: students, neighbors, and Kendall Sq. movie enthusiasts. Weekend evenings are busy, as are weekday lunches when the crowd pulls from the neighborhood tech firms.
EXTRAS/NOTES	Owners Wendy and Dave inherited the name from their old location on Huron Ave. where they took over a longstanding West Cambridge neighborhood institution run by the original Emma and her husband. Although they kept the name, they updated the pizza with a choice of sauces: traditional, rosemary, and olive oil infused with garlic; cheeses: cow, goat, and sheep; and infinite toppings of the gourmet and not-so variety. Soon their custom-made pies became so popular that patrons had to order hours in advance if they wanted pizza for dinner. About three years ago, Emma's moved into its Kendall Sq. location where business is busy as ever.

—Katie Stone

Hungry? MIT:
The Best Food Stops for the
Starving Student

For a university its size, MIT has surprisingly few cheap food options within walking distance of campus. A few spots in nearby Kendall Square cater to the starving student, but the real competition is among the food trucks parked on campus at lunch.

Best Truck: Gooseberry's

Calling it the best truck damns it with faint praise. The Gooseberry's truck is the best food on campus. The curry tofu (don't call it the Viet curry tofu; only rookies do that) is the best bet. *Parked on Massachusetts Ave. during lunch hours.*

Best Falafel: Moshe's Chicken Truck

The falafel is cheap, spicy, tasty, and served by a Jesse Ventura look-alike. *Parked by Sloan during lunch hours.*

Best Sandwich: Rebecca's Café & K2 Café

Rebecca's does great sandwiches but watch out: they're (a) overpriced and (b) your chance of getting exactly what you ordered is only 50%. **K2 Café** does a better job on (b) but even worse on (a). *Rebecca's: 290 Main St., Cambridge 02142, (617) 494-6688. K2 Café: see p. 160. 290 Main St., Cambridge 02142, (617) 583-7000.*

Best Pizza: Emma's

Not much competition here. The excellent paper-thin crust and variety of gourmet toppings make the high prices easier to swallow. *See p. 157. 40 Hampshire St., Cambridge 02139, (617) 864-8534.*

Best Deal: Au Bon Pain

Don't miss the daily "bake sale" (Mon–Fri: 4 PM–6 PM) during which all pastries are half off. *3 Cambridge Ctr., Cambridge 02142, (617) 494-9726.*

Best Place to Bring a Date: The Helmand

Afghan leader Hamid Karzai's brother runs a slightly expensive but delicious Afghan restaurant, a 10-minute walk from campus. *See p. 159. 143 First St., Cambridge 02142, (617) 492-4646.*

Best Coffee: Toscanini's

Any comparison to other nearby coffee shops would be the biggest mismatch since the Bears-Patriots Super Bowl. *84 Massachusetts Ave., Cambridge 02139, (617) 491-1558.*

Most Overrated: Legal Seafood

It speaks to the lack of local dining options that Legal is always as mobbed as it is. The high prices and "authentic" New England experience make it the classic spot to take the 'rents. *5 Cambridge Ctr., Cambridge 02142, (617) 864-3400.*

—*Tyler Doggett*

The Helmand

An ethnic dining delight.

$$$$

143 First St., Cambridge 02142
(at Bent St., near CambridgeSide Galleria)
Phone (617) 492-4646
www.helmandrestaurant.sbweb.switchboard.com

CATEGORY	Afghan
HOURS	Sun–Thurs: 5 PM–10 PM Fri/Sat: 5 PM–11 PM
MASS TRANSIT	T: Green line to Lechmere
PAYMENT	VISA MasterCard AMERICAN EXPRESS
POPULAR FOOD	*Kaddo*, a mouthwatering appetizer of baby pumpkin baked in a garlic yogurt sauce; *chowpan*, half a rack of lamb marinated and grilled, served with eggplant and *pallow* rice; vegetarian diners will find appealing appetizers and entrees aplenty
UNIQUE FOOD	*Dolma*, eggplants stuffed with spinach and baked with cauliflower, peppers, corn, peas, onions, tomatoes, and spices; *mantwo*, pastry shells filled with onions and beef and topped with a beef sauce
DRINKS	Extensive wine list with selections from Italy, Germany, Spain, South America, Portugal, South Africa, America, and France; beer, soft drinks, tea, and coffee
SEATING	Seats 100 people, readily accommodating large and small parties; reservations are essential, and be warned, they are given away after 15 minutes
AMBIENCE	The ambience is a highlight here—with its muted earth tones, open brick oven, and well-placed Afghan art, it charms first-daters as well as groups of old friends
EXTRAS/NOTES	Hamid Karzai, the brother of the owners of The Helmand, was named head of Afghanistan's post-Taliban provisional government in 2002. Their father, Abdul Ahad Karzai, served in the Afghan Legislature in the early 1970s and was killed by a Taliban assassin three years ago.
OTHER ONES	• The Karzai family also has restaurants by the same name in Baltimore and San Francisco.

—Sarah Duggan & Stephanie Carlin

"I'm at the age when food
has taken the place of sex in my life.
In fact I've just had a mirror put
over my kitchen table."

—Rodney Dangerfield

K2 Café

*K2 belongs in the 2K—a cafe for
the new millennium.*

$

290 Main St., Cambridge 02142

(at Carleton St.)

Phone (617) 583-7000

CATEGORY	Café
HOURS	Mon–Thurs: 10 AM–7 PM Fri: 10 AM–6 PM
MASS TRANSIT	T: Red line to Kendall/MIT
PAYMENT	VISA MasterCard AMERICAN EXPRESS
POPULAR FOOD	Specialty sandwiches (London broil hoagie, ham and asparagus with brie) and wraps (grilled summer veggie, pulled beef); specialty pizzas (with names like Heaven or Hell and Uncle Vinny); amazing, fully loaded, and well-labeled salad bar; home-baked desserts and soups
UNIQUE FOOD	BBQ chipotle chicken wrap; smoked turkey and apple sandwich; jalapeño corn muffins
DRINKS	Sodas, juices, sparkling waters, full coffee bar, wide array of fresh fruit smoothies
SEATING	A large, high-ceilinged room facing large windows contains a number of tables, booths, bright vinyl couches, and bar stools
AMBIENCE	A funky, modern interior, with upbeat music and speedy, friendly service; decorated with industrial-looking exposed pipes, slabs of aluminum siding, and bright orange, blue, and yellow walls and couches; MIT students and urban professionals crowd the place during weekday lunch hours
EXTRAS/NOTES	Because it is raised above street level, the K2 Café's modest sign and inconspicuous door conceal one of Cambridge's best-kept secrets: a hip, bustling café with gourmet-caliber food.

—Meaghan Mulholland

Legal Sea Foods

(see p. 27)
Seafood/Chowder
5 Cambridge Ctr., Cambridge 02141
Phone (617) 864-3400

Toscanini's

(see p. 131)
Ice Cream Shop
84 Massachusetts Ave., Cambridge 02139
Phone (617) 491-1558

CENTRAL SQUARE

The Asgard

(see The Kinsale, p. 6)
Irish Pub
350 Massachusetts Ave., Cambridge 02139
Phone (617) 577-9100

Bertucci's

(see p. 175)
Gourmet Pizza
799 Main St., Cambridge 02139
Phone (617) 661-8356

Carberry's

(see p. 214)
Bakery/Café
79 Prospect St., Cambridge 02139
Phone (617) 576-3530

Izzy's

Homestyle Puerto Rican flavor.
$$
169 Harvard St., Cambridge 02139
(at Windsor St.)
Phone (617) 661-3910

CATEGORY	Puerto Rican
HOURS	Mon–Fri: 10 AM–8:30 PM
	Sat: 10 AM–8 PM
MASS TRANSIT	T: Red line to Central
PAYMENT	Cash only
POPULAR FOOD	Huge combo plates with pepper steak, pork chops, or crispy chicken legs and white or yellow rice, beans, and salad; daily specials include roast pork with pigeon peas, steak in sauce, and stewed beef; chicken soup; steak bombs; plantains (sweet or fried with garlic)
UNIQUE FOOD	Stewed goat; oxtail; tripe stew; cassava and garlic; fish cakes; Jamaican beef patties; beef turnovers
DRINKS	Ginger beer; Caribbean cola; Goya juices
SEATING	Seats 15 to 20, but most orders are for takeout
AMBIENCE	Order at the counter and they'll bring the food to your table; Latin music; Puerto Rican flags and pictures of Latino sports stars decorate the place

—Carol Alves & Kaya Stone

Mama Gaia's

*Everybody wins at
this community-centric
café extraordinaire.*

$$

401 Massachusetts Ave., Cambridge 02139

(at Columbia St. and Main St.)

Phone (617) 441-3999

www.mamagaiascafe.com

CATEGORY	Café
HOURS	Mon–Wed: 8 AM–midnight
	Thurs–Sat: 8 AM–1 AM
	Sun: 9 AM–midnight
MASS TRANSIT	T: Red line to Central
PAYMENT	*VISA* MasterCard AMERICAN EXPRESS
POPULAR FOOD	The perfect place to bring together friends of all food-peculiarity stripes. You can eat a chicken sandwich next to your vegan friend chomping on the tempeh wrap with soy cheese. The burritos, tacos, and quesadillas are all excellent; the rest of the menu is mostly hearty sandwiches (baked tofu, spicy portobello, Peruvian chicken) and extraordinary salads—all under $6.
UNIQUE FOOD	On weekends the place goes all out, bringing out their special Mexican brunch and other dishes that are dormant during the work week, from a bagel with lox to a breakfast burrito (wheat tortilla packed with black beans, avocado, pico de gallo, and scrambled eggs).
DRINKS	Homemade Mexican *aguas frescas*, bottled juices, smoothies, coffee, and espresso drinks
SEATING	About 15 small tables (two to three chairs each) that can be arranged to accommodate groups; plus, a great bar with stools along the window, perfect for single diners
AMBIENCE	Like the name suggests, (Mama Gaia = Mother Earth), the "crunchiness" factor is high; while not a traditional first date place, it is a good second or 100th date place with a great atmosphere for conversation
EXTRAS/NOTES	The café was opened with the intention of becoming a place where the community could come together (they've hosted Ralph Nader and went all out for a Cinco de Mayo celebration). With a staff that makes you feel like a regular instantly, free Internet access, improv comedy on Fridays, and live music, the community-centric mindset becomes apparent. The outside wall on Columbia St. was made available to the community after 9/11 to depict their reaction to the tragedy. Mama Gaia's also chooses products that embrace responsible business practices.

—Jodi Hullinger

Mary Chung

A cold-cash stash of great Chinese.

$$

464 Massachusetts Ave., Cambridge 02139

(at Brookline St.)

Phone (617) 864-1991 • Fax (617) 864-1661

CATEGORY	Chinese
HOURS	Mon, Wed/Thurs: 11:30 AM–10 PM Fri–Sun: 11:30 AM–11 PM
MASS TRANSIT	T: Red line to Central
PAYMENT	Cash only
POPULAR DISHES	Yu-hsiang eggplant; sweet sesame lemon chicken; $5 lunch specials
UNIQUE FOOD	Their well-loved Dun Dun spicy sauce, hot and sweet, can be had with noodles, bean curd, sprouts, or shredded chicken
DRINKS	Beer, wine, sake
SEATING	About 75
AMBIENCE	Extremely bland atmosphere; filled with MIT students and faculty
EXTRAS/NOTES	On Sundays sample their full dim sum menu from 11:30 AM–3 PM; try some pig feet with soup noodles or for those less courageous, more pedestrian items like steamed pork buns and scallion pie.

—Paula Foye

Miracle of Science

Geeky, but good.

$$

321 Massachusetts Ave., Cambridge 02139

(near Main St.)

Phone (617) 868-2866

CATEGORY	Bar & Grill
HOURS	Daily: 11:30 AM–1 AM
MASS TRANSIT	T: Red line to Central
PAYMENT	VISA MasterCard AMERICAN EXPRESS DISCOVER
POPULAR DISHES	Huge burgers; spicy turkey chipotle chili
UNIQUE DISHES	Grilled shrimp skewers with pineapple salsa
DRINKS	A good selection of beers, bottled and on tap; drinks served in lab beakers
SEATING	During the school year, this place gets packed with MIT grads, undergrads, and professors
AMBIENCE	Décor matches the techy clientele: a photo of Einstein, a machinery-decorated bar

—Kyle Konrad

"Cheese—milk's leap toward immortality."
—Clifton Fadiman (Any Number Can Play)

Moody's Falafel

First-rate, quick-stop falafel, plain and simple.

$

25 Central Sq., Cambridge 02139
(near the corner of Massachsetts Ave. and River St.)
Phone (617) 864-0827

CATEGORY	Middle Eastern
HOURS	Daily: 11 AM–midnight
MASS TRANSIT	T: Red line to Central
PAYMENT	Cash only
POPULAR FOOD	Cheap, excellent falafel, crispy on the outside and soft inside topped with tahini sauce
UNIQUE FOOD	The most you'll spend here is $6 and that'll get you a combo plate with *everything* on the menu
SEATING	Four counter stools and two tables
AMBIENCE	Not much bigger than a walk-in closet, most folks take their falafel to go

—Kyle Konrad

Picante Mexican Grill

(see p. 220)
Mexican
735 Massachusetts Ave., Cambridge 02139
Phone (617) 576-6394

Rangzen Tibetan Restaurant

Homestyle Tibetan cuisine in the heart of Cambridge.

$$

24 Pearl St., Cambridge 02139
(at Green St.)
Phone (617) 354-8881 • Fax (617) 354-8882

CATEGORY	Tibetan
HOURS	Mon–Sat: 11:45 AM–2:45 PM, 5 PM–10 PM
MASS TRANSIT	T: Red line to Central
PAYMENT	VISA MasterCard AMERICAN EXPRESS DISCOVER
POPULAR FOOD	Tibetan food focused on seasonal ingredients, simply prepared and carefully spiced. The excellent weekday luncheon buffet features a large rotating selection of both vegetarian and meat-based dishes (at least nine entrees, plus appetizers, sides, pickles, and salads). Start with basmati rice and some of the breads—look especially for the *shogo phaley* (a pancake-like potato and ginger bread), fat spears of asparagus (perfectly steamed and lightly seasoned—simple and delicious), and thin slices of eggplant fried in a savory but light chickpea batter. The meat dishes are

equally tasty, especially the sweet-salty chicken stir-fry with mushrooms, and the thin-sliced beef with ginger, garlic, onion, and tomato. Finish the plate with some pickles and salads, and don't forget to come back for ripe chunks of melon and other seasonal fruits for dessert.

UNIQUE FOOD	Steamed doughy Tibetan flour buns (*tingmo*); *tsel numtak* (string beans and scallions in chickpea batter)
DRINKS	Beer, wine, full bar, soft drinks, free tea
SEATING	Seats 37 at tables for two, four, and one larger round table
AMBIENCE	The interior feels like a calm retreat from the city, with Tibetan music in the background and the requisite picture of the Dalai Lama gazing down upon the comfortable and attractive dining room. The friendly staff keeps the buffet well replenished, and happily answers any and all questions about the more unfamiliar dishes.

—*Michael Beckett*

Rhythm and Spice

*The "total Caribbean experience"
just outside of Central Square.*

$$$$

315 Massachusetts Ave., Cambridge 02139

(between Blanche St. and Village St.)

Phone (617) 497-0977

www.rspice.com

CATEGORY	Caribbean
HOURS	Sun: 2 PM–9:30 PM Mon–Wed: 5 PM–9:30 PM Thurs: 5 PM–10 PM Fri: 5 PM–11 PM Sat: 4 PM–11 PM (Appetizers/sides/roti until 1:30 AM on Fri/Sat)
MASS TRANSIT	T: Red line to Central
PAYMENT	VISA MasterCard AMERICAN EXPRESS
POPULAR FOOD	Roti; boneless jerk pork; Bahamian conch fritters; roasted eggplant
UNIQUE FOOD	Fried plantain; stewed oxtail (Thurs–Sun); *ackee* and saltfish (Sunday only)
DRINKS	Beer; liquor; soft drinks (including ginger beer and other Caribbean special sodas); Caribbean fruit juices; great mixed drinks like the Natty Dread and the Mellow Mood
SEATING	There is a small bar in the front of the restaurant and a dining room with good-sized, close-set tables that seat around 40.
AMBIENCE	Flags from Caribbean nations decorate the high walls, but aside from that the furniture and décor are plain. Show nights are the busiest (see below). The service, like the pace of life in the Caribbean is a little slower than most Americans are used to, but that's part of the experience, *mon*.

EXTRAS/NOTES	Thursday night DJs spin hip-hop, R&B, and dancehall (21+, $10) until 1 or 2 AM. On Friday and Saturday, there's live reggae, calypso, or soca (check web site for listings) and on Sunday night there is soca music from 10:30 PM to 1 AM (21+, $5).

—*Matthew Isles*

River Gods

A promising new bar with live DJs and a creative menu.

$$

125 River St., Cambridge 02139
(at Kinnaird St.)
Phone (617) 576-1881

CATEGORY	Irish Pub
HOURS	Daily: 3 PM–1 AM
MASS TRANSIT	T: Red line to Central
PAYMENT	VISA MasterCard AMERICAN EXPRESS
POPULAR FOOD	The starters are the real attraction: clever, reasonably priced, deftly executed; a sampling of the appetizers and a few drinks will make as satisfying a meal as the entrees
UNIQUE FOOD	Sausage and beans; Thai curry; bruschetta
DRINKS	Full bar
SEATING	There's a bar, and then several large, low tables; it's likely you'll end up sharing one of these with complete strangers, but even on a Saturday night, it rarely feels cramped
AMBIENCE	Somewhat Gothic, without the geekiness that this implies. The owner calls it "new Irish," but it's open to interpretation. There are church pews, mismatched chairs, and an old desk. The room is dim, and the lights are a study in form over function. A DJ booth perches over one corner of the bar, and there is a regular rotation of local jockeys, spinning a variety of genres.

—*James Haynes*

Toscanini's

(see p. 131)
Ice Cream Shop
899 Main St., Cambridge 02139
Phone (617) 491-5877

INMAN SQUARE

B Side Lounge

(see p. 168)
Gourmet Comfort Food
92 Hampshire St., Cambridge 02139
Phone (617) 354-0766

Café China

A cut above the usual Chinese,
with a European twist.
$$$$
1245 Cambridge St., Cambridge 02139
(at Prospect St.)
Phone (617) 868-4300
www.cafechina.com

CATEGORY	Chinese
HOURS	Tues–Thurs: noon–9:45 PM
	Fri/Sat: noon–10:15 PM
	Sun: noon–9:30 PM
MASS TRANSIT	Bus: #69, 83, or 91
PAYMENT	VISA MasterCard
POPULAR FOOD	The standard General Tso's Chicken and beef with broccoli but prepared with unusual lightness and flavor; lo mein is steamed and thus not so oily; several interesting variations of the Chinese, including warm marinated duck salad and spicy ginger-cilantro chicken
UNIQUE FOOD	While most dishes are wholly Asian, the European influence of the half-Swiss ownership comes through in the preparation (and description) of dishes— where else would you find bean sprouts "quickly blanched" or dumplings "wrapped in a light pasta"? this Continental *je ne sais quoi* also shows in desserts, like Swiss chocolate torte and mocha cognac truffles; even the fortune cookies are chocolate-flavored
DRINKS	Italian-style coffee; American, European, and Asian beers; a short list of affordable aperitifs and wines
SEATING	An intimate dining room with tables for two and four; seats about 35
AMBIENCE	Walls colored a bold shade of salmon and lined with work from local artists

—*Esti Iturralde*

Central Bakery

(see p. 111)
Bakery
732 Cambridge St., Cambridge 02141
Phone (617) 547-2237

Lowering the Bar on Fine Dining

A limited pocketbook combined with a reliance on public transportation has made me narrow my choices when eating out in Boston. Nevertheless, I have found a way to lower the bar on fine dining. Rather than fighting for an elusive reservation at one of the city's fine restaurants, I often grab a seat at their bar, where dining is not only welcomed but encouraged—many otherwise unaffordable restaurants have special bar menus with reasonably priced selections. While the search for great cheap eats is always a worthy undertaking, it's natural to occasionally pamper yourself. Give this strategy a try at the following fine restaurants.

Chez Henri

Located on a quiet street just off Mass. Ave. in Cambridge, this French-Cuban restaurant caters to a mixed crowd of academics from nearby Harvard, MIT, and Tufts, along with urban hipsters, hungry travelers, and food cognoscenti. The barroom is relatively small with a few tables and stools at the counter, all open for dining, and all on a "first come, first served" basis. The lighting is just low enough to make everyone look good and the mixologists are amiable and seasoned, but the real attraction is the food, and at the top of the list is the Cuban sandwich. Chef Paul O'Connell's Cuban sandwich is no small thing—pulled pork, ham, gruyere cheese, chopped pickles, and dijon mustard—served on grilled bread with a salad of mixed baby greens, fresh plantain chips, and salsa. There is also a vegetarian version. At around $11 this sandwich is an embarrassment of riches. *Porter Square: 1 Shepard St., Cambridge 02138, (617) 354-8980.*

B Side Lounge

On the outside this establishment looks like a neighborhood bar, or perhaps a bowling alley, but the inside is another story. Retro with rock 'n' roll swagger may be the best way to describe it. Hard-boiled eggs and Tabasco sauce are ever-present at the bar, not to mention gratis. Chef Tomás García has put together a fine menu—a mixture of updated comfort foods and modern dishes. Some favorites, all under $10, include the arugula salad with pears, bleu cheese, toasted pecans, and cider vinaigrette, a roasted beet plate with goat cheese, curried raisins, and crostini, and the meatball grinder with espagnole sauce, melted provolone, mashed potatoes, and hot peppers. *Inman Square: 92 Hampshire St., Cambridge 02139, (617) 354-0766.*

Franklin Café

Ask anyone who works in the local food service business, "Where do you go out to eat in Boston?" and invariably the answer will be the

Franklin Café. It is small and dark, the kitchen is open until 1 AM, and it is very cool. Everything on the appetizer menu goes for $8 or less—the portions are sizable and served with fresh bread and hummus. Chef David DuBois offers choices such as PEI mussels with pernod, scallions, and garlic, eggplant and tomato salad with fresh mozzarella, mini lamb osso buco, duck quesadilla, and crisp batter-fried calamari. *South End: 278 Shawmut Ave., Boston 02118, (617) 350-0010.*

—*R. B. Michael Oliver*

Christina's Homemade Ice Cream

(see p. 132)
Ice Cream Shop
1255 Cambridge St., Cambridge 02139
Phone (617) 492-7021

Court House Seafood

So cheap, it's just not Legal (Seafood, that is).
Since 1912
$$$
498 Cambridge St., Cambridge 02141
(at Sixth St.)
Phone (617) 491-1213 • Fax (617) 661-6380
www.courthouseseafood.com

CATEGORY	Historic/Seafood
HOURS	Mon: 11 AM–3 PM
	Tues–Thurs: 11 AM–7 PM
	Fri: 11 AM–8 PM
	Sat: 11 AM–6 PM
MASS TRANSIT	Bus: #69
PAYMENT	VISA MasterCard
POPULAR FOOD	No frills seafood; fried clams, haddock, smelt, mackeral, and more; homemade fish cakes; linguica
UNIQUE FOOD	Every Thursday, fresh sardines and stickleback is flown in directly from Portugal; if you don't see the fish you want on the menu, find something in their adjoining fish market and they'll cook it up for you
DRINKS	Sodas and juices
SEATING	Less than ten small tables; no table service
AMBIENCE	Order at the counter and wait for your name to be called; at lunchtime, the neighborhood's lawyers and clerks crowd the place

—*Laura Stone*

Mr. Pie

A shockingly cheap shoebox-sized Middle Eastern joint.

$$

645 Cambridge St., Cambridge 02141
(at Lambert St.)
Phone (617) 661-4555

CATEGORY	Middle Eastern
HOURS	Daily 10 AM–10 PM
MASS TRANSIT	Bus: #69
PAYMENT	VISA MasterCard
POPULAR FOOD	The excellent tahini sauce graces a number of sandwiches, including their fluffy falafel and zesty *baba ganoush*; meat and chicken kebabs and $1 pizza slices also forge a loyal clientele; great deals on meals, including free soups with purchase of a meal and drink
UNIQUE FOOD	Surely Mr. Pie should serve dishes to justify its name, and it does—cheese, meat, spinach, and *zaatar* (a mix of spices in a lemony sauce) pies, served on fresh-baked pita
DRINKS	Soft drinks, juice, and fruit cocktails
SEATING	Three small tables, and six counter seats
AMBIENCE	An easy-to-overlook, tiny corner restaurant frequented by grad students and neighborhood residents; a steady, trickling traffic of eat-in and carry-out eaters churns through from noon–1 PM.

—Alex Speier

O Cantinho

*Adorable, family-run spot
for Portuguese home-cooking.*

$$

1128 Cambridge St., Cambridge 02139
(between Norfolk St. and Elm St.)
Phone (617) 354-3443 • Fax (617) 354-2877
www.atasca.com

CATEGORY	Portuguese
HOURS	Mon–Thurs: 11 AM–10 PM Fri/Sat: 11 AM–11 PM Sun: 10 AM–10 PM
MASS TRANSIT	Bus: #69
PAYMENT	Cash only
POPULAR FOOD	The way real Europeans eat and the way we should: a plate of salad with tuna, sardines, or soft cod cakes; simple sandwiches of cured ham and sharp cheeses; a pork loin sautéed in white wine and garlic with rice; crispy, fried potatoes sliced thin, and soft, gently toasted bread.

UNIQUE FOOD	Come here for the Portuguese-style snack, or *petisco*: little dishes of linguiça, a typical sausage grilled; white cheese with sliced tomatoes in a vinaigrette; stewed octopus or chicken giblets; and, on the side, get an order of the typical black-eyed pea salad.
DRINKS	Hot and iced coffees; beer and wine
SEATING	A small room seats no more than 20
AMBIENCE	Lunchtime beckons a loyal East Cambridge Portuguese-speaking clientele with kids in tow; pretty painted plates adorn the wall, and other accents like a pot full of wine corks exude charm; cute, and so clean you will want to eat your lunch off the shiny wooden floors
EXTRAS/NOTES	Come here for an afternoon glass of white wine with your fish; then go home and take a nap, Iberian-style.
OTHER ONES	O Cantinho is the cafe counterpart to the more expensive Atasca, with two locations:

- East Cambridge: 279A Broadway, Cambridge 02139, (617) 354-4355
- Kendall Square: 50 Hampshire St., Cambridge 02139, (617) 621-6991

—Esti Iturralde

Punjabi Dhaba

Incredibly affordable and authentic Indian "roadside truck stop" in Inman.

$$

225 Hampshire St., Cambridge 02139
(at Cambridge St.)
Phone (617) 547-8272

CATEGORY	Northern Indian
HOURS	Daily: noon–11:30 PM
MASS TRANSIT	Bus: #69, 83, or 91
PAYMENT	Cash only
POPULAR FOOD	The thick, spicy curries are the real deal, delicious, and filling, but not for the faint of heart. Don't expect the watered-down *tikka masalas* found at most Indian restaurants in the U.S. (even the *saag paneer* here has a bit of a kick). There's an extensive vegetarian menu, less spicy *tandoori* offerings, and huge combos fit for a Maharajah or a light meal for two ($8-10, includes main dish, bread, rice, samosa, chutney, and yogurty *raita*).
UNIQUE FOOD	One of the few places in the area that serves *chaat*, yogurt- or curry-based streetside snacks popular in India; they're small in size but not in flavor.
DRINKS	Canned soft drinks and juices, various flavors of chai, *lassis* (including a salt version)

SEATING	Small and ambience-less; perfect for takeout; 15 booth seats downstairs and 25 seats almost hidden upstairs
AMBIENCE	As one of the few late-night dining options in the area, the Dhaba is busiest at night, and also on weekends, but there's rarely more than a 15-minute wait for your food. In keeping with its attempt to recreate the sights, sounds, and tastes of a traditional *dhaba* (Indian roadside truck stop), the restaurant offers its mostly local clientele no-frills, self-service dining, with the kitchen in full view (and smell) and lots of tacky posters, Hindi music, and the occasional Bollywood film. Luckily, it more than adequately makes up in taste what it lacks in tasteless décor.
EXTRAS/NOTES	Indian restaurants are a rupee a dozen in Cambridge, but this local favorite stands a head above the rest with its incredibly cheap, hearty curries, and traditional specialties.

—Ankur Ghosh

Rosie's Bakery

(see p. 111)
Bakery
243 Hampshire St., Cambridge 02138
Phone (617) 491-9488

Royal Pastry Shop

(see p. 111)
Italian Bakery
738 Cambridge St., Cambridge 02141
Phone (617) 547-2053

Ryle's

*This joint's not just
for jazz junkies.*
$$
212 Hampshire St., Cambridge 02139
(at Inman St.)
Phone (617) 876-9330
www.rylesjazz.com

CATEGORY	Bar & Grill
HOURS	Tues–Thurs: 7:30 PM–1 AM Fri/Sat: 7:30 PM–2 AM Sun: 10 AM–3 PM
MASS TRANSIT	Bus: #69, 83, or 91
PAYMENT	VISA MasterCard AMERICAN EXPRESS DISCOVER
POPULAR DISHES	Owned by the S&S Deli across the street, Ryle's Sunday jazz brunch features the great omelettes and other brunch goodies that have made S&S a Cambridge institution; special sweet and spicy wings; gourmet individual pizzas; burgers and salads
DRINKS	Full bar and a good selection of beer and wine
SEATING	Approximately 50 seats downstairs and another 50 upstairs

EXTRAS/NOTES   In the mood to feel a groove with your grub, wine and dine with some rhythm, swing to some soul, or get your sashay sassing? Check out the always auspicious Ryle's line-up. A moderate cover charge of $7-10 will get you in the door (sometimes more for big head-liners).Upstairs at Ryle's offers dance parties three nights a week: salsa and merengue on Thursdays with a dance lesson at 8:30 PM for $10; Brazilian dance parties start at 9 PM on Fridays; and a mix of Latin, swing, and tango on Saturday starts at 9 PM ($10).

—Paula Foye

S&S
Restaurant

This comfy, "kosher-style"
brunch spot is a Cambridge institution.
Since 1919

$$

1334 Cambridge St., Cambridge 02139
(at Hampshire St.)
Phone (617) 354-0777 • Fax (617) 354-6924
www.sandsrestaurant.com

CATEGORY   Deli

HOURS   Mon–Wed: 7 AM–11 PM
Thurs–Fri: 7 AM–midnight
Sat: 8 AM–midnight
Sun: 8 AM–10 PM

MASS TRANSIT   Bus: #69, 83, or 91

PAYMENT   VISA   MasterCard   AMERICAN EXPRESS

POPULAR FOOD   As the lines out the door attest, weekend brunch at S&S is a Cambridge favorite, and despite the fair quality (and massive quantity) of their regular menu, it's breakfast food they do best. Luckily, S&S serves breakfast all day, every day (the official "brunch" served Sat/Sun 7 AM–4 PM has only a few extra dishes). Whether it's noon or midnight, you can't beat the tasty omelettes, thick pancakes, French toast, and fluffy quiche lorraine. Their reubens are made with homemade corned beef, sauerkraut, Swiss cheese, and dressing.

UNIQUE FOOD   The menu is overwhelming: aside from the legendary breakfast staples, there's an end-less array of meat and seafood entrees, salads, soups, burgers, deli sandwiches, gourmet pizzas, and "kosher-style" favorites (not ac-tually cooked kosher, but decidedly old-school deli-style), like knishes and delicious, if slightly overpriced, blintzes. The oft-forgotten desserts (cakes, pies, and cheesecakes) are all deca-dent and delicious, and perfect for sharing.

DRINKS   Full bar, various wines and bottled beers, a few frozen cocktails, and even champagne by the bottle; but nothing goes better with S&S's diner-style food than the bottomless cup of coffee; skip the miniscule and pricey OJ ($2.50) and the too-sweet, brunch-only spe-cialty drinks like bellinis and bloody marys

SEATING Despite S&S's seemingly endless rooms of booths and tables, there's always a wait (of about 15 minutes) for weekend brunch—after all, S&S is the best place in Cambridge to nurse a Sunday morning hangover. The deli tables at the front of the store (serving ready-made food from the takeout deli) are great if you're in a rush.

AMBIENCE A great place to come in to from the cold: cozy booths and tables are the perfect match for the genial, welcoming waitresses and the comfort food on the menu. The deli area in the front of the restaurant will put you in a New York state of mind in no time.

EXTRAS/NOTES The name comes from the Yiddish "ess and ess" ("eat and eat") that original owner Ma Edelstein used to greet all her customers. That was over 80 years ago, but this homey restaurant still serves tasty, heart-warming food (most of it at a reasonable price) just like Ma used to make.

—Ankur Ghosh

HARVARD SQUARE

Algiers

An exotic coffeehouse—not as ancient as the Kasbah, but still an institution.

$$

40 Brattle St., Cambridge 02138
(at Story St.)
Phone (617) 492-1557 • Fax (617) 868-4953

CATEGORY Middle Eastern

HOURS Daily: 8 AM–midnight

MASS TRANSIT T: Red line to Harvard

PAYMENT VISA MasterCard AMERICAN EXPRESS

POPULAR FOOD Middle Eastern favorites like hummus, *baba ganoush*, and tabouli; falafel grilled to perfection and served with a side of spicy onions

UNIQUE FOOD A variety of local North African dishes including barbecued Chicken Ajami and tasty *merguesa* (lamb sausage) served with a side of hummus and salad; *besbousa*, a nougat filled semolina pastry

DRINKS As the name suggests, Algiers is known for its unique coffee blends, including the restaurant's namesake, the Algiers Special Mint Coffee. The not-so-faint-of-heart should try the strong, but intensely flavorful Arabic coffee, served by the pot in a beautiful copper vessel. Algiers also offers a wide variety of exotic teas, including the fine spearmint and *karkadale* (hibiscus flower) teas. To cool off during hot summer days, try a strawberry frappe or the iced chocolate; in winter, there's hot orange mint chocolate or hot cider with cinnamon. Italian sodas, from *orzata* (almond) to *tamarindo* (tamarind) also punctuate the menu.

SEATING　Forty tables spread across its two levels, seating about 95 people; the upstairs is a smoking area, killer for the (wannabe) literary crowd; non-smokers find a friendly haven downstairs; plans are in the works to create an elegant rooftop dining terrace that would seat about 20

AMBIENCE　This is a place to kick back, sip coffee from huge mugs, and read your favorite book. The staff doesn't really care how long you stay, as long as you don't create a ruckus. The crowd is very international, ranging from young professionals living in the area to students studying for their next exam. Downstairs, the warm terracotta-painted walls are warm and inviting, serving as the perfect accent to the bejeweled mirrors and antiques of yore; upstairs, the hand-carved tiered hexagonal ceiling opens up the dining area and lifts one's spirits. A mix of classical and Arabic music fills the air and transports you to a bygone era—the only thing missing is a magic carpet ride.

EXTRAS/NOTES　Owner Emil opened the Algiers in 1971, co-locating the coffeehouse with Casablanca, an upscale Moroccan restaurant located in the basement. Since its move up to the street level, the restaurant has grown in popularity for its laid-back atmosphere and no-frills international coffee. Canned goods are forever banished from the Algiers kitchen while homemade yogurt finds its way into the pantry each day.

—Priti Chinai

Bertucci's
Pizza, pasta, and oh the rolls.
$$
21 Brattle St., Cambridge 02138
(off Massachusetts Ave.)
Phone (617) 864-4748 • Fax (617) 864-5823
www.bertuccis.com

CATEGORY　Gourmet Pizza
HOURS　Sun–Thurs: 11 AM–10 PM
　　　　　Fri/Sat: 10 AM–11 PM
MASS TRANSIT　T: Red line to Harvard
PAYMENT　VISA　MasterCard　AMERICAN EXPRESS
POPULAR FOOD　A special take on typical pizza and pasta dishes. The Carmine pizza combines fresh mozzarella with caramelized onions. Satisfying salads make good use of baby field greens, plum tomatoes, grilled chicken, and homemade bread sticks. Make-your-own toppings include roasted vegetables, pesto sauce, and portobello mushrooms. Lunch is the best deal, with unlimited salad, rolls, and choice of pizza, pasta, or panini sandwich.

UNIQUE FOOD Lobster ravioli, with a sauce made of diced plum tomatoes, scallions, and a saffron orange cream

DRINKS Beer, wine, soda, tea, coffee, and juice

SEATING Mix of booths and tables seats 82; a handful of tables outside exposes you to free entertainment from street musicians and clowns

AMBIENCE A rustic-looking chain, Bertucci's displays large black-and-white pictures of old Italian families next to wine bottles and old wooden buckets and tools. The clientele consists of everybody in the area, not just Harvard kids, and it shows in the line of people outside. Very kid-friendly, Bertucci's will give young 'uns real dough to shape and then bake it for them.

EXTRAS/NOTES The original 20-seat Bertucci's—with a bocce court in back—was opened on Elm St. in Somerville. Back in 1982, Joey Crugnale, then owner of Steve's Ice Cream next door, bought the space with the idea of installing a restaurant that would complement his booming ice cream shop. Bertucci's succeeded in its own right, launching dozens of locations across New England. But much has changed. Bertucci's went public in 1991, and Joey lost all say after a large restaurant company bought the chain in 1998. The Elm St. location closed for good in July 2002.

OTHER ONES
- Faneuil Hall Marketplace: 22 Merchants Row, Boston 02109, (617) 227-7889
- Copley Sq./Back Bay: 43 Stanhope St., Boston 02116, (617) 247-6161
- Brookline Village: 4 Brookline Pl., Brookline 02215, (617) 731-2300
- Alewife: 5 Cambridge Park Dr., Cambridge 02140, (617) 876-2200
- Central Square: 799 Main St., Cambridge 02139, (617) 661-8356
- Seventy other locations on the East Coast.

—*Dara Olmsted*

"Sharing food with another human being is an intimate act that should not be indulged in lightly."

—*M.F.K. Fisher*

Border Café

Noisy, lively, and soaked in tequila.
$$$
32 Church St., Cambridge 02138
(between Brattle St. and Church St.)
Phone (617) 864-6100

CATEGORY	Tex-Mex and Cajun
HOURS	Mon–Thurs: 11 AM–11 PM Fri/Sat: 11 AM–midnight Sun: noon–11 PM
MASS TRANSIT	T: Red line to Harvard
PAYMENT	VISA MasterCard AMERICAN EXPRESS DISCOVER
POPULAR FOOD	Great appetizers including *chile queso* (green peppers in melted cheese); the usual enchiladas, tacos, burritos
UNIQUE FOOD	Jambalaya; blackened tuna; Cajun shrimp coated with coconut, fried, and served wth a marmalade sauce
DRINKS	Full bar with great margaritas and many Mexican beers (Dos Equis, Negra Modelo)
SEATING	Two floors that seat many people; still, oddly, there is always a wait
AMBIENCE	Very loud and very young; always filled with local students drinking and crowded in among the kitschy Mexican décor; one of the best places in the Square to spend an evening just sipping margaritas and catching up with friends.
EXTRAS/NOTES	Be prepared to wait a long time for a table (usually 45 minutes to one hour for dinner). While the food is not quite worth that long of a wait, the atmosphere and the drinks are.

—*Christopher Russell*

R.I.P.
The Blue Parrot

This small café in the Brattle Theater was born in the 1950s when the movie house started screening Humphrey Bogart films during a Harvard exam period—a step that was met with cult-like success. The Blue Parrot was named for the café rival of Rick's, the club run by Bogart's character in *Casablanca*. The nearby Casablanca Restaurant, which still survives, also opened as part of this '50s Brattle Square Bogart craze.

The Blue Parrot displayed *Casablanca*-themed paraphernalia, and the food wasn't bad, but the quality that truly marked the eatery was the way it fostered intense discussions. Something about the environment encouraged diners to put their feelings right out on the table. Inevitably there would be at least two couples breaking up in a given evening. One did not go to the Blue Parrot to have fun or an enjoyable meal. One always went to "work things out."

—*Sandy Ruben*

Café India

A taste of India in an intimate and ornate setting.

$$$

52A Brattle St., Cambridge 02138
(at Farwell Pl.)
Phone (617) 661-0683 • Fax (617) 661-5922

CATEGORY	Indian
HOURS	Sun–Thurs: 7:30 AM–11 PM
	Fri/Sat: 7:30 AM–midnight
MASS TRANSIT	T: Red line to Harvard
PAYMENT	VISA MasterCard AMERICAN EXPRESS
POPULAR FOOD	The $8 lunch buffet is the biggest draw, usually including various vegetarian options, a chicken entree, a pork or lamb dish, basmati rice, choice of plain or garlic *naan*, onion or tamarind chutney, *raita* (yogurt) sauce, soup, vegetable samosas (savory stuffed turnovers), and *kheer* (rice, milk, and raisin dessert). The vegetable masala and the mutter mushroom (green peas with mushrooms, herbs, and spices) are excellent.
UNIQUE FOOD	*Nariyal* (creamy shredded coconut milk soup) with nuts and flavored with Indian cardamom; *bhindi masala kadahi* (fresh okra cooked with onions, ginger, tomatoes, and Indian spices) served in a miniature wok; special biryani (basmati rice with shrimp, fish, chicken, lamb, beef, paneer cheese, vegetables, almonds, cashews, raisins, and garnished with fresh coriander)
DRINKS	Full bar, assortment of cocktails, yogurt *lassis*, tea, coffee, espresso, cappuccino
SEATING	One large room with a fair number of tables, some by the windows in an area that opens to the street in the summer; also, booths and a small bar
AMBIENCE	Café India is smaller and more intimate than its Harvard Square competition, but peppier and a bit more casual, with hip, upbeat Indian music, cool ornate plated chairs, and tapestries of elephants and Hindu gods.
EXTRAS/NOTES	The food is by no means amazing, but it is satisfying and a hearty, quality meal for a low price. The service is extremely attentive, and though the restaurant is busy there is hardly ever a wait at lunchtime.

—*Meaghan Mulholland*

Café Pamplona

*An underground
hole in the ground with
a lot of history.
Since 1956*

$$

12 Bow St., Cambridge 02138
(near Quincy St.)
No phone

CATEGORY	Café
HOURS	Daily: 11 AM–midnight
MASS TRANSIT	T: Red line to Harvard
PAYMENT	Cash only
POPULAR FOOD	The daily special is the way to go for lunch; over the years three international chefs have contributed their personal recipes to Pamplona's recipe book, and there's always a unique surprise
UNIQUE FOOD	Fantastic fruit tarts and other desserts
DRINKS	A range of strong coffee, tea, frappes, and Italian sodas
SEATING	This basement restaurant has a cozy interior, with small tables slightly cramped together under a low ceiling; the umbrella-tabled patio is nice in the summer, where you can stretch out and hang with coffee and friends far into the night
AMBIENCE	Most visitors to Café Pamplona pop by during lunch hours to take advantage of the specials on the menu; however, Harvard students abound at all hours, huddled in intense conversations in the corners of the restaurant. Back before smoking was banned, Pamplona was the place to go for a double whammy caffeine-and-nicotine-induced buzz—now the basement air is a bit clearer.
EXTRAS/NOTES	Pamplona's reputation as a cult hangout is confirmed by the restaurant's sole decoration: a fading fresco painted in the 1970s by an art school student in exchange for a year's supply of coffee. Josefina Yanguas, Cafe Pamplona's 87-year-old owner, has been baking delicious desserts by hand daily since 1956.

—Sylvia Kindermann

Caffe Paradiso

*An Italian respite
in Harvard Square.
Since 1962*

$$

1 Eliot Sq., Cambridge 02138
(at JFK St.)
Phone (617) 868-3240
www.caffeparadiso.com

CATEGORY	Italian Café
HOURS	Daily 7 AM–midnight
MASS TRANSIT	T: Red line to Harvard
PAYMENT	VISA MasterCard AMERICAN EXPRESS
POPULAR FOOD	Tiramisu with just the right hint of liqueur, chocolate mousse cake; gelati served with a heart shaped wafer cookie in a fluted parfait glass; salads, sandwiches, focaccia, quiches, and soups, all priced under $7
DRINKS	Coffee, espresso, cappuccino, lattes, loose teas, Italian sodas
SEATING	Seating for 40 inside; on a warm summer night, you'll find 15 or so outdoor tables
AMBIENCE	A vase with fresh roses perched on a green Corinthian column greets you upon entering Caffe Paradiso, a garden patio atmosphere perfect for sipping an Italian style latte; an eclectic mix of students, professors, and bohemian teenagers bask in the reserved bustle of Harvard Square
OTHER ONES	• North End: 253-255 Hanover St., Boston 02113, (617) 742-1768

—Paula Foye

Campo De' Fiori

*Surprisingly excellent
pizza stand with thin crusts,
Roman style.*

$

1350 Massachusetts Ave., Cambridge 02138
(at Holyoke St., inside Holyoke Center Arcade)
Phone (617) 354-3805 • Fax (617) 354-3873

CATEGORY	Pizza by the Slice
HOURS	Mon–Fri: 8:30 AM–8 PM
	Sat: 11:30 AM–6 PM
MASS TRANSIT	T: Red line to Harvard
PAYMENT	VISA MasterCard AMERICAN EXPRESS
POPULAR FOOD	The *pane romano* is not the usual pizza— it's very flat and crunchy, and only the margherita *pane* has tomato sauce on it. The Pane Combo is an especially good deal: for around six bucks you get a slice of *pane romano*, a half-sandwich of your choice, and a drink. *Pane* also come in sweet varieties, for example with Nutella or jam.

UNIQUE FOOD	The *ciambella*, a light and fluffy breakfast doughnut covered in sugar
DRINKS	Coffee, tea, hot chocolate, sodas, lemonade, *frullati di frutta* (Italian fresh fruit shakes)
SEATING	There are about five small tables available in the Holyoke Center
AMBIENCE	Strictly takeout and very very busy from noon to 2 PM on weekdays

—*Amélie Cherlin*

Charlie's Kitchen

A gritty hold-out in the face of Harvard Square mall-ification.
Since 1950
$$

10 Eliot St., Cambridge 02138
(at Bennett St.)
Phone (617) 492-9646

CATEGORY	Bar & Grill
HOURS	Sun–Wed: 11 AM–1 AM Thurs–Sat: 11 AM–2 AM
MASS TRANSIT	T: Red line to Harvard
PAYMENT	VISA MasterCard
POPULAR FOOD	The famous double cheeseburger special for $5; diner dishes like meatloaf, mouth-wateringly good beer-battered fries, and chili
UNIQUE FOOD	Themed monthly specials like Lobster Fiesta or "Stews of the World"
DRINKS	Beer by the pitcher is the most popular deal, especially of Sam Adams; full bar
SEATING	Booths downstairs seat a couple dozen alongside a long counter; the upstairs is bigger, with tables, booths, and a bar, for a capacity of around 50
AMBIENCE	Downstairs, Charlie's is a '50s-style greasy spoon. It might take the accidental visitor a few trips to notice the staircase upstairs to the spacious and smoky bar; up here there's a jukebox, trashy programs playing on several TVs, and tattooed waitresses pulling pints with attitude you can't fake. The crowd is student-heavy—Charlie's is one of the few pubs in the area to stay open this late—but it remains true to folks who have lived here for decades.

—*Esti Iturralde & Kaya Stone*

"Hunger is not debatable."

—*Harry Hopkins*

Darwin's

*All neighborhoods should have
this kind of corner store.*

$$

148 Mt. Auburn St., Cambridge 02138
(between Ash St. and Brewer St.)
Phone (617) 354-5233

CATEGORY	Sandwich Shop
HOURS	Mon–Sat: 6:30 AM–11 PM
	Sun: 7 AM–9 PM
MASS TRANSIT	T: Red line to Harvard
PAYMENT	Cash only
POPULAR FOOD	Darwin's sandwiches are all named for nearby streets, from modest Story (prosciutto, mozzarella, a vinaigrette) to opulent Brattle (smoked salmon, cream cheese, capers, cucumbers). All are made with excellent breads (nine varieties), and simple but high-quality and wholesome meats and vegetables, even green apples. Great pasta salads in the deli case, and a couple of satisfying soups are always available.
UNIQUE FOOD	Some groceries, and a small selection of good, in-season produce
DRINKS	The Busch sign out front might indicate otherwise, but Darwin's sells a wide variety of beers, including foreign and New England selections; some are available by the case; many wines by the bottle; for the usual lunchers, there are shelves upon refrigerated shelves of juices
SEATING	A handful of seats indoors at a table squeezed between the bottled beverages and the register; on a sunny day bring your sandwich down to the grassy bank of the Charles or the little park at the end of Longfellow on Mt. Auburn St.
AMBIENCE	Darwin's corner-store looks belie the charms within; the tight space means that only the best foods make it inside; the young, cool, friendly staff move the oft-present line along quickly

—Esti Iturralde

Formaggio's

*Impressive sandwiches
among the wonders
of a minimall.*

$$

81 Mt. Auburn St., Cambridge 02138
(at JFK St., inside the Garage)
Phone (617) 547-4795

CATEGORY	Sandwiches
HOURS	Mon–Sat: 9:30 AM–9 PM
	Sun: 10 AM–7 PM
MASS TRANSIT	T: Red line to Harvard
PAYMENT	VISA MasterCard

POPULAR FOOD	Fat sandwiches on substantial, fresh-baked breads: almost a pound of smoked turkey, juicy roast beef, or baked ham—eat half and save the rest for later; fresh pastas, salads, and pasta salads
UNIQUE FOOD	Curried tuna salad sandwich
DRINKS	Soda and fruit juices by the bottle
SEATING	Capacity for a couple dozen at simple tables
AMBIENCE	A fast food setup: follow your sandwich along the preparation counters, from the meat-slicer to the register

—*Kyle Konrad*

Formaggio Kitchen

(see p. 57)
Gourmet Grocery
244 Huron Ave., Cambridge 02138
Phone (617) 354-4750

R.I.P.
The Tasty

City planners might as well rename Harvard Square "New Harvard Square" because, in the last ten years, the area has been remodeled into a shiny outdoor mall replete with four Starbucks and countless chains. No single event symbolized the Square's millennial demise more than the 1997 closing of **The Tasty**, which, despite impassioned local pleas, was pushed out by its landlord Cambridge Savings Bank by escalating rents to make room for the desperately needed Californian clothing store Pacific Sunwear, where nary a Bostonian has ever set foot or ever will. The countdown to the closing of The Tasty was met with more hype than Y2K, garnering enormous apocalyptic headlines for weeks in advance.

What was all the fuss about?

Rewind to February 1997, 5 AM. The wind chill brings the air temperature down to 20 below. There's only one beacon of light extending across the heart of the Square from a surprising diner. Inside, a unique mix of eminent professors, homeless people, and stressed, raccoon-eyed students huddle together, warming their hands with french fries cooked in a Fryolater practically older than Harvard itself, and tearing into a "cardiac burger" (fried egg, cheese, and bacon on a quarter pound of beef) like it were the last scrap of food on earth—all at a tiny counter, where the salt shakers jitter to blaring Beatles and Doors. And the wait staff—who breathe grease from their pores—try not to ash into your coffee.

—*Nick Grossman*

Grendel's Den

*Where it's always
happy hour (almost).*

$$

89 Winthrop St., Cambridge 02138
(near the corner of JFK St. and Mt. Auburn St.)
Phone (617) 491-1160

CATEGORY	Bar & Grill
HOURS	Mon–Sat: noon–1 AM
	Sun: 4 PM–1 AM
MASS TRANSIT	T: Red line to Harvard
PAYMENT	VISA MasterCard AMERICAN EXPRESS DISCOVER
POPULAR FOOD	From 5 PM–7 PM daily (and Sun–Thurs: 9 PM–11:30 PM), everything on the menu becomes a mere $3 with purchase of more than $3 in beverages. The nachos supreme are a good choice, as are the straw and hay pasta, and the mussels (yes, just $3). The hamburgers are fine if a little oddly presented—Grendel's doesn't serve fries.
DRINKS	Pitchers of (not very strong) sangria; standard draft and bottled beer; full bar
SEATING	Booths, tables, and bar typical of a pub setting, and thick with fun-loving atmosphere; there are a few tables outside when the weather's nice, but drinking alcohol outside is a no-no in dear Cambridge
AMBIENCE	Extremely busy starting around 10 PM from Thursday to Saturday; the crowd consists of grad students, college seniors (Grendel's cards hard), and other twentysomething folk
EXTRAS/NOTES	Grendel's is in business thanks to a 1982 Supreme Court ruling, which declared unconstitutional a Massachusetts statute allowing churches to veto liquor applications from establishments within 500 ft. of them. Grendel's is ten feet from the Holy Cross Armenian Catholic Church.

—Amélie Cherlin

Herrell's

(see p. 131)
Ice Cream Shop
15 Dunster St., Cambridge 02138
Phone (617) 497-2179

Hi Rise Bread Company

(see p. 205)
Bakery
56 Brattle St., Cambridge 02138
Phone (617) 492-3003

Il Panino Express

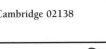

(see p. 23)
Italian
1001 Massachusetts Ave., Cambridge 02138
Phone (617) 547-5818

Johnny's Luncheonette

(see p. 252)
Retro '50s Diner
1105 Massachusetts Ave., Cambridge 02138
Phone (617) 495-0055

L.A. Burdick

(see p. 111)
European Bakery
52 Brattle St., Cambridge 02138
Phone (617) 491-4340

Lee's Sandwich Shop

*Inexpensive and deli-icious
greasy spoon fare.*
$
61 Church St., Cambridge 02138
(at Brattle St.)
Phone (617) 876-4090

CATEGORY	Sandwich Shop
HOURS	Mon–Fri: 7 AM–9 PM
	Sat: 8 AM–9 PM
	Sun: 9 AM–9 PM
MASS TRANSIT	T: Red line to Harvard
PAYMENT	Cash only
POPULAR FOOD	French toast, muffins, western omelette, chicken parm, cheeseburger, pastrami and cheddar, BLT, two-egg special with homefries and toast
DRINKS	Soft drinks, tea, coffee, bottled juices
SEATING	Large counter (14 stools); three booths
AMBIENCE	A long and narrow diner, whose long counter and food prep line occupy most of the restaurant's space; simple, unobtrusive decorations; especially busy at breakfast and lunch during the week
EXTRAS/NOTES	One of the few places in the Square whose prices haven't inflated in pace with local rent, a place where patrons are more important than the bottom line.
OTHER ONES	• Lee's Beehive: Harvard Square: 24 Dunster St., Cambridge 02138, (617) 661-6722 (a sister diner)

—Matthew Isles

Mr. Bartley's Burger Cottage

A burger shack where the rich and powerful get slung right on the grill.
Since 1961

$$$

1246 Massachusetts Ave., Cambridge 02138
(at Plympton St.)
Phone (617) 354-6559
www.mrbartleys.com

CATEGORY	Burger Joint
HOURS	Mon–Wed, Sat: 11 AM–9 PM
	Thurs/Fri: 11 AM–10 PM
	Sat: 11 AM–9 PM
MASS TRANSIT	T: Red line to Harvard
PAYMENT	Cash only
POPULAR FOOD	A long list of big, greasy, seven- or even 14-ounce hamburgers, each named for a celebrity (Elvis, Tiger Woods) or political figure (like the Ted Kennedy, "a plump, liberal amount of burger" with cheddar and mushrooms). Legendary thin and crispy onion rings and sweet potato fries; wraps, club sandwiches, and salads—but who are you kidding? You're here for the meat.
UNIQUE FOOD	Fries and gravy; sloppy joes; baked mac 'n' cheese with bacon; Cajun meatloaf with gravy; maple bread pudding
DRINKS	Award-winning frappes (malted, chocolate with banana and peanut butter, peppermint patty) that also come in Godzilla size; lime rickeys; root beer floats; egg creams; cream soda; lemonade
SEATING	Tables are within arms' distance of each other
AMBIENCE	Ironic, vintage paraphernalia on the walls, like "Aliens Are Here" bumper stickers; the constant burger slinging fills the air with a beefy smell that wafts out the door and sticks to you on the way out
EXTRAS/NOTES	Bartley's is recognized as the classic place in the neighborhood to get a classic burger—on a real bun, no goat's cheese (except on the Yuppie Burger, of course). Located across the street from Harvard Yard, Bartley's is a fond stop for tourists, visiting alumni, and the occasional undergrad or grad student hungering for a quick dose of cholesterol. Some drop by to get a frappe on the run, which is a meal in a drink— and we're not talking Slim-Fast either.

—Esti Iturralde

New Asia

(see p. 228)
Chinese
1105 Massachusetts Ave., Cambridge 02138
Phone (617) 491-1188

One Arrow St. Crêpes

*A small side-street tribute
to France's greatest fast food export.*

$$

1 Arrow St., Cambridge 02138
(off Massachusetts Ave.)
Phone (617) 661-2737 • Fax (617) 547-2737

CATEGORY	Crêpes
HOURS	Tues–Thurs: 10 AM–11 PM
	Fri/Sat: 10 AM–midnight
	Sun: 10 AM–10 PM
MASS TRANSIT	T: Red line to Harvard
PAYMENT	VISA MasterCard
POPULAR FOOD	Smoked chicken crêpe with sautéed spinach, caramelized onions, sundried tomatoes, and brie; homemade basil and walnut pesto crêpes with marinated mozzarella and big juicy hothouse tomatoes; crêpes with two eggs, spinach, tomatoes, scallions, black olives, and jack cheese; sweet varieties with brie, fresh apples, toasted walnuts, and honey drizzle or some combination of Nutella, Belgian white chocolate, raspberries, and pirouline cookie crumbles
UNIQUE FOOD	Lamb crêpes
DRINKS	Variety of fancy coffees, juice, soda, tea, smoothies, and lemonade
SEATING	Small and comfy, with a few tables tucked into odd places, and a bar with stools
AMBIENCE	This homey yellow house decorated with incongruous Native American accessories attracts Harvard students and other locals who have made the tucked-away crêperie a hot spot; chill out to the eclectic music, read, study, or watch your crêpe being made in front of you

—Dara Olmsted

Pho Pasteur

*Harvard Square's heartiest,
healthiest Asian cuisine.*

$$$

36 Dunster St., Cambridge 02138
(at Mt. Auburn St., inside the Garage)
Phone (617) 864-4100

CATEGORY	Vietnamese
HOURS	Sun–Wed: 11 AM–10 PM
	Thurs–Sat: 11 AM–11 PM
MASS TRANSIT	T: Red line to Harvard
PAYMENT	VISA MasterCard AMERICAN EXPRESS
POPULAR FOOD	Giant bowls of *pho hoac mi* (noodle soups) with choice of beef, chicken, or fish in a zesty broth with scallions, onions, cilantro, and either white or yellow noodles. Fried or vegetarian spring rolls; beef or chicken teriyaki skewers; stir-fried noodles; and

great lunch specials under $8 consisting of chicken, shrimp, or tofu dishes served in a savory, light curry sauce with fresh vegetables and rice vermicelli (*bun*).

UNIQUE FOOD   The *banh hoi* dishes are presented traditional Vietnamese style in which grilled shrimp, fresh mint, roasted peanuts, lettuce, and steamed vermicelli are rolled by hand (by you) into softened rice paper at the table and seasoned with *nuoc cham sauce*. Pan-fried salmon with black bean sauce; caramelized chicken or pork; and soft shell crab sautéed with ginger roots and scallions. Unusual desserts such as *che ba mau*, translated as Three Color Sweet, with coconut milk, beans, and gelatin strips over ice, or *che dau trang*, sweet rice pudding, coconut milk, and black-eyed peas, served warm.

DRINKS   Soft drinks, bottled water, full bar, tea, and coffee; exotic options like fresh limeade (*da chanh*), available in sparkling, salty, or jasmine flavors; sweet soy bean milk; egg soda; chilled fruit from the Far East; coconut juice; fruit, coconut, avocado, and mung bean shakes

SEATING   One large high-ceilinged room with several small, close-spaced tables, always fairly crowded; additional bar area

AMBIENCE   Expect to wait for a table at dinnertime (although efficient, attentive service makes the longest wait only about 30 minutes). Lunch specials make Pho a popular mid-day spot with the locals as well. The atmosphere is funky and upbeat, with the typical mixed crowd of artists, academics, and international tourists. Bright colored walls, interesting modern paintings, Asian fans, and hanging paper lanterns create a festive atmosphere.

OTHER ONES
- Theater District: 123 Stuart St., Boston 02116, (617) 742-2436
- Chinatown: 682 Washington St., Boston 02111, (617) 482-7467
- Back Bay: 119 Newbury St., Boston 02116, (617) 262-8200
- Allston: 137 Brighton Ave., Allston 02134, (617) 783-2340

—*Meaghan Mulholland*

Pinocchio's

The Sicilian slice kings.

$

74 Winthrop St., Cambridge 02138
(at Dunster St.)
Phone (617) 876-4897

CATEGORY   Pizza by the Slice

HOURS   Mon–Sat: 1 PM–1 AM
          Sun: 11 AM–midnight

MASS TRANSIT   T: Red line to Harvard

PAYMENT   VISA MasterCard

POPULAR FOOD	All the Sicilian slices are favorites, but especially the tomato basil. The delicious cheeseburger sub almost trumps the pizza in popularity. The slices are pre-made and warmed up in the oven upon ordering, but somehow they maintain their fresh, cheesy puffiness—never stale or too greasy; quality ingredients through and through.
SEATING	A small square room with seating for at most 15 at little tables crowded together
AMBIENCE	'Noch's, as it is known to the many Harvard students who frequent it, is a lifesaver—providing quality grub during those nebulous late-night study and party hours. A friendly team of pizza makers keep up an energetic, almost rhythmic pace of service; everyone who lives or labors nearby is eventually drawn into this tight little gem of a pizza parlor.

—*Esti Iturralde*

Sabra

*Heavenly hummus
with a smile.*

$$

20 Eliot St., Cambridge 02138
(at JFK St.)
Phone (617) 868-5777

CATEGORY	Middle Eastern
HOURS	Daily: 10 AM–10 PM
MASS TRANSIT	T: Red line to Harvard
PAYMENT	Cash only
POPULAR FOOD	Arguably the best place to get cheap, authentic Middle Eastern food in a hurry; generous falafel and *shawarma* sandwiches and platters; grape leaves; the perennial grilled vegetable special sandwich; baklava
UNIQUE FOOD	Chef's special: the baked *kibbee* sandwich, a combo of cracked bulgar wheat, ground beef, sautéed onions, and special herbs
DRINKS	Zesty carrot juice freshly made; homemade lemonade; standard soft drinks and iced teas
SEATING	Table seating for 15; counter for five
AMBIENCE	An inviting place with few frills where *shawarma* is carved with gusto and good cheer; an eager line forms during lunchtime; many notes and comments on the wall offer well-deserved praise

—*Christopher Russell*

Skewers

Filling, tasty Middle Eastern awaits downstairs.

$$

92 Mt. Auburn St., Cambridge 02138

(at JFK St.)

Phone (617) 491-3079 • Fax (617) 491-3571

CATEGORY	Middle Eastern
HOURS	Mon–Sat: 11 AM–11 PM
	Sun: 11 AM–10 PM
MASS TRANSIT	T: Red line to Harvard
PAYMENT	VISA MasterCard AMERICAN EXPRESS DISCOVER
POPULAR FOOD	Falafel; beef, chicken, or lamb shish kabob; *shawarma* from lamb or chicken; the Maza sampler features Skewers' wonderful hummus and *baba ganoush*; nothing too fancy, just hearty meals that taste good and make you very full
UNIQUE FOOD	*Moussaka*, a zesty combo of potatoes, eggplant, and meat cooked in herbs and spices and topped with bechamel sauce
DRINKS	Soda, juices, Turkish coffee, and very good mango and plain yogurt *lassis*
SEATING	About ten tables, as well as a counter where you can wait for a takeout order or eat if you're on the run
AMBIENCE	This underground hole-in-the-wall evades most of Harvard Square's tourists; instead it's filled with college kids and locals, but somehow there's rarely much of a wait.

—*Lara Fox*

Tanjore

Just the answer for your chicken tikka cravings.

$$$

18 Eliot St., Cambridge 02138

(near JFK St.)

Phone (617) 868-1900 • Fax (617) 868-1906

CATEGORY	Southern Indian
HOURS	Daily: 11:30 AM–3 PM, 5 PM–11 PM
MASS TRANSIT	T: Red line to Harvard
PAYMENT	VISA MasterCard AMERICAN EXPRESS DISCOVER
POPULAR FOOD	The chicken *tikka masala* is a classic; grandiose lunch buffet
UNIQUE FOOD	Vast selection of superb dishes spanning the Indian subcontinent, with many vegetarian choices
DRINKS	Five kinds of yogurt *lassi*, chai tea, full bar
SEATING	Modest, comfortable dining room good for small groups
AMBIENCE	Soft lighting and gentle conversational babble make for pleasant dining
OTHER ONES	• Allston: Rangoli: 129 Brighton Ave., Allston 02134, (617) 562-0200. (owned/operated by the same family)

—*Nick Grandy*

Hungry? Harvard:
The Best Food Stops for the Starving Student

With chains popping up everywhere and beloved student dives like Elsie's, The Tasty, and the original Grendel's now long gone, Harvard Square has fully transformed from a dingily hip (if slightly pretentious) student stomping ground to full-on mall. Tourists pay through the teeth by day, while area yuppies (or Harvard yuppies-in-training) happily shell out major cash by night. However, there are still a number of places to eat for cheap in the Square.

Best Ice Cream: Herrell's

In a photo finish, the wacky flavors at Herrell's (how 'bout jalapeño?) barely beat out the smoother scoops at Toscanini's. *Harvard Square: 15 Dunster St., Cambridge 02138, (617) 497-2179.*

Best Truck/Cart/Stand:
Chinese Kitchen Food Truck

This darling of the Biolabs lunchtime crowd promises a lot of greasy Chinese food for very little money. Plus no MSG! *Oxford St. near the Science Center.*

Best Late-Night: Hong Kong

Fuel up for Scorpion Bowl races—the fiercest competition in town—with scallion pancakes or an order of crab(less) rangoon. *Harvard Square: 1236 Massachusetts Ave., Cambridge 02138, (617) 864-5311.*

Best Pizza: Pinnochio's

The fat slices of 'Noch's signature Sicilian-style pizza are dished out by some of the nicest guys around. See p. 188. *Harvard Square: 74 Winthrop St., Cambridge 02138, (617) 876-4897.*

Best Pizza Delivery: Pizza Ring

Their chewy double-deckers will satisfy even the hungriest dorm room's munchies. *Harvard Square: 212 Western Ave., Cambridge 02139, (617) 864-1800.*

Best Hangover Food: Johnny's Luncheonette

The huge breakfast plates and bottomless cups of coffee are perfect for when the dining hall's hangover chicken just ain't cutting it. See p. 252. *Harvard Square: 1105 Massachusetts Ave., Cambridge 02138, (617) 495-0055.*

Best Place to Eat While Drinking:
Charlie's Kitchen

What could be better than a pitcher of Sam Adams and a Charlie's double cheeseburger special? (Answer: the Charlie's jukebox.) See p. 181. *Harvard Square: 10 Eliot St., Cambridge 02138, (617) 492-9646.*

Best Place to Drink While Eating: Cambridge Common

Shh! Quadlings don't want River folk to know that this low-key law school watering hole also serves some of the best American comfort food in the city (don't forget the sweet potato chips). See p. 199. *Porter Square: 1667 Massachusetts Ave., Cambridge 02138, (617) 547-1228.*

Second Best Place to Drink While Eating: Grendel's Den

Happy Hour at this undergound bar means the entrees are cheaper than the beer you're washing them down with. See p. 184. *Harvard Square: 89 Winthrop St., Cambridge 02138, (617) 491-1160.*

Best Food on the Run: Campo de' Fiori

A huge *pane romano* from Campo—thin-crust pizza topped with things like mozzarella and Nutella—is perfectly suited for that between-lecture dash. See p. 180. *Harvard Square: 1350 Massachussetts Ave. (inside Holyoke Center Arcade), Cambridge 02138, (617) 354-3805.*

Best Happy Hour: John Harvard's Brewhouse

Join everyone else in your class for beer and half-priced appetizers on Monday nights. *Harvard Square: 33 Dunster St., Cambridge 02138, (617) 868-3585.*

Best Burger: Mr. & Mrs. Bartley's Burger Cottage

The hilarious celebrity monikers given to the thick, juicy burgers at this carnivores' paradise make the heartburn pangs worth it. See p. 186. *Harvard Square: 1246 Massachusetts Ave., Cambridge 02138, (617) 354-6559.*

Best Cheap Date: Pho Pasteur

Soft colors, unobtrusive service, and huge portions of Vietnamese food that are perfect for sharing set the scene for your dinnertime seduction. See p. 187. *Harvard Square: 36 Dunster St., Cambridge 02138, (617) 864-4100.*

—Ankur Ghosh

Tealuxe

(see p. 76)
Bakery
0 Brattle St., Cambridge 02138
Phone (617) 927-0400

Toscanini's

(see p. 131)
Ice Cream Shop
1310 Massachusetts Ave., Cambridge 02139
Phone (617) 354-9350

Veggie Planet

An innovative vegetarian pizzeria and much more—great food with a conscience.

$$

47 Palmer St., Cambridge 02138
(at Church St.)
Phone (617) 661-1513
www.clubpassim.com/cafe

CATEGORY	Vegetarian
HOURS	Daily: 11:30 AM–10:30 PM (Closed some Mondays for Open Mic Nights; best to call ahead)
MASS TRANSIT	T: Red line to Harvard
PAYMENT	Cash only
POPULAR FOOD	Try chef Didi Emmons' (of DeLux and Pho Republique fame) provocative and delicious weekly soup, salad, and pizza specials. You'll forget your carnivorous cravings as soon as you sample the Caesar salad with tofu croutons or Dinner for Henry pizza, topped with roasted butternut squash, caramelized onions, sage, and creamy goat cheese.
UNIQUE FOOD	Best described as "ethnic food on flat bread," you can get any of the unique pizza toppings over steamed, brown, or coconut rice. The red peanut curry and portobello redhead pizzas are particularly suited for the rice substitutions. The Sunday brunch menu (served 'til 3:30 PM) stars green apple compôte-topped waffles, pecan sticky buns, homemade granola, and much more. Add live musicians, board games, and a laid-back atmosphere for the perfect weekend non-activity.
DRINKS	Organic is the key word here—from natural fruit sodas to organic cola; summertime is partial to the Kashmiri chai iced tea and fresh-squeezed lemonade; also organic coffees, cocoa, and herbal and fruit-flavored teas
SEATING	Located adjacent to the legendary music lounge, Club Passim, Veggie Planet avails of the club's surprisingly airy 100-person seating capacity till 6:30 PM every day. After 6:30 PM, the seating capacity dwindles down to 20 if you don't plan to pay the cover to watch the Club Passim performance du jour. From then 'til closing, Veggie Planet customers can either find themselves seated at one of three tightly packed tables or along a long, narrow counter, straining to hear the chords emanating from next door.
AMBIENCE	Hippie throwbacks, fresh-faced Harvard students, and tree-huggers abound, varying greatly with the Club Passim performances each day; service is unhurried and insightful. Be patient as your pizza is fired up in the restaurant's special eco-friendly oven.

EXTRAS/NOTES Chef Didi Emmons and her partner, Adam Penn, cater to people with adventurous taste buds on a budget. This makes for an innovative and bold menu where everything is made from scratch. The pizza crust is 100% organic, produced fresh daily by Haley House, a homeless services provider in the South End. If that's not enough, 2% of Veggie Planet's profits and 100% of T-shirt profits go to Food For Free, a non-profit organization feeding the hungry in Cambridge.

—*Priti Chinai*

PORTER SQUARE

Andy's Diner

A breakfast deal
with family appeal.
Since 1958
$$

2030 Massachusetts Ave., Cambridge 02140
(at Creighton St.)
Phone (617) 497-1444

CATEGORY	Diner
HOURS	Mon–Fri: 6 AM–3 PM
	Sat: 6 AM–2:30 PM
	Sun: 6:45 AM–1 PM
MASS TRANSIT	T: Red line to Porter; bus: #77
PAYMENT	Cash only
POPULAR FOOD	A few dollars buy a pair of eggs, home fries, and toast—just enough salt and fat to fix what you did to yourself the night before. Most breakfasts fall under six bucks and cover the homestyle diner basics: waffles, omelettes, pancakes, French toast, and sausage-and-egg specials. Lunch is about 50 cents more and includes hot and cold sandwiches, meatloaf, and hamburgers.
DRINKS	Soda, juice, bottomless coffee, chocolate milk
SEATING	A counter with half-a-dozen swivel stools, a dozen comfortable booths, and tables
AMBIENCE	Frequented by families with kids, Andy's is family-run. The younger staff bus the tables and seat you while the grownups pour your coffee. The mood is efficient, quiet, and kind.
EXTRAS/NOTES	Andy's has always been biased to the early riser. Eggs start cracking at 6 AM, and an especially early closing on Sunday means that weekend snoozers lose. However, the genial staff has been known to take pity on a certain reviewer whose aversion to the morning hours makes her push the boundaries of politeness and punctuality and drag herself to the lunch counter for a cup of joe—but bless 'em, they pour it for her every time.

—*Esti Iturralde*

Of Pilgrims and Munchkins: The Story of Boston Donuts

The rugged air of Yankee individualism marks your typical New Englander as a living monument to American history. The blob of custard on his chin marks him as a living monument to the history of donuts.

The Pilgrims are said to have brought *olykoeks*, Dutch "oil cakes," to the shores of Massachusetts and to have called them "dough-nuts" because the little balls of fried dough looked like walnuts. Sadly, despite their noble spirit of exploration, the Pilgrims would fail to discover the donut hole. And it would be another 200 years before anyone did.

The town of Clam Cove, Maine has a monument to the New Englander who, in 1850, finally joined holes and donuts in blessed union. This "o" pioneer, Captain Hanson Gregory, is said to have been eating one of his mother's homemade donuts at the ship's wheel during a storm, and, unwilling to sacrifice ship or donut, stuck the latter on a spoke of his wheel, leaving both hands free to steer—and giving the donut its hole.

Some sources, however, claim that Gregory was simply a cheap man who cut the middle to cut costs. Or that he created the hole in hopes that it would make the donut easier to digest. We may never know the hole truth. Gregory himself cast doubt on the spoke story when, at the turn of the century, he told the *Boston Post* that he had used the top of a tin pepper box to cut "the first doughnut hole ever seen by mortal eyes."

For years, donuts kept mostly to themselves as true products of New England—until duty called. In World War I, American soldiers in France were served millions of donuts by women volunteers, who made the first wartime donuts with a wine bottle for a rolling pin and a camphor ice sucking tube for making holes—though eventually they'd use a seven-pound shell fitted with a one-pound shell to cut the dough. Soldiers' helmets on a stove served as deep-fryers on the front.

When the doughboys—a term possibly related to their diet—returned Stateside, they were still hungry for donuts, which became so popular that in 1920 a New York City vendor, Adolph Levitt, invented the first donut machine to keep up with demand. The automation of donut-making created "the food hit of the Century of Progress," according to the buzz that surrounded donuts at the 1934 World's Fair in Chicago. A decade later, after going to war with another generation of American troops, their popularity would swell once more.

In 1950, the Open Kettle donut shop in Quincy was renamed **Dunkin' Donuts**. Five years later, the first Dunkin' Donuts franchise agreement was signed in Worcester, Massachusetts. Today there are almost 5,000 Dunkin' Donuts locations in 40 countries. They sell 20 cups of coffee a second, and almost 6.4 million donuts every day—in one year, that's enough donuts to circle the earth twice. Dunkin' Donuts is still based in Massachusetts, with its corporate headquarters in Randolph.

The most popular Dunkin' Donut is the humble glazed, but it was the Boston Cream Donut—or "Boston Kreme" in Dunkin' Donuts parlance—that was made the official donut of the Commonwealth by the Massachusetts legislature in 2001.

The donut connoisseur will want to visit:
Dunkin' Donuts *Find one of the 600 Massachusetts locations at www.dunkindonuts.com*

Lori-Ann Donut Shop *Charlestown: 198 Bunker Hill St., Charlestown 02129, (617) 241-7808.*

Verna's *Porter Square: 2344 Massachusetts Ave., Cambridge 02140, (617) 354-4110.*

And, try out cider donuts at the following farms:
Atkins Farms *Western Massachusetts: Rte. 16 and Bay Rd, South Amherst 01002, (413) 253-9528. www.atkinsfarms.com*

Honey Pot Hill Orchards *Cider donuts made daily mid-August through December. Central Massachusetts: 144 Sudbury Rd., Stow 01775, (978) 562-5666. www.honeypothill.com*

—*Katie Wink*

Anna's Taquería

Step in line for the Boston area's top burrito.
$
822 Somerville Ave., Cambridge 02140
(inside the Porter Square Galleria)
Phone (617) 661-8500

CATEGORY	Mexican/Burrito Joint
HOURS	Daily: 10 AM–11 PM
MASS TRANSIT	T: Red line to Porter; bus: #77 along Mass. Ave.
PAYMENT	Cash only
POPULAR FOOD	A butcher's knife, tongs, and a spatula—"Next!"—these are the elements of the Anna's experience. The men make the burritos, stabbing a hunk of meat and chopping it up, placing it on the tortilla with tongs, slopping on your choice of ingredients, and wrapping it up in half a minute flat (the ladies work the cash register). Perhaps the secret's in the steamer, a hissing machine that melds the cheese with the tortilla into a moist, pliant wrap, juices oozing out. The aptly titled

Super Burrito has rice, beans, pico de gallo, and cheese with your choice of add-ins: fresh guacamole, sour cream, meats, and sauces. Especially recommended are the *carnitas* (pork), hot sauce, and black beans; also a treat are warm, greasy, hot tortilla chips with homemade salsa.

UNIQUE FOOD   Might as well just get the Super Burrito—regardless of name all the dishes are identical except maybe in presentation.

DRINKS   Sodas from a fountain; Mexican drinks like Jarritos bottled sodas and JuMex juices in mango, guava, strawberry

SEATING   Small tables seat about 25 total; many just take out, or eat quick and run

AMBIENCE   If you are under 30 and make less than $30,000 a year, you have eaten at Anna's. With various food groups represented, many have found it possible to live on Anna's burritos alone. Always seems like there are 20 people in line but the wait is about a minute, that's how fast the assembly line works.

EXTRAS/NOTES   Despite the Mexican and Central American staff, the Anna's empire is owned by a Japanese-American visionary from California. The name "Anna's"? He chose it because it sounded motherly and would appear near the top of any alphabetical listing. Editors' note: When asked what restaurants they would most like to review for this book, over half of our contributors listed Anna's. It's just that cheap and that good.

OTHER ONES
• Coolidge Corner: 1412 Beacon St., Brookline 02446, (617) 739-7300
• Coolidge Corner: 446 Harvard St., Brookline 02446, (617) 277-7111
• Davis Square: 236A Elm St., Somerville 02144, (617) 666-3900

—Esti Iturralde & Kaya Stone

Blue Fin

Ichiban for combining inexpensive sushi, quality, atmosphere, and alcohol.

$$$

1815 Massachusetts Ave., Cambridge 02140
(inside Porter Square Exchange)
Phone (617) 497-8022

CATEGORY   Japanese

HOURS   Daily: noon–11 PM

MASS TRANSIT   T: Red line to Porter; bus: #77

PAYMENT   VISA MasterCard

POPULAR FOOD   Sushi combo specials with 18–32 pieces comprised of a selection of your choice; udon noodle soup with kimchee, spicy radish, or seaweed

UNIQUE FOOD	The thick, hearty, and savory Japanese rice curry confirms once again that curry dishes from the land of Pokemon are better than a 30-minute stay at a Tokyo love hotel; offers a standard selection of Japanese noodle dishes and sushi choices including vegetarian options
DRINKS	Six different types of *sake*, beer, soft drinks, and Japanese green tea
SEATING	Even though the place seats up to 60, expect to wait outside with other expectant sushi aficionados during meal times. Luckily it's inside a mall catered to the local Japanese community, so you can walk 20 feet to the Japanese grocery store or to the food court around the corner for something to nibble on. The mall setting also provides free parking in the lot.
AMBIENCE	Youngish crowd from around Boston sit comfortably in this very clean, bright, and casual restaurant decorated with Eastern flair

—Charlene X. Wang

Boca Grande

Feisty fast food that won't leave you faint.

$

1728 Massachusetts Ave., Cambridge 02138
(at Linnaean St.)
Phone (617) 354-7400

CATEGORY	Mexican
HOURS	Daily: 11:30 AM–11:30 PM
MASS TRANSIT	T: Red line to Porter; bus: #77
PAYMENT	VISA MasterCard AMERICAN EXPRESS
POPULAR FOOD	Fat burritos stuffed with beans, rice, cheese salsa, and choice of meat (try the Chicken Colorado or *carnitas*); cheesy enchiladas
UNIQUE FOOD	1/4 and 1/2 grilled chickens; homemade tamales (fresh cornmeal wrapped in corn husk)
DRINKS	Homemade lemonade, *aguas frescas* (tamarindo and jamaica), coffee, tea, soda
SEATING	Small tables with room for about 20
AMBIENCE	A good place to go solo or with a platonic friend if you want Mexican food without the aftertaste of Taco Bell or the prices of a more upscale Mexican restaurant. Mexican lanterns, blue skies painted on the ceiling, and red walls make it very bright and very casual. There's no wait service; the large student clientele primarily takes their burritos to-go.
OTHER ONES	• Coolidge Corner: 1294 Beacon St., Brookline 02446, (617) 739-3900
	• Kendall Square: 149 First St., Cambridge 02142, (617) 354-5550

—Ana Laguarda

Cambridge Common

A billion beers—everybody goes home happy from Cambridge Common.

$$

1667 Massachusetts Ave., Cambridge 02138
(between Wendell St. and Sacramento St.)
Phone (617) 547-1228 • Fax (617) 661-3852

CATEGORY	Bar & Grill/Comfort Food
HOURS	Mon–Wed: 10:30 AM–1 AM
	Thurs–Sat: 10:30 AM–2 AM
	Sun: 10 AM–1 AM
MASS TRANSIT	T: Red line to Porter; bus: #77
PAYMENT	VISA MasterCard AMERICAN EXPRESS DISCOVER
POPULAR FOOD	Pub grub but a little fancier and very generous: Angus burgers, sliced sweet potato fries, nachos, curly fries, boneless buffalo wings; the homemade salsa kicks ass; lots of vegetarian options, too; great fruit crisp of the day
UNIQUE FOOD	Portobello burger with marinated red peppers, gorgonzola, and spinach
DRINKS	Twenty-four beers on tap, full bar, soft drinks, and their very own specialty brew, Liquid Lizard Ale
SEATING	About 175 at booths, tables, and the bar
AMBIENCE	This comfortable, neighborhood restaurant is busiest at night and at dinnertime; frequented by Harvard Law students and undergrads; walls of dark red finished wood display an ever-changing array of local artwork that's pretty good and available for sale
EXTRAS/NOTES	The funky Lizard Lounge is right downstairs—a popular live music club.

—Dara Olmsted

Chez Henri

(see p. 168)
French/Cuban
1 Shepard St., Cambridge 02138
Phone (617) 354-8980

"If you are what you eat, then I'm fast, cheap and easy."

—Anon

Christopher's

*Organic grub
in a traditional pub.*

$$

1920 Massachusetts Ave., Cambridge 02140
(at Davenport St.)
Phone (617) 876-9180

CATEGORY	Bar & Grill
HOURS	Mon–Fri: 4 pm–midnight
	Sat: 11:30 am–2 am
	Sun: 10:30 am–2 am
MASS TRANSIT	T: Red line to Porter; bus: #77
PAYMENT	VISA MasterCard AMERICAN EXPRESS DISCOVER
POPULAR FOOD	Nachos and fajitas (chicken to shrimp); baby spinach salad; tofu, chicken, or vegetable stir-fry; *enchiladas suizas*; thick veggie or beef burgers with choice of 14 toppings
UNIQUE FOOD	Yuppie nachos with goat cheese and sun-dried tomatoes; roasted eggplant sandwich with hummus and roasted red peppers; foccacia pizza with chicken and pesto; sesame spinach burrito
DRINKS	Long list of microbrews, full bar, coffee drinks
SEATING	Two floors or dark wood tables and chairs seat close to 100; reservations accepted for parties of six or more
AMBIENCE	Dark, lively setting with exposed-beam ceilings, wrap-around bar, and fireplace
EXTRAS/NOTES	The owners only use meat from animals that are raised on natural foods and the menu caters to a large vegetarian following.

—*Kyle Konrad*

Forest Café

*Real-deal Mexican cooking with that
laid-back, hole-in-the-wall charm.*

$$$

1682 Massachusetts Ave., Cambridge 02138
(at Sacramento St.)
Phone (617) 661-1603 • Fax (617) 354-1944

CATEGORY	Mexican
HOURS	Sun–Thurs: 11:30 am–2:30 pm, 5 pm–10 pm
	Fri/Sat: 11:30 am–2:30 pm, 5 pm–11 pm
MASS TRANSIT	T: Red line to Porter; bus: #77
PAYMENT	VISA MasterCard AMERICAN EXPRESS DISCOVER
POPULAR FOOD	A number of enchilada platters that ooze with melted Mexican cheeses and other delectable flavors: a creamy avocado and cilantro sauce, green and red salsas, and best of all, the bittersweet *mole*, a chili and chocolate sauce rarely found in these parts
UNIQUE FOOD	Even though Cambridge is not known for its Mexican eats, Forest avoids the easy clichés; the menu is skimpy on burritos and tacos, while featuring plenty of pork chop dishes smothered in spicy sauces
DRINKS	A host of Mexican beers, powerful margaritas
SEATING	The often-crowded watering-hole of a bar

extends the length of this narrow restaurant, with foursomes taking up booths along the opposite wall

AMBIENCE While the quality of its dishes might indicate otherwise, the Forest still maintains the worn-in feel of a dive

EXTRAS/NOTES A Mexican restaurant with as Anglo a name as "Forest Café" inevitably screams identity crisis, but regulars are as drawn to this cantina's quirks as they are to its dead-on *mole*. With its aged, incongruous decor and general low profile, the Forest stands out (or better said, stands in) from its more glitzy Mass. Ave. neighbors.

—Esti Iturralde

Greek Corner

Greek comfort food in a homey atmosphere.
$$
2366 Massachusetts Ave., Cambridge 02140
(at Dudley St.)
Phone (617) 661-5655

CATEGORY	Greek
HOURS	Mon–Sat: 11 AM–10 PM
	Sun: noon–9:30 PM
MASS TRANSIT	T: Red line to Davis; bus: #77
PAYMENT	VISA MasterCard AMERICAN EXPRESS DISCOVER
POPULAR FOOD	Roast lamb, souvlaki, kebabs, calamari; all the Greek mainstays are here
UNIQUE FOOD	Not many other places in town to get octopus
DRINKS	Beer and wine, including a variety of Greek offerings
SEATING	The restaurant holds 70 in two rooms, mostly in tables of two or four; the front is a bit more casual and exposed to the elements; can be a bit cold on a winter night
AMBIENCE	Isolated from the hustle and bustle of Mass. Ave.'s more crowded neighborhoods, the Greek Corner is down home, straightforward, and practical. No candlelit dinners here, but a relaxed atmosphere with warm, hearty food. The place makes a decent attempt to recall a Greek taverna with plenty of Athenian knick-knacks and a beautiful seascape mural dominating the rear wall. It gets packed on weekend nights, especially during the summer.
EXTRAS/NOTES	The Boretos brothers take great pride in serving authentic Greek dishes and can often be found waiting tables and chatting up the guests.
OTHER ONES	• Harvard Square: 8 1/2 Eliot St., Cambridge 02138, (617) 661-3433

—Joe Goss

Kotobukiya

Great sushi at rock-bottom prices.

$$

1815 Massachusetts Ave., Cambridge 02140
(inside Porter Square Exchange)
Phone (617) 354-6914

CATEGORY	Japanese
HOURS	Mon–Fri: 10 AM–9 PM
	Sat: 9 AM–9 PM
	Sun: noon–7 PM
MASS TRANSIT	T: Red line to Porter; bus: #77
PAYMENT	VISA MasterCard AMERICAN EXPRESS
POPULAR FOOD	Inside-out California roll with roe, various yummy sashimi
DRINKS	A variety of canned Japanese concoctions; tea
SEATING	Small counter seats around 12; seats are hard to come by around dinnertime
AMBIENCE	Very loud, very crowded, and very mixed crowd, including people looking for authentic sushi and gym rats who just finished working out at the nearby Bally's
EXTRAS/NOTES	Stop by the grocery store within to buy supplies for making sushi at home.

—*Christopher Russell*

Oxford Spa

*Friendly neighborhood
lunch spot—but sorry,
no facials.*

$$

102 Oxford St., Cambridge 02138
(between Garfield St. and Crescent St.)
Phone (617) 661-6988 • Fax (617) 661-9018

CATEGORY	Sandwich Shop
HOURS	Mon–Fri: 7 AM–8 PM
	Sat/Sun: 8 AM–6 PM
MASS TRANSIT	Bus: #77 bus down Mass. Ave. to Sacramento St.
PAYMENT	VISA MasterCard DISCOVER
POPULAR FOOD	Sandwiches with names ranging from the pedantic (Dissertation) to the provocative (Bikini), all drawing from the same set of exceptional ingredients: crusty breads, savory slices of ham and turkey, three kinds of lettuce, and cheeses that seem to have sprung from the bosoms of cows or goats in the south of France.
UNIQUE FOOD	Indication of its past life as a convenience store, Oxford Spa also stocks baking and breakfast supplies
DRINKS	Fresh brewed coffee and bottled juices
SEATING	A few tables indoors and out
AMBIENCE	This big square room feels like a casually cluttered kitchen; mismatched chairs mingle with vintage Coca-Cola memorabilia; a friendly staff of hipsters

serves brainy grad students and other folk who live and work nearby; at lunchtime the line leads through the shop and out the door

EXTRAS/NOTES Despite fancy ingredients, Oxford is a neighborhood hangout from another era. Hence the "spa" in the name, an old-fashioned eastern New England term for a corner store and soda fountain where you might catch up with neighbors at lunchtime.

—*Esti Iturralde*

Verna's

(see p. 196)
Donut Shop
2344 Massachusetts Ave., Cambridge 02140
Phone (617) 354-4110

WEST CAMBRIDGE/ALEWIFE

Bertucci's

(see p. 175)
Gourmet Pizza
5 Cambridge Park Dr., Cambridge 02140
Phone (617) 876-2200

Cheddar's

A sub shop with personality—and one mean steak and cheese.
$
201 Alewife Brook Pkwy., Cambridge 02138
(at Concord Ave.)
Phone (617) 661-3366

CATEGORY	Sub Shop
HOURS	Mon–Fri: 10 AM–8 PM
	Sat: 10 AM–6 PM
MASS TRANSIT	T: Red line to Alewife
PAYMENT	Cash only
POPULAR FOOD	One of the best steak and cheese subs around; fresh baked and thick-sliced turkey and ham subs with very fresh veggies including red peppers; hummus pockets; greasy, but good thin-crust pizza
UNIQUE FOOD	Mammoth chicken Caesar pocket with marinated mushrooms; spinach pie
DRINKS	Juices and soda
SEATING	Eight small tables for two or four
AMBIENCE	At lunchtime there's always a line out the door; Charlie and Dino keep it moving yelling "Hey Guy, Next!" pausing only to charm the female customers; pass the wait by watching the drama playing out both on the hanging mini-TV and behind the counter

EXTRAS/NOTES   Truly a son and mom operation: Owner Charlie and his buddy Dino whip up the sandwiches, while Charlie's mom works the register. There's no need to order anything but a small sub unless you're eating for two.

—*Kaya Stone*

R.I.P.
The Restaurants of Joyce Chen

For much of the '60s, '70s, and '80s, Joyce Chen achieved with Chinese food what Betty Crocker did with cake mix. While a few Chinese restaurants were dishing out chop suey and chow mein, Joyce Chen was one of the first to introduce Mandarin specialties such as Peking duck, moo shu pork, and hot and sour soup. Through TV shows and supermarket soy sauces, this longtime Cambridge restaurateur is credited with bringing stir-fry to homes across America.

Chen and her husband left China during the revolution in 1949, and by 1958 had begun their empire on Concord Ave. in West Cambridge. Business flourished, and in 1973 a larger Cambridge restaurant opened on Rindge Ave. in the Alewife section of Cambridge. Joyce Chen became the most famous Chinese restaurant in America, with patrons like economist John Kenneth Galbraith, Julia Child, and Henry Kissinger chowing down on Chen's stir-fries. Soon the chef herself could be seen slicing and dicing on her very own nationally syndicated PBS show, *Joyce Chen Cooks*. There were Joyce Chen cookbooks, Joyce Chen sauces, Joyce Chen knives, and even the brilliant, Chen-invented flat-bottomed wok.

Although the brand continues to thrive, the Cambridge restaurant has since departed. For $6.95, the Joyce Chen lunch buffet was the epitome of what every Middle America Chinese buffet can only aspire to be. Delicious noodle, chicken, and beef dishes were continually replenished as poor students and businesspeople piled heaps on their plates. Every child left with a Tootsie Pop. At its peak, Joyce Chen was serving close to 400,000 meals a year divided between its Theater District and Cambridge locations. In the early 1990s, the business fell on hard times and was ordered to close its doors for nonpayment of rent.

Years after closing down, the mark of Joyce Chen can be seen on nearly every Chinese menu in the region. It is Chen, after all, who coined the term "Peking Ravioli," the New England name for dumplings. How else could she explain to her patrons in an Italian neighborhood what pan-fried potstickers were like?

—*Kaya Stone*

Hi Rise Bread Company

High-end sandwiches and baked goods in a rustic bakery-café.

$$$

208 Concord Ave., Cambridge 02138
(at corner of Huron Ave.)
Phone (617) 876-8766

CATEGORY	Bakery
HOURS	Mon–Fri: 8 AM–8 PM
	Sat: 8 AM–5 PM
	Sun: 8 AM–4 PM
MASS TRANSIT	Bus: #74 or 78
PAYMENT	*VISA* MasterCard
POPULAR FOOD	Everything sold here is excellent, as it should be at the sometimes eye-popping prices, but the generously sized sandwiches (each about $8) are exceptional. Made on Hi Rise's own breads, the whimsically named combinations from Linda's Swinging Single (grilled smoked pork loin, sharp cheddar, cole slaw, and honey mustard on toasted corn loaf) to Fern's Problem Solver (smoked turkey, Monterey Jack, avocado, and Russian dressing on Semolina bread, grilled), reflect a chef's sensibility in their careful balance of flavors and textures. All the breads are baked in-house, sandwich fillings like grilled chicken are cooked to order, and everything that goes into the sandwiches (and salads and soups), from the vegetables and meats to the cheeses and mustards, is the best available.
DRINKS	Coffee, tea, lemonade, fancy sodas
SEATING	One large table seating 12 to 16, four smaller tables seating two to four
AMBIENCE	As you wait to order, the line to the register runs along a counter covered with an abundant spread of fresh-baked breads, tarts, scones, muffins, cookies, and cakes. Place your order, then join the West Cambridge crowd of handsome young couples with babies in tow, creatively tattooed singletons, and tastefully well-heeled locals who happily share the long wooden table running down the center of the room, but compete discreetly for the three prized window tables. Watch the bakers carry enormous tubs of dough to an immense wooden table, where they shape loaves and rolls for their final rise before baking.
EXTRAS/NOTES	Chef/Owner René Becker indulges his more ambitious culinary ideas in a takeout dinner menu that changes weekly—two different entrees with accompanying sides offered every weeknight, in oven-ready containers, for $14 each. (The main dish and sides are also available separately.) The walls are lined with Becker's hand-picked selection of wines, along with jars of preserves and other artisanal foodstuffs.

OTHER ONES   A slightly reduced selection of sandwiches and baked goods:
- Harvard Square: 56 Brattle St., Cambridge 02138, (617) 492-3003

—Michael Beckett

Il Buongustaio

A veritable pantry of doughy Italian delights.

$$

370 Huron Ave., Cambridge 02138

(at Gurney St.)

Phone (617) 491-3133

CATEGORY	Italian
HOURS	Mon–Sat: 11 AM–10 PM
	Sun: noon–9 PM
MASS TRANSIT	Bus: #72
PAYMENT	Cash only
POPULAR FOOD	Delicate, thin-crust pizzas; the dough is made with virgin olive oil, not butter or yeast, which is then spread with fresh plum tomato sauce; for those more interested in sandwiches, there's the Il Buongustaio panini with Italian beef, thick fresh mozzarella, roasted peppers, fresh basil, and olive oil
SEATING	A handful of seats at the counter, but there is hardly enough room to fit a pizza pan; most take their pies to go
AMBIENCE	Like eating in an Italian family's kitchen; the customer is privy to all of the preparation that goes into every fresh, baked-to-order pie; big jars of marinated peppers and olive oil left casually around the eatery set the scene for serious Italian cooking

—Kaya Stone

Real Pizza

A hipster's pizza paradise.

$$

359 Huron Ave., Cambridge 02138

(at Gurney St.)

Phone (617) 497-4497 • Fax (617) 497-7325

CATEGORY	Gourmet Pizza
HOURS	Mon–Thurs: 9 AM–9 PM
	Fri: 9 AM–10 PM
	Sat: 5 PM–9 PM
MASS TRANSIT	Bus: #72
PAYMENT	Cash only
POPULAR FOOD	The #1 ("REAL Pizza") is the most popular—fresh-made mozzarella, tomato sauce, and oregano—12 inches of goodness for $10; other favorites include prosciutto-covered Olbers' Paradox, mushroom-laden Planck Time and the Chandra, topped with caramelized onions, roasted peppers, and gorgonzola

UNIQUE FOOD	Real Pizza's mozzarella cheese is made on site and its dough comes direct from the Hi Rise Bakery down the street. Creative toppings include shrimp, white clams, very smoky bacon, pancetta, andouille sausage, and two kinds of pesto. In addition to Real Pizza there are also Real Dinners—main courses of meat with veggie sides, complete with suggested wine matches.
DRINKS	Made-to-order, old timer's drugstore-style Coca Colas—flavor shots include cherry, vanilla, grenadine, raspberry, blackberry, and chocolate; also, coffee shop-quality teas, coffees, and cold drinks.
SEATING	More of a takeout kind of place; it seats about seven in small booths and tables
AMBIENCE	A hipster's pizzeria, complete with staff and soundtrack
EXTRAS/NOTES	If you love the Real Pizza dough, check out Hi Rise Bakery (see p. 205), under the same ownership, down the street.

—*Alissa Farber*

SOMERVILLE

DAVIS SQUARE/BALL SQUARE

Amelia's Kitchen

A onetime sandwich counter, but now all grown up.

$$$

1137 Broadway, Somerville 02144
(at Holland St.)
Phone (617) 776-2800 • Fax (617) 628-3388

CATEGORY	Italian
HOURS	Mon–Sat: 11 AM–11 PM Sun: 5 PM–10 PM
MASS TRANSIT	T: Red line to Davis
PAYMENT	VISA MasterCard AMERICAN EXPRESS
POPULAR FOOD	Pasta of all kinds; lobster ravioli, foccacia; gnocchi made from scratch by Amelia herself; incredible tiramisu and cannoli
DRINKS	Beer and wine—after a several-year wait for a liquor license; espresso and cappuccino
SEATING	Eleven tables in tight quarters; most of the tables are fours, meaning the romance is expected to be shared; a couple of outdoor tables in the summer
AMBIENCE	The restaurant has taken on a more romantic air, with subdued lighting and darkly attired wait staff. A definite step up from the Italian soccer posters and cartoons of a few years ago, the restaurant has aspirations for an inspired meal. Summer evenings are a little crowded, but most times you can get a table without a wait. The crowd is slightly upscale, having migrated slightly to a more yuppie crowd.
EXTRAS/NOTES	Not that long ago, Amelia's was a sandwich counter with very upscale tastes in pasta and other offerings. Run by Amelia and Delio Susi who live in the neighborhood, you felt at home and learned something from the drawings, amateur artwork, and newspaper articles under the tabletops and on the walls. Now, it aspires to be a full-fledged restaurant, with candlelight, table service, and a wine list. Times have changed for the bistro, but it still offers incredible pastas, panini, and other Italian treats.
OTHER ONES	• Kendall Square: Amelia's Trattoria, 111 Harvard St., Cambridge 02139, (617) 868-7600

—Joseph Goss

Anna's Taquería

(see p. 196)
Mexican
236A Elm St., Somerville, 02144
Phone (617) 666-3900

Blue Shirt Café

West Coast-style grub to cure what ails you.

$$$

424 Highland Ave., Somerville 02143
(at College Ave.)
Phone (617) 629-7641

CATEGORY	Wrap/Sandwich Shop
HOURS	Sun–Wed: 8 AM–9 PM
	Thurs–Sat: 8 AM–10 PM
MASS TRANSIT	T: Red line to Davis
PAYMENT	Cash only
POPULAR FOOD	Sandwiches and wraps with accents from the Far East and the Near West (California): curried Indonesian tuna salad; Thai seared peanut chicken; the Davis Square sandwich, chicken breast, spinach, tomatoes, and sundried tomato spread; the I'll Just Pick Breakfast, a sampling of eggs, bacon (or tofu sausage), multigrain pancakes, homefries, and fruit for around $7
UNIQUE FOOD	Carrot-based juice remedies with ingredients like ginger, garlic, and bee's pollen; organic multigrain pancakes
DRINKS	Fresh-squeezed juices, coffee, tea; a dozen fruit smoothies, some with choice of "booster" (Echinacea, ginseng, and the like)
SEATING	Room for only about 15 inside, but with a few outdoor seats during the warmer months and with many customers ordering takeout, there's rarely a wait for a table
AMBIENCE	A friendly and efficient place. Large, handmade menus adorn the upper halves of three walls, with the space below dedicated to a few pictures, several bright-colored publicity posters, and an inconspicuous blue shirt. Just step up to the counter, tell them what you want, and watch them prepare the food in the exposed kitchen. The majority of patrons tend to be students or young professionals.

—Matt Bloomer

Café de Crêpe

(see p. 212)
Crêpes
283 Boston Ave., Medford 02155
Phone (781) 391-3833

Hungry? Tufts:
The Best Food Stops for the
Starving Student

Tufts students enjoy quick and easy access to the old favorites of rising star Davis Square, including **Denise's Homemade Ice Cream** (see p. 132), **Carberry's** for sandwiches (see p. 214), the **Rosebud Diner** (see p. 221), and the ever-popular **Johnny D's** for live music and bar-and-grill food (see p. 216). But there are plenty of other cheap, local eats that Tufties enjoy outside as well as inside of Davis.

Best Breakfast: SoundBites

Just about the only place that can drag Tufties out of bed before noon, SoundBites in Ball Square is famous for huge portions, friendly staff, and unbeatable home fries. In blazing heat, blizzards, or thunderstorms, you can always see loyal patrons lining up on the sidewalk to get in for a little taste of heaven. See p. 224. *Ball Square: 708 Broadway, Somerville 02144, (617) 623-8338.*

Best Sandwiches: Tasty Gourmet

A hole in the wall on Boston Ave. with a variety of wraps and sandwiches that will make your mouth water. Try the Summer Turkey Wrap, and be sure to get a side of their incredible seasoned fries. *Medford: 321B Boston Ave., Medford 02155, (781) 391-9969.*

Best Service: Jay's Deli

There's no Jay, but Perry will hook you up with standard deli fare, throw in some chips, round down the price, and smile at you like you're the prodigal son returned. Eating at Jay's becomes a matter of loyalty, and the more time you spend in this laid-back little deli, the more like home it feels. *Medford: 340 Boston Ave., Medford 02155, (781) 391-0370.*

Best Chinese: Wang's Fast Food

Start off with the best spinach dumplings you'll ever taste, and move on down the menu from there. Far from your standard greasy Chinese, the offerings at Wang's will melt in your mouth, not all over your napkin. See p. 231. *Union Square: 509 Broadway, Somerville 02145, (617) 623-2982.*

Best Dessert: Café de Crêpe

A great stop on the way home from dinner, the Nutella and banana crêpe is a must. Or, if you want to do one-stop shopping for dinner and dessert, their Signature Crêpes—especially the Chicken Crêpe—can provide a satisfying meal in a pinch. *Medford: 283 Boston Ave., Medford 02155, (781) 391-3833.*

Best Pizza: Espresso Pizza

A mainstay of Tufts dining, Espresso is on the Merchants on Points program, which means Tufties can use their dining points to pay for a speedy slice or a giant calzone. Their Caesar salad wraps are also popular with those who object to dripping grease. *Medford: 336 Boston Ave., Medford 02155, (781) 396-0062.*

Best Delivery: Urban Gourmet

Flexibility is the key at Urban: build your own sandwiches, mix and match your pizza toppings (or have your favorite pizza made into a calzone), and have any of the nine pasta sauces on spaghetti, bow ties, or rigatoni. With a million options (often vegetarian-friendly), and offering eat-in, takeout, and free delivery, Urban is a blessing for Tufties who can only stomach so much dining hall grub. See p. 225. *Davis Square: 688 Broadway, Somerville 02144, (617) 628-2322.*

Best Classy Date: Sabur

The delectable fusion of Mediterranean cuisines here is matched only by the friendly and knowledgeable service. After dropping your (borrowed) car in the off-street parking (a premium in Somerville), grab a quiet booth in the corner and impress your date by recommending the outstanding Peasant Fritatta. *Davis Square: 212 Holland St., Somerville 02144, (617) 776-7890.*

—Dan Rosenberg

Café Rossini

A well-kept Somerville secret.
$$
278 Highland Ave., Somerville 02143
(at Cedar St.)
Phone (617) 625-5240

CATEGORY	Café
HOURS	Sun–Tues: 7 AM–9 PM
	Wed–Sat: 7 AM–10 PM
MASS TRANSIT	T: Red line to Davis; bus: #88 or 90
PAYMENT	Cash only
POPULAR FOOD	Caffe Rossini seeks to feed as well as caffeinate you; popular breakfast treats include apple turnovers, cinnamon rolls, triple berry scones, and great big blueberry muffins; for afternoon and evening fare, try one of their Italian sandwiches, or pizza topped with seven cheeses
UNIQUE FOOD	Homemade candy bars
DRINKS	Coffee however you like it; good selection of tea and soft drinks, including fresh lemonade; fruit smoothies
SEATING	Cozy tables provide indoor seating for about 12, plus three or four tables outside in warm weather
AMBIENCE	Bright and cheerful; artwork, flowers, and hanging decorations adorn the one-room café; regulars are mostly over 25 and longtime locals

—Melissa Carlson

Carberry's

Settle in with the paper
and baked goods to die for.

$$

187 Elm St., Somerville 02144
(at Russell St.)
Phone (617) 666-2233

CATEGORY	Bakery
HOURS	Mon–Sat: 6 AM–8 PM
	Sun: 7 AM–7 PM
MASS TRANSIT	T: Red line to Davis
PAYMENT	Cash only
POPULAR FOOD	Baked goods of all kinds made on site fresh throughout the day; fabulous sweets such as tiramisu and mousses; design-your-own sandwich on great bread
UNIQUE FOOD	Many of the baked goods are one-of-a-kind including Icelandic pastries courtesy of the immigrants on the staff
DRINKS	Lattes, espressos, mochas, chai—and all else a caffeine-lover could ask for
SEATING	Spacious with seating for about 50; they put a few tables on the sidewalk in good weather
AMBIENCE	A bit industrial in feel, but the large quarters allow plenty of sunlight and air, making Carberry's a welcoming place for enjoying a cup of coffee, a scone, and the Sunday Globe; fairly yuppie clientele base; order your meals at the counter and pick up when your number is called
EXTRAS/NOTES	Heed the signs and "ask the baker what's hot" for best treats right out of the oven.
OTHER ONES	• Central Square: 79 Prospect St., Cambridge 02139, (617) 576-3530
	• Western Suburbs: 600 Massachusetts Ave., Arlington 02476, (781) 641-0007
	• Malden: 20 Riverside Park, Malden 02148, (781) 397-9511

—*Joe Goss*

Denise's

(see p. 132)
Ice Cream Shop
4 College Ave. Somerville 02144
Phone (617) 628-2764

"I never worry about diets. The only carrots that interest
me are the number you get in a diamond."

—*Mae West*

Diesel Café

*De rigeur coffee shop for funky
Somervillians—with pool tables.*
257 Elm Street, Somerville 02144
(in Davis Sq.)
Phone (617) 629-8717

CATEGORY	Café
HOURS	Mon–Thurs: 7 AM–midnight
	Fri: 7 AM–1 AM
	Sat: 8 AM–1 AM
	Sun: 8 AM–midnight
MASS TRANSIT	T: Red line to Davis
PAYMENT	Cash only
POPULAR FOOD	Simple sandwiches, salads, soup, pastries from Rosie's Bakery, and ice cream from Toscanini's
UNIQUE FOOD	Excellent selection of vegan baked goods and veggie sandwiches
DRINKS	Strong and flavorful coffee. Great creative concoctions with fun names, like the Rusty Slide (a chai drink with ice cream); the Tuck's Turtle (hot chocolate with caramel, hazelnut, whipped cream, and chocolate shavings); and the Solid Six (six long shots of espresso for $4). Also, Vietnamese coffee (coffee with condensed milk); Italian sodas; and fresh squeezed lemonade (add your own sugar).
SEATING	Seats 30–40, with very small tables, two counter areas, and booths and a communal couch in the back; it gets incredibly full on weekends and evenings.
AMBIENCE	A funky artistic coffeehouse feel, while staying clean, functional, and friendly to just about anyone. Lots of writers tapping on laptops, newspaper browsers, and friends hanging out, laughing, and talking. The front window panels are a garage door that can be slid open on nice days. Local artists' work decorates the walls. The female baristas here are buff and thoroughly pierced, while the music runs toward the Tori Amos or Ani DiFranco variety.
EXTRAS/NOTES	Starbucks opened up a shop right across the street from Diesel about a year ago, much to the chagrin (and fury) of locals. So far, Diesel seems to be remaining ahead of the game.

—Amy Cooper

Espresso Pizza

(see p. 212)
Pizza
336 Boston Ave., Medford 02155
Phone (781) 396-0062

House of Tibet Kitchen

A jewel in the funky crown of Davis Square.

$$

235 Holland St., Somerville 02144

(at Broadway)

Phone (617) 629-7567

CATEGORY	Tibetan
HOURS	Tues–Sun: 5 PM–9:30 PM
MASS TRANSIT	T: Red line to Davis; bus: #87, 88, or 89
PAYMENT	VISA MasterCard AMERICAN EXPRESS
POPULAR FOOD	This is one restaurant where vegetarian dishes outnumber meat ones; recommended is the *tsel baklab*, fried patties filled with potato and vegetables; *momo* appetizer (steamed dumplings); all dishes are served with the soup of the day and a bean sprout salad
DRINKS	A variety of Tibetan shakes and teas; to cool fires stoked by chili sauce, try hot Tibetan apple cider sprinkled with cottage cheese
SEATING	Scattered tables seat about 25 in a cozy room
AMBIENCE	A Tibetan flag guards the doorway of this Asian treat perched on a hill by Teele Square. Dine under the benevolent gaze of the Dalai Lama whose likeness adorns the walls. The restaurant's owner may emerge from the kitchen to give you a lively lecture on Tibetan culture.

—*Sylvia Kindermann*

Jay's Deli

(see p. 212)

Deli

340 Boston Ave., Medford 02155

Phone (781) 391-0370

Johnny D's

Jazz brunch, catfish burritos, and Liquid Viagra—oh, my!

$$$

17 Holland St., Somerville 02144

(in Davis Sq.)

Phone (617) 776-2004 • Fax (617) 628-1028

www.johnnyds.com

CATEGORY	Bar & Grill
HOURS	Tues–Fri: 4:30 PM–11:30 PM
	Sat: 9 AM–2:30 PM, 4:30 PM–11:30 PM
	Sun: 9 AM–2:30 PM, 4:30 PM–7:30 PM
MASS TRANSIT	T: Red line to Davis
PAYMENT	VISA MasterCard AMERICAN EXPRESS DISCOVER
POPULAR FOOD	Everything on the weekend jazz brunch menu is a hit: mix-and-match oatmeal, blintzes, multigrain pancakes with walnuts and raisins, and over a dozen

other choices for $8. Spa chicken in a garlic and wine sauce; Asian stir fry over noodles; baby back ribs; and Johnny's Cheeseburger, a half-pounder with bacon and cheddar. There's half-price dining Tues–Fri: 4:30 PM–6:30 PM.

UNIQUE FOOD Catfish burrito; Cajun meatloaf

DRINKS A dozen craft beers on tap; complete by-the-glass wine selection; full bar; inventive drink menu includes such mixtures as Liquid Viagra, Surfer on Acid, and the Chocolate-Covered Peach Margarita; fresh-squeezed juices

SEATING The dining room seats 100 around a performance stage and includes booths; the casual bar seats 40

AMBIENCE Davis Square is eclectic, and Johnny D's clientele reflects it—from Somerville natives to Tufts frosh; jazz brunch often jumps with customers, but the talent on stage is smooth

EXTRAS/NOTES Go for dinner and stay for a show most nights—if you pay the cover charge. Johnny D's books diverse sounds— "everything from blues to Bulgarian wedding music, bagpipes to bongos."

—*Reg Brittain*

Kelly's Diner

Be-bop and a Burger Deluxe.
Since 1953
$$

674 Broadway, Somerville 02144
(at Rogers Ave.)
Phone (617) 623-8102 • Fax (617) 623-8062

CATEGORY Historic Diner

HOURS Mon–Sat: 5:30 AM–3 PM
Sun: 6 AM–2 PM

MASS TRANSIT T: Red line to Davis

PAYMENT Cash only

POPULAR FOOD There's more to do at Kelly's Diner than just punch up Elvis and Patsy on the tableside jukeboxes—you can eat, too. While the heaping breakfast specials are by far the most popular meals here, the menu features everything from cheeseburgers to knockwurst.

DRINKS Coffee, tea, and juices; if you're out with your sweetie, grab two straws and split a delicious ice cream frappe.

SEATING Seats 70 people at booths, a counter, and a few small tables.

AMBIENCE With Tufts University nearby, Kelly's is as popular with students and young professionals as it is with the blue-collar crowd.

EXTRAS/NOTES At Kelly's Diner, don't be surprised if you hear Buddy Holly on the jukebox. In fact, don't be too startled if you see him eating Belgian waffles in the booth next to you. This 1953 diner is the real deal. One of the largest dining cars ever manufactured, this model features a 20-stool counter, classic Formica tables, and sparkling chrome on nearly every surface. Kelly's didn't get to its current location in Ball Square until 1996 when it moved from its original spot along Route 13 in Delaware and was fully restored.

—*Mark Ferguson*

Mr. Crêpe

Fresh and tasty, sweet or savory, Mr. Crêpe has it all.
$$

83 Holland St., Somerville 02144
(at Irving St.)
Phone (617) 628-1500

CATEGORY	Crêpes
HOURS	Tues–Sat: 11 AM–10 PM Sun: 9 AM–9 PM
MASS TRANSIT	T: Red line to Davis
PAYMENT	Cash only
POPULAR FOOD	Savory crêpes mixing cheese and fruit: try the brie with green apples and grapes, or the spiced pear with bleu cheese, arugula, and walnuts; sweet crêpes filled with Nutella and fresh fruit; and tasty and eclectic soups
UNIQUE FOOD	While-you-wait crêpes in the French tradition: brie and fruit; Belgian chocolate; butter and sugar; the kitchen is up front and behind glass, allowing you to watch the magic at work; Merguez crêpe with Algerian sausage, spinach, and basil
DRINKS	Good variety of both cold and hot: fresh lemonade, sparkling water, juices, cocoa, coffees, and tea
SEATING	One-room restaurant with small tables; inside seats 15 to 20; sidewalk seating can fit eight to 12, when New England weather permits
AMBIENCE	Bright and cheery with high ceilings, big windows, and local artists' work decorating the walls. A nice mix of Tufts students, twentysomethings, and families make the place friendly and easygoing. The small tables fit two to three and easily lend themselves to a casual date—plus, with the Somerville Theatre just a few blocks away, make a night of it. There is usually only one chef, so the wait can be long, especially on Friday and Saturday nights and during the summer.

—*Melissa Carlson*

R.I.P.
Steve's Ice Cream

Whenever I went to my grandparents' house, we always had ice cream for dessert. Either Friendly's or Brigham's Spumoni or Neopolitan. No nuts or chunks. Just light and fluffy, air-packed ice cream. Sure, I always finished my bowl, but even at the age of three I was a bit snooty about my frozen treats. After all, I lived right around the corner from Steve's Ice Cream, the home of the Smoosh-in.

It was Somerville's own Steve's that originated the art of mixing candy bars and nuts into ice cream—the art of the Smoosh-in. It was here that some of the first Oreo Cookie and Heath Bar ice creams were made.

The employees at Steve's were true chefs and ice cream was made to order. The entrees were the rotating list of rich flavors posted on the wall, and the Smoosh-in options were displayed in small buckets across the counter. Because my parents were '70s-era hippies, I always passed up on Oreos for the more wholesome nuts and raisins to smoosh into my chocolate. A scoop of rich chocolate ice cream would be pounded on a cutting board, thrown side to side using two flat sliver scoops until it was soft, and then mixed with my raisins and nuts—a more artistic take on the Dairy Queen Blizzard.

When Steve Herrell, a former high school English teacher, first opened his small shop on Elm Street in Davis Square, Somerville in 1973, the only other premium ice cream on the market was Häagen Dazs. While other brands were filling their ice creams with air, Herrell slowed the motor of his maker down, reducing the amount of air whipped in. Since then, everyone from Ben and Jerry's to J.P. Licks have operated their ice cream makers at a slower speed, creating a denser ice cream that takes longer to melt in your mouth.

In 1976, just as Steve's was becoming a local legend, Herrell sold his business for $80,000 to Joey Crugnale, the owner of Joey's, a small ice cream shop in nearby Ball Square known for its make-your-own sundaes. By the early '80s, with the help of a *Time Magazine* feature, Steve's had gone national with as many as 26 stores nationwide and a line of pints on supermarket shelves across the country.

However, by the late 1980s and early 1990s, Steve's could not compete with the increasing number of premium ice cream shops in the area. Steve Herrell had gone on to open Herrell's (now with four locations in the Boston area) and Joey Crugnale turned his attention to **Bertucci's**—the now 80-restaurant national chain that started with a single pizza place next door to the original Steve's (see p. 175). Now owned by CoolBrands International—the ice cream conglomerate behind Swensen's, Eskimo

Pies, and I Can't Believe It's Yogurt!—the legacy of Steve's hangs by a thread at its Faneuil Hall Marketplace location.

Next time you're enjoying one of Ben and Jerry's flavors packed with nuts, candies, cookie dough, and every other sweet goodie under the sun, remember the Smoosh-in that started it all.

—Kaya Stone

Picante Mexican Grill

Good Mexican food to help you relax the day away.

$$

217 Elm St., Somerville 02144
(between Cutter St. and Grove St.)
Phone (617)-628-6394
www.picantemex.com

CATEGORY	Mexican
HOURS	Mon–Fri: 11 AM–10:30 PM Sat/Sun: 10 AM–11 PM
MASS TRANSIT	T: Red line to Davis
PAYMENT	Cash only
POPULAR FOOD	Salsa bar with homemade *salsa roja*, pico de gallo, super picante, chipotle, and *salsa yanque*; Mexican brunch on weekends features omelettes, quesadillas, and huevos rancheros; at lunch, most go for the burritos; everything is relatively healthy, without added lard or extra sugar and oil on the beans
UNIQUE FOOD	*Camotes*, sweet potatoes topped with a cinnamon and clove syrup; *panqueques*, Mexican pancakes covered with fruit
DRINKS	During the summer, there's special limeade (*agua fresca*); soda and juice; bottomless cup of Seattle's Best Coffee
SEATING	Fairly tight with ten tables seating two to four each and several bar stools along a very small counter
AMBIENCE	Most times it's counter service, except during brunch when you can get service at your table. There's not as much sunlight as one might hope, so Picante is best on a warm day when you can get out of the heat and enjoy good Mexican food with a little Latin music to keep up the mood.
OTHER ONES	• Central Square: 735 Massachusetts Ave., Cambridge 02139, (617) 576-6394

—Joe Goss

Redbones

*Somerville's succulent tribute
to the almighty Rib.*

$$$

55 Chester St., Somerville 02144
(between Elm St. and Cottage Ave.)
Phone (617) 628-2200
www.redbonesbbq.com

CATEGORY	Southern Barbecue
HOURS	Daily: 11:30 AM–10 PM
MASS TRANSIT	T: Red line to Davis
PAYMENT	Cash and check only
POPULAR FOOD	A star on every point of the barbecue map: sauce-drenched brisket from Texas, Memphis pork ribs with meat that falls away from the bone, thick Arkansas pork ribs, great big Texas beef ribs for the cowboys, and slighter baby back ribs for their womenfolk. All-you-can-eat lunch from 11:30 AM to 4 PM for $9 ($10 on weekends). Nearly everything available in bulk for takeout.
UNIQUE FOOD	White Trash Sundae (a variation on the brownie a la mode); every kind of side dreamed up in a Southern kitchen: succotash, hush puppies (with a little garlic and scallion), fried okra; corn bread to accompany your meal
DRINKS	Enormous selection of beers, 24 on tap, including locally produced brews; full bar with inventive cocktails
SEATING	Two floors of seating, upstairs in booths and long tables, downstairs in Underbones, which is smokier with a bar
AMBIENCE	A gritty un-self-conscious rib shack with Formica tabletops, linoleum floors, wood cut-outs of hogs, and jelly jars. The reputation is enough to bring diners from all over: Somerville lifers alongside students, expatriated Southerners, and diehard rib aficionados; the wait for a seat is notorious.

—Esti Iturralde

Rosebud Diner

*Irresistible retro kitsch—
but the food's good, too.*
Since 1941

$$$

381 Summer St., Somerville 02144
(at Elm St.)
Phone (617) 666-6015

CATEGORY	Historic Diner
HOURS	Sun–Thurs: 8 AM–11 PM Fri/Sat: 8 AM–midnight
MASS TRANSIT	T: Red line to Davis
PAYMENT	VISA MasterCard AMERICAN EXPRESS
POPULAR FOOD	Homestyle classics, particularly the juicy burgers and stellar club sandwiches. The huge and fluffy Mega Omelettes are a great deal, served with home fries and toast for just over $5. The Texas breakfast doesn't mess around

at $6 for three eggs, fries, bacon, sausage, and toast; too bad breakfast ends at 3 PM.

DRINKS	Coffee and juice; a full bar that serves a popular bloody mary for brunch
SEATING	A long counter with classic swivel stools that seat a dozen, which is especially suitable to solo dining; another dozen cushy booths seat four each
AMBIENCE	The Rosebud's pride is its old-fashioned box-car architecture—classic booths and stools, blue tile, wood paneling—bringing you back to the days when these Worcester-manufactured diners were sprinkled along the highways and byways of New England, stayed open 24 hours, and served a full turkey dinner for 50 cents. Today, the Rosebud packs them in during brunch when there is often a wait. Service is fast, friendly, and generous with words like "sweetheart" and "hon." A billion photos of the very photogenic Rosebud with its hot pink neon sign line the walls.

—Esti Iturralde

Rudy's Café

A fiery combination of tequila and Tex-Mex.

$$$

248 Holland St., Somerville 02144

(at Broadway)

Phone (617) 623-9201 • Fax (617) 623-6144

www.rudyscafe.com

CATEGORY	Tex-Mex
HOURS	Mon–Wed: 5 PM–midnight Thurs–Sat: 11:30 AM–1 AM Sun: 11:30 AM–midnight
MASS TRANSIT	T: Red line to Davis; bus: #87, 88, or 89
PAYMENT	VISA MasterCard AMERICAN EXPRESS DISCOVER
POPULAR FOOD	El Grande Burrito; Super Taco Salad; *chili con queso*
UNIQUE FOOD	Spinach quesadilla with feta and corn
DRINKS	Forty-one tequilas and five mezcals; ten draft and 20 bottled beers; *blancos, reposados, anejos*; primo margaritas
SEATING	Newly redesigned to make it more open and easier to get into; it still gets pretty crowded on weekend nights.
AMBIENCE	If it has been a couple of years since you have been to Rudy's, you won't recognize the place. Gone are the tight dinner tables and obstacle course of stairs. Instead you find a relocated entrance, jazzed up seating, a fancy bar, and a circular fireplace. The stucco walls and the basic red and yellow colors remain, but they have been muted and lighting changed to make the place more intimate and more upscale. It definitely has a classier feel than the Rudy's of old that had been in Teele Square for 15 years.

—Joseph Goss

Sabur

(see p. 213)
Mediterranean
212 Holland St., Somerville 02144
Phone (617) 776-7890

Savannah Grill

A welcome lunch/brunch oasis
tucked away in busy Davis Square
$$$
233A Elm St., Somerville 02144
(at Grove St.)
Phone (617) 666-4200

CATEGORY	Café
HOURS	Daily: 11:30 AM–10:30 PM
MASS TRANSIT	T: Red line to Davis
PAYMENT	VISA MasterCard AMERICAN EXPRESS DISCOVER
POPULAR FOOD	Owner Omar Mhiuldin (who formerly ran Club Passim in Harvard Sq.) investigated the prices and presentation of entrees at other Davis Square restaurants, and wisely decided to offer dishes that nearby places don't, such as: a warm spinach salad with meaty portobello mushrooms, crispy prosciutto, and rich chevre; a frisee salad tossed with pistachios, pears, and crumbled bleu cheese; and a lamb and rice entree. The portions are uncommonly large.
UNIQUE FOOD	The generously large lentil soup is seasoned perfectly with cumin. Grilled chicken or lamb roll-ups are most popular at lunch (and for $5.25, you cannot err); for brunch, the made-to-order omelette (served with home fries, toast, and seasonal fruit) reigns supreme. Flaky and delicious baklava with just the right amount of honey.
DRINKS	Sodas, coffee, tea, and iced coffee and tea
SEATING	Seats 38
AMBIENCE	One room with soft, muted yellow walls; blond wood wainscoting, and matching light wood tables and chairs make this a most comforting atmosphere; beautiful Japanese nature prints, depicting trees, birds, and blossoms add to the tranquil setting

—Christina Tuminella

SoundBites

Cheerful, jam-packed brunch with no-nonsense efficiency.

$$

708 Broadway, Somerville 02144
(at Willow Ave.)
Phone (617) 623-8338

CATEGORY	Diner
HOURS	Daily: 7 AM–3 PM
MASS TRANSIT	Bus: #89
PAYMENT	Cash only
POPULAR FOOD	Huge omelettes, waffles, muffins, challah French toast; soft, smooth NoPlaceLike Homefries with a touch of garlic; a fleet of fruity pancakes
UNIQUE FOOD	Several Middle Eastern accents like Moroccan eggs—fried with tomato, onion, and peppers, and flavored with cumin— and kebabs and falafel for lunch
DRINKS	All beverages are self-service to speed up dining; variety of teas and juices; coffee is bottomless, and offered to those standing in line
SEATING	It's hard to imagine squeezing one more table into the place; it's elbow-to-elbow for 37 seats, mostly in twos; moving tables together is no problem, but expect to wait a long time for more than four seats
AMBIENCE	While most brunch places pride themselves on the leisurely pace of their experience, you'll find a strong sense of urgency to SoundBites. No lingering over coffee or reading the Sunday paper—they need your table for the 20 or so folks standing out in the rain, snow, cold, or heat. For a more relaxed meal, come before 9:30 AM or after 1 PM, or try it during the week.

—*Joe Goss*

Tacos Lupita

Homemade Mexican and Salvadoran dishes that keep this neighborhood dive busy at all hours.

$$

13 Elm St., Somerville 02143
(at Porter St., just off Somerville Ave.)
Phone (617) 666-0677

CATEGORY	Salvadoran
HOURS	Daily: 11 AM–11 PM
MASS TRANSIT	T: Red line to Porter
PAYMENT	Cash only
POPULAR FOOD	Slight variations revolving around these magical 11 words, "fresh corn tortilla with cheese, beans, lettuce, and choice of meat"; choose from grilled steak, roast pork, tongue, and chicken

UNIQUE FOOD	Known for their chicken and beef soups, only available Friday through Sunday; the chicken soup is a huge bowl filled with chunks of roast chicken (bones and all), veggies, cumin, and onion
DRINKS	Tropical juices and sodas, and iced coffee
SEATING	This isn't a large place—it seats about 30
AMBIENCE	Strictly tables and chairs; just a hanging sombrero and a small TV decorate the place; without wait service, this would qualify as fast food if the staff didn't put so much time into making your meal.

—Glen Strandberg

Tasty Gourmet

(see p. 212)
Sandwich Shop
321B Boston Ave., Medford 02155
Phone (781) 391-9969

Urban Gourmet

*Neighborhood pizza place
for the discerning palate.*
$$
688 Broadway, Somerville 02144
(between Josephine Ave. and Rogers Ave.)
Phone (617) 628-2322

CATEGORY	Gourmet Pizza
HOURS	Mon, Wed–Fri: 11:30 AM–2 PM; 4 PM–11 PM Tues: 4 PM–11 PM Sat/Sun: 11:30 AM–11 PM
MASS TRANSIT	Bus: #89
PAYMENT	
POPULAR FOOD	Slow-cooked pizza with toppings like goat's cheese, linguica, and pineapple; gourmet sandwiches on focaccia; lots of vegetarian options; try the daily specials for the chef's more creative dishes
UNIQUE FOOD	Shrimp and bacon pizza; pan-roasted cod with tomatoes, basil, and white wine
DRINKS	Soda and juices
SEATING	Eight tables for four; roomy enough but expect everyone in the place to hear your conversation
AMBIENCE	Busy is the word for this place, especially during dinner hours, when the place is hopping with delivery and takeout orders; delivery drivers run in and out of the open-air kitchen
EXTRAS/NOTES	You know you aren't in your average pizza place when the menu warns that your pizza will take about 25 minutes. Using his grandfather's recipe, the owner-chef cooks every pie with a rich, crispy crust and adds an incredible array of toppings.

—Joe Goss

Wing Works

*Enough gutsy wings
to feed the locals by the thousands.*

$$

201 Elm St., Somerville 02144

(at Cutter Ave.)

Phone (617) 666-9000 • Fax (617) 666-9069

CATEGORY	Wings
HOURS	Daily: 11 AM–11 PM
MASS TRANSIT	T: Red line to Davis
PAYMENT	Cash or check only
POPULAR FOOD	The Buffalo wings are so special that even those who sold their Somerville houses for princely sums in the '90s make the trip back to eat them; these folks come from far and wide—Billerica, Worcester, Newburyport, New Hampshire—for this Wing of Desire.
UNIQUE FOOD	In addition to the expected fare—Buffalo, Texas barbecue, honey barbecue, Hawaiian teriyaki, and the like—these guys have the guts to serve the humble Buffalo wing's natural rival, the Rochester wing, which the menu describes best: "sweet and spicy with a dash of honey mustard." Even better, however, are the garlic parmesan wings, dripping with savory, garlicky sauce.
DRINKS	Sodas, Snapple, bottled water
SEATING	Mostly takeout and not suited to eating in, since there's no real dining area, only a tiny vestibule and a few tall chairs with no tables
AMBIENCE	Lots of Tufts students and as brightly lit as the inside of a bug zapper; you're not paying for the décor—you're paying for the zing in the wings
EXTRAS/NOTES	Their largest order to date was a thousand wings, which they delivered to a Tufts fraternity. Another noteworthy order was when they catered the Lord of The Wings event at Harvard to mark Elijah Wood's visit to the campus.

—*Ray Misra*

"Food is the most primitive form of comfort."

—*Sheila Graham*

UNION SQUARE

Café Belo

(see p. 88)
Brazilian
120 Washington St., Somerville 02108
Phone (617) 623-3696

La Hacienda

Cheap beer and old-school Italian
frozen in time.
Since 1939
$$
46 Medford St., Somerville 02143
(at Ward St.)
Phone (617) 864-2553

CATEGORY	Italian-American
HOURS	Mon–Sat: 11 AM–10 PM
MASS TRANSIT	Bus: #69 down Cambridge St.
PAYMENT	VISA MasterCard DISCOVER
POPULAR FOOD	Thin-crust pizza served with a loaf of cold white Italian bread; sirloin tips; chicken parm; lunch specials served until 3:30 PM include $4.50 individual pies
UNIQUE FOOD	Linguica pizza; honeycomb tripe in tomato sauce; homemade gnocchi
DRINKS	Miller Lite, Bud, or Bud Light for a measly $2/mug, $7/pitcher; there are also some other beers on tap, but this is a Bud Light sort of place; root beer, soft drinks
SEATING	Twelve hard wood benches that match the tables and walls; very low ceilings; though La Hacienda was not the inspiration for *Cheers*, it could have been, with a dark old tavern feel; a brighter non-smoking room in back has 10–15 more comfortable tables
AMBIENCE	La Hacienda is thick with character—thick Boston accents, thick air filled with cigarette smoke, and thick-around-the-middle patrons; it's frequented by white-haired ladies and potbellied men decked out in sweatpants and their softball jersey of choice

—*Kaya Stone*

Neighborhood Restaurant

A quiet gem for brunch
with your neighbors.
$$
25 Bow St., Somerville 02143
(at Walnut St.)
Phone (617) 623-9710 • Fax (617) 628-2151

CATEGORY	Portuguese
HOURS	Daily: 7 AM–3 PM
MASS TRANSIT	Bus: #85, 86, 87, or 91
PAYMENT	VISA MasterCard

POPULAR FOOD	Known for its unique thickly packed omelettes (lobster-mushroom, shrimp-mushroom, etc.), banana or raspberry-blueberry pancakes
UNIQUE FOOD	All of the breakfast specials come with an absurd amount of food: homefries, fruit salad, a bread/baked good plate, OJ, and bottomless coffee. At dinner they roll out seafood specialties such as Portuguese sardines and mussels in tomato sauce. Another rare treat is pork and clams in red sauce.
DRINKS	Soft drinks, coffee, Brazilian-style fruit juices; beer served during dinner hours
SEATING	An approximate capacity of 25 people indoors, but twice that in the outdoor patio where everyone sits under a shady canopy in warm weather
AMBIENCE	A usually mellow atmosphere except during lunchtime and Friday nights; the most common patrons are Portuguese and Brazilian locals, as well as senior citizens; a wider variety of diners come for brunch, drawn to the intimate feel of the place

—*Melvin Cartagena*

New Asia

*A diverse menu serves up
Chinese fresh, fast, and cheap.*

$$$

328 Somerville Ave., Somerville 02143

(at May Pl.)

Phone (617) 628-7710

www.newasia.com

CATEGORY	Chinese
HOURS	Daily: 11 AM–10 PM
MASS TRANSIT	Bus: #85, 86, 87, or 91
PAYMENT	VISA MasterCard AMERICAN EXPRESS
POPULAR FOOD	New Asia's varied menu serves up large portions in little time; particularly good are the numerous vegetarian options; other favorites include General Gau's Chicken and Sesame Chicken
UNIQUE FOOD	This culinary trip around Asia includes China, Polynesia, and Thailand; also featured: Temple's Delight, a high-protein, low-cholesterol, meat-like soy product
DRINKS	Soft drinks, tea, Bud, and Bud Lite
SEATING	Standard tables in a large, open space.
AMBIENCE	Mealtimes at New Asia are punctuated by constantly ringing phones for takeout orders, which account for most of their business; most traffic in the restaurant is from staff on delivery duty
EXTRAS/NOTES	There's no minimum charge for delivery, but a $2 fee will be added to your order
OTHER ONES	• Harvard Square: 1105 Massachusetts Ave., Cambridge 02138, (617) 491-1188

- Western Suburbs: 194 Massachusetts Ave., Arlington 02474, (781) 643-6364
- Western Suburbs: 93 Trapelo Rd., Belmont 02478, (617) 484-7000
- Danvers: 180 Endicott St., Danvers 01923, (978) 774-8080
- Western Suburbs: 211 Massachusetts Ave., Lexington 02420, (781) 863-5533

—*Alissa Farber*

Panini Bakery

(see p. 111)
Bakery/Café
406 Washington St., Somerville 02143
Phone (617) 666-2770

R.F. O'Sullivan and Sons

To those serious about burgers, listen up.
$$
282 Beacon St., Somerville 02143
(at Sacramento St.)
Phone (617) 492-7773 • Fax (617) 492-7775

CATEGORY	Burgers
HOURS	Daily: 11 AM–1 AM
MASS TRANSIT	Bus: #83
PAYMENT	VISA MasterCard
POPULAR FOOD	Best known for its half-pound burgers (voted best burgers in town by seemingly everyone five years running). Over 20 choices of toppings from the Black and Blue (ground black pepper and blue cheese) to the Papa (bacon, cheddar, mushrooms, onions), served with Sullies' fries (big potatoes, cut thick, and fried with skin and all).
UNIQUE FOOD	Big Daddy hot dog served over chili and onions with a side of fries; the "Two Pound Delight", an 8 oz. burger, 20 oz. beer, and a pound of fries for $10 (Mon–Thurs: 3 PM–5:30 PM and 9:30 PM–11:30 PM)
DRINKS	Full bar; wide choice of draft or bottled beer; root beer floats
SEATING	A large, U-shaped bar gives the best seating, but there are a few tables and booths, bringing the total capacity to approximately 25
AMBIENCE	Smooth paneling and frosted glass, staunchly Irish in feel and look—there are black-and-white pictures of Kerry County, Ireland. Older patrons exchange jokes comparing the difference in efficiency between the Irish and Polish military, or compare who is the hardest working Joe there.

—*Melvin Cartagena*

Taquería La Mexicana

*The Somerville source for tamales
and other authentic Mexican.*

$

247 Washington St., Somerville 02143

(at Prospect St.)

Phone (617) 776-5232 • Fax (617) 776-0243

www.lataqueria.com

CATEGORY	Mexican
HOURS	Daily: 11 AM–10 PM
PAYMENT	Cash only
MASS TRANSIT	Bus: #85, 86, 87, or 91
POPULAR FOOD	Tamales: either cooked for immediate consumption or frozen/uncooked for reheating at home; chicken, beef, pork, or veggie all for $1 each; burros with meat, rice, beans, guacamole, cheese, sour cream, and pico de gallo
UNIQUE FOOD	Potato and chorizo enchiladas; *chiles rellenos*; stuffed *poblanos*; beef and vegetable soup
DRINKS	Mexican soda, homemade lemonade and other fruit juices
SEATING	About 15 seats
AMBIENCE	No wait service and not much in the way of décor; takeout is your best bet

—*Kyle Konrad*

The Thirsty Scholar

A little Irish near Inman Square.

$$$

70 Beacon St., Somerville 02143

(at Waldo Ave.)

Phone (617) 497-2294

www.thirstyscholarpub.com

CATEGORY	Irish Pub
HOURS	Daily: 11 AM–10 PM
MASS TRANSIT	Bus: #83
PAYMENT	VISA MasterCard
POPULAR FOOD	American dishes along with Irish offerings, as well as pasta dishes; there are great Italian influences, as in the caprese salad, but it's hard not to go back to the standby beef and Guinness pie for your entree
UNIQUE FOOD	Irish breakfast on Sunday morning
DRINKS	Full bar, many beers on tap, coffee, tea
SEATING	Many small tables, a long bar, few booths
AMBIENCE	You are likely to see an old man or two at the bar, an intellectual crowd from Harvard or MIT, blue-collar guys having a drink after work, and a young crowd when the weekends start swinging
EXTRAS/NOTES	There are live music nights, beer promo nights, and Boston sports nights for hockey, baseball, and football.

—*John Newton*

Wang's Fast Food

It's all about the dumplings.

$$

509 Broadway, Somerville 02145
(at Medford St.)

Phone (617) 623-2982

CATEGORY	Chinese
HOURS	Mon–Fri: 4 PM–1 AM
	Sat/Sun: 11:30 AM–1 AM
MASS TRANSIT	Bus: #89
PAYMENT	VISA MasterCard
POPULAR FOOD	One of the best places in Boston for authentic Chinese dumplings; there are eight choices of filling, but the spinach variety stands out from the crowd; a dozen dumplings go for $4 or $5
UNIQUE FOOD	Leek and cabbage dumplings
DRINKS	Tea, soft drinks
SEATING	It is more of a takeout place, but you can sit in the simple, 20-seat dining area
AMBIENCE	Exactly what you'd expect of a place called "Wang's Fast Food"; there are few efforts at decoration or coziness—just simple tables and chairs and wood-paneled walls
EXTRAS/NOTES	A great spot for vegetarians and vegans. You can take home a package of 50 frozen dumplings for about $12.

—*Amy Cooper*

WESTERN
SUBURBS

The Farmer in the City

This may be the big city, but that doesn't mean you can't get fresh fruit and vegetables straight from the farm. From June through October, these farmstands and farmer's markets provide some of the healthiest and cheapest food around.

Farmstands

Wilson Farm For the past 118 years, the Wilson family has been treating the area to fresh produce, house-baked breads and sweets, their own hen house eggs, almost 200 cheeses from around the world, and a fresh-squeezed juice bar. In their farm out back they grow a huge selection of salad greens, tomatoes, carrots, cucumbers, squashes, peppers, apples, pumpkins, berries, and melons. *Western Suburbs: 10 Pleasant St., Lexington 02421, (781) 862-3900. www.wilsonfarm.com*

Allandale Farm The last working farm in Boston, Allandale grows their own corn, apples and tomatoes among a plethora of other fruits and vegetables. *Brookline: 259 Allandale Rd., Brookline 02467, (617) 524-1531. www.allandalefarm.com*

Marino Lookout Farm Established in 1680, Lookout Farm is one of the oldest continually oper- ated farms in the country. You can pick your own strawberries (June), apples and raspberries (Sept–Oct), and eggplants and tomatoes. Everything in their 115-acre farm is organically grown. *Western Suburbs: 89 Pleasant St., Natick 01760, (508) 655-4294. www.lookoutfarm.com*

Brooksby Farm This eight-acre farm, just 20 min- utes north of Boston, is owned and operated by the City of Peabody. While they stock all the regular farmstand goodies, they are best known for their apple orchard and pick-your-own strawberries, raspberries, and blueberries. *North Shore: 38 Felton St., Peabody 01960, (978) 531-1631.*

Farmer's Markets

Boston City Hall Plaza *Financial District: Late May–late Nov, Mon and Wed: 11 AM–6 PM.*

Copley Square *Back Bay: Along St. James Ave. at Dartmouth St.: Late May–late Nov, Tues and Fri: 11 AM–6 PM.*

Charlestown *Thompson Sq. on Main St. and Austin St.: June–Oct, Wed: 2 PM–7 PM.*

South Boston *West Broadway: June–Oct, Mon: noon–6 PM.*

South End *Corner of Tremont St. and Clarendon St.: July–Oct, Wed: 3 PM–7 PM.*

Brighton *Fleet Bank Parking lot, 5 Chestnut Hill Ave.: Mid-July–Oct, Sat: 11 AM–3 PM.*

Jamaica Plain *Fleet Bank Parking lot on Centre St.: July–Oct, Tues: noon–5 PM; Sat: noon–3 PM.*

Coolidge Corner, Brookline *Harvard St. parking lot: Mid-June–Oct, Thurs: 1:30 PM–dusk.*

Central Square, Cambridge *Parking lot at Norfolk St. and Bishop Allen Dr.: Late May–late Nov, Mon: noon–6 PM.*

Harvard Square, Cambridge *Charles Hotel Courtyard: Early June–late Nov, Fri: 1 PM–7 PM; Sun: 10 AM–3 PM.*

Davis Square, Somerville *Day St. and Herbert St.: Mid-June–Oct, Wed: noon–6 PM.*

—Kaya Stone

ARLINGTON

Arlington Restaurant and Diner

Classic diner fare in a tidy, modern restaurant.

$$

134 Massachusetts Ave., Arlington 02474
(between Milton St. and Varnum St.)
Phone (781) 646-9266

CATEGORY	Diner
HOURS	Mon–Fri: 6:30 AM–9 PM
	Sat: 6 AM–9 PM
	Sun: 6 AM–1 PM
MASS TRANSIT	Bus: #77 or #79
PAYMENT	VISA · MasterCard · DISCOVER
POPULAR FOOD	Eggs in countless ways, including delicious Mykonos (scrambled with tomatoes and feta), on top of some the best corned beef hash around, and traditional eggs benedict—all piled high with red-potato homefries. A large selection of nightly dinner specials and homemade soups.
UNIQUE FOOD	Great Grape-Nut pudding
DRINKS	Coffee, tea, juices, soft drinks, a small selection of bottled beer, and wine
SEATING	This expanded location—they moved from a smaller space next door a few years ago—is a mixture of cute pink and turquoise booths, tables, and stools at the counter. The booths are prized and worth a little wait.
AMBIENCE	Where the locals and all their friends go; on weekend mornings, especially in nice weather, the line is out the door. Friday and Saturday are also packed at dinnertime.
EXTRAS/NOTES	Favorite waitresses like Angela and Diane will remember how you like your eggs fried and if you drink regular or decaf. Even when the place is jammed, everyone here is friendly and efficient.

—Mary Beth Doyle

Blue Plate Express

Scrumptious home-style cooking
$$

315 Broadway, Arlington 02474
(off Massachusetts Ave.)
Phone (781) 646-4545
www.blueplateexpress.com

CATEGORY	Gourmet Café
HOURS	Tues–Sun: noon–9 PM
MASS TRANSIT	Bus: #77 or #79
PAYMENT	VISA MasterCard AMERICAN EXPRESS
POPULAR FOOD	Caramelized balsamic glazed chicken; herb grilled salmon filet topped with citrus-thyme butter; mac 'n' cheese; hearty chicken soup; roasted garlic mashed potatoes
UNIQUE FOOD	Vital Veggies, an array of unique fixings (such as jicama, chick peas, dried cranberries) cooked in your choice of sauces (balsamic vinaigrette, yogurt curry) and served over hot couscous; tender beef brisket served with a tomato, garlic, and sweet onion sauce; spinach and portabello lasagna topped with a dollop of pesto
DRINKS	Hank's Root Beer, Nantucket Nectars, soda
SEATING	Limited seating of 14 barstools at black granite counters; mostly a takeout place
AMBIENCE	The restaurant, like its cuisine, combines a homey-vibe with accents of American nouveau. The walls are decorated with collages of Dizzy Gillespie, Louis Armstrong, and Billie Holiday, combined with framed paintings of French bistro scenes; and large mirrors and cobalt blue hanging lamps add a contemporary air.
EXTRAS/NOTES	Entrees are served with delicious warm rosemary grilled bread and your selection of one to two sides from 15 choices. If you have room for dessert, choose from two to three flavors of delectable home-baked brownies.

—*Lauren Dozier-Abbate*

Blue-Ribbon Bar-B-Q

Authentic Southern barbecue in northern climes.
$$$

908 Massachusetts Ave., Arlington 02476
(at Highland Ave.)
Phone (781) 648-RIBS • Fax (781) 648-9100
www.blueribbonbbq.com

CATEGORY	Barbecue
HOURS	Sun: noon–8 PM
	Mon–Sat 11:30 AM–9 PM
MASS TRANSIT	Bus: #77 or #79
PAYMENT	VISA MasterCard

POPULAR FOOD	All those sauce-smothered favorites from Carolina, Texas, Tennessee, Missouri, and the Caribbean: pulled pork, ribs, burnt ends, brisket, jerk chicken, and various specials like catfish or turkey. Choose from a half-dozen or so sauces, from mild to hot, to slather on or dip into. Excellent sides like mashed potatoes with gravy, mac 'n' cheese, baked beans, and cornbread pudding.
UNIQUE FOOD	Potlikker with cornbread, which is…oh maybe it's better if you ask them. Excellent homemade pickles. Barbecued burrito filled with pulled pork, burnt ends, or barbecued chicken.
DRINKS	Just soft drinks
SEATING	A few tables and a small counter that faces the street; in summer there are some tables out on the sidewalk
AMBIENCE	A funky retro look, with Southern state license plates and old-fashioned signs next to Blue-Ribbon T-shirts and ball caps for sale. The best albeit warped decoration has been taken down—a row of chicken, pig, and cow bean bag animals strung up by their feet as if waiting to be smoked. This may be Southern cooking but one can't ignore those Northeastern PC sensibilities.
OTHER ONES	• Western Suburbs: 1375 Washington St., West Newton 02465, (617) 332-2583

—Mary Beth Doyle

Neillio's

*An appetizing blend
of Mediterranean cuisines.*

$$

218 Massachusetts Ave., Arlington 02474
(at Winter St., next to the Capitol Theater)
Phone (781) 643-6644 • Fax (781) 646-6457
www.neillios.com

CATEGORY	Mediterranean
HOURS	Mon–Fri: 8 AM–8 PM
	Sat: 8 AM–4 PM
MASS TRANSIT	Bus: #77 or #79 down
PAYMENT	VISA MasterCard AMERICAN EXPRESS
POPULAR FOOD	The lasagna is layered perfectly with either meat and cheese or vegetables and cheese, and topped with an herbed tomato sauce. Or try the roasted portabello panini topped with roasted red peppers and mozzarella cheese; or vegetable stir-fry tossed with a sumptuous light wine sauce and served over linguini. For dessert, choose cannoli filled to order, homemade cookies, or espresso brownies.
UNIQUE FOOD	The chicken with artichokes, lemon, and capers served over linguini is light and delectable.

237

DRINKS	Fresh Samantha juices, soft drinks, coffee, tea
SEATING	The cafe seats 16 at intimate tables and a large white counter overlooking Mass. Ave.
AMBIENCE	Lemon-colored walls are adorned with bright Italian pottery and bunches of garlic; mostly a takeout and pre-movie crowd; friendly staff await your order from behind the counter
EXTRAS/NOTES	If you would prefer to cook at home, fresh-made ravioli, pasta sauces, salads, and a variety of pre-made frozen dinners (lasagna, shepherd's pie, beef bourginnionne) are also available.

—Lauren Abbate

BELMONT

Café Fiorella

No frills, but delicious, high-quality Italian.

$$

263 Belmont St., Belmont 02478
(east of White St.)
Phone (617) 489-1361

CATEGORY	Italian
HOURS	Mon–Sat: 10 AM–10 PM
MASS TRANSIT	Bus: #73 to Waverly Sq.
PAYMENT	VISA MasterCard AMERICAN EXPRESS DISCOVER
POPULAR FOOD	Best known for its wood-fired brick-oven pizza; top it with everything from prosciutto to breaded eggplant to fresh basil; also serving pasta dishes, calzones, salads, and subs
DRINKS	Self-serve soft drinks from a fridge, coffee, espresso
SEATING	For about 20 in tables of two and four
AMBIENCE	A very casual spot with locals ordering at the counter and picking up their purchases at the window; go right ahead and seat yourself; great for a quick but authentic meal
OTHER ONES	• Western Suburbs: 187 North St., Newton 02460, (617) 969-9990 (Full service restaurant)

—Christine Laurence

Rancatore's

(see p. 132)
Ice Cream Shop
283 Belmont St., Belmont 02478
Phone (617) 489-5090

WATERTOWN

Aegean

$$$

640 Arsenal St., Watertown 02472
(at Coolidge Ave.)
Phone (617) 923-7771

CATEGORY	Greek
HOURS	Mon–Sat: 11 AM–10 PM
	Sun: noon–9 PM
MASS TRANSIT	Bus: #70
PAYMENT	VISA MasterCard AMERICAN EXPRESS
POPULAR FOOD	Mousaka, spinach pie, stuffed grape leaves, kebab skewers, Greek salads
UNIQUE FOOD	Fried calamari, chicken egg lemon soup, broiled shrimp with feta
DRINKS	Soft drinks, beer, wine
SEATING	Table and bar seating
AMBIENCE	White tablecloths and fireplace make it a classy-looking establishment frequented by an older Greek clientele
EXTRAS/NOTES	Good size portions and attentive staff.

—Laura Stone

Demos

The shish kebab specialists.

$$

64 Mt. Auburn St., Watertown 02472
(at Summer St.)
Phone (617) 924-9660

CATEGORY	Greek/Middle Eastern
HOURS	Mon–Sat: 11 AM–9:30 PM
	Sun: 11:30 AM–9:30 PM
MASS TRANSIT	Bus: #70 or #71
PAYMENT	Cash only
POPULAR FOOD	Demos does shish kebabs best—a kebab dinner "for one" can really feed two—and you can enjoy two skewers of chicken, beef, or lamb, with vegetables, and a salad and bread for under ten bucks. The Greek sausage is mildly spiced in a wonderful way. For an even cheaper but filling meal, have the meatloaf, a combination of beef and lamb, or the spinach pie, both around $5.
UNIQUE FOOD	Knockwurst
DRINKS	A small selection of beer and wine
SEATING	Room for 50; order at the counter—there'll be a list of specials on a blackboard behind the cashier; find a table and they will bring your meal to you
AMBIENCE	There can be a wait from 6:30 to 8:30 PM most nights, when the place is packed with families and locals and the atmosphere is jovial.
OTHER ONES	• Western Suburbs: 146 Lexington St., Waltham 02452, (781) 893-8359

—Ted Kulik

Iggy's

(see p. 112)
Bakery/Café
205-4 Arlington St., Watertown 02472
Phone (617) 924-0949

Low Fat No Fat Grille and Café

Banishes the boredom
of healthy eating!
$$

222 Arsenal St., Watertown 02472
(near Paul St.)
Phone (617) 923-7686 • Fax (617) 923-0183

CATEGORY	Café
HOURS	Mon–Fri: 10 AM–9:30 PM
	Sat: 10:30 AM–9 PM
	Sun: 11 AM–9 PM
MASS TRANSIT	Bus: #70
PAYMENT	VISA MasterCard AMERICAN EXPRESS
POPULAR FOOD	An extensive wrap menu devoted to healthy eating with a multitude of flavors in mind; follow the crowd and enjoy the chicken meatball with marinara and skim cheese; or break out with a Ginger Thai Chicken Wrap or Bison burger wrap; standout entrees include lean steak or turkey tips
UNIQUE FOOD	Amazing "Air Fries," air-cooked in a special machine; taste-wise you won't know the difference; occasionally they have low fat sweet potato brownies
DRINKS	Berry Blast, Razzapple Burst, California Rainbow, Peach Dream—a fruity array of nutritious smoothies; gourmet Prolattas, a unique blend of high protein mixtures in a variety of flavors from chocolate banana to pineapple cream
SEATING	The cafe seats about 45 people, mostly tables and chairs and it extends into the next door vitamin and health store also owned by the cafe's management
AMBIENCE	Weekday lunchtimes catch the biggest crowd from 11:45 AM–1:30 PM; amid the hustle and bustle, friendly cashiers take orders for wraps, smoothies; the staff aim to have you served within three minutes of ordering; quick and efficient without the typical fast food atmosphere
EXTRAS/NOTES	The Low Fat menu details the fat, protein, carbs, and fiber in each item and no item on the menu has more than three grams of fat or 400 calories. The owner is a former competitive bodybuilder; you can't miss him.

—*Liz McEachern-Hall*

New England's
Landmark Diners

Nowadays, any restaurant with a decent-sized counter and some booths can be called a diner. But if you wanted to open a diner 60 years ago, you had to look in a catalog. Back then, diners were factory-manufactured from floor to ceiling, then transported to their ultimate location. Even though they usually stayed in place, diners bore a vague resemblance to railroad cars with their curvy steel shells, as though they were expected to move around. This ostensibly weird concept for a restaurant can still be found along the highways and byways of Massachusetts, around Boston, and elsewhere in New England, and this ubiquity is no coincidence. The people of Massachusetts were among the diner's greatest champions—helping to spread the restaurant style across America. The Worcester Lunch Car Company, the state's foremost diner manufacturer, rolled out hundreds between 1907 and 1957, many of which still stand today.

Like much in Worcester, the rise and fall of the diner was closely tied to the industrial age. It all started with the lunch cart, a horse-drawn wagon that opened on the street at night to feed factory workers on their late shifts. Samuel Messer Jones brought the first of these to Massachusetts in 1884 (the first lunch cart had been a converted train car opened in Providence some 10 years earlier) and Messer's Worcester lunch wagon was just big enough to allow patrons to eat inside—an important innovation. It was not long before these curbside food carts gave way to a more permanent type of eatery that could stay open at all hours. And these new lunch places did not have to remain in industrial neighborhoods either. They found a growing market along the nation's highways now that Americans were hitting the roads.

The term "diner" arose out of a marketing necessity. Manufacturers wanted to distinguish their spiffy new lunch wagons from the cheaper variety made out of old horse-drawn trolley cars (which had been scrapped with the advent of electric trolleys in the 1920s). The new carts became known as dining cars in order to associate themselves with the fancy restaurant compartments of railroads. "Dining car" led to "diner" and an American symbol was born.

To many, the diner was a dream come true. It didn't matter if you had experience with restaurants. The Worcester Lunch Car Company provided all the basics: counter, refrigerator, stove with fans, interior paneling, cutlery, dishes—even a pie warmer and cake display. In the 1920s and '30s, all this could be yours for under $10,000 with a convenient monthly payment plan.

By the Great Depression, and especially after World War II, diners expanded in size and reached out to a wider audience. A high premium was placed on booths versus counters, which created a better environment for family-style dining. (The notion of a woman scrambling up onto a stool to eat her food was quite unthinkable.) In the 1960s, diners began to resemble more traditional restaurants, pushing family appeal at a time when McDonald's was becoming the new American standard. The diner experience would be associated with leisure rather than with a quick, greasy, or cheap meal. Gone were the aerodynamic steel barrel roofs. Tables were now more common than booths, and even in cases where the diner was manufactured elsewhere (probably sectionally), it was made to appear as organic to the site as possible.

The steel-roofed originals are now considered classics, and some old diners are being refurbished and actually moved across the country to new locations. Of the long list of old-fashioned diners around New England, here are a few of our favorites.

Kelly's Diner, manufactured in 1953, formerly located in Delaware. See p. 217. *Davis Square: 674 Broadway, Somerville 02144, (617) 623-8102.*

Rosebud Diner, manufactured in Worcester, 1941. See review p. 221. *Davis Square: 381 Summer St., Somerville 02144, (617) 666-6015.*

South Street Diner, see p. 12. *Waterfront: 178 Kneeland St., Boston 02111, (617) 350-0028.*

Town Diner *Western Suburbs: 627 Mount Auburn St., Watertown 02472, (617) 924-9789.*

Wilson's Diner, manufactured in Worcester, 1949. *Western Suburbs: 507 Main St., Waltham 02452, (781) 899-0760.*

—Esti Iturralde

Massis Bakery

(see p. 112)
Middle Eastern/American Bakery
569 Mt. Auburn St., Watertown 02472
Phone (617) 924-0537

Sevan Bakery

(see p. 112)
Middle Eastern Bakery
599 Mt. Auburn St., Watertown 02472
Phone (617) 924-3243

Strip-T's

An arousing menu at enticing prices, but the clothes stay on.

$$

93-95 School St., Watertown 02472

(near Arsenal St)

Phone (617) 923-4330 • Fax (617) 923-8062

www.stripts.com

CATEGORY	American Bar & Grill
HOURS	Mon–Fri: 11 AM–9 PM
MASS TRANSIT	Bus: #70 down Arsenal St.
PAYMENT	VISA MasterCard AMERICAN EXPRESS DISCOVER
POPULAR FOOD	Good soups and sandwiches, and the dinner entrees are a bargain at around $10; soft and chewy cookies
UNIQUE FOOD	The rotating blackboard menu, with some Southern and Cajun specials and lots of fish, adds some zest to an otherwise meat-and-potatoes menu
DRINKS	Beer and wine
SEATING	About ten tables, plus a good-sized lunch counter
AMBIENCE	A fun place, but not for the faint of heart—Friday is "customer abuse day"
EXTRAS/NOTES	Although the true origin of the unique name is the restaurant's original specialty sandwich, the roast sirloin strip, the staff says the name is designed "to keep out the pretentious people…it's tough enough serving people all day long." Apparently, it worked—the wait staff knows most of its clientele by name (or "makes one up") and are always quick with a joke (or insult).

—Brendan Gibbon

Sushi King

Raw power, served fresh and cheap.

$$$

600 Mt. Auburn St., Watertown 02472

(at corner of Irma Ave.)

Phone (617) 972-8580 • Fax (617) 972-8505

CATEGORY	Japanese
HOURS	Mon–Sat: 11:30 AM–10 PM Sun: 11:30 AM–9 PM
MASS TRANSIT	Bus: #71
PAYMENT	VISA MasterCard AMERICAN EXPRESS DISCOVER
POPULAR FOOD	Extremely fresh sushi specials named simply A to K and one to ten; for lunch they're a generous eight bucks or less. The appetizer menu is incredible and each can easily make a meal for one. No visit is complete without sampling the Korean pancakes, a combination of scallions, crab, and green peppers.
UNIQUE FOOD	There are Thai, Korean, and non-sushi Japanese dishes; of these, the *pad* Thai and tempura deserve a special nod.
DRINKS	Soft drinks, mineral water, and green tea; plum wine or sake is strictly BYOB

SEATING	Modest; seats up to 36
AMBIENCE	This small cafe is filled with professors and PhD student types
EXTRAS/NOTES	Though South Korean, restaurant owners/husband-wife team Cheh Yoon Bak and Johng Wan Bak know their sushi through studying in Japan during their more than 20 year restaurant career. Their experience shows in the kind and competent service and in every delicious item on the menu.

—*Barry Willingham*

Town Diner

(see p. 242)

Old-fashioned Diner

627 Mount Auburn St., Watertown 02472

Phone (617) 924-9789

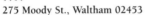

(see p. 242)

WALTHAM

Bison County

Where the 'twain shall meet:
the wild West in the heart of the Northeast.

$$$$

275 Moody St., Waltham 02453

(at Pine St.)

Phone (781) 642-9720 • Fax (781) 642-9313

www.bisoncountybbq.com

CATEGORY	Southern Barbecue
HOURS	Mon–Wed: 5 PM–midnight
	Thurs/Fri: 11:30 AM-midnight
	Sat/Sun: noon–midnight
MASS TRANSIT	T: Commuter Rail-Fitchburg to Waltham
PAYMENT	
POPULAR FOOD	South Carolina- and Texas-style barbecue; the pulled pork sandwiches and all varieties of ribs make it a force to be reckoned with for nearby Blue-Ribbon Barbecue
UNIQUE FOOD	Where else in New England (or anywhere east of the Rockies for that matter) can you get your hands on a buffalo burger or bison tips? And the pulled pork quesadilla is not only unique, but amazing.
DRINKS	Dixie lagers and 15 beers on tap; full bar
SEATING	Tons of seating available in the bar and the dining rooms
AMBIENCE	The ambience of Bison County is ultra casual. For females, it's a great place to be waited on by attractive, nice male waiters and be outnumbered by a cross-section of mostly men who work in the area. Men—it's your ideal food emporium (meat slathered in sauce) with TVs to watch sports while drinking with your buddies at the bar.

—*Jodi Hullinger*

Carl's

Nondescript dive proves yummy.

$$

55 Prospect St., Waltham 02453
(at Vernon St.)
Phone (781) 893-9313

CATEGORY	Sub Shop
HOURS	Mon–Sat: 11 AM–9 PM Sun: noon–6 PM
MASS TRANSIT	T: Commuter Rail-Fitchburg to Waltham
PAYMENT	Cash only
POPULAR FOOD	The burritos are huge and super good, directly in contrast to this hole-in-the-wall's own size and ambience. Get the Carl's Original stuffed with the usual suspects—grilled chicken, rice, beans, salsa, and a mix of jack and cheddar cheeses.
UNIQUE FOOD	Innovative and entertaining subs including the Budster (cold chicken cutlet with barbecue sauce, cheese, and bacon) and Giambotta (a hot "Big Boy" sub with steak, cheese, green peppers, onions, mushrooms, sausage, pepperoni, salami, and tomato sauce)
DRINKS	Sodas
SEATING	No seating during the colder months, but there are about five tables outside in warmer weather
AMBIENCE	Carl's is a dive frequented by area employees and high school/Brandeis students alike

—Jodi Hullinger

Demos

(see p. 239)
Greek/Middle Eastern
146 Lexington St., Waltham 02452
Phone (781) 893-8359

Domenic's Paninoteca

Waltham's go to Paninoteca.

$$

987 Main St., Waltham 02451
(near South St.)
Phone (781) 899-3817 • Fax (781) 899-3664

CATEGORY	Italian
HOURS	Mon–Fri: 10:30 AM–5:30 PM
PAYMENT	Cash only
MASS TRANSIT	T: Commuter Rail-Fitchburg to Waltham
POPULAR FOOD	Domenic's has mastered the lunch rush; they pre-make their Parma, Verde, Melenzane, Tonno, and Pollo paninis and then display them on a shelf above hot dishes like homemade gnocchi, chicken parm, and pizza slices. The panini aren't cheap (around $7), but they are huge and

worth it. You can also make your own deli sandwich with homemade ciabattini and focaccia breads and Boar's Head meats.

UNIQUE FOOD	Anise cookies—black licorice flavored sugar cookies topped with yummy icing and multi-colored sprinkles (the more icing the better)
DRINKS	Italian imported beverages like San Benedetto bottled water
SEATING	Mostly a takeout place with a few tables inside the cramped space; on warmer days, the seating doubles with a few more tables outside on Main St.
AMBIENCE	A family-owned Italian deli boasting pictures of grandchildren behind the register; with a huge lunch clientele, there is often up to a 15-minute wait between noon and 2 PM

—*Jodi Hullinger*

Iguana Cantina

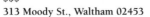

A food fiesta featuring muchos margaritas and one grande iguana.
$$$
313 Moody St., Waltham 02453
(at Spruce St., next to Jordan's Furniture)
Phone (781) 891-3039 • Fax (781) 891-1154
www.theiguanacantina.com

CATEGORY	Mexican/Southwestern
HOURS	Mon:11:30 AM–9:30 PM Tues–Thurs: 11:30 AM–10 PM Fri/Sat: 11:30 AM–11 PM Sun: 3 PM–9:30 PM
MASS TRANSIT	T: Commuter Rail-Fitchburg to Waltham
PAYMENT	VISA MasterCard AMERICAN EXPRESS DISCOVER
POPULAR FOOD	Fresh and plentiful fajitas; extra grande Burrito Grande; and Rosie's Club Wrap with chicken, avocado, and salsa mayo
UNIQUE FOOD	Menu incorporates Southwestern, Caribbean, and even Asian influences; notables include coconut shrimp (six jumbo shrimp encrusted in coconut, flash-fried, and served with a unique honey mustard sauce), blackened red snapper, and curried chicken
DRINKS	Fifteen homemade margarita concoctions, 20 varieties of tequila, and a handful of Mexican beers in addition to a full bar
SEATING	About 100–125 can snugly fit indoors while the red brick patio out back (open from late April to early November) adds room for an extra 50
AMBIENCE	Red adobe, colorful tiles, and the ever-present iguana give the Cantina one of the most festive dining spaces around. Brandeis students, families, and first date types play out their usual dinnertime chaos. Gen-X working types congregate

on the patio for group therapy in the form
of a couple of stiff 'ritas.

OTHER ONES • Western Suburbs: 1656 Worcester Rd.,
Framingham 01702, (508) 875-1188
• Western Suburbs: 66 Chestnut St.,
Needham 02492, (781) 444-9976

—Jesse Crary

Joan and Ed's Deli

Knishes and kugel in Metro-West.
$$
1298 Worcester St., Natick 01760
(Sherwood Plaza, at Dean Rd., near Rte. 9)
Phone (508) 653-4442

CATEGORY	Deli
HOURS	Sun: 8 AM–8 PM
	Mon–Thurs: 9:30 AM–9 PM
	Fri: 9:30 AM–10 PM
	Sat: 8 AM–10 PM
PARKING	Free lot
PAYMENT	VISA MasterCard AMERICAN EXPRESS DISCOVER
POPULAR FOOD	Older folks and former city-dwellers come for traditional Jewish favorites, such as matzo ball soup, whitefish, reubens, and latkes; others just come for the impressive length and variety of the menu
UNIQUE FOOD	Latke Stuffers are a Joan and Ed's invention: deli sandwiches that include a potato pancake along with meat and sauce in a bulkie roll. Another unusual dish is the Jewish Pu Pu Platter, a sampling of several traditional favorites that makes a good introduction for newcomers to New York deli fare.
DRINKS	Beer, wine, soft drinks, tea, and coffee are also available, but so are two kinds of drink rarely found in the Metro-West region: Dr. Brown's Kosher carbonated beverages and made-to-order fountain sodas, like root beer floats, chocolate Cokes, and New York egg creams
SEATING	Booths and tables of various sizes
AMBIENCE	A combination of the traditional Kosher deli and 1950s-style diners, the walls are covered with Jewish food and culture items while vintage rock 'n' roll plays in the background. Typical patrons vary from the early bird set in the late afternoon to high school kids looking for a post-movie sandwich and Coke on weekend nights.
EXTRAS/NOTES	Call ahead when making late-night runs to Joan and Ed's as all closing times are flexible; 9 PM could actually come as early as 8:30 PM if business is slow on a particular evening.

—John Woodford

Lizzy's

(see p. 132)
Ice Cream Shop/Vegan-friendly
367 Moody St., Waltham 02453
Phone (781) 893-6677

Taqueria Mexico

Cheap, authentic Mexican with heart.
$$
24 Charles St., Waltham 02453
(one block from Moody St.)
Phone (781) 647-0166

CATEGORY	Mexican
HOURS	Daily: 10 AM–11 PM
MASS TRANSIT	T: Commuter Rail-Fitchburg to Waltham
PAYMENT	VISA MasterCard AMERICAN EXPRESS
POPULAR FOOD	Burritos and quesadillas, (spicy chorizo, *carnitas*); tamales; *chiles rellenos*
UNIQUE FOOD	Tacos, burritos, quesadillas or tortas come filled with authentic fillings such as *carne asada*, steamed beef, tongue, pastor (pork and chili), mushrooms, or potatoes; *pollo con mole*
DRINKS	Fresh fruit smoothies and shakes; mango milkshake; *jugo especial* packed with six types of fruit; Corona; $2 sangria
SEATING	Good-sized booths and tables with seating for about 75
AMBIENCE	No-frills crowd for a no-frills place: Mexican and Guatemalan families, college students, and the occasional yuppie; service can be slow, but it's always pleasant; Spanish jukebox
EXTRAS/NOTES	Family-owned and operated; everything is homemade and fresh, including the two types of salsa that accompany every meal

—*Melissa Carlson*

Wilson's Diner

(see p. 242)
Old-fashioned Diner
507 Main St., Waltham 02452
Phone (781) 899-0760

LEXINGTON

Wilson Farm

(see p. 234)
Farm Stand
10 Pleasant St., Lexington 02421
Phone (781) 862-3900

NATICK

Marino Lookout Farm

(see p. 234)
Farm Stand
89 Pleasant St., Natick 01760
Phone (508) 655-4294

NEWTON

Amarin of Thailand

The mecca of Thai food.
$$$
1 Newton Pl., 287 Centre St., Newton 02458
(at Pearl St.)
Phone (617) 527-5255

CATEGORY	Thai
HOURS	Mon–Thurs: 11:30 AM–3 PM, 5 PM–9:30 PM Fri/Sat: 11:30 AM–3 PM, 5 PM–10 PM Sun: 4 PM–9:30 PM
PARKING	Free validated parking in the garage above the restaurant
PAYMENT	VISA MasterCard AMERICAN EXPRESS DISCOVER
POPULAR FOOD	Chicken or beef masaman curry, which unlike northern Thai curries incorporates coconut milk; spicy classic hot salmon or chon-buri squid; coconut ice cream; lychees in syrup on ice
UNIQUE FOOD	*Todman,* which is minced shrimp and sliced Thai long beans served with a cucumber dipping sauce; *som-tum,* a shrimp and papaya salad seasoned with garlic and chili
DRINKS	Beer and wine; Thai iced tea
SEATING	Seats approximately 100; reservations are definitely needed on the weekends; there is traditional floor seating in the center of the restaurant, complete with a canopy of gold lotus flowers and elephant statues
AMBIENCE	A peaceful atmosphere and Thai artifacts hang on the walls amidst plants and flowers.
OTHER ONES	• Western Suburbs: 27 Grove St., Wellesley 02482, (781) 239-1350

—Heidi Solomon

Baker's Best

$$
27 Lincoln St., Newton 02458
(at Adams St.)
Phone (617) 332-4588 • Fax (617) 332-9188

CATEGORY	Café
HOURS	Daily: 7:30 AM–9:30 PM
MASS TRANSIT	T: Green line-D to Newton Highlands
PAYMENT	VISA MasterCard AMERICAN EXPRESS

POPULAR FOOD	Fabulous fresh sandwiches, soups, and desserts
UNIQUE FOOD	The chicken piccata is one of the most frequently ordered items for dinner.
DRINKS	Soft drinks, juices, teas, coffees
SEATING	Plenty of tables available, with some along the large sunny windows
AMBIENCE	Casual, homey, and laid-back; bigger than most cafés but steers clear of any cafeteria feel; the walls are a warm yellow dotted with intriguing and haunting pictures of mysterious landscapes.

—Jenny Bengen

Blue-Ribbon Bar-B-Q

(see p. 236)
Southern Barbecue
1375 Washington St., West Newton 02465
Phone (617) 332-2583

Buff's Pub

*Suburban pub famous
for its buffalo wings.*
$$
317 Washington St., Newton 02458
(at Peabody St.)
Phone (617) 332-9134 • Fax (617) 332-9134

CATEGORY	Bar & Grill
HOURS	Mon–Fri: 11:30 AM–11:30 PM Sat/Sun: 5 PM–11:30 PM
MASS TRANSIT	T: Commuter Rail-Framingham to Newtonville
PAYMENT	Cash only
POPULAR FOOD	Heralded as the best buffalo wings for miles around; wings come in barbecue, honey hot, or honey barbecue, and are served in half ($3.95) or full ($7.95) orders. You can order each flavor of wings in varying degrees of heat, although the way that they subtract heat is just to subtract sauce, making the milder wings rather dry.
UNIQUE FOOD	A notable feature of Buff's menu is simply the low prices; there are no meals over $8.50.
DRINKS	A full bar with an especially good beer selection and about ten different wines
SEATING	There is a line of booths against one wall, and about ten other smaller tables.
AMBIENCE	Weekday lunch hours are busy at Buff's, as there are a number of businesses in the immediate area, and any night that there's a pro team game on TV, it's sure to be bustling. Décor is simple but inviting, with a giant buffalo head and a multitude of beer mirrors on the walls, rows of beer mugs for the regulars hanging on the ceiling above the bar, and not much else.

EXTRAS/NOTES As small as Buff's is, there is a shoulder-
height partition between the bar and the
dining area to lean on. It doesn't really do
much to separate the diners from the bar
crowd, which in this case is fine. It's a
neighborhood bar where everyone pretty
much wants to be able to see and mingle
with everyone else.

—*Kimberly Loomis*

Café Fiorella

(see p. 238)
Italian
187 North St., Newton 02460
Phone (617) 969-9990

Flat Breads Café

Sandwiches, pizza, pasta, and more.
$$
11 Commonwealth Ave., Newton 02467
(near Waban Hill Rd.)
Phone (617) 964-8484 • Fax (617) 964-4685

CATEGORY	Café
HOURS	Mon–Fri: 7 AM–8 PM
	Sat/Sun: 8 AM–7 PM
MASS TRANSIT	T: Green line-B to Boston College
PAYMENT	VISA MasterCard AMERICAN EXPRESS
POPULAR FOOD	Wraps, including Plymouth Plantation (turkey, cranberry chutney, bread stuffing, mayo, lettuce, tomato, and onion in a pita), and a variety of other vegetarian, chicken, beef, pork, or seafood options; the Chicken Acapulco (grilled chicken, roasted green tomato cilantro salsa, mozzarella, cheddar, avocado, and onions in a tortilla); Philly steak and cheese
UNIQUE FOOD	Teriyaki Trio, a mixture of grilled chicken breast, beef or stir-fried vegetables, white rice, teriyaki sauce, carrots, onions, bean sprouts, leeks, red peppers, snow peas, and mozzarella in a pita; La Fiesta, a tasty combo of avocado, cheddar, Swiss, American, roasted red tomato cilantro salsa, and onions in a pita; *pad* Thai wrap; pesto or barbecued chicken pizza
DRINKS	Sodas, juices, and bottled waters
SEATING	The main entrance is a takeout counter, but a side room contains a number of small tables
AMBIENCE	Bright and upbeat, with checkered floors, mirrors, and clean white walls; across the street from BC, Flat Breads (and Sweet Basil, the pizza "section" of the restaurant) is obviously a favorite with college students, faculty, and staff

—*Meaghan Mulholland*

J.P. Licks

(see p. 131)
Ice Cream Shop
46 Langley Rd., Newton 02459
Phone (617) 244-0666

Johnny's Luncheonette

Milkshakes to matzo balls: Johnny's be good.
$$$
30 Langley Rd., Newton Centre 02159
(between Beacon St. and Center St.)
Phone (617) 527-3223 • Fax (617) 527-4103

CATEGORY	Retro '50s Diner
HOURS	Mon–Sat: 7 AM–10 PM
	Sun: 8 AM–9 PM
MASS TRANSIT	T: Green line-D to Newton Centre
PAYMENT	VISA MasterCard
POPULAR FOOD	Breakfast belt-busters with names like The 18-Wheeler (three eggs with flapjacks, home fries, and your choice of bacon, sausage links, ham, or homemade turkey and apple sausage). More modern health-conscious fare such as the You Look Mahvelous Omelette (egg beaters, low-fat mozzarella, broccoli, and tomato, served with cantaloupe wedges). Also, waffles, cheese blintzes, and salmon or portobello burger.
UNIQUE FOOD	Thick, hand-cut crispy sweet potato fries with honey-mustard dip; French toast on thick golden slabs of homemade challah bread in such varieties as crunchy and cornbread crunchy (sprinkled with toasted almonds); Johnny's Penicillin (chicken soup) with matzoh balls—the ultimate stick-to-your-ribs comfort food; turkey apple sausages
DRINKS	Dig it, Daddy-o! Traditional 1950s soda-shop fare including shakes, floats, egg creams, and malted frappes. Also non-fat yogurt shakes and smoothies, specialty sodas, soft drinks, beer, and wine.
SEATING	Always crowded intimate space; booths, some tables, and a small bar space; expect a wait on weekend mornings
AMBIENCE	Upon entering Johnny's luncheonette (the former site of a Jewish deli, now remodeled to '50s-era Americana perfection, complete with Formica table tops, red vinyl booths, mirrors, and black-and-white school photos), one almost expects girls in ponytails and poodle skirts to be sipping milkshakes, high school boys in varsity lettermen jackets chomping burgers in a crowded booth, and maybe even some black-leather-coated hoodlums loitering by the jukebox. The atmosphere is vibrant and traditional without being cliched, and offers distinctly modern touches to the standard diner grub one would expect.

OTHER ONES • Harvard Square: 1105 Massachusetts Ave.,
Cambridge 02138, (617) 495-0055
—Meaghan Mulholland

New England Soup Factory

(see p. 121)
Soup
244 Needham St., Newton 02464
Phone (617) 558-9988

Rosie's Bakery

(see p. 111)
Bakery
**Chestnut Hill Shopping Center,
9 Boylston St., Chestnut Hill 02467**
Phone (617) 277-5629

Sweet Tomatoes

*Some of the tastiest pizza you'll
find in Boston, period.*
$$
47 Langley Rd. Newton Centre 02459
(at Beacon St.)
Phone (617) 558-0222
www.sweettomatoespizza.com

CATEGORY	Pizza by the Slice
HOURS	Daily: 11:30 AM–9 PM
MASS TRANSIT	T: Green line-D to Newton Centre
PAYMENT	VISA MasterCard AMERICAN EXPRESS
POPULAR FOOD	In addition to the made-to-order pizza pies, really big individual slices are served here every day until 4 PM; you can choose between the Specialty Slice of the Day or a cheese slice. Go for the former—specialties of the day are fabulous, especially the Pesto Splash (with light pesto, mozzarella, tomatoes, and garlic), The Hawaiian (which uses real Canadian bacon), and the White Greek (spinach, feta, garlic); the crust is light and thin.
UNIQUE FOOD	The tomato sauce here isn't cooked and you can find a few more toppings here than you will at most pizza parlors, including eggplant, portobello mushrooms, goat cheese, Canadian bacon, and ricotta cheese; all pizzas can be served without sauce and/or cheese; there are also huge calzones
DRINKS	Sodas and juices
SEATING	Things can get a bit crowded here during lunch and dinner with people vying for space at one of the three sit down tables and the two standing tables; there's usually a table outdoors as well, and a large bench inside for those who'd like to eat and run.

AMBIENCE	A favorite spot among the health conscious because the dough and sauce are both non-fat, Sweet Tomatoes gets more requests for its healthy spinach and mushroom pizzas than almost any other; people come here for the peppers, not the pepperoni.
OTHER ONES	• Cape Cod: 770 Main St., Osterville 02655, (508) 420-1717
	• Cape Cod: 148 Rte. 6A, Sandwich 02563, (508) 888-5979

— Jenny Bengen

White Mountain Creamery

(see p. 101)
Ice Cream Shop
19 Commonwealth Ave., Chestnut Hill 02467
Phone (617) 527-8790

NEEDHAM

Bai Thong

Visually appealing without all the lines.
$$$
1257 Highland Ave., Needham 02492
(west of Pickering St., in small shopping center across from the Needham High School field)
Phone (781) 433-0272 • Fax (781) 433-0274

CATEGORY	Thai
HOURS	Mon–Thurs: 11:30 AM–9:30 PM
	Fri/Sat: 11:30 AM–10 PM
	Sun: 4 PM–9 PM
PAYMENT	
POPULAR FOOD	Classic Hot Salmon, which provides a nice five ounces or so of tenderly steamed fish; the sauce is a little hot and lemony, with basil, green beans, and red and green peppers over rice
UNIQUE FOOD	Swordfish Choo Choo; Hot Crazy Noodle with ground chicken, eggplant, and peppers
DRINKS	Thai iced tea and coffee, lemonade, sodas
SEATING	Fits about 50
AMBIENCE	Green plants hang from wooden trellises, and a fresh flower adorns every table; service is prompt and portions are good.
EXTRAS/NOTES	Bai Thong is tucked away in a nondescript strip mall, but inside it's a secret garden of Thai freshness and quiet respite from office life.

—Paula Foye

Iguana Cantina

(see p. 246)
Mexican/Southwestern
66 Chestnut St., Needham 02492
Phone (781) 444-9976

Zathmary's Specialty Foods Marketplace

(see p. 118)
Gourmet Cafeteria
1000 Highland Ave., Needham Heights 02494
Phone (781) 449-9090

WELLESLEY

Amarin of Thailand

(see p. 249)
Thai
27 Grove St., Wellesley 02482
Phone (781) 239-1350

Vidalia's Truck Stop

*Blue-collar wannabe dining
in the land of lunching ladies.*
$$
13 Central St., Wellesley 02482
(at Crest Rd.)
Phone (781) 431-0011

CATEGORY	Diner
HOURS	Sun–Thurs: 8 AM–8 PM
	Fri/Sat: 8 AM–9 PM
MASS TRANSIT	T: Commuter Rail-Framingham to Wellesley Square
PAYMENT	VISA MasterCard AMERICAN EXPRESS
POPULAR FOOD	Burgers, spicy chicken fingers, and vegetarian chili
UNIQUE FOOD	Prides itself on nothing unique—only hearty, carefully prepared, albeit overpriced, all-American favorites
DRINKS	Beer, wine, and soft drinks
SEATING	Up to 90 fit in the booths, tables, and counter
AMBIENCE	The movie-set perfection inside Vidalia's—that only an interior designer could have achieved—is a microcosm of the pristine movie-set quality of the town of Wellesley. This crowded, noisy, and friendly neighborhood establishment where customers greet the manager by name attracts local lunching ladies, business types, young families, and even an old guard of the American Legion in his entire get up—pins on hat and all.

—*Charlene X. Wang*

FRAMINGHAM

Café Belo

(see p. 88)
Brazilian
94 Union Ave., Framingham 01702
(508) 620-9354

Desmond O'Malley's
(see The Kinsale, p. 7)
Irish Pub
30 Worcester Rd., Framingham 01701
Phone (508) 875-9400

Iguana Cantina
(see p. 246)
Mexican/Southwestern
1656 Worcester Rd., Framingham 01702
Phone (508) 875-1188

Rami's
(see p. 114)
Israeli/Kosher
341 Cochichuate Rd. (Rte. 30), Framingham 01701
Phone (508) 370-3577

NORTH SHORE

Brooksby Farm

(see p. 234)
Farmstand
38 Felton St., Peabody 01960
Phone (978) 531-1631

Clam Box of Ipswich

*Fried clams served in the world's
largest takeout container.*
Since 1935
$$$
246 High St. (Rte. 1A), Ipswich 01938
(south of Mile Ln.)
Phone (978) 356-9707
www.ipswichma.com/clambox/

CATEGORY	Seafood Shack
HOURS	Wed–Mon: 11 AM–8 PM (Early Mar.–late Nov. only, hours vary slightly by season)
PAYMENT	Cash only
POPULAR FOOD	Whole-bellied fried clams—not too greasy, not too rubbery, and extremely flavorful; thick and crispy onion rings; lobster rolls
UNIQUE FOOD	Fisherman's platter with sweet scallops; fish chowder
DRINKS	Soft drinks
SEATING	Outside deck seating as well as booths and tables indoors
AMBIENCE	The stand is shaped like a takeout clam box; long lines are almost inevitable
EXTRAS/NOTES	While nearby Woodman's (see p. 263) claims to have "invented the fried clam," the Clam Box counters that "we perfected it."

—*Kyle Konrad*

Farnham's

Fried clams with tender loving care.
$$$
88 Eastern Ave. (Rte. 133), Essex 01929
(north of Lufkin St.)
Phone (978) 768-6643

CATEGORY	Seafood Shack
HOURS	Sun–Thurs: 11 AM–8 PM Fri/Sat: 11 AM–9 PM (Mar.–Nov. only)
PAYMENT	Cash only
POPULAR FOOD	Woodman's and the Clam Box may get all the attention but many locals would argue that Farnham's has the best fried clams around; they cook every order individually and dip their shellfish in egg before battering to give them a more golden color
UNIQUE FOOD	They also serve breakfast
DRINKS	Beer and wine
SEATING	Wooden seats and benches in addition to a small counter with stools

AMBIENCE	The eating area is quite small; your best bet is to take your meal outside for a picnic on the edge of the marsh

—*Kyle Konrad*

Iggy's

(see p. 112)
Bakery/Café
5 Pleasant St., Marblehead 01945
Phone (781) 639-4717

J. Pace & Son

(see p. 6)
Italian
325 Main St., Saugus 01906
Phone (781) 231-9599

Kelly's Roast Beef

A beachside icon.
Since 1951
$$

410 Revere Beach Blvd., Revere 02151
(at Oak Island)
Phone (781) 284-9129 • Fax (781) 284-5199
www.kellysroastbeef.com

CATEGORY	Stand
HOURS	Daily: 6 AM–3 AM
MASS TRANSIT	T: Blue line to Revere Beach
PAYMENT	Cash only
POPULAR FOOD	Kelly's invented the roast beef sandwich. "On a hot summer's day, two large roast beefs were cooked on rotisseries, sliced and piled high on a sandwich roll. Before that time, no one had ever heard of serving such a sandwich," proclaims the family-run eatery. In addition to the famous roast beef sandwiches, try Kelly's burgers and fried seafood.
DRINKS	No beer, no wine, not even milkshakes; just sodas that taste perfect with a burger and onion rings.
SEATING	After you walk away from the walk-up window, you have two options; if it's warm, you eat at the classically styled pavilion overlooking Revere Beach; if it's cold, you eat in your car.
AMBIENCE	A summertime visit to Kelly's isn't simply picking up food; it's a night on the town. Along Revere Beach Blvd., buff boys cruise in jacked up muscle cars and half-clad girls play with their cell phones. Under wrought-iron pavilions, elderly couples shuffle cards and sometimes shuffle their feet to music from portable boom boxes. The air smells like sea salt, and the flavor on everyone's tongue is from Kelly's.

EXTRAS/NOTES	Kelly's Roast Beef is more than a beachside, walk up window. It is an institution. Founded in 1951, it has outlasted the elegant dance halls and wild rides that once made Revere shine. As the new century unfolds, Kelly's remains a vibrant and constant link to 20th-century Boston. It closes only on Christmas and Thanksgiving, but even then someone sticks around to hand out free coffee and danishes.
OTHER ONES	• North Shore: Liberty Tree Mall, 165 Endicott St., Danvers 01923, (978) 777-1290
	• Western Suburbs: 2 Under Price Way, Natick 01760, (508) 872-4900
	• North Shore: Rte. 1 South, Saugus 01906, (781) 233-5700

—Mark Ferguson

Kowloon

Kitschy Polynesian palace.
Since 1950

$$$

948 Broadway (Rte. 1), Saugus 01906
(South of Thomas St.)
Phone (781) 233-0077

CATEGORY	Chinese/Thai/Tiki
HOURS	Daily: 11:30 AM–2 AM; food served until 1 AM
PAYMENT	VISA MasterCard AMERICAN EXPRESS DISCOVER
POPULAR FOOD	Kowloon has created the *War and Peace* of restaurant menus with over 200 Chinese, Thai, and American dishes; in a typical week Kowloon serves 1,000 pu-pu platters, 2,500 orders of fried rice, and over 5,200 pounds of pork
UNIQUE FOOD	There's a separate quieter, classier Thai dining room with its own large Thai menu
DRINKS	An endless list of fruity, umbrella decorated drinks served in fancy tiki mugs; the Mai Tai is their specialty
SEATING	Over 1,200 seats
AMBIENCE	Pure Polynesian heaven; everywhere you turn there's more tiki kitsch—from a huge fountain spurting tiki colored water to tiki masks adorning the bamboo walls to the fake palm trees lining the booths
EXTRAS/NOTES	In 1950, the Wong family opened a small 40-seat restaurant in a former ice cream parlor. Four generations later, Kowloon is the busiest Chinese restaurant in the country feeding over 20,000 people every week. It is also home to Nick's Comedy Stop and has hosted such stars as Jerry Seinfeld and The Temptations.

—Kyle Konrad

Of Gold, Glory, and Cod: A Fish 'n' Chips Tale

Boston is an overgrown seaside town. Go anywhere near the water and you can expect to be tempted by the sight of heaping portions of thick, greasy, batter-fried fish fillets with a dollop of tartar sauce and fries. The ubiquity of fish 'n' chips suits a place with such Old World leanings as New England, but fried fish is also an artifact of Boston's seafaring past, a history that runs as deep as its European roots.

The long, storied history of fish in Boston begins with cod. If your people came over on the Mayflower this silvery fish had something to do with it, and you may consider yourself a descendant of what has been known as "the codfish aristocracy." While the Pilgrims were certainly seeking religious freedom, they were also lured by a place that promised a never-ending feast of fruits from the sea, a place seductively named "Cape Cod." In those days cod was far more valuable than lobster which, unlike today, could be seen in piles washed up on the beach, to be eaten only in moments of abject desperation. Cod, on the other hand, could be cured with salt, thus providing food during lean months and lasting long voyages by ship to be exported abroad for a handsome profit. The coast of Massachusetts positively teemed with it.

The Pilgrims were terrible fishermen at first, which may explain the conspicuous absence of salt cod on Thanksgiving, but as more skilled countrymen arrived on their shores, fisheries grew in places like Gloucester, Salem, and Dorchester. Cod was gold—a flaky, scaly sort of gold—and pretty soon the Boston-Bilbao cod-for-wine-and-iron trade was pouring money into Boston harbor, helping to drive the city's ascent to a capital of the New World.

The role of the cod in nation building has been immortalized in the Massachusetts House of Representatives where a painted, five-foot long wooden carving of the "Sacred Cod" has overseen lawmaking for decades (except when it was "codnapped" briefly in 1933 by pranksters from the Harvard Lampoon) and points in a different direction depending on which party holds the majority (north for Democrats, south for Republicans). Why sacred? Could be fish favoritism, or if you believe old fishing tales, it's because the identifying stripe on either side of the cod is the very mark of Jesus' grasp. Even Puritans bend the rule about worshipping strange gods.

In 1974, cod was officially named the state fish of Massachusetts.

Fish 'n' chips is typically made of cod or haddock. But what of scrod, one might ask? Scrod is not actually a unique species of fish. The term was thought to be coined many years ago by the restaurant at the Parker House (also noteworthy for its rolls). At market, the restaurant would always purchase the newest, firmest fish, which would have rested at the top of a large fishing vessel's hold. There was no telling what kind of fish would have ended up on top, whether cod, haddock, pollack, or something else, so the restaurant saved itself from printing headaches by listing the single name of "scrod," which signified the freshest catch. The word itself could have been a contraction of, once again, "sacred cod." Today, the name is usually applied to young haddock or cod—with indifference toward which may have more sacred qualities.

Overfishing has significantly depleted cod, the one-time plentiful "beef of the sea." The biggest culprits have been trawling and gillnetting, practices that catch large numbers of cod near the ocean floor, right where they dwell. In Gloucester, the most famous of Massachusetts fishing towns, the population of cod dropped so steeply in the '90s that long-overdue regulation was introduced to reduce the length of the fishing season. Families that once thrived on cod fishing for generations have left the trade now that their costs have far exceeded their expected revenue. An enormous quantity—five million pounds—of cod are hauled into Gloucester's port each year, but it is doubtful whether the fish, once even more abundant in these waters, will ever completely rebound.

While supporting one of the region's oldest industries, you can find some of the best (and cheapest) fish 'n' chips at the following restaurants in and around Boston:

No Name (see p. 10) *Waterfront: 15 Fish Pier St. West, Boston 02210, (617) 338-7539*

Fish Pier (see p. 148) *South Boston: 667 E. Broadway, Boston 02127, (617) 269-2111*

Matt Murphy's (see p. 120) *Brookline Village: 14 Harvard St., Brookline 02445, (617) 232-0188*

Courthouse Seafood (see p. 169) *Inman Square: 498 Cambridge St., Cambridge 02141, (617) 491-1213*

The Clam Box (see p. 258) *North Shore: 246 High St. (Rte. 1A), Ipswich 01938, (978) 356-9707*

Farnham's (see p. 258) *North Shore: 88 Eastern Ave. (Rte. 133), Essex 01929, (978) 768-6643*

Woodman's (see p. 262) *North Shore: 121 Main St., Essex 01929, (978) 768-6451*

—Esti Iturralde

Porthole Restaurant

Family restaurant with nautical flare.
Since 1967
$$$

98 Lynnway, Lynn 01902
(Rte. 1A South. towards the coast)
Phone (781) 595-7733 • Fax (781) 596-0020
www.portholerestaurant.com

CATEGORY	Seafood
HOURS	Daily: 11:30 AM–9:30 PM
PAYMENT	VISA MasterCard AMERICAN EXPRESS DISCOVER
POPULAR FOOD	Thick, hearty chowder; large portions of fresh fried seafood; baked stuffed jumbo shrimp
UNIQUE FOOD	Deep fried pickles; haddock and shrimp Rockefeller (with spinach, cheese, and bread crumbs)
DRINKS	Full bar, wine, beer, cream soda, lime rickeys, root beer
SEATING	A huge restaurant with hundreds of wooden seats split between two levels; still, expect a 30-minute wait on weekends
AMBIENCE	Old seafaring feel with sea signs, anchors, and fish art decorating the walls; overlooking the harbor
EXTRAS/NOTES	There's karaoke, DJs, and live bands on weekends.

—*Laura Stone & Carol Alves*

Woodman's of Essex

The original Cape Ann clam shack.
Since 1914
$$$

121 Main St., Essex 01929
(East of Willow Ct.)
Phone (800) 649-1773
www.woodmans.com

CATEGORY	Seafood
HOURS	Daily: 11 AM–9 PM (Shorter hours in off-season)
PAYMENT	Cash only
POPULAR FOOD	Anyone who lives anywhere close to the North Shore will surely have a memorable Woodman's story. For over four generations, the name has been synonymous with fried clams— Woodman's claims to have invented the dish. However with such huge crowds pounding down their door, Woodman's is often forced to produce their delicacy in mass quantities; as a result quality sometimes suffers during the busy season.
UNIQUE FOOD	Boiled lobsters; raw bar with clams on the half shell
DRINKS	Full bar with frozen drinks, beer, wine

SEATING   Picnic tables and booths in a large noisy dining area

AMBIENCE   All self-service dining; there's also an upstairs deck with a raw bar

EXTRAS/NOTES   Back in 1914, Dexter "Chubby" Woodman was running a roadside stand selling homemade potato chips, fresh fruit, and fresh clams dug from the nearby Essex River. Seeing success with his chips, Chubby decided that rather than just steaming the shellfish he'd coat them with batter and fry them up. And thus the fried clam was born.

—Kyle Konrad

SOUTH SHORE

Christo's

"Home of the Greek Salad King."
Since 1966

$$$

782 Crescent St., Brockton 02302
(at Burrill Ave.)
Phone (508) 588-4200

CATEGORY	Greek
HOURS	Mon–Wed: 11 AM–11 PM
	Thurs–Sat: 11 AM–midnight
	Sun: noon–11 PM
PARKING	Street
PAYMENT	VISA MasterCard Discover
POPULAR FOOD	Christo's sells over 12,000 Greek salads a week, and it's no wonder why: the salads are always prepared with crisp greens and flavorful vegetables, the feta cheese is unmatched in freshness and taste, and their dressing has become so legendary that it is now bottled and sold in local supermarkets.
UNIQUE FOOD	Southern fried chicken; excellent grape-nut pudding and baklava
DRINKS	A full-fledged, hoppin' bar with a pollution index higher than Mexico City; but if you're single, over 60, and want to experience temporary emphysema, it doesn't get any better.
SEATING	Christo's is divided into five main parts: the bar, the function rooms, the Red Room, the Blue Room, and the famous Gold Room. Although the décor throughout Christo's varies from slightly tacky to outlandish, the Gold Room has nonetheless earned a reputation for being the room where everyone wants to sit; graced with a giant, gold, concave tree trunk-like structure in the center, the room is gaudy, but strangely appealing. The Red and Blue Rooms are acceptable alternatives if you don't want to tack on an extra 20-minute wait; reservations are not accepted.
AMBIENCE	The clientele tends to be older—mostly forty- or fiftysomethings going out with friends; families, however, have also discovered Christo's economical prices.
EXTRAS/NOTES	Keep your eye out for Christo—he's always around the restaurant. His charming Greek accent ("Smiiiiith, party of four") soothes you while you wait.

—*Amy Kirkcaldy*

Circe's Grotto

It's all about the swine.

$$

344 Gannet Rd., Scituate 02066
(East of Mordecai Lincoln Rd.)
Phone (781) 545-6007

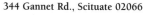

CATEGORY	Cafe
HOURS	Mon–Fri: 6 AM–6 PM
	Sat/Sun: 7 AM–4 PM
PARKING	Street
PAYMENT	Cash only
POPULAR FOOD	Pastries, cookies, soup, sandwiches, and to-go stuff. Circe's makes great sandwiches with hummus, not to mention ingredients like roast beef, goat's cheese, and pb&j. Choose from the Daily Hog chalkboard for specials like La Fiesta (grilled chicken, fresh corn and cilantro salsa, thick slices of avocado, and romaine lettuce), or a rustic sausage and tomato soup served with warm focaccia.
UNIQUE FOOD	Circe's meat and produce is ultra-fresh with little bonuses like high-quality mustards, kosher salt and pepper on the sandwiches, cucumbers sliced long and thin, and of course, the beautiful bread from Pain D'Avignon in Hyannis. The to-go cooler is equally as tempting, stocked full of quarts of carrot-ginger and chicken-noodle soup, assorted pasta, grain, and fruit salads.
DRINKS	Coffee, juices, milk
SEATING	A neo-cave: three tables, one counter, a deep windowsill with four stools, two coolers, and enough room to turn around
AMBIENCE	Tucked next to a day spa in North Scituate Village; mid-morning through lunch you will encounter local landscapers and contractors with shamrocks stenciled on the sides of their trucks, SUV mommies, truant high school students, old-timers, and out-of-towners
EXTRAS/NOTES	There are pigs everywhere in Circe's, and it's not just a quirk of the ownership. In Homer's *Odyssey*, Circe was a bewitching enchantress who turned Odysseus' men to swine by giving them a delicious, magical beverage. No word from Circe's on which of their drinks turns customers to swine, but we speculate that it might be the whole chocolate milk in glass bottles from Hornstra Farms, a nearby dairy. Watch out!

—Leigh Belanger

Great Chow

The name speaks for itself.

$$$

15-17 Beale St., Wollaston 02170
(at Hancock St.)
Phone (617) 328-1338 • Fax (617) 328-8166

CATEGORY	Chinese
HOURS	Mon–Wed: 11 AM–11 PM
	Thurs–Sat: 11 AM–11:30 PM
	Sun: 11 AM–10:30 PM
MASS TRANSIT	T: Red line-Braintree to Wollaston
PAYMENT	VISA MasterCard AMERICAN EXPRESS DISCOVER
POPULAR FOOD	The combination dinners, which include an entree and one or two appetizers for $7–10, are the best bet for price, portion size, and variety; get the General Gau's—you won't be disappointed
UNIQUE FOOD	A special gourmet menu includes delicacies like spicy salted scallops, calamari with pickled mustard green, and Cantonese-style pork
DRINKS	Beer, wine, soda
SEATING	Seats about 60 at closely arranged tables
AMBIENCE	Bright lights and quite noisy at busy times; the open kitchen can be seen behind a large glass window

—*Lisa Johnson*

La Dalat

Southeast Asian delicacies served with casual style.

$$$

181 Nantasket Ave., Hull 02045
(on The Strip north of Park Ave.)
Phone (781) 925-4587

CATEGORY	Vietnamese
HOURS	Tues–Sun: 4 PM–10 PM
PARKING	Street
PAYMENT	VISA MasterCard AMERICAN EXPRESS DISCOVER
POPULAR FOOD	Spicy ginger hot pot, served with slices of ginger and covered in a sweet but tangy sauce; Japanese shu-mai dumplings; a full array of sushi and sashimi
UNIQUE FOOD	Duck Tataki, a pan-fried marinated duck breast sauce, mirin sake, and vinegar and layered on top of watercress; La Dalat Banana Leaf Salmon, filleted and steamed in a banana leaf with mushroom sauce
DRINKS	Full bar
SEATING	Seats approximately 100
AMBIENCE	Decorated with traditional Asian artifacts such as rice paper and bamboo screens, wooden boats, tropical flowers, and dim lighting

—*Heidi Solomon*

La Paloma

*A mini Mexican vacation
in the middle of Quincy.*

$$

195 Newport Ave., Newport Center, Quincy 02170
(South of Hobart St.)
Phone (617) 773-0512 • Fax (617) 376-8867

CATEGORY	Mexican
HOURS	Tues–Sat: 11:30 AM–10 PM
	Sun: 3 PM–9 PM
MASS TRANSIT	T: Red line-Braintree to Wollaston
PAYMENT	VISA MasterCard AMERICAN EXPRESS
POPULAR FOOD	La Paloma's own salsa is so well received that you don't even have to go there to try it; their tasty, full-bodied, aromatic version is sold at supermarkets statewide. You can't go wrong with the homemade chorizo or excellent fajitas.
UNIQUE FOOD	They have an unusually wide selection of desserts, which includes not only flan and deep fried ice cream, but apple chimichangas, caramel apple or key lime pie, and *bunuelos* (fried dough with cinnamon and sugar).
DRINKS	Soft drinks, beer, full bar
SEATING	Between the two rooms and small bar, there is room for about 100 people
AMBIENCE	The terra cotta-colored walls covered with colorful posters, dried chilis, and copper pots, and high ceilings with fans give a tropical airy feeling. The minute you walk in the door, you might just forget that you are in a Quincy strip mall.

—Lisa Johnson

Punjab Café

*The Southern Artery's
best Indian secret.*

$$$$

653 Southern Artery, Quincy 02169
(East of Mill St.)
Phone (617) 472-4860 • Fax (617) 472-4889

CATEGORY	Indian
HOURS	Daily: 11:30 AM–10 PM
PARKING	Street
PAYMENT	VISA MasterCard AMERICAN EXPRESS DISCOVER
POPULAR FOOD	They have an all you can eat lunch buffet every day; lamb *saag*; chicken tikka masala; tandoori specials; *aloo naan*
UNIQUE FOOD	Child portions with less spice available for the youngsters; low cholesterol and low sodium preparation available for the old-timers
DRINKS	Smooth and creamy mango lassis; also sweet lassis and salty lassis; mango juice, coffee, plain black tea, and Indian-style spiced tea with cardamom and milk

| SEATING | Seating for about 50 with several tables seating four or six each |
| AMBIENCE | The ambience is a bit romantic at night; there are candles on the tables with low light; the tables have red tablecloths with glass on top |

—Lisa Johnson

Tennesee's BBQ.

Authentic smoked barbecue worth leaving the city for.

$$$

173 Pearl St., Braintree 02184

(at Ivory St.)

Phone (781) 843-0999 • Fax (781) 843-0984

CATEGORY	Southern Barbecue
HOURS	Daily: 11 AM–10 PM
PARKING	Street
PAYMENT	VISA MasterCard AMERICAN EXPRESS DISCOVER
POPULAR FOOD	Known for its ribs, Tennesee's draws a loyal lunch crowd with a selection of sandwiches, sides, and drinks that could feed the fattest Southern sheriff, and still leave enough change on $10 for a piece of homemade pecan pie.
UNIQUE FOOD	The pulled pork sandwich: smoky, slightly sweet, and not overly greasy
DRINKS	Soft drinks
SEATING	Ample seating at booths, a counter top, and long tables for larger parties
AMBIENCE	Often packed during lunch; the décor tries to approximate a Southern barbecue dive, not entirely successfully, but stops short of contrived Dixie décor
EXTRAS/NOTES	Using Southern Pride brand smokers, and a mix of various fruitwoods, Tennesee's turns out the sort of barbecue that is a rare and precious find above the Mason Dixon line. Tennesee's has held its own outside the Northeast as well, making it to the finals of the Jack Daniel's World Champ BBQ competition.
OTHER ONES	• Western Suburbs: 341 Cochituate Rd., Framingham 01701, (508) 626-7140
	• Milford: 201 E. Main St., Milford 01757, (508) 634-3902
	• North Shore: 260 Andover St., Peabody 01960, (978) 977-9977

—James Haynes

Town Spa Pizza

*Some of the best pizza
outside the North End.*

$$

1119 Washington St. (Rte. 138), Stoughton 02072
(at Plain St.)
Phone (781) 344-2030

CATEGORY	Italian
HOURS	Mon–Sat: 11 AM–midnight Sun: noon–midnight
PARKING	Street
PAYMENT	Cash only
POPULAR FOOD	An Italian family-style restaurant with excellent thin-crust pizza; prices start at a measly $5 for a 12-inch cheese pie; make sure to order it crispy
UNIQUE FOOD	Chicken fingers and honey mustard sauce
DRINKS	Sodas (fountain drinks as well as IBC bottles), beer, wine, full bar
SEATING	A huge place; the main dining room is filled with 50 tables and booths (on both the main floor and a balcony), and the center of the room is comprised of the full bar with 20 seats spread around three sides.
AMBIENCE	A very popular bar and eating spot during all hours of the day and night; fish sculptures hang on the walls, there's a full-screen projection TV, and one section of the room is filled with trophies from community events
EXTRAS/NOTES	Founded by Henry "the Pizza King" Phillips and his wife Rena in 1955, their original location was in Stoughton Square on Porter Street. In 1986, they moved to the current location.

—Ari Herzog

NEW ENGLAND

Introduction to New England

Bostonians may call their city "the hub of the universe," but more directly, Boston is the gateway to New England. Many of the unique culinary mainstays of this town actually arrived here from somewhere else in the region. The **diner** made its name in Worcester (see p. 241). **Chowder** was perfected from Maine to Connecticut (see p. 27). And **cod** came from, well, Cape Cod (see p. 261). What better way to appreciate so many of Boston's food artifacts than to make a pilgrimage to the **cranberry** bogs of Cape Cod (see p. 277) or the **fried clam shacks** of Maine where they got their start?

We have provided below abbreviated reviews of some of the best pit stops for travelers to New England: charming greasy spoons and roadside clam shacks, family restaurants by the sea, and historic burger and hot dog joints. The following eateries have been selected for their adherence to *Hungry?* ideals: true regional character, excellent food, and the availability of a meal for around $10 or less.

WESTERN MASSACHUSETTS

Atkins Farm
(see p. 196)
Cider Donuts
Rte. 16 and Bay Rd., South Amherst, MA 01002
Phone (413) 253-9528

Charlie's Diner
**344 Plantation St.,
Worcester, MA 01604**
Phone (508) 752-9318
www.charliesdiner.com

HOURS	Mon–Fri: 6 AM–2:30 PM
	Sat/Sun: 7:30 AM–11:30 AM
PAYMENT	Cash only
THE LOWDOWN	Since 1950, this tried and true classic diner has been dishing out good ol' American favorites: steak and eggs, burgers, meatloaf, mashed potatoes, and beans. Steve, Charlie's son, still runs the place, but rumors are the diner will be relocating down the street to Lake Ave.

—Ari Herzog

Chef Wayne's Big Mamou

63 Liberty St., Springfield, MA 01103

Phone (413) 732-1011

HOURS	Mon–Sat: 11 AM–9:30 PM
PAYMENT	Cash only
THE LOWDOWN	You might not expect to find good Cajun and Creole cooking in Western Mass., but Hartford-born Chef Wayne Hooker's spicy crawfish, scrumptious cornbread, and blackened shrimp and catfish have folks lining up outside this small restaurant. The Zydeco music and stuffed gator in the window add to the Bayou experience.

—*Kyle Konrad*

Herrell's

(see p. 131)

Ice Cream Shop

8 Old South St., Northampton, MA 01060

Phone (413) 586-9700

La Cucina Di Pinocchio

30 Boltwood Walk, Amherst, MA 01002

(Off Rte. 116)

Phone (413) 256-4110

www.pinocchiosamherst.com

HOURS	Mon–Fri: 11:30 AM–2 PM, 5 PM–9 PM Sat/Sun: 11:30 AM–2 PM, 5 PM–10 PM
PAYMENT	VISA MasterCard AMERICAN EXPRESS
THE LOWDOWN	This is *the* place for calzones. With 35 combinations to choose from and toppings ranging from tortellini to smoked mozzarella to Cajun hamburger there's something for everyone. All calzones (up to four fillings) are just under $5 and are served with fresh tomato sauce. While there is no seating available, the nearby UMass duck pond makes for a nice picnic spot.

—*Mary Beth Doyle*

Ralph's Chadwick Square Diner

95 Prescott St., Worcester, MA 01605

Phone (508) 753-9543

HOURS	Wed–Sat: 6 PM–2 AM
PAYMENT	Cash only
THE LOWDOWN	A Worcester institution for 22 years, Ralph's triples as a diner, billiards/jukebox/arcade room, and saloon with live music. Burgers (ham, cheese, and veggie) and chili highlight the minimal menu. On Fridays at 4 PM there are free hot dogs.

—*Ari Herzog*

CAPE COD

Arnold's

3580 State Hwy., Eastham, MA 02642

Phone (508) 255-2575

www.arnoldsrestaurant.com

HOURS Daily: 11:30 AM–9:30 PM
(hours vary with season)

PAYMENT Cash only

THE LOWDOWN Arnold's is one of the best of the Cape's many lobster and clam bars. The fried clams virtually melt in your mouth while the crispy onion rings and sweet corn make perfect sides. The raw bar is owned and operated by a local shellfisherman.

—*Jesse Peck*

Baxter's Fish 'n' Chips and Boathouse Club

Since 1955

177 Pleasant St., Hyannis, MA 02601

Phone (508) 775-4490

www.baxtersboathouse.com

HOURS Summer only: Thurs–Sun: 11:30 AM–9:30 PM

PAYMENT VISA MasterCard AMERICAN EXPRESS

THE LOWDOWN Since 1955 Baxter's has been a Hyannis landmark. From the fried clams to lobster to fish 'n' chips everything is delicious and served in very generous portions. Picnic tables are set up on an old floating ferry in the heart of Hyannis Harbor.

—*Jesse Peck*

Bob Briggs Wee Packet Restaurant and Bakery

Since 1950s

79 Depot St., Dennisport, MA 02639

(at Lower County Rd.)

Phone (508) 398-2181

www.weepacket.com

HOURS Daily: 11:30 AM–8:30 PM
(May to Sept. only)

PAYMENT VISA MasterCard

THE LOWDOWN For over 50 years, Bob Briggs has been running this wee restaurant whose name is a term for "small ship." Try one of the seafood rolls (lobster, scallop, crab, clam, shrimp, scrod) along with an order of bread pudding or one of their homemade pies from their neighboring bakery.

—*Jesse Peck*

The New England Cranberry: Where Sassamanash got its Start

The cranberry is truly a New England fruit. Called Sassamanash by the Native Americans, the cranberry is one of only three fruit endemic to North American soil. Southeastern Massachusetts provides the perfect boggy conditions for cranberry vines, which are nestled in layers of sand, peat, gravel, and clay that were formed by glaciers thousands of years ago. Because cranberry plants can live for hundreds of years at a time, some Massachusetts growing families still rely on the same vines their ancestors used 150 years ago.

Cranberry cultivation is a relatively new industry. In Dennis, Massachusetts, in 1816, Captain Henry Hall realized that sand blowing into his wild cranberry bogs made the fruit grow faster, and he began spreading sand over the vines himself. Nowadays the cranberry industry plays an integral part in the state's economy: the tiny berry brings more than $200 million to Massachusetts every year. **Ocean Spray**, a grower-owned cooperative of over 800 cranberry and 126 grapefruit growers nationwide, is the country's largest cranberry juice producer. In Massachusetts alone, there are 500 cranberry growing families, which together, take on the responsibility of supplying 38 percent of America's cranberries.

Yet despite many years of success, cranberries have taken a beating since the late '90s. Efficiency has led to overproduction, and prices have dropped. In 1996, a 100-pound barrel of the fruit fetched $60, but in 1999 the same barrel earned growers a piddling $11. In 1999 Ocean Spray was forced to lay off over 500 workers, or 20 percent of its work-force. Still, Ocean Spray strives to buy all of its growers' berries despite the difficult economic climate.

For those who would like to observe cranberry growing firsthand, it's not quite as easy as going strawberry or apple picking. Bog tours are hard to come by, as most bogs are in growers' backyards. However, visitors can witness the cranberry harvest season in full swing with a trip down Rte. 44 or Rte. 58 in Carver, MA between mid-September and early November. On Nantucket, **Windswept Bog** in Siasconset offers bike and hiking trails through the 205-acre bog habitat.

—*Amy Kirkaldy*

Captain Frosty's Fish and Chips

219 Rte. 6A, Dennis, MA 02638
Phone (508) 385-8548

HOURS	Daily: 11 AM–8 PM (Apr. to end of Sept. only)
PAYMENT	Cash only
THE LOWDOWN	Seafood and ice cream. Cream and grease. It's the perfect combo and not many places do it better. The fish 'n' chips and fried clams are done in canola oil and the lobster rolls contain big, fresh pieces of lobster meat. There's seating inside as well as outside on a shady brick patio.

—Jesse Peck

Kream 'n' Kone

Since 1953
527 Main St. (Rte. 28), Dennisport, MA 02639
Phone (508) 394-0808

HOURS	Mon–Fri: 11 AM–9:30 PM Sat/Sun: 11 AM–10 PM (Feb. to Oct. only)
PAYMENT	VISA MasterCard AMERICAN EXPRESS DISCOVER
THE LOWDOWN	Contrary to the name, this place is known for its heaping portions of fried seafood. Since 1953 they've attracted huge crowds with their clams, shakes, and onion rings. Another location sits further down Rte. 28 in Chatham.

—Kyle Konrad

Land Ho!

Rte. 6A, Orleans, MA 02653
(at Cove Rd.)
Phone (508) 255-5165
www.land-ho.com

HOURS	Daily: 11:30 AM–10 PM
PAYMENT	VISA MasterCard AMERICAN EXPRESS DISCOVER
THE LOWDOWN	Simple is the way to go at "the Ho." Start with a huge stuffed clam or some Ho! Made chowder. Then, the beer-boiled hot dogs or fish 'n' chips are good bets to top it off. Live entertainment is provided year round and the Ho even features a new piece from a different artist every month. Another location is in Playa Junquillal, Costa Rica.

—Tim Leonard

Eastham Lobster Pool

4380 Rte. 6, Eastham, MA 02642

Phone (508) 255-9706

HOURS	Mon–Fri: 11:30 AM–9 PM
	Sat–Sun: 11:30 AM–9:30 PM
	(Apr. to Oct. only)
PAYMENT	VISA MasterCard AMERICAN EXPRESS DISCOVER
THE LOWDOWN	Upon first walking in customers are greeted by tanks full of live lobsters awaiting their fate. They quickly end up on your plate steamed, grilled, broiled, or in a nice lobster cream soup. There is indoor seating as well as an outside area with picnic benches and garden tables.

—*Jesse Peck*

Moby Dick's

Rte. 6, Wellfleet, MA 02667

(on Truro side of town center)

Phone (508) 349-9795

www.mobydicksrestaurant.com

HOURS	Daily: 11:30 AM–9 PM
	(May to Oct. only)
PAYMENT	VISA MasterCard
THE LOWDOWN	Only the freshest fish is served at this down-home Cape Cod fish shack. Order the clambake special (a lobster, native Monomoy steamed clams, and corn on the cob) or a fried seafood plate from the giant blackboard menu, then take a seat on the screened-in porch.

—*Kyle Konrad*

Sweet Tomatoes

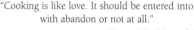

(see p. 253)

Pizza

770 Main St., Osterville, MA 02655

Phone (508) 420-1717

and

148 Rte. 6A, Sandwich, MA 02563

Phone (508) 888-5979

> "Cooking is like love. It should be entered into with abandon or not at all."
>
> —*Harriet Van Horne* (Vogue)

RHODE ISLAND

Angelo's Civita Farnese

Since 1924

141 Atwells Ave., Providence, RI 02903

Phone (401) 621-8171

HOURS	Mon–Thurs: 11 AM–8:30 PM
	Fri/Sat: 11 AM–9 PM
	Sun: noon–6:30 PM
PAYMENT	Cash only
THE LOWDOWN	From the long communal tables packed with old locals to the generous portions to the absurdly low-priced dishes it's apparent that time stopped about 40 years ago at Angelo's. *Civita* means a local meeting place, and Farnese is a region on the outskirts of Rome. While the prices have increased ever so slightly since 1924, the food remains the same. Eggplant parmigiana goes for less than $4 and daily specials like braciola, lasagna, and calamari just $4–6.

—Kathy Morelli

Aunt Carrie's

1240 Ocean Rd., Narragansett, RI 02882

Phone (401) 783-7930

HOURS	Wed–Mon: noon–9 PM (Apr. to Sept. only)
PAYMENT	VISA MasterCard
THE LOWDOWN	For a real New England splurge, order the Aunt Carrie's Shore Dinner, a lobster feast that includes chowder, clam cakes, steamers, fish, corn, fries, and warm Indian pudding. There are also three types of chowder—creamy white (New England), brothy (Southern New England-style), and tomato-based (New York-style).

—Kathy Morelli

Caserta Pizzeria

Since 1946

121 Spruce St., Providence, RI 02903

Phone (401) 272-3618

HOURS	Sun, Tues–Thurs: 9:30 AM–10 PM
	Fri/Sat: 9:30 AM–11 PM
PAYMENT	Cash only
THE LOWDOWN	Nobody goes to Caserta without ordering pizza, but the "Wimpy Skippy" has been Caserta's claim to fame since 1946. This anything-but-wimpy spinach pie stuffed with cheese and pepperoni is beyond anything Popeye ever dreamed of chugging.

—Amy Kirkcaldy

Geoff's Superlative Sandwiches

163 Benefit St., Providence, RI 02903

Phone (401) 751-2248

HOURS	Mon–Fri: 9 AM–9 PM
	Sat/Sun: 9:30 AM–9 PM
PAYMENT	
THE LOWDOWN	Geoff's is known for its dizzying number of sandwich choices named for both local Providence figures and national luminaries, including Marlene Dietrich, Dr. Kevorkian, and Judy Garland. Other playful titles include the E-Z Wider and the Embryonic Journey. Interesting condiments (or "Active Ingredients") are available at no additional cost, such as Russian dressing, many types of mustards, picante sauce, cranberry sauce, Frank's Hot Sauce, and proprietary concoctions like Shedd's Sauce (mayo, mustard, and horseradish) and Tiger Sauce (mayonnaise and horseradish).

—Nina West

Mike's Kitchen

170 Randall St., Cranston, RI 02920

Phone (401) 946-5320

HOURS	Mon: 11 AM–3 PM, 5 PM–8 PM
	Wed–Fri: 11 AM–3 PM, 5 PM–8:30 PM
	Tues, Sat: 11 AM–3 PM
	Sun: 5 PM–8 PM
PAYMENT	Cash only
THE LOWDOWN	Nearly impossible to find, this unassuming eatery is located inside the Tabor-Franchi Veterans of Foreign Wars post off Atwood Ave. in Cranston. Italian favorites like fried calamari (called "squid" here), spaghetti and meatballs ($6), and tripe are consumed in mass quantities surrounded by the military paraphernalia you'd expect in a VFW Hall.

—Kathy Morelli

The Modern Diner

Since 1941

364 East Ave., Pawtucket, RI 02860

Phone (401) 726-8390

HOURS	Mon–Sat: 6 AM–3 PM
	Sun: 9:30 AM–9 PM
PAYMENT	Cash only
THE LOWDOWN	The Modern puts a contemporary twist on traditional diner fare with specials like custard French toast topped with a Kentucky bourbon custard sauce, blueberries, strawberries, and pecans, as well as omelettes made with chili and linguica.

This red and yellow 1941 Sterling Stream-
liner is the first diner to be added to the
National Register for Historic Places.

—*Kathy Morelli*

Spike's Junkyard Dogs

273 Thayer St., Providence, RI 02906
Phone (401) 454-1459

HOURS   Mon/Tues: 11 AM–1:30 AM
Wed–Sat: 11 AM–2 AM
Sun: noon–1:30 AM

PAYMENT   Cash only

THE LOWDOWN   The name says it all—Junkyard Dogs.
They are anything but ordinary. You can
get anything and everything on an
incredible tasting "all natural" jumbo dog
from chili to buffalo wing sauce to blue
cheese. Eat six or more dogs in one sitting
and get your picture on the wall. Eat 17
dogs and you're the new record holder.

OTHER ONES   • Rhode Island: 1623 Warwick Ave.,
Warwick 02889, (401) 732-5858
• Rhode Island: 640 Reservoir Ave.,
Cranston 02910, (401) 781-7556

—*Tim Leonard*

Tealuxe

(see p. 76)
Café
231 Thayer St., Providence, RI 02906
Phone (401) 734-9920

CONNECTICUT

Gail's Station House

378 Main St., Ridgefield, CT 06877
Phone (203) 438-9775

HOURS   Mon–Sat: 7 AM–3 PM
Sun: 7 AM–8 PM

PAYMENT   VISA | MasterCard | AMERICAN EXPRESS | DISCOVER

THE LOWDOWN   A breakfast connoisseur's dream, Gail's is
known for its corn and cheddar pancakes,
omelettes stuffed with ingredients like
gorgonzola and jalapeños, as well as
scrumptious scones. The walls are
decorated with local art and a fine
collection of vintage ladies' hats.

—*Jamie Drummond*

New Haven Pizza

Ask a group of New Haven natives where to find the city's best pizza and a heated battle will inevitably erupt. In what may be the fiercest food rivalry in New England, Pepe's, the original, is pitted against Sally's, the off-shoot, and the Modern, the upstart. As the story goes, in the early part of the 20th century, Frank Pepe immigrated to New Haven, where he created the first American pizza by putting tomatoes on top of old bake-shop bread. By 1925, Pepe opened his first pizzeria on Wooster Street. Business took off, causing Pepe's nephew Sal to open in 1938 his own pizzeria, Sally's, just a few blocks away. Today, the tradition continues as both spots specialize in thin-crust pizzas, while Pepe's is especially known for its excellent white clam and garlic pie. At the Modern, you can't go wrong with the Bomb, a thin-crust pie topped with sausage, peppers, onions, meatballs, pepperoni, and more.

Frank Pepe's Pizzeria Napoletana
> *157 Wooster St., New Haven, CT 06511,* (203) 865-5762.

Sally's
> *237 Wooster St., New Haven, CT 06511,* (203) 624-5271.

Modern's Famous Brick Oven Apizza
> *874 State St., New Haven, CT 06511,* (203) 776-5306.

—Kaya Stone

Harry's Place

Since 1920s
104 Broadway,
Colchester, CT 06415
Phone (860) 537-2410

HOURS	Sun–Thurs: 11 AM–7 or 8 PM Fri/Sat: 11 AM–8 or 9 PM
PAYMENT	Cash only
THE LOWDOWN	Toothpicks are the only thing separating a Harry's burger topped with lettuce, tomato, onions, pickles, hot peppers, ketchup, mustard, and mayonnaise from a total mess. This nearly 80-year-old stand designated in the National Register of Historic Places is known for its foolishly tall burgers and foolishly good shakes.

—Jamie Drummond

Louis' Lunch

Since 1895
263 Crown St.,
New Haven, CT 06511

Phone (203) 562-5507

HOURS	Tues/Wed: 11 AM–4 PM
	Thurs–Sat: noon–2 PM
PAYMENT	Cash only
THE LOWDOWN	As the story goes, Louis Lassen invented the hamburger here back in 1895 when a man came into his steak sandwich shop looking for a quick bite he could eat on the run. Not wanting to waste any beef, Louis ground up the meat, grilled it, and stuck it between a couple pieces of white bread. The man went on his way and the hamburger was born. While many have put their own twists on this classic American food, there is no changing the original. Customers at Louis's can top their Wonder bread-wrapped burger with cheese, tomato, or onion—that's it. Ketchup and mustard are simply out of the question.

—*Kaya Stone*

Super Duper Weenie

306 Black Rock Turnpike,
Fairfield, CT 06432

Phone (203) 334-DOGS

HOURS	Sun–Wed: 11 AM–4 PM
	Thurs–Sat: 11 AM–8 PM
PAYMENT	Cash only
THE LOWDOWN	Named one of the top ten hot dogs in the country by *USA Today*, Super Duper has weenies down to an art. "Chef" and owner Gary Zemola may have moved his stand from his 1973 GMC van to a small shop, but he still makes all of his own relishes from scratch, freshly bakes his buns, and fries Idaho russets to order.

—*Jamie Drummond*

"There is no sincerer love than the love of food."

—*George Bernard Shaw*

VERMONT

Al's French Fries

1251 Williston Rd.,
South Burlington, VT 05403
Phone (802) 862-9203

HOURS	Mon–Thurs: 10:30 AM–11 PM
	Fri/Sat: 10:30 AM–midnight
	Sun: 11 AM–11 PM
PAYMENT	Cash only
THE LOWDOWN	Every day, Al's dishes out upwards of one ton of Russet potatoes. By the quart, pint, or cup; plain, or with cheese sauce or gravy; they have fries down to a science. While you can easily make a nice (albeit heart-clogging) meal with fries alone, Al's also has some great burgers, dogs, and old-fashioned milkshakes.

—*Dorothy Dwyer*

Curtis BBQ

Rte. 5, Putney, VT 05346
Phone (802) 387-5474

HOURS	Tues–Sun: 10 AM–7 PM
	(Mar. to Oct. only)
PAYMENT	Cash only
THE LOWDOWN	Curtis' looks like something you might find in rural Mississippi. Inside two old blue school buses and a tin-roof cooking shack, pitmaster Curtis Tuff turns out some seriously good barbecue. From the smoky pork ribs down to the Vermont maple syrup-flavored beans, this self-serve dive is worth the drive.

—*Dorothy Dwyer*

Nectar's

188 Main St.,
Burlington, VT 05401
Phone (802) 658-4771

HOURS	Mon–Fri: 5:45 AM–2 AM
	Sat/Sun: 7 AM–2 AM
PAYMENT	Cash only
THE LOWDOWN	It's all about the gravy fries. Owner Nectar Rorris carved out his niche nearly 30 years ago combining long, narrow-cut Idaho spuds with turkey and roast beef gravy prepared fresh daily. While the fries are served from late morning, Nectar's take-out window really heats up after the bars close. Phish began playing at Nectar's in 1984 and were regulars until breaking onto the national scene. Their album *A Picture of Nectar* is named after Nectar Rorris, the restaurant's owner. Look closely at the album cover and you'll see Nectar's face superimposed onto an orange.

—*Jesse Crary*

Food Factory Fun

When in Vermont, do as Vermonters do: EAT. Anchored by ice cream kings Ben and Jerry, northern Vermont is home to an impressive trio of food factory tours. Check out these three, along with one Cape treat worth the trip:

Ben & Jerry's

Hands down the best and most well-known food factory tour in New England. Over the course of the 30-minute tour, you'll learn how social entrepreneurs Ben Cohen and Jerry Greenfield went from a $5 correspondence course in ice cream making to becoming the masterminds behind Chunky Monkey, Cherry Garcia, and Phish Food. You'll also see the production line in action and enjoy a tiny sample at the end of the tour. *Rte. 100, Waterbury, VT 05676, (866) BJ-TOURS. Take Exit 10 off of I-89 and head north on Rte. 100 towards Stowe; the factory will be a mile up on the left. Admission $2, seniors $1.75, 12 and under free. Daily: 9 AM–5 PM. www.benjerry.com*

Cabot Creamery

New Englanders will by and large agree that not much beats Cabot's sharp cheddar. At the company's Montpelier factory, visitors receive a guided tour that explains the history of the over 80-year-old company, gives a peak at how the award-winning cheese is made, and provides the usual free samples at the end. On November 4, 2000, Cabot entered the *Guinness Book of World Records* using 120 pounds of their sharp cheddar to grill the world's largest grilled cheese sandwich in history. *1 Home Farm Way, Montpelier, VT 05602, (800) 837-4261. From I-89, take Exit 8 to Rte. 2 East. At Marshfield, go left on Rte. 215, then 5 miles to Cabot Village. Admission $1, 12 and under free. Open June–Oct., Daily: 9 AM–5 PM; Nov–May, Mon–Sat: 9 AM–4 PM. www.cabotcheese.com*

Maple Grove Farms

This two-floor guided tour takes visitors through the syrup packaging and maple candy making processes. Check out the Sugar House Museum to learn more about "The Whole Sugaring Experience." Taste and compare grades of pure syrup at the end of your tour. *1052 Portland St., St. Johnsbury, VT 05819, (802) 748-5141. From I-91, take Exit 20, go north on Rte. 5 through town to Rte. 2 east; the farm will be about 1 mile down on the right. Admission $1, 13 and under free. Mon–Fri: 8 AM–4 PM. www.maplegrove.com*

Cape Cod Potato Chips

You're on your own for this no-frills, no hype factory tour. On one side of the short narrow hallway, there's a nice history of the company. On the other, there are windows that allow visitors to gawk at workers as they take sliced raw potatoes, dump them in a sizzling 200-gallon kettle of hot oil, and miraculously transform them into over 200,000 bags of greasy, crispy, kettle-cooked chips every day. A free

bag and potato chip gift store await at the end.
100 Breed's Hill Rd., Hyannis, MA 02601, (508) 775-3206.
From Rte. 6 East, take Exit 6 and turn right onto Rte. 132;
take a left at the fourth traffic light onto Independence Dr.
and then your second right onto Breed's Hill Rd. Free ad-
mission. Mon–Fri: 9 AM–5 PM. www.capecodchips.com

—Kaya Stone

Papa Frank's Italian Restaurant

13 West Center St., Winooski, VT 05404
Phone (802) 655-2423

HOURS	Mon–Fri: noon–10 PM
	Sat/Sun: 11 AM–10 PM
PAYMENT	VISA MasterCard AMERICAN EXPRESS DISCOVER
THE LOWDOWN	Frank Sciara has built his great reputation on the cheap eats Triple Crown: huge portions, dirt-cheap prices, and legendary wait service. The authentic Italian daily specials go for just $4 and the huge calzones have earned a large following.

—Dorothy Dwyer

Sneakers Bistro/Café

36 Main St., Winooski, VT 05404
Phone (802) 655-9081

HOURS	Daily: 7 AM–3 PM
PAYMENT	VISA MasterCard AMERICAN EXPRESS DISCOVER
THE LOWDOWN	A hip eatery with a creative twist on break- fast. Folks line up for morning concoctions like Kahlua batter-dipped French toast and smoked turkey eggs benedict with arti- choke hearts and spinach. Artwork from lo- cal artists adorn the walls on the restaurant.

—Dorothy Dwyer

Vermont Pub & Brewery

144 College St., Burlington, VT 05401
Phone (802) 865-8500
www.vermontbrewery.com

HOURS	Sun–Thurs: 11:30 AM–1 AM
	Fri/Sun: 11:30 AM–2 AM
PAYMENT	VISA MasterCard AMERICAN EXPRESS DISCOVER
THE LOWDOWN	The Pub & Brewery's solid fare centers around tried-and-true favorites from both sides of the pond. English influences in- clude shepherd's pie, bangers 'n' mash (beer-steamed sausage with mashed pota- toes, gravy, and apple chutney), and fish 'n' chips. On the American end nothing beats the Angus Brewburger (locally raised, hor- mone-free Angus beef burger for under $5) along with a side order of some of the best sweet potato fries slathered in their own

special honey mustard sauce. After three years of lobbying the state legislature to allow pub brewing, the law passed in the spring of 1988. Soon after, VPB opened as Vermont's first brewpub (and only the fourth on the East Coast).

—Jesse Crary

NEW HAMPSHIRE

Country Life Vegetarian

(see p. 3)
Vegetarian
15 Roxbury St., Keene, NH 03431
Phone (603) 357-3975

Gilley's

Since 1940
175 Fleet St.,
Portsmouth, NH 03801
Phone (603) 431-6343
www.gilleyspmlunch.com

HOURS   Mon: 11:30 AM–6:30 PM
     Tues–Sun: 11:30 AM–2:30 AM

PAYMENT   Cash only

THE LOWDOWN   Gilley's is in the *Guinness Book of World Records* not for its legendary hot dogs or burgers, but for receiving the most number of consecutive parking tickets. Every day for over 60 years, Gilley's lunch cart was towed into Market Square and every day Gilley's received a parking ticket. Today, nearly 30 years after settling in its current permanent Fleet Street location in 1974, the prices still have a '70s ring: burgers still go for $2, and hot dogs are just $1.25.

—Kyle Konrad

Mary Ann's Diner

29 E. Broadway, Derry, NH 03038
Phone (603) 434-5785
www.maryannsdiner.com

HOURS   Mon–Sat: 6 AM–2 PM
     Sun: 7 AM–2 PM

PAYMENT   VISA   MasterCard   AMERICAN EXPRESS   DISCOVER

THE LOWDOWN   Mary Ann's takes customers back to the fabulous '50s. Waitresses decked in poodle skirts and ponytails serve old-fashioned egg and bacon breakfasts along with creative twists on the originals like banana-stuffed French toast. At dinner, classic chicken-fried steak or biscuits and gravy can be had for under $6.

—Kyle Konrad

Parker's Maple Barn

1316 Brookline Rd., Mason, NH 03048

Phone (800) 832-2308

www.parkersmaplebarn.com

HOURS	Mon–Thurs: 8 AM–2 PM
	Fri: 8 AM–8 PM
	Sat: 7 AM–8 PM
	Sun: 7 AM–4 PM
PAYMENT	VISA MasterCard AMERICAN EXPRESS DISCOVER
THE LOWDOWN	Parker's prepares anywhere from 2,000 to 3,500 meals per week which amounts to two to three times the population of Mason. Clearly, folks are coming from miles around to sample the huge waffles and stacks of pancakes featuring their own rich maple syrup tapped and made here. Parker's also makes a mean maple frappe and maple syrup ribs.

—*Kyle Konrad*

Polly's Pancake Parlor

Since 1938

Hildex Maple Sugar Farm
Rte. 117, Sugar Hill, NH 03585

(2 mi. from Exit 38 on I-93)

Phone (603) 823-5575

www.pollyspancakeparlor.com

HOURS	Daily: 7 AM–3 PM
	(May to Oct. only)
PAYMENT	VISA MasterCard AMERICAN EXPRESS DISCOVER
THE LOWDOWN	This adorable log cabin with sweeping mountain views always hosts a crowd for some of New England's finest pancakes. They are made almost entirely from scratch—from the oatmeal, buckwheat, cornmeal, or whole wheat batter to the maple butter you spread on top—and served by a charming staff. The parlor was opened by Pauline Dexter in 1938 as a way of promoting the family's maple farm, and it remains in the family still. To this day, the adjacent store does a brisk business in Polly's luscious maple spread, homemade pancake mixes, and various bright red-and-yellow maple leaf-themed paraphernalia. The only conceivable complaint? The limited seasonal hours and mid-afternoon closing time.

—*Esti Iturralde*

"Love and scandal are the best sweeteners of tea."
—*Henry Fielding* (Love in Several Masques)

Sugar Shack

314 Rte. 4, Barrington, NH 03825

Phone (800) 576-2753

www.maplesugarshack.net

HOURS	Sat/Sun: 7:30 AM–1 PM (Mar. to May only)
PAYMENT	VISA MasterCard
THE LOWDOWN	On weekends during the Spring, the Sugar Shack rolls out their famous all-you-can-eat pancake breakfast served with pure maple syrup made right on the premises. The rest of the year, they offer self-guided tours around the sugarhouse and property.

—Kyle Konrad

MAINE

Bob's Clam Hut

Rte. 1, Kittery, ME 03904

Phone (207) 439-4233

HOURS	Sun–Thurs: 11 AM–8 PM Fri/Sat: 11 AM–9 PM
PAYMENT	VISA MasterCard AMERICAN EXPRESS
THE LOWDOWN	While there are plenty of good deals to be had in outlet-crazed Kittery, Bob's fried clam or lobster rolls top any half-price sale. Succulent clams are fried to perfection then topped with homemade tartar sauce and stuffed in a toasted bun. Bob's is strictly a takeout-window-and-picnic-table sort of place, but then again, who needs atmosphere when shopping awaits.

—Mark Sloan

The Clam Shack

Rte. 9, Kennebunkport, ME 04046

Phone (207) 967-3321

HOURS	Mon–Thurs: 11 AM–6 PM Fri/Sat: 11 AM–7 PM
PAYMENT	Cash only
THE LOWDOWN	The lobster rolls here are fit for a president. For years, Kennebunkport has been the Bush summer vacation destination and for years the Clam Shack has been satisfying crowds with their Hot Lobster Roll packed with large pieces of meat and topped with butter. The fried clams aren't bad either.

—Mark Sloan

Flo's Hot Dogs

Rte. 1, Cape Neddick, ME 03902

No phone

HOURS Thurs–Tues: 11 AM–2 PM

PAYMENT Cash only

THE LOWDOWN At this coastal Maine legend, you will never be asked, "Whaddaya want?" because there's only one item on the menu: Flo's legendary dogs, best accompanied by a decades-old family-recipe hot sauce. A more likely question will be "How many?" since Flo's dogs are small—enough so that a normal-sized man could probably down a dozen for lunch. Best way to fit in? Place your order with mayo and the fiery sauce, and don't be surprised at the feisty attitude that comes along with it.

—Mark Sloan

Thurston's Lobster Pound

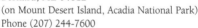

Steamboat Wharf Rd., Bernard, ME 04612

(on Mount Desert Island, Acadia National Park)

Phone (207) 244-7600

HOURS Daily: 11 AM–8 PM (late Apr. to Oct. only)

PAYMENT VISA MasterCard

THE LOWDOWN Without frills and run with maximum efficiency, Thurston's demands that you order before you sit down—and then face a mad dash for an empty table. The two-floor mosquito-screened porch of a dining area overlooks the quietly picturesque harbor with its rows upon rows of stacked lobster traps. Most patrons order the top-notch soft or hard shell lobster, choosing the weight and then paying per pound—a deal that's hard to beat. There's a large selection of beer served by the bottle or the plastic cup.

—Esti Iturralde

GLOSSARY

Our glossary covers basic ethnic dishes that you will probably come across in the Boston area, as well as those peculiar menu terms that you sort of know but are not always sure about—are frappes really different from milkshakes? Is chicken fried steak chicken or steak?

ackee and saltfish (Jamaican)—a traditional dish made of soaked salt cod and ackee, a yellow fleshy fruit that is usually poured out of a can because it can be toxic if unripe.

aloo ghobi (Indian)—cauliflower and potatoes cooked in herbs and spices.

antojitos (Latin American)—appetizers (in Spanish, "little whims").

arepas (Colombian)—corn cakes.

au jus (French)—meat (usually beef) served in its own juices.

ayran (Middle Eastern)—yogurt-based drink, like *lassi* but flavored with cardamom.

baba ganoush (Middle Eastern)—smoky eggplant dip.

baklava (Greek/Turkish)—pastry made of filo layered with honey, nuts, and spices.

bandeja paisa (Colombian)—A hearty "mountain dish" with steak, rice, beans, sweet plantains, *chicharrón, arepas,* and a fried egg.

bangers 'n' mash (British)—sausage and mashed potatoes.

banh xeo (Vietnamese)—a crêpe stuffed with shrimp, pork, and bean sprouts.

bao (Chinese)—sweet stuffed buns either baked or steamed; a very popular dim sum treat.

barbecue (Southern)—not to be confused with putting hamburgers on the grill; real barbecue slow-cooks tough pieces of meat over smoky heat; a sauce may be applied or a dry "rub" of spices.

bean curd (Pan-Asian)—tofu.

bibimbap (Korean)—also *bibibap,* served cold or in a heated clay bowl, a mound of rice to be mixed with vegetables, beef, fish, egg, and red pepper sauce.

biryani (Indian)—meat, seafood, or vegetable curry mixed with rice and flavored with spices, especially saffron.

black cow (American)—frosty glass of root beer poured over chocolate ice cream.

blintz (Jewish)—thin pancake stuffed with cheese or fruit then baked or fried.

bo ba milk tea (Taiwanese)—see pearl milk tea.

borscht (Eastern European)—beet soup, served chilled or hot, topped with sour cream.

bourekas (Middle Eastern)—a puffed sesame pastry filled with potatoes, spinach, or apples.

bratwurst (German)—roasted or baked pork sausage.

bul go gi (Korean)—slices of marinated beef, grilled or barbecued.

bun (Vietnamese)—rice vermicelli.

caesar salad (American)—named not for the Roman emperor but for César Cardini, the chef who invented the salad at his Tijuana restaurant in the 1920s; consists of romaine lettuce and croutons with a dressing made of mayonnaise, parmesan, and sometimes anchovies.

calzone (Italian)—pizza dough turnover stuffed with cheesy-tomato pizza gooeyness (and other fillings).

cannoli (Italian)—a tube of pastry filled with a sweet ricotta cream.

caprese (Italian)—fresh mozzarella, tomatoes, and basil drizzled with olive oil and cracked pepper.

carne asada (Latin American)—thinly sliced, charbroiled beef, usually marinated with cumin, salt, lemon, and for the bold, beer; a staple of the Latin American picnic.

carnitas (Mexican)—juicy, marinated chunks of pork, usually fried or grilled; a very good burrito stuffer.

Cel-Ray (American)—Dr. Brown's celery-flavored soda; light and crisp—found in the best delis.

ceviche (Latin American)—also *cebiche*, raw fish or shellfish marinated in citrus juice or pepper acids, which sort of cooks the fish.

chacarero (Chilean)—sandwich made of tomatoes, mashed avocado, muenster cheese, hot sauce, marinated green beans, and a choice of barbecued meat.

challah (Jewish)—plaited bread, sometimes covered in poppy seeds, enriched with egg and eaten on the Sabbath.

cheese steak (American)—see Philly cheese steak.

Chicago-style hot dog (American)—you can't even see the bun or Vienna brand weenie; they're topped with lettuce, tomato, relish, green pepper, pickles, something called sport peppers, cucumber, and celery salt.

chicharrón (Latin American)—deep-fried pork rinds.

chicken fried steak (Southern)—it's steak—floured, battered, and fried à la fried chicken.

chiles rellenos (Mexican)—green poblano chilis, typically stuffed with jack cheese, battered, and fried; occasionally found grilled instead of fried.

chimichangas (Mexican)—fried burritos.

chowder (New England)—a stew thickened with cream, usually with clams as the main ingredient; in Rhode Island and Connecticut may also include tomato; "farmhouse" chowders use ingredients such as corn or chicken.

chow foon (Chinese)—wide, flat rice noodles.

chorizo (Latin American)—spicy sausage much loved for its versatility—grill it whole, fry it in pieces, or scramble it with eggs for breakfast.

churrasco (Latin American)—charcoal-grilled meat or chicken.

ciambella (Italian)—a light and fluffy breakfast doughnut covered in sugar.

clambake special (New England)—lobster, steamed clams, and corn on the cob.

congee (Chinese)—also *jook*, rice-based porridge, usually with beef or seafood.

corn dog (American)—hot dog dipped in cornbread batter, usually served on a stick.

Cuban sandwiches (Cuban)—roasted pork sandwich with cheese, mustard, and pickles pressed on Cuban rolls, which have a crusty, French bread-like quality.

dal (Indian)—lentil bean-based side dish with an almost soupy consistency, cooked with fried onions and spices.

Denver (or Western) omelette (American)—eggs scrambled with ham, onions, and green pepper.

dim sum (Cantonese)—a brunch or lunch meal consisting of various small appetizers served by waiters pushing carts around the restaurant, which allows diners to choose whatever they want that comes by; literally translated means, "touching your heart."

dolmades (Greek)—also *warak enab* as a Middle Eastern dish, grape leaves stuffed with a rice and herb or lamb and rice mixture.

döner kebab (Middle Eastern)—thin slices of raw lamb meat with fat and seasoning, spit roasted with thin slices carved as it cooks.

dosa (South Indian)—also *dosai*, an oversized traditional crispy pancake, often filled with onion and potato and folded in half.

edamame (Japanese)—soy beans in the pod, popularly served salted and steamed as appetizers.

eggs Benedict—poached eggs, typically served with Canadian bacon over an English muffin with hollandaise sauce.

empanada (South American)—a flaky turnover, usually stuffed with spiced meat.

escovish (Jamaican)—a spicy marinade of onions, herbs, and spices.

étouffe (Creole)—highly spiced shellfish, pot roast, or chicken stew served over rice.

falafel (Middle Eastern)—spiced ground chickpea fava bean balls and spices, deep fried and served with pita.

feijoada (Brazilian/Portuguese)—the national dish of Brazil, which can range from a pork and bean stew to a more complex affair complete with salted beef, tongue, bacon, sausage, and more parts of the pig than you could mount on your wall.

filo (Greek/Turkish)—also phyllo, a very thin flaky pastry prepared in multiple layers.

flautas (Mexican)—akin to the taco except that it is rolled tight and deep fried; generally stuffed with chicken, beef, or beans and may be topped with lettuce, guacamole, salsa, and cheese; they resemble a flute, hence the name.

focaccia (Italian)—flatbread baked with olive oil and herbs.

frappe (New England)—what non-New Englanders might call a milkshake: ice cream, syrup, and milk blended together.

frites (Belgian/French)—also *pommes frites*, french or fried potatoes.

gefilte fish (Jewish)—white fish ground with eggs and matzo meal then jellied. No one—and we mean no one—under 50 will touch the stuff.

gelato (Italian)—ice cream or ice.

gnocchi (Italian)—small potato and flour dumplings served like a pasta with sauce.

grinder (Italian-American)—also called a sub, hoagie, or torpedo—a long sandwich on a split roll containing cold cuts or meatballs.

grits (Southern)—also hominy, a breakfast side dish that looks like a grainy white mush topped with butter or a slice of American cheese.

gumbo (Creole)—rich, spicy stew thickened with okra, often including crab, sausage, chicken, and shrimp.

gyros (Greek)—spit-roasted beef or lamb strips, thinly sliced and served on thick pita bread, garnished with onions and tomatoes.

horchata (Mexican/Central American)—cold rice and cinnamon drink, sweet and heavenly.

huevos rancheros (Mexican)—fried eggs atop a fried tortilla with salsa, *ranchero* cheese, and beans.

hummus (Middle Eastern)—banded garbanzo beans, *tahini*, sesame oil, garlic, and lemon juice; somewhere between a condiment and a lifestyle.

hush puppies (Southern)—deep-fried cornmeal fritter in small golf ball-sized rounds; said to have been tossed at dogs to keep them quiet.

injera (Ethiopian)—flat, spongy, sour unleavened bread; use it to scoop up everything when you eat Ethiopian food, but be forewarned: it expands in your stomach.

jambalaya (Creole)—spicy rice dish cooked with sausage, ham, shellfish, and chicken.

jimmies (New England)—bizarre local term for what is known everywhere else as sprinkles for ice cream.

kabob (Middle Eastern)—also called shish kabob, this refers to chunks of meat, chicken, or fish grilled on skewers, often with vegetable spacers.

kibbee sandwich (Middle Eastern)—a combo of cracked bulgur wheat, ground beef, sautéed onions, and special herbs.

kielbasa (Polish)—smoked sausage.

kimchi (Korean)—pickled vegetables, highly chilied- and garlicked-up; some are sweet, some spicy—there are limitless variations.

knish (Jewish)—a thin dough enclosing mashed potatoes, cheese, or ground meat.

knockwurst (German)—a small, thick, and heavily spiced sausage.

korma (Indian)—a style of braising meat or vegetables, often highly spiced and using cream or yogurt.

lahmejune (Armenian)—flat bread soaked with oil, herbs, chicken or beef, and tomato.

lassi (Indian)—yogurt drink served salted or sweetened with rose, mango, or banana.

latkes (Jewish)—potato pancakes.

linguica—Portuguese sausage.

lychee (Southeast Asian)—red-shelled fruit served in desserts and as a dried snack known as lychee nuts.

macrobiotic—diet and lifestyle of organically grown and natural products.

maduros (Latin American)—fried ripe plantains.

maki (Japanese)—sushi rolled up in a seaweed wrap coated with rice and then cut into sections.

mariscos (Latin American)—seafood.

masala (Indian)—blend of ground spices, usually including cinnamon, cumin, cloves, black pepper, cardamom, and coriander seed.

mesclun salad (French)—a mix of young lettuce and greens, which have a tender quality.

milkshake (New England)—in New England, just milk and syrup mixed together; see also frappe.

mofongo (Dominican)—mashed green plantains with pork skin, seasoned with garlic and salt.

mole (Mexican)—a thick poblano chili sauce from the Oaxacan region served over chicken or other meats; most popular is a velvety black, *mole negro* flavored with unsweetened chocolate; also available in a variety of colors and levels of spiciness depending on the chilis and other flavors used (*amarillo*, or yellow, for example, uses cumin).

moussaka (Greek)—alternating layers of lamb and fried eggplant slices, topped with Béchamel sauce, an egg and cheese mixture, and breadcrumbs, finally baked and brought to you with pita bread.

naan (Indian)—flatbread cooked in a tandoor oven.

niçoise salad (French)—salad served with all the accoutrements from Nice, i.e. French beans, olives, tomatoes, garlic, capers, and of course, tuna and boiled egg.

pad Thai (Thai)—popular rice noodle stir-fry with tofu, shrimp, crushed peanuts, and cilantro.

paella (Spanish)—a rice jubilee flavored with saffron and sprinkled with an assortment of meats, seafood, and vegetables, all served in a sizzling pan.

panini (Italian)—a sandwich from the Old World: prosciutto, mozzarella, roasted peppers, olive oil, or whatever, grilled between two pieces of crusty bread.

pastitsio (Greek)—cooked pasta layered with a cooked meat sauce (usually lamb), egg-enriched and cinnamon-flavored Béchamel, grated cheese, and topped with a final layer of cheese and fresh breadcrumbs.

patty melt (American)—grilled sandwich with hamburger patty and melted Swiss cheese.

pearl milk tea (Taiwanese)—served hot or cold, made of tea, milk, flavoring, and chewy tapioca beads, slurped through a fat straw; also called *zhen zhu nai cha* and *bo ba* milk tea.

Peking ravioli (Chinese)—the New England term for dumplings, coined by Joyce Chen who wanted a more evocative menu description that would make sense to her Italian-American patrons.

penicillin (Jewish)—delicatessen talk for chicken soup emphasizing its curative qualities, sometimes including matzo balls.

Philly cheese steak (American)—hot, crispy, messy sandwich filled with thin slices of beef, cheese, and relish from…where else? Philadelphia.

pho (Vietnamese)—hearty rice noodle soup staple, with choice of meat or seafood, accompanied by bean sprouts and fresh herbs.

pico de gallo (Mexico)—also *salsa cruda*, a chunky salsa of chopped tomato, onion, chili, and cilantro.

pierogi (Polish)—potato dough filled with cheese and onion boiled or fried.

pigs-in-a-blanket (American)—sausages wrapped in pastry or toasted bread then baked or fried; or, more informally, breakfast pancakes rolled around sausage links.

pizzelle (Italian)—thin, round wafer cookie, made in a press resembling a waffle iron.

plantains (Latin American)—bananas that are cooked; when ripe and yellow they're served fried as a sweet side dish called *maduros*; when green and unripe they're twice-fried and called *tostones*, or can be used to make chips.

po' boy (Cajun)—New Orleans-style hero sandwich with seafood and special sauces, often with lemon slices.

pollo a la brasa (Latin American)—rotisserie chicken.

porgy (American)—various deep-bodied seawater fish with delicate, moist, sweet flesh.

puddings, black and white (Irish)—traditional breakfast sausages made of grains and pork products; the black pudding contains pork blood.

pupusa (Salvadoran)—round and flattened cornmeal filled with cheese, ground pork rinds, and refried beans, cooked on a flat pan known as a *comal*; this indigenous term literally means "sacred food."

quesadilla (Mexican)—soft flour tortilla filled with melted cheese and possibly other things.

raita (Indian)—yogurt condiment flavored with spices and vegetables (often cucumber) or fruits—a great relish to balance hot Indian food.

ramen (Japanese)—thin, squiggly egg noodle, often served in a soup.

reuben (Jewish)—rye bread sandwich filled with corned beef, Swiss cheese, and sauerkraut and lightly grilled.

roti (Indian/Indo-Caribbean)—round flat bread served plain or filled with meat or vegetables.

rugelach (Jewish)—a cookie made of cream cheese dough filled with fruit and nuts.

saag paneer (Indian)—cubed mild cheese with creamed spinach.

samosa (Indian)—pyramid-shaped pastry stuffed with savory vegetables or meat.

sashimi (Japanese)—fresh raw seafood thinly sliced and artfully arranged.

satay (Thai)—chicken or shrimp kabob, often served with a peanut sauce.

sauerkraut (German)—chopped, fermented sour cabbage.

schnitzel (English/Austrian)—thin fried veal or pork cutlet.

scrod—a restaurant term for the day's catch of white fish, usually cod or haddock; possibly a conjunction of "sacred cod."

seitan (Chinese)—wheat gluten marinated in soy sauce with other flavorings.

shaved ice—ice with various juices or flavorings, from lime or strawberry to sweet green tea and sweetened condensed milk.

shawarma (Middle Eastern)—pita bread sandwich filled with sliced beef, tomato, and sesame sauce.

shish kabob (Middle Eastern)—see kabob.

soba (Japanese)—thin buckwheat noodles, often served cold with sesame oil-based sauce.

soda bread (Irish)—a simple bread leavened by baking soda instead of yeast.

souvlaki (Greek)—kebabs of lamb, veal or pork, cooked on a griddle or over a barbecue, sprinkled with lemon juice during cooking, and served with lemon wedges, onions, and sliced tomatoes.

spanakopita (Greek)—filo triangles filled with spinach and cheese.

sushi (Japanese)—the stuff of midnight cravings and maxed out credit cards. Small rolls of vinegar infused sticky rice topped (or stuffed) with fresh raw seafood or pickled vegetables and held together with sheets of seaweed (*nori*).

tabouli (Middle Eastern)—light salad of cracked wheat (bulgur), tomatoes, parsley, mint, green onions, lemon juice, olive oil, and spices.

tahini (Middle Eastern)—paste made from ground sesame seeds.

tamale (Latin American)—each nation has its own take on the tamale, but in very basic terms it is cornmeal filled with meat and veggies wrapped in corn husk or palm tree leaves for shape, then steamed; there are also sweet varieties, notably the *elote*, or corn, tamale.

tamarindo (Mexican)—popular *agua fresca* made from tamarind fruit.

tandoori (Indian)—literally means baked in a tandoor (a large clay oven); a sauceless, but still very tender, baked meat.

tapas (Spanish)—small dishes with dozens of meat, fish, and vegetable possibilities—a meal usually consists of several; this serving style is thought by some to have originated when Spaniards covered their glass with a piece of ham to keep flies out of the wine (*tapar* means to cover).

tapenade (Provençale Italian)—chopped olive garnish; a delightful spread for a hunk of baguette.

taquitos (Mexican)—also called *flautas*, shredded meat or cheese rolled in a tortilla, fried, and served with guacamole sauce.

taramosalata (Greek)—a caviar spread.

teriyaki (Japanese)—boneless meat, chicken, or seafood marinated in a sweetened soy sauce, then grilled.

tikka (Indian)—marinated morsels of meat cooked in a tandoor oven, usually chicken.

tilapia—a healthy and delicious white fish that originated in Africa but is raised by aquaculture throughout the tropics.

tiramisu (Italian)—a classic non-bake dessert made of coffee-dipped ladyfingers layered with mascarpone cream and grated chocolate cake that is refrigerated.

tom yum gung (Thai)—lemongrass hot-and-sour soup.

torta (Mexican)—Spanish for sandwich or cake.

tortilla (Spanish)—an onion and potato omelette much like an Italian frittata.

tostada (Mexican)—traditionally a corn tortilla fried flat; more commonly in the U.S. vernacular the frilly fried flour tortilla that looks like an upside down lampshade and is filled with salad in wannabe Mexican restaurants.

tostones (Latin American)—fried green plantains.

tzatziki (Greek)—fresh yogurt mixed with grated cucumber, garlic, and mint (or coriander, or both).

udon (Japanese)—thick white rice noodles served in soup, usually *bonito* broth.

ALPHABETICAL INDEX

Bold indicates main entry.

A

Addis Red Sea Ethiopian Restaurant, 53
Aegean, 239
Al's French Fries, 285
Algiers, 174
Ali's Roti Restaurant, 139
Allandale Farm, 119, **234**
Amarin of Thailand, **249**, 255
Amelia's Kitchen, 210
Amelia's Trattoria, 156
Amrheins, 148
Anchovies, 53
Andy's Diner, 194
Angelo's Civita Farnese, 280
Angora Café, 99, **102**
Anna's Taquería, 106, **196**, 210
Antonio's Cucina Italiana, 32
Appleton Bakery, 54
Arlington Restaurant and Diner, 235
Arnold's, 276
Asgard, The, 161
Athan's, **110**, 124
Atkins Farm, **196**, 274
Atlantic Fish Co., **28**, 62
Au Bon Pain, 158
Audubon Circle, 80
Aunt Carrie's, 280

B

B Side Lounge, 167, **168**
B&D Deli, 124
Bai Thong, 254
Baja Betty's, 119
Baja Cantina, **62**, 68
Baker's Best, 249
Bamboo, 99
Bangkok Bistro, 100
Bangkok City, 63
Baxter's Fish 'n' Chips and Boathouse Club, 276
Bay State Chowda Co., 2, **28**
Bella Luna, 126
Ben & Jerry's Factory, 286
Bertucci's, 2, 64, 119, 161, **175**, 203, 219
Betty's Wok and Noodle Diner, 64
Big Burrito, 88
Bison County, 244
Blue Fin, 197
Blue Parrot, The, (R.I.P.), 177
Blue Plate Express, 236
Blue Shirt Café, 211
Blue-Ribbon Bar-B-Q, **236**, 250
Bluestone Bistro, **102**, 103
Bob Briggs Wee Packet Restaurant and Bakery, 276
Bob the Chef's, 55
Bob's Clam Hut, 290
Boca Grande, 106, 156, **198**
Bodhi Café, 65
Bombay Bistro, 107
Border Café, 177
Boston Chipyard, 11
Boston Daily Bread Company, 107, **110**

Boston Speed's Famous Hot Dogs, 139
Bottega Fiorentina, 107
Bova's Bakery, 15
Bow & Arrow Pub, 150
Brooksby Farm, **234**, 258
Brown Derby Deli, 11
Brown Sugar Café, 80
Buddha's Delight, 37
Buddha's Delight, Too, 107
Buff's Pub, 250
Bukowski Tavern, 65
Bull & Finch, 150
Burrito Max, 81
Buteco Restaurant, 82
Buzzy's Fabulous Roast Beef (R.I.P.), 32

C

Cabot Creamery, 286
Cactus Club, 68
Café 300, 2
Café Belo, 82, **88**, 227, 256
Café Brazil, 89
Café China, 167
Café de Crêpe, 211, **212**
Café Fiorella, **238**, 251
Café India, 178
Café Jaffa, 66
Café Pamplona, 179
Café Rossini, 213
Caffe Vittoria, 16
Caffe Paradiso, 15, **180**
Cambridge Brewing Company, 156
Cambridge Common, 192, 199
Camino Real, 90
Campo De' Fiori, **180**, 192
Cape Cod Potato Chips Factory, 286
Captain Frosty's Fish and Chips, 278
Carberry's, 161, 212, **214**
Carl's, 245
Carlo's Cucina Italiana, 91
Caserta Pizzeria, 280
Central Bakery, **111**, 167
Centre Street Café, 127
Chacarero, 2
Charlie's Sandwich Shoppe, 55
Charlie's Kitchen, **181**, 191
Charlie's Diner, 274
Chart House, 3, **28**
Cheddar's, 203
Chef Chang's, 108
Chef Lee's, 140
Chef Wayne's Big Mamou, 275
Chez Henri, **168**, 199
China Pearl, 38
Chinatown Café, 39
Chinatown Festival, 144
Chinese Kitchen Food Truck, 191
Chowderfest, 143
Chris' Texas B.B.Q., 140
Christina's Homemade Ice Cream, 132, 169
Christo's, 266
Christopher's, 200
Cindy's Planet, 44

Circe's Grotto, 267
Clam Box of Ipswich, **258**, 262
Clam Shack, The, 290
Clear Flour Bread, 108, **110**
Coffee Cantata Bistro and Beans, 128
Common Ground Café, 141
Corner Café, **19**, 68
Cornwall's, 82
Corrib Pub, 103, **108**
Country Life Vegetarian, **3**, 288
Court House Seafood, **169**, 262
Cranberry Harvest Festival, 144
Crazy Dough's, 67
Crescent Ridge Dairy Bar, 132
Curtis BBQ, 285

D

D'Amores, 19
Darwin's, 182
Delux, 56
Demos, **239**, 245
Denise's, **132**, 212, 214
Desmond O'Malley's, 256
Diesel Café, 215
Ding Ho, 40
Dino's Café, 20
Domenic's Paninoteca, 245
Doyle's Café, **129**, 150
Dunkin' Donuts, 195
Durgin Park, 4, **5**

E

Eagles Deli, **101**, 104
East Ocean City, 40
Eastham Lobster Pool, 279
El Cafetal, 89
El Oriental de Cuba, 135
El Pelón Taquería, 84
El Phoenix Room (R.I.P.), 93
Elbow Room, 104
Eldo Cake House and Bakery, 44
Emma's, **157**, 158
Ernesto's Pizzeria, 21
Espresso Pizza, **212**, 215

F

Fajitas & 'Ritas, 4, **120**
Faneuil Hall, 11
Farnham's, **258**, 262
Fish Pier Restaurant and Market, The, **148**, 262
Flat Breads Café, 251
Flo's Hot Dogs, 291
Forest Café, 200
Formaggio Kitchen, **57**, 183
Formaggio's, 182
Fornax Bread Company, **111**, 130
Frank Pepe's Pizzeria Napoletana, 283
Franklin Café, 57, **168**

G

Gail's Station House, 282
Galleria Umberto, 22
Garden of Eden, 59
Geoff's Superlative Sandwiches, 281
Giacomo's Ristorante, **23**, 60

Gilley's, 288
Gooseberry's, 158
Gloucester Seafood Festival, 144
Gourmet India, 109
Grand Chau Chow, 41
Grasshopper, 92
Great Chow, 268
Greek Corner, 201
Grendel's Den, 68, **184**, 191
Guido's, 105

H

Hampton Beach Seafood Festival, 144
Harrison Café, 44
Harry's Place, 283
Harvard Business School Dining Hall, 92
Hayes Bickford (R.I.P.), 58
Hedge School, The (R.I.P.), 85
Helmand, The, 158, **159**
Herrell's, 67, 83, 94, **131**, 184, 191, 275
Hi Rise Bread Company, 184, **205**
Ho Yuen Bakery, **41**, 110
Honey Pot Hill Orchards, 196
Hong Kong, 191
Hot Dog Safari, 144
House of Tibet Kitchen, 216
Hu Tieu Nam Vang, 44
Hub Pub, The, 4

I

Ice Creamsmith, 131, 142
Iggy's, **112**, 240, 259
Iguana Cantina, **246**, 255, 256
Il Buongustaio, 206
Il Panino Express, **23**, 185
India Quality, 83
Irie Jamaica, 142
Island Hopper, 69
Istanbul Café, 33
Izzy's, 161

J

J. Pace & Son, **6**, 33, 259
J.P. Licks, 70, 109, **131**, 130, 252
Jacob Wirth, 42
Jake's Boss BBQ, 130
James's Gate, 133
Jay's Deli, **212**, 216
Jeveli's, 26
Joan and Ed's Deli, 247
Joe and Nemo's, 33
John Harvard's Brewhouse, 68, **192**
Johnny D's, 212, **216**
Johnny's Luncheonette, 185, 191, **252**
JP Seafood, 134
Juice Bar, 45
Jumbo Seafood, 43

K

K2 Café, 158, **160**
Keith's Place, 144
Kelly's Roast Beef, 259
Kelly's Diner, **217**, 242
Khao Sarn, 112

King and I, The, 34
King Fung Garden, 45
Kinsale, The, 6
Kotobukiya, 202
Kowloon, 260
Kream 'n' Kone, 278
Kupel's, **110**, 113

L

L Street Diner, 149
L Street Tavern, 150
L.A. Burdick, **111**, 185
La Cucina Di Pinocchio, 275
La Dalat, 268
La Famiglia Giorgio's, **21**, 70
La Hacienda, 227
La Paloma, 269
La Pupusa Guanaca, 136
La Terraza, 30
Land Ho!, 278
Le Gamin, 60
Lee's Sandwich Shop, 185
Legal Sea Foods, **28**, 158, 160
Little Stevie's Pizza, 70
Lizzy's, **132**, 248
Loaf and Ladle, 149
Lori-Ann Donut Shop, 26, **196**
Louis' Lunch, 284
Low Fat No Fat Grille and Café, 240

M

M&M Ribs, 145
Maine Lobster Festival, 144
Mama Gaia's, 162
Maple Grove Farms, 286
Marché, 71
Maria's Pastry Shop, 17
Marino Lookout Farm, **234**, 249
Marshall House, The, **7**, 28
Mary Ann's, **101**, 105
Mary Ann's Diner, 288
Mary Chung, 163
Massis Bakery, **112**, 242
Matt Murphy's Pub, **120**, 262
McCormick and Schmick's, 68
Miami Restaurant, 135
Mike's City Diner, 60
Mike's Kitchen, 281
Mike's Pastry, 17
Milk Street Café, 8
Miracle of Science, 163
Moby Dick's, 279
Modern Diner, The, 281
Modern Pastry, 17
Modern's Famous Brick Oven
    Apizza, 283
Mondo's (R.I.P.), 58
Monica's Salumeria, 17
Moody's Falafel, 164
Moshe's Chicken Truck, 158
Mr. Bartley's Burger Cottage, **186**,
    192
Mr. Crêpe, 218
Mr. Pie, 170
Mr. Sushi, 113
Mul's Diner, 151
Mykonos Fair, 11

N

Nashoba Brook Bakery, 61
Nectar's, 285
Neighborhood Restaurant, 227
Neillio's, 237
New Asia, 186, **228**
New England Barbecue
    Championship, 144
New England Soup Factory, **121**,
    253
New Lei Jing, 46
New Shanghai, 46
New York Soup Exchange, 9
No Name Restaurant, **10**, 28,
    262
North End Summer Street
    Festivals, 143

O

O Cantinho, 170
One Arrow St. Crêpes, 187
Other Side Cosmic Café, The, 71
Our House, 69, **94**
Oxford Spa, 202

P

Panificio, 35
Panini Bakery, **111**, 229
Papa Frank's Italian
    Restaurant, 287
Paramount, The, 36
Parish Café, 72
Parker's Maple Barn, 289
Parziale and Sons Bakery, 18
Pat's of Lower Mills, 146
Peach Farm, 47
Penang, 48
Pho Hòa, 146
Pho Lemongrass, 114
Pho Pasteur, 48, 73, 94, **187**,
    192
Pho Vietnam, 48
Picante Mexican Grill, 164, **220**
Pinocchio's, **188**, 191
Pit Stop Barbecue, 147
Pizza Etc., **102**, 105
Pizza Ring, 191
Pizzeria Regina, 10, **24**
Pizzeria Rico, 10
Polcari's Coffee, 18
Polly's Pancake Parlor, 289
Pomodoro Ristorante, 25
Porthole Restaurant, 263
Pour House, 69, 73
Presto Pizzeria Restaurant, **102**,
    105
Punjab Café, 269
Punjabi Dhaba, 171
Purity Cheese Company, 18
Purple Cactus, 136

Q

Quiet Man Pub, 151

R

R.F. O'Sullivan and Sons, 229
R & L Deli, 152
Ralph's Chadwick Square Diner,
    275
Rami's, **114**, 256

Rancatore's, 132, 238
Rangoli, 95
Rangzen Tibetan Restaurant, 164
Rebecca's Café, 158
Real Pizza, 206
Redbones, 221
Remington's, 49
Rhythm and Spice, 165
River Gods, 166
Rod Dee Thai Cuisine, 85, **115**
Rod Thai, 50
Roggie's Brew & Grille, **101**, 105
Rosebud Diner, 212, **221**, 242
Rosie's Bakery, 12, **111**, 172, 253
Royal Pastry Shop, **111**, 172
Rudy's Café, 222
Ryle's, 172

S

S&S Restaurant, 173
Sabra, 189
Sabur, **213**, 223
Sài Gòn, 96
Sally's, 283
Salsa's, 152
Salumeria Italiana, 18
Salumeria Toscana, 18
Sam Hop Eatery, 50
Santarpio's Pizza, 28
Sausage Guy, 85
Savannah Grill, 223
Scooper Bowl, 143
Scoozi, 74
Seoul Bakery, 96, **110**
Sevan Bakery, **112**, 242
Shawarma King, 102, **115**
Shino Express, 75
Sichuan Garden, 122
Silvertone Bar & Grill, 12
Skewers, 190
Sneakers Bistro/Café, 287
Sorella's, 137
Sorelle, 29
SoundBites, 212, **224**
South Street Diner, **12**, 242
Spike's Junkyard Dogs, 282
Steve's Ice Cream (R.I.P.), 219
Steve's Kitchen, 96
Steve's Restaurant, 75
Strip-T's, 243
Sugar Shack, 290
Sullivan's, 153
Sultan's Kitchen, 13
Sunset Grill and Tap, The, 69, **97**
Super Duper Weenie, 284
Sushi Express, 116
Sushi King, 243
Sweet Tomatoes, **253**, 279

T

Tacos El Charro, 138
Tacos Lupita, 224
Taiwan Café, 51
Tanjore, 190
Taquería La Mexicana, 230
Taqueria Mexico, 248
Tasca, 101, **106**
Taste of Hartford, 144
Taste of Home Bakery, 153

Taste of Northampton, 144
Taste of Rhode Island, 144
Tasty, The (R.I.P.), 150, **183**
Tasty Gourmet, **212**, 225
Tealuxe, **76**, 192, 282
Tennesee's BBQ, 270
Terri's Place, 154
Thai Dish, 77
Thirsty Scholar, The, 230
Thornton's Fenway Grill, 86
Thurston's Lobster Pound, 291
Tim's Bar & Grill, 62
Torrefazione Italia, 78
Toscanini's, **131**, 158, 160, 166, 192
Town Diner, **242**, 244
Town Spa Pizza, 271
Trident Booksellers and Café, 78
Trio's Ravioli, 18
Tu Do, 51

U

Uncle Pete's Hickory Ribs, 30
Union Oyster House, 14, **27**, 28
Upper Crust, The, 36
Urban Gourmet, 213, **225**

V

Vegetarian Food Festival, 143
Veggie Planet, 193
Vermont Pub & Brewery, 287
Verna's, **196**, 203
Via Via Café, 116
Vidalia's Truck Stop, 255
Village Pizza House, 122
Village Smokehouse, 123

W

Wang's Fast Food, 212, **231**
Warren Tavern, 31
White Horse Tavern, 69, **98**
White Mountain Creamery, **101**, 254
Wildflower, 14
Wilson Farm, **234**, 248
Wilson's Diner, **242**, 248
Wing Works, 226
Wing-It, 99
Wisteria House, 45
Wonder Spice Café, 138
Woodman's of Essex, 262, **263**

Y

Yan's Best Place Restaurant, 52

Z

Zaftigs Delicatessen, 117
Zathmary's Specialty Foods Marketplace, **118**, 255

CATEGORY INDEX

Afghan
Helmand, The, 158, **159**

American Pub (also see Bar & Grill)
Corrib Pub, 103, 108
Remington's, 49
Warren Tavern, 31

Bakery
Appleton Bakery, 54
Athan's, **110**, 124
Boston Chipyard, 11
Boston Daily Bread Company, 107, **110**
Bova's Bakery, 15
Carberry's, 161, 212, **214**
Central Bakery, **111**, 167
Clear Flour Bread, 108, **110**
Eldo Cake House and Bakery, 44
Hi Rise Bread Company, 184, **205**
Ho Yuen Bakery, 41, **110**
Iggy's, **112**, 240, 259
Fornax Bread Company, **111**, 130
Kupel's, **110**, 113
L.A. Burdick, **111**, 185
Maria's Pastry Shop, 17
Massis Bakery, **112**, 242
Mike's Pastry, 17
Modern Pastry, 17
Panini Bakery, **111**, 229
Parziale and Sons Bakery, 18
Rosie's Bakery, 12, **111**, 172, 253
Royal Pastry Shop, **111**, 172
Seoul Bakery, 96, **110**
Sevan Bakery, **112**, 242
Sorelle, 29
Taste of Home Bakery, 153

Bar & Grill
Amrheins, 148
Audubon Circle, 80
Buff's Pub, 250
Bukowski Tavern, 65
Cambridge Brewing Company, 156
Cambridge Common, 192, 199
Charlie's Kitchen, **181**, 191
Christopher's, 200
Corner Café, **19**, 68
Delux, 56
Grendel's Den, 68, **184**, 191
Hub Pub, The, 4
John Harvard's Brewhouse, 68, **192**
Johnny D's, 212, **216**
Mary Ann's, **101**, 105
Miracle of Science, 163
Our House, 69, **94**
Pour House, 69, 73
Roggie's Brew & Grille, **101**, 105
Ryle's, 172
Silvertone Bar & Grill, 12
Strip-T's, 243
Sunset Grill and Tap, The, 69, **97**
Thornton's Fenway Grill, 86
Tim's Bar & Grill, 62
Vermont Pub & Brewery, 287

Barbecue
Bison County, 244
Blue-Ribbon Bar-B-Q, **236**, 250
Chris' Texas B.B.Q., 140
Curtis BBQ, 285
Jake's Boss BBQ, 130
M&M Ribs, 145
Pit Stop Barbecue, 147
Redbones, 221
Tennesee's BBQ, 270
Uncle Pete's Hickory Ribs, 30
Village Smokehouse, 123

Burger Joint
Al's French Fries, 285
Eagles Deli, **101**, 104
Gilley's, 288
Louis' Lunch, 284
Mr. Bartley's Burger Cottage, **186**, 192
R.F. O'Sullivan and Sons, 229

Burrito Joint
Anna's Taquería, 106, **196**, 210
Baja Betty's, 119
Big Burrito, 88
Burrito Max, 81
Harry's Place, 283

Brazilian
Buteco Restaurant, 82
Café Belo, 82, **88**, 227, 256
Café Brazil, 89

Café
Angora Café, 99, **102**
Appleton Bakery, 54
Au Bon Pain, 158
Baker's Best, 249
Blue Plate Express, 236
Bodhi Café, 65
Café Pamplona, 179
Café Rossini, 213
Caffe Vittoria, 16
Circe's Grotto, 267
Coffee Cantata Bistro and Beans, 128
Common Ground Café, 141
Diesel Café, 215
Dino's Café, 20
Garden of Eden, 59
Low Fat No Fat Grille and Café, 240
Mama Gaia's, 162
Milk Street Café, 8
Nashoba Brook Bakery, 61
New York Soup Exchange, 9
Other Side Cosmic Café, The, 71
Panificio, 35
Paramount, The, 36
Parker's Maple Barn, 289
Polcari's Coffee, 18
Savannah Grill, 223
Sorella's, 137
Sorelle, 29
Sugar Shack, 290
Tealuxe, **76**, 192, 282
Torrefazione Italia, 78
Trident Booksellers and Café, 78
Wildflower, 14

CATEGORY INDEX

Cafeteria

Harvard Business School Dining
    Hall, 92
Marché, 71
Zathmary's Specialty Foods
    Marketplace, **118**, 255

Cajun/Creole

Border Café, 177
Chef Wayne's Big Mamou, 275

Cambodian

Wonder Spice Café, 138

Chilean

Chacarero, 2

Chinese

Chef Chang's, 108
Café China, 167
China Pearl, 38
Chinatown Café, 39
Chinese Kitchen Food Truck, 191
Cindy's Planet, 44
Ding Ho, 40
East Ocean City, 40
Grand Chau Chow, 41
Great Chow, 268
Hong Kong, 191
Jumbo Seafood, 43
King Fung Garden, 45
Mary Chung, 163
New Asia, 186, **228**
New Shanghai, 46
Peach Farm, 47
Sam Hop Eatery, 50
Sichuan Garden, 122
Taiwan Café, 51
Wang's Fast Food, 212, 231
Yan's Best Place Restaurant, 52

Colombian

Camino Real, 90
El Cafetal, 89
La Terraza, 30

Cuban

Chez Henri, **168**, 199
El Oriental de Cuba, 135
Miami Restaurant, 135

Cuban-Asian Fusion

Betty's Wok and Noodle Diner, 64

Deli

B&D Deli, 124
Bova's Bakery, 15
Brown Derby Deli, 11
Jay's Deli, **212**, 216
Joan and Ed's Deli, 247
R & L Deli, 152
S&S Restaurant, 173
Zaftigs Delicatessen, 117

Diner

Andy's Diner, 194
Arlington Restaurant and Diner,
    235
Charlie's Diner, 274
Charlie's Sandwich Shoppe, 55
Johnny's Luncheonette, 185, 191,
    252
Kelly's Diner, **217**, 242
Mary Ann's Diner, 288
Mike's City Diner, 60
Modern Diner, The, 281
Mul's Diner, 151
Ralph's Chadwick Square Diner,
    275
Rosebud Diner, 212, **221**, 242
SoundBites, 212, **224**
South Street Diner, **12**, 242
Terri's Place, 154
Town Diner, **242**, 244
Vidalia's Truck Stop, 255
Wilson's Diner, **242**, 248

Donuts

Dunkin' Donuts, 195
Lori-Ann Donut Shop, 26, **196**
Verna's, **196**, 203

Editors' Pick

Anna's Taquería, 106, **196**, 210
Blue-Ribbon Bar-B-Q, **236**, 250
Boston Speed's Famous Hot
    Dogs, 139
Brown Sugar Café, 80
Centre Street Café, 127
Charlie's Kitchen, **181**, 191
Charlie's Sandwich Shoppe, 55
Coffee Cantata Bistro and Beans,
    128
Delux, 56
Doyle's Café, **129**, 150
El Cafetal, 89
El Oriental de Cuba, 135
El Pelón Taquería, 84
Galleria Umberto, 22
Jacob Wirth, 42
King Fung Garden, 45
M&M Ribs, 145
Matt Murphy's Pub, 120, 262
Mike's City Diner, 60
Milk Street Café, 8
Neighborhood Restaurant, 227
O Cantinho, 170
Pat's of Lower Mills, 146
Pho Pasteur, 48, 73, 94, **187**,
    192
Pit Stop Barbecue, 147
Pizzeria Regina, 10, **24**
Polly's Pancake Parlor, 289
R.F. O'Sullivan and Sons, 229
Rami's, **114**, 256
Rangoli, 95
Redbones, 221
Santarpio's Pizza, 28
Sorella's, 137
SoundBites, 212, **224**
Sultan's Kitchen, 13
Tim's Bar & Grill, 62
Warren Tavern, 31
Zaftigs Delicatessen, 117

English Pub
Cornwall's, 82
White Horse Tavern, 69, **98**

Ethiopian
Addis Red Sea Ethiopian
    Restaurant, 53

Farm Stand
Allandale Farm, 119, **234**
Atkins Farm, **196**, 274
Brooksby Farm, **234**, 258
Maple Grove Farms, 286
Marino Lookout Farm, **234**, 249
Wilson Farm, **234**, 248

Food Stand
Kelly's Roast Beef, 259
Sullivan's, 153

French/Crêpes
Café de Crêpe, 211, **212**
Chez Henri, **168**, 199
Le Gamin, 60
Mr. Crêpe, 218
One Arrow St. Crêpes, 187

Fries
Curtis BBQ, 285
Nectar's, 285

German
Jacob Wirth, 42

Gourmet/Nouveau American
Appleton Bakery, 54
B Side Lounge, 167, **168**
Bella Luna, 126
Blue Plate Express, 236
Bluestone Bistro, **102**, 103
Café 300, 2
Centre Street Café, 127
Elbow Room, 104
Emma's, **157**, 158
Franklin Café, 57, **168**
Gail's Station House, 282
Nashoba Brook Bakery, 61
Paramount, The, 36
Parish Café, 72
Real Pizza, 206
Scoozi, 74
Sneakers Bistro/Café, 287
Upper Crust, The, 36
Urban Gourmet, 213, **225**
Zathmary's Specialty Foods
    Marketplace, **118**, 255

Gourmet Grocery
Formaggio Kitchen, **57**, 183
Zathmary's Specialty Foods
    Marketplace, **118**, 255

Greek
Aegean, 239
Christo's, 266
Demos, **239**, 245
Greek Corner, 201
Mykonos Fair, 11
Steve's Kitchen, 96
Steve's Restaurant, 75

Historic (in business since 1969 or earlier)
Amrheins, 148
Andy's Diner, 194
Anchovies, 53
Angelo's Civita Farnese, 280
B&D Deli, 124
Baxter's Fish 'n' Chips and
    Boathouse Club, 276
Bob Briggs Wee Packet
    Restaurant and Bakery, 276
Bob the Chef's, 55
Bova's Bakery, 15
Café Pamplona, 179
Caffe Paradiso, 15, **180**
Caffe Vittoria, 16
Caserta Pizzeria, 280
Charlie's Diner, 274
Charlie's Kitchen, **181**, 191
Charlie's Sandwich Shoppe, 55
Christo's, 266
Clam Box of Ipswich, **258**, 262
Court House Seafood, **169**, 262
Doyle's Café, **129**, 150
Flo's Hot Dogs, 291
Gilley's, 288
Harry's Place, 283
Jacob Wirth, 42
Jeveli's, 26
Joe and Nemo's, 33
Kelly's Diner, **217**, 242
Kelly's Roast Beef, 259
Kowloon, 260
Kream 'n' Kone, 278
La Hacienda, 227
Louis' Lunch, 284
Modern Diner, The, 281

Mr. Bartley's Burger Cottage, **186**,
    192
No Name Restaurant, **10**, 28,
    262
Polly's Pancake Parlor, 289
Porthole Restaurant, 263
Rosebud Diner, 212, **221**, 242
S&S Restaurant, 173
Santarpio's Pizza, 28
South Street Diner, **12**, 242
Sullivan's, 153
Town Diner, **242**, 244
Union Oyster House, **14**, **27**, 28
Warren Tavern, 31
Woodman's of Essex, 262, **263**

Hot Dogs/ Sausages
Boston Speed's Famous
    Hot Dogs, 139
Flo's Hot Dogs, 291
Joe and Nemo's, 33
Sausage Guy, 85
Spike's Junkyard Dogs, 282
Super Duper Weenie, 284

CATEGORY INDEX

Ice Cream

Christina's Homemade Ice Cream, **132**, 169
Crescent Ridge Dairy Bar, 132
Denise's, **132**, 212, 214
J.P. Licks, 70, 109, **131**, 130, 252
Herrell's, 67, 83, 94, **131**, 184, 191, 275
Ice Creamsmith, **131**, 142
Lizzy's, **132**, 248
Toscanini's, **131**, 158, 160, 166, 192
White Mountain Creamery, **101**, 254

Indian

Bombay Bistro, 107
Café India, 178
India Quality, 83
Gourmet India, 109
Punjab Café, 269
Punjabi Dhaba, 171
Rancatore's, **132**, 238
Rangoli, 95
Tanjore, 190

International

Marché, 71

Irish

Loaf and Ladle, 149
Taste of Home Bakery, 153

Irish Pub

Asgard, The, 161
Desmond O'Malley's, 256
Doyle's Café, **129**, 150
James's Gate, 133
Kinsale, The, 6
Matt Murphy's Pub, **120**, 262
Quiet Man Pub, 151
River Gods, 166
Thirsty Scholar, The, 230

Italian

Amelia's Kitchen, 210
Amelia's Trattoria, 156
Anchovies, 53
Angelo's Civita Farnese, 280
Antonio's Cucina Italiana, 32
Bottega Fiorentina, 107
Bova's Bakery, 15
Café Fiorella, **238**, 251
Caffe Paradiso, 15, **180**
Caffe Vittoria, 16
Carlo's Cucina Italiana, 91
D'Amores, 19
Dino's Café, 20
Domenic's Paninoteca, 245
Giacomo's Ristorante, **23**, 60
Il Buongustaio, 206
Il Panino Express, **23**, 185
J. Pace & Son, **6**, 33, 259
Jeveli's, 26
La Cucina Di Pinocchio, 275
La Famiglia Giorgio's, **21**, 70
La Hacienda, 227
Mike's Kitchen, 281
Monica's Salumeria, 17
Panificio, 35

Papa Frank's Italian Restaurant, 287
Pomodoro Ristorante, 25
Purity Cheese Company, 18
Salumeria Italiana, 18
Salumeria Toscana, 18
Torrefazione Italia, 78
Town Spa Pizza, 271
Trio's Ravioli, 18

Japanese/ Sushi

Blue Fin, 197
Kotobukiya, 202
Mr. Sushi, 113
Shino Express, 75
Sushi Express, 116
Sushi King, 243

Kosher/Jewish

B&D Deli, 124
Joan and Ed's Deli, 247
Milk Street Café, 8
Rami's, **114**, 256
S&S Restaurant, 173
Zaftigs Delicatessen, 117

Korean

JP Seafood, 134

Malaysian

Penang, 48

Mexican

Anna's Taquería, 106, **196**, 210
Baja Cantina, **62**, 68
Boca Grande, 106, 156, **198**
El Pelón Taquería, 84
Forest Café, 200
Iguana Cantina, **246**, 255, 256
La Paloma, 269
Picante Mexican Grill, 164, **220**
Salsa's, 152
Tacos El Charro, 138
Taquería La Mexicana, 230
Taqueria Mexico, 248

Middle Eastern/ Mediterranean

Algiers, 174
Café Jaffa, 66
Moody's Falafel, 164
Mr. Pie, 170
Neillio's, 237
Sabra, 189
Sabur, **213**, 223
Skewers, 190
Shawarma King, 102, **115**
Via Via Café, 116

Night Owl

Algiers, 174
Anchovies, 53
Audubon Circle, 80
Bison County, 244
Bukowski Tavern, 65
Café India, 178
Café Pamplona, 179
Caffe Vittoria, 16
Cambridge Brewing Company, 156
Cambridge Common, 192, 199

305

CATEGORY INDEX

Charlie's Kitchen, **181**, 191
Christo's, 266
Christopher's, 200
Corner Café, **19**, 68
Cornwall's, 82
Corrib Pub, 103, **108**
Diesel Café, 215
East Ocean City, 40
Elbow Room, 104
Franklin Café, 57, **168**
Gilley's, 288
Grand Chau Chow, 41
Grendel's Den, 68, **184**, 191
Hub Pub, The, 4
Jeveli's, 26
Jumbo Seafood, 43
Kelly's Roast Beef, 259
Kinsale, The, 6
Kowloon, 260
Le Gamin, 60
Little Stevie's Pizza, 70
Mama Gaia's, 162
Marché, 71
Miracle of Science, 163
Moody's Falafel, 164
Nectar's, 285
Other Side Cosmic Café, The, 71
Our House, 69, **94**
Parish Café, 72
Peach Farm, 47
Pinocchio's, **188**, 191
Pit Stop Barbecue, 147
Pour House, 69, 73
R.F. O'Sullivan and Sons, 229
Ralph's Chadwick Square Diner, 275
Remington's, 49
River Gods, 166
Rudy's Café, 222
Ryle's, 172
Sam Hop Eatery, 50
Santarpio's Pizza, 28
Sausage Guy, 85
Spike's Junkyard Dogs, 282
Sunset Grill and Tap, The, 69, **97**
Thornton's Fenway Grill, 86
Tim's Bar & Grill, 62
Town Spa Pizza, 271
Trident Booksellers and Café, 78
Vermont Pub & Brewery, 287
Via Via Café, 116
Wang's Fast Food, 212, **231**
White Horse Tavern, 69, **98**
Wing-It, 99

Pan-Asian
Buddha's Delight, 37
Grasshopper, 92
Island Hopper, 69
New Lei Jing, 46
Tu Do, 51

Pizza
Bella Luna, 126
Bertucci's, 2, 64, 119, 161, **175**, 203, 219
Bluestone Bistro, **102**, 103
Campo De' Fiori, **180**, 192
Caserta Pizzeria, 280
Crazy Dough's, 67
Emma's, **157**, 158
Ernesto's Pizzeria, 21
Espresso Pizza, **212**, 215
Frank Pepe's Pizzeria Napoletana, 283
Galleria Umberto, 22
Little Stevie's Pizza, 70
Modern's Famous Brick Oven Apizza, 283
Pat's of Lower Mills, 146
Pinocchio's, **188**, 191
Pizza Etc., **102**, 105
Pizza Ring, 191
Pizzeria Regina, 10, **24**
Pizzeria Rico, 10
Presto Pizzeria Restaurant, **102**, 105
Real Pizza, 206
Sally's, 283
Santarpio's Pizza, 28
Scoozi, 74
Sweet Tomatoes, **253**, 279
Town Spa Pizza, 271
Upper Crust, The, 36
Urban Gourmet, 213, **225**
Village Pizza House, 122

Polynesian/ Tiki
Kowloon, 260

Portuguese
Neighborhood Restaurant, 227
O Cantinho, 170

Puerto Rican
Izzy's, 161

Salvadoran
La Pupusa Guanaca, 136
Tacos Lupita, 224

Sandwich Shop (also see Café)
Blue Shirt Café, 211
Carl's, 245
Cheddar's, 203
Darwin's, 182
Flat Breads Café, 251
Formaggio's, 182
Geoff's Superlative Sandwiches, 281
Guido's, 105
K2 Café, 158, **160**
Lee's Sandwich Shop, 185
Oxford Spa, 202
Parish Café, 72
Purple Cactus, 136
R & L Deli, 152
Rebecca's Café, 158
Tasty Gourmet, **212**, 225

CATEGORY INDEX

Seafood

Arnold's, 276
Atlantic Fish Co., **28**, 62
Aunt Carrie's, 280
Baxter's Fish 'n' Chips and
    Boathouse Club, 276
Blue Fin, 197
Bob Briggs Wee Packet Restaurant
    and Bakery, 276
Bob's Clam Hut, 290
Brown Sugar Café, 80
Captain Frosty's Fish and Chips,
    278
Chart House, 3, **28**
Clam Box of Ipswich, **258**, 262
Clam Shack, The, 290
Court House Seafood, **169**, 262
East Ocean City, 40
Eastham Lobster Pool, 279
Farnham's, **258**, 262
Fish Pier Restaurant and Market,
    The, **148**, 262
Jumbo Seafood, 43
JP Seafood, 134
Kream 'n' Kone, 278
Land Ho!, 278
Legal Sea Foods, **28**, 158, 160
Marshall House, The, **7**, 28
Moby Dick's, 279
No Name Restaurant, **10**, 28, 262
Peach Farm, 47
Porthole Restaurant, 263
Shino Express, 75
Thurston's Lobster Pound, 291
Union Oyster House, 14, **27**, 28
Woodman's of Essex, 262, **263**

Soup Shop

Bay State Chowda Co., 2, **28**
New England Soup Factory, **121**,
    253
New York Soup Exchange, 9

Southern/ Soul Food

Bob the Chef's, 55
Chef Lee's, 140
Keith's Place, 144

Spanish/ Tapas

Tasca, 101, **106**

Tex-Mex

Border Café, 177
Fajitas & 'Ritas, 4, **120**
Rudy's Café, 222

Thai

Amarin of Thailand, **249**, 255
Bai Thong, 254
Bamboo, 99
Bangkok Bistro, 100
Bangkok City, 63
Brown Sugar Café, 80
Khao Sarn, 112
King and I, The, 34
Kowloon, 260
Rod Dee Thai Cuisine, 85, **115**
Rod Thai, 50
Thai Dish, 77
Wonder Spice Café, 138

Tibetan

House of Tibet Kitchen, 216
Rangzen Tibetan Restaurant, 164

Turkish

Istanbul Café, 33
Sultan's Kitchen, 13

24/7

Bova's Bakery, 15
South Street Diner, **12**, 242

Vegetarian/ Vegan-Friendly

Betty's Wok and Noodle
    Diner, 64
Buddha's Delight, 37
Buddha's Delight, Too, 107
Café India, 178
Centre Street Café, 127
Christopher's, 200
Common Ground Café, 141
Country Life Vegetarian, **3**, 288
Grasshopper, 92
Low Fat No Fat Grille and Café,
    240
Mama Gaia's, 162
Milk Street Café, 8
New Asia, 186, **228**
Other Side Cosmic Café, The, 71
Punjabi Dhaba, 171
Rangzen Tibetan Restaurant, 164
Sorella's, 137
Urban Gourmet, 213, **225**
Veggie Planet, 193
Wildflower, 14

Vietnamese

Hu Tieu Nam Vang, 44
La Dalat, 268
Pho Hòa, 146
Pho Lemongrass, 114
Pho Pasteur, 48, 73, 94, **187**, 192
Pho Vietnam, 48
Sài Gòn, 96

West Indian/ Caribbean

Ali's Roti Restaurant, 139
Irie Jamaica, 142
Rhythm and Spice, 165

Wings

Wing-It, 99
Wing Works, 22

Lauren Abbate is a well-traveled food lover. She has enjoyed visiting various countries and tasting their cuisine, but still loves living in Boston best.

Jennifer Adams, an aspiring food writer/restaurateur, is learning the ropes serving at the North End's Florentine Café, and as an Editorial Assistant at Slammed Magazine. She can be seen working off some "research" around her North End neighborhood.

Carol Alves was born and raised in Somerville. She knows a thing or two about Italian and Portuguese food.

Michael Beckett, a native New Yorker and lifelong Yankee fan, has lived a life of constant peril and vigilance in the Boston area for over ten years. He has a deep appreciation for all forms of cupcakes.

Leigh Belanger has plenty of experience scoping out cheap eats in Scituate, Cohasset, and her current place of residence, Norwell.

Jenny Bengen is a North End regular and fan of Back Bay's cobbled streets and cafes. She is currently mastering the perfect smoothie at Emack and Bolio's on Newbury St.

Jerry Berndt photographed in Boston for 30 years, cluttering up the pages of the *Globe*, the *Phoenix*, and *Boston Magazine*. In 1998 he moved to Paris for the food—where there are more than 200 varieties of cheese.

Matt Bloomer is a web developer in the Back Bay and resides in Porter Square. He temporarily gave up the staples of his diet—cereal and peanut butter—in order to contribute to this book.

Reg Brittain eats. He recently recouped some of the money he spent eating in Boston from 1998 to 2002 by supplying restaurant content to the web. Now a Northampton resident, Reg still eats.

Melissa Carlson is a New England native, Somerville Barney, and master of ceremonies at the Tofu Day Parade. She has previously written for WGBH Boston and several web sites.

Pete Carpenter, a lifelong resident of the Boston area, spends an inordinate amount of time thinking about, reading about, talking about, seeking out, and eating great food. In order to support his habit, he occasionally designs microprocessors for a living.

Mel Cartagena works as a surveyor with a marine construction firm that works up and down the eastern seaboard, but tackles writing in all its various forms (fiction, nonfiction, scripts), either as himself, or under the nom de plume Jay Corso.

Amélie Cherlin is a former managing editor of *Let's Go* travel guides and nightlife writer for their Boston edition. She turned to *Hungry? Boston* with the sole intention of proclaiming her undying love for Campo de' Fiori.

Priti Chinai has eaten her way across 23 countries in search of the best in vegetarian cuisine. She is a corporate ladder-climber by day, experimental chef by night, and mixed media painter on the weekends.

Eric Cho is a longtime Cantabridgian and fabulous dining companion.

Amy Cooper has lived in Boston for four years. You can usually locate her at the local farmer's markets buying yellow cucumbers, in a field snapping photos of old factories, or about town continuing her arduous quest to find the perfect brownie.

Nicole Cotroneo, a recent Boston College grad, was one of few to burst through the "BC Bubble" in search of great eats beyond Harvard Ave. on the B-line. After four years she has exchanged the T for the subway, continuing her writing in New York.

Rhonda Cozier works in tax law in Salem.

Colleen Craig is a writer who lives and works in Boston. Among other things, she likes to eat.

Jesse Crary's acute nose for bargain burgers and bulging burritos have developed during his nomadic 20s while surviving as a writer/editor in such locales as Burlington, VT, Portland, OR, and Waltham, MA.

Laura & Ben D'Amore, a wife-husband contributor team, pride themselves on finding the "gourmet" in the inexpensive off-the-beaten-path restaurants of Boston.

Tyler Doggett is a grad student at MIT and is now, reluctantly, a Red Sox fan.

Amanda Dorato is a transplanted Bostonian, a freelance writer for magazines in New York and Boston, and a seeker of the perfect Caesar salad.

Mary Beth Doyle works for the MSPCA and moonlights as a Harvard student. She is a bargain-loving native Bostonian who has eaten nearly every day for the past 29 years.

Jamie Drummond is looking for love in all the wrong places, so he'll content himself with a corndog instead.

Sarah Duggan lives in Jamaica Plain.

Dorothy Dwyer is returning to New England after a year in Ecuador. True to her name she will tell anyone who'll listen there's no place like home.

Alissa Farber commits the lion's share of her paycheck to prowl local restaurants and supermarkets in search of verdant feeding grounds. She spends the rest of her waking hours with middle school students in West Roxbury.

Mark Lynn Ferguson, like any good Southerner, has the essence of iced tea and bacon drippings pumping through his veins. He can smell a pulled pork plate from six miles away if it costs under $3.50.

Lara Fox, seven years a Boston-area resident, is an editor who spends her free time doing things like writing creatively and eating out often with friends.

Paula Foye learned to eat well for cheap after spending her college years in NYC surviving on slices and scones. She has edited for Marvel Comics, made films at NYU, and now spends her time making a high school geometry textbook palatable fare.

Ankur Ghosh researched and edited the 2003 edition of *Let's Go Boston* and is the former editor-in-chief of the *Let's Go* series.

Brendan Gibbon, a former *Let's Go* managing editor, recently got dragged around the U.S. in an RV to search for $20-per-night motels and the perfect plate of ribs.

Jon Gorey is a well-traveled musician who believes that food is one of the last true forms of cultural expression and tradition.

Joe Goss has lived and traveled all over the place, but now considers the Boston area home. When not writing restaurant reviews and lengthy letters to the editor, he works as an independent recruiting consultant.

Nick Grandy now lives in Brooklyn, relishes pasta, and occasionally whips up a croque-en-bouche.

Melinda Green believes food tastes better in a restaurant. When she isn't eating, Melinda is also a graphic designer and online content writer.

Nick Grossman recently left his native Boston and managing editor post at *Let's Go* travel guides to write for a Bangkok magazine.

James Haynes moved to Boston five years ago, and has split his time between reporting for several local newspapers, cooking, and searching out restaurants that don't believe that good food is synonymous with "tastes like cod."

Becky Hays is a cooking instructor for Brookline Adult Education and an editor at *Cook's Illustrated* magazine in Brookline. She is a not-so-strict vegetarian that won't turn down good food of any kind.

Ari Herzog, a Boston-area native, writes about travel, technology, and the arts. He has traveled the country in a Subaru and has never met a green chili or a garlic clove he hasn't liked.

Hadley Hudson is a former food editor from NYC who frequents as many places to eat as possible. She is the mother of three children and enjoys flying airplanes in her free time.

Jodi Hullinger is in her seventh year in greater Boston via Poland via Wyoming. She is desperately trying to eat her way out of the culinary void that was her antelope meatloaf and Wonder Bread childhood.

Matthew Isles is a West Cantabridgian born and raised, at various dining tables is where he spent most of his days; eating out, drinking, enjoying most foods, and always shooting off jokes to liven up the mood.

ABOUT THE CONTRIBUTORS

Esti Iturralde likes to eat everything, but has learned the best lesson from the one food she won't eat: the sea cucumber. When attacked, this underwater creature ejects its intestine as an offering and flees. The lesson? Don't fight your enemies—feed them. She has edited travel guides for *Let's Go*, and currently serves as a travel editor for a major publishing company.

Lisa Johnson makes her first bread of the season around October and bakes her famous gingerbread by special request. She is an attorney with a green thumb and has lived in Quincy for 12 years.

Sylvia Kindermann thinks Café Pamplona in Harvard Square is just great.

Stephanie Kinnear, a former waitress and current high school teacher with college loans, considers cheap yet tasty foods to be a matter of survival.

Amy Kirkcaldy is a native of Bridgewater, MA. She is currently living, writing, and learning to digest wicked spicy food in Monterrey, Mexico.

Kyle Konrad is a large and lovely fried food aficionado.

Ted Kulik enjoys the neighborhoods of Boston almost as much as the food, particularly lingering over wine and dessert among the vibrant streets of Boston's North and South End.

Ana Laguarda was an associate editor for *Let's Go USA*, and likes not-necessarily-healthy diner-style portions.

Christine Laurence lives in Watertown.

Tim Leonard, the vagabond, has lived in ten different places in the Boston area. He does business development for a consulting company in Boston when not looking for the best Guinness and pub grub in town.

Kimberly Loomis is a Maine native who hates lobster. After eight seasons in Boston without a World Series championship, she still believes that you can't beat Fenway Park for the town's best meal with a view.

Joel Lowden is a hotel concierge because he is a lover of all foods/drinks and enjoys telling people where to go. A transplanted Texan, he resides in Southie amid the sub shops and Irish pubs.

Donna M. Mancusi, founder of LawSchoolConnections.com, graduated from UPenn Law School, moved to Boston, and began wandering the streets searching for an authentic Italian meal.

Liz McEachern-Hall is a temporarily displaced Aussie who decided to brave the big, bad US of A for love. She currently lives in Cambridge with her amazing husband and works at a local radio station. She loves trying new tastes, has a sad weakness for dessert, but thankfully doesn't mind exercise.

Ray Misra, a 20-year Boston resident, comes to us after writing comic book reviews and advice columns for publicists. He loves to cook, particularly Mexican and Italian food, but presently has no kitchen.

Kathy Morelli has lived in Providence for 25 years.

Anna Morris, in a somewhat clichéd manner, fell in love with food while living among the cuisine-obsessed in France. She has mild aspirations to be a famous food writer, but really prefers eating to hard work.

Meaghan Mulholland grew up in Massachusetts, attended college in Boston, and has recently relocated to Washington D.C. to work for *National Geographic*.

John Newton is a writer living in Jamaica Plain who tours about the city looking for story ideas, but mostly finds himself poor and hungry.

R.B. Michael Oliver was born in Gloucester, MA. By day he's a mild-mannered criminal justice policy writer. By night he's a pop music writer and performer, working on his third CD. He'll eat anything that doesn't run away from him.

Dara Olmsted spent her first four years in Cambridge locked in a dining hall and is happy to have escaped in order to bask in the gooey deliciousness that is Cambridge cuisine.

Sarah Pascarella, when not cooking for friends and family, is a full-time editor and grad student in Boston. She lives and dines out frequently in the North End.

Estelle Paskausky began her career as a culinary bargain hunter when she started grad school at Boston College four years ago. Currently she's a technology consultant and aspiring children's writer, and spends most weekends feeding her food cravings with friends.

Zachary Patten lives in Jamaica Plain.

Jesse Peck could live many a lifetime without growing tired of fried clams.

Alison Pereto is so obsessed with food, a lemon poppyseed muffin once took out a restraining order on her. She stays off the street by typing 97 w.p.m. for charity.

Chris Railey is a writer in Boston's South End whose unforgiving epicureanism depends on the kind of insight contained in this guide.

Dan Rosenberg has learned the importance of enjoying a good meal when it comes his way. Why? His pantry is stocked entirely with nonperishable processed items and fruit juices.

Sandy Ruben has been a pie-eating contest winner, occasional writer, and professional and amateur cook who has never prepared a meal without cheese or butter.

Christopher Russell is one hot South Ender—and soon to become a doctor.

Mark Sloan misses his pretty lake in Croydon, New Hampshire.

Juan Smith enjoys pixie stix.

Heidi Solomon, a born and bred Bostonian, is an avid backpacker and environmentalist. When she's not hitting the trails or exploring the latest caverns, she's obtaining an MA in Desert Ecology and hanging with the girls.

Alex Speier remains hell-bent on finding cheap eats to subsidize his lifestyle of sloth, lethargy, and time spent covering the Red Sox for *Boston Metro*.

Caroline Stanculescu has recently relocated to Inman Square, an ideal place to satisfy her insatiable appetite. She eats a lot, too.

Jason Stevenson makes a mean bruschetta. But it's a good thing he eats out because, left to his own devices, he will put carrots in his omelettes.

Katie Stone is a Boston native and gallerist by day. She's moving to London in search of an MA and the best fish 'n' chips in the city. (She is not Kaya Stone's long-lost twin sister.)

Kaya Stone has been writing restaurant reviews since the age of 12. His dream of completing a kid's food guide to his native Boston fell through somewhere between a short-lived Little League hitting streak and eighth-grade graduation. Since then he has written and edited *Let's Go* guides to Boston and the USA, as well as serving as the series' publishing director.

Laura Stone may have raised her son Kaya on tofu and brown rice, but she is now more versatile—still a great cook and an even better mother.

Glen Strandberg enjoys food so much he once devoured enough spaghetti to make him sick. He achieved this feat again four years later. Sadly, these accomplishments did not occur during Olympic years.

Tina Tuminella's zest for food was acknowledged early when a waitress proclaimed, "I've never seen a little girl enjoy prime rib so much!" Today, Tina seeks the type of spiritual contentment only reached via tomato salad, steak frites, and baklava.

Megan Valentine is a Harvard Physics PhD student by day and webmaster of LawSchoolConnections.com by night. She has spent the past four years exploring the city and scoping out new restaurants as much for the food as for the clientele.

Charlene Wang, a transplanted Southern Californian, divides her time between studying International Development at Wellesley College, searching for either the perfect lemonade or corned beef hash, and making weekly pilgrimages to Chinatown to satisfy her stomach and soul.

Nina West is a Massachusetts native who has spent the past few years feeding her life-long hunger for food and knowledge in culinary school and the food industry. She's currently looking to become involved in food writing.

Barry Willingham is partial to dives—those sorts of holes in the wall one walks into expecting to contract an unnamed disease and comes out overjoyed for the find.

Katie Wink gets too hungry for dinner at eight.

John Woodford does it all. Among other things, he's a fiction writer (unpublished), a psychotherapist (unlicensed), and a computer expert (unqualified).